HTML for the
Business Developer

HTML

for the Business Developer

with JavaServer Pages, PHP, ASP.NET, CGI, and JavaScript

Kevin Forsythe
&
Laura Ubelhor

MC Press Online, LP
Lewisville, TX 75077

HTML for the Business Developer: *with JavaServer Pages, PHP, ASP.NET, CGI, and JavaScript*
Kevin Forsythe & Laura Ubelhor

First Edition

First Printing—July 2008

MC Press offers excellent discounts on this book when ordered in quantity for bulk purchases or special sales, which may include custom covers and content particular to your business, training goals, marketing focus, and branding interest.

For information regarding permissions or special orders, please contact:
MC Press
Corporate Offices
125 N. Woodland Trail
Lewisville, TX 75077 USA

For information regarding sales and/or customer service, please contact:
MC Press
P.O. Box 4300
Big Sandy, TX 75755-4300 USA

ISBN: 978-158347-079-4

First and foremost, I'd like to thank Laura Ubelhor and Merrikay Lee. Without their help, encouragement, and support, this work would not have been possible. As a publisher, Merrikay provided guidance and encouragement. Laura provided most of the technical know-how for this book. Her experience and drive helped push me to keep my nose to the grindstone and finish the tasks as needed. I'd also like to thank her husband, Paul, and her dog, Duke, for putting up with her being even busier than normal and probably not having as much time for them as they'd have liked.

I'd also like to thank my own family. The loving support and encouragement I receive is far more meaningful and important to me than I could ever say. Life challenges us and forces us to grow or wither on the vine. This book represents a small step forward in my life, and I hope that others find it useful in theirs.

—Kevin Forsythe

I'd like to thank Kevin for asking me to be a part of this project. It has been a great experience, and we have worked well together. I've always appreciated Kevin's writing and teaching style. I'd also like to thank Merrikay Lee. Merrikay is a pleasure to work with and has made writing this book a very comfortable project.

I'd also like to thank my family for their support. A special thanks to Paul for his love and patience. I have always felt fortunate to have a large, loving, supportive family. I'd especially like to thank my dad for all that he has taught me—teaching me to dig in and do so happily. There is always something positive to be found if you seek it, and if you really want and are passionate about something, with effort, you are capable of achieving your goal.

My hope is that this book inspires business developers with experience to feel comfortable learning Web skills and those new to development to dive in and learn how to get down to business with HTML. I've been very fortunate to have a career that I enjoy and am very passionate about. I hope this book is an inspiration to others to realize the same career satisfaction.

—Laura Ubelhor

Contents

Introduction

HTML is a topic of great interest. Getting down to business with HTML is, in our opinion, even more interesting. It is a topic all business developers must take into consideration today. We have enjoyed writing this book and have put in a lot of effort to provide an inclusive source for business developers.

Why Another Book on HTML?

With so many books already written on HTML, why write another? We felt that few, if any, books capture the real needs of business application programmers. All too often, books on Web development focus on a single technology or language. Learning to write HTML is only half the battle. It is reminiscent of a commercial that ran years ago, in which a young programmer excitedly shows off his latest company Web page, complete with flaming, spinning logos, to his boss. The boss nods in appreciation, and then says, "Great, now can you integrate it with Accounts Payable?"

How many veteran application developers, with many years' worth of experience building complex and productive applications, have suddenly been thrown off balance when asked to develop an application for the Web? That is why we wrote this book. It provides a comprehensive guide not just to HTML, but to many aspects of browser-based applications. You will learn to do more than create Web pages with flaming logos. You will learn to actually deploy real-time data to Web-based applications, and create fully interactive modern applications.

How Is This Book Arranged?

The early chapters of the book introduce HTML, the foundational language for browser-based applications. The HTML covered within this book is extensive, but also focused. Rather than trying to teach every possible feature of HTML, we focus on those portions most useful to business programmers. Later chapters introduce common methods for integrating real application data into Web applications.

When reviewing specific coding techniques, highlighted code such as is shown below contains the commands/tags as well as any pertinent parameters:

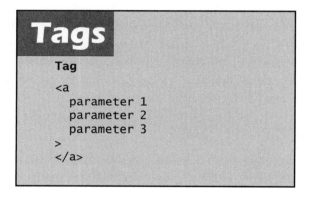

```
Tags

Tag

<a
    parameter 1
    parameter 2
    parameter 3
>
</a>
```

Consistently displaying commands like this will make it easier for you to use this book as a reference, flipping through the pages looking for the one you need.

You'll review simple HTML pages for a hypothetical business, Bill's Barbeque Barn. The first examples show the creation of a home page for the business that provides a Web presence and contact information. Later pages add additional content and more sophisticated design techniques. After that, browser-based application programs are reviewed. You will see example applications that present practical, day-to-day business uses. Use these examples to help develop your own applications.

Figure I.1 shows our starting point for the Bill's Barbeque Barn Web site. It's not much—just a simple, static HTML document. Very little is happening on this Web page, as far as images, formatting, or style sheets.

These features will be added later in the book, but since we're application developers, not graphic designers, we'll begin with just the code involved, not on creating aesthetically snazzy Web pages.

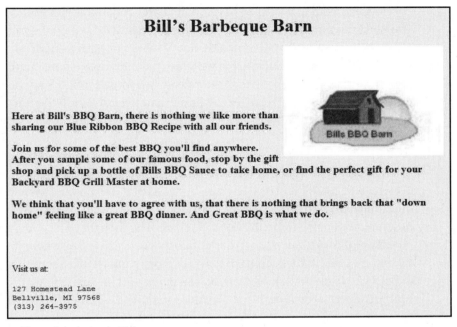

Figure 1.1: A simple Web page.

Once we've covered the basics of the HTML, we'll discuss other languages that interact with HTML. It's inconceivable to have a business Web application created with just HTML. Virtually every Web application incorporates something else to produce the necessary dynamic content. We've selected several of the most common languages used to develop Web applications. Each one has its own chapter in this book.

Intended Audience

The intended audience for this book is business developers or those who are considering or are interested in becoming business developers. We assume that most of you have experience developing business applications. Developers might be very familiar with traditional mainframe/midrange programming environments, but know little about Web-based applications. The world is ever-changing, and many business programmers find themselves needing to learn about doing business on the Web.

In larger shops, the business application developer might not be the one to create and support the organization's Web site, but might still be expected to develop new business applications to deploy through the site. This kind of collaborative environment is nothing new. Most IT staffs are comfortable with team-based development and collaborative effort. Do you need to know all of the Web site development bits and pieces to code business applications? No, probably not. We intentionally included many of the pieces for a traditional site with the intent to give you insight into how it works, so you can make better decisions throughout the application development process. We cover the basics and then dive into the fun stuff, with the business developer in mind.

As a business developer, you likely already have a programming language or languages with which you are very literate and comfortable. It might be C++ on a PC, RPG on IBM's System i, or COBOL on a mainframe. While traditional developers often work on a single platform, Web development might require using more than one platform. The thought of stepping outside of the box, outside of your comfort zone, can be overwhelming. Our intention in this book is to make you feel more comfortable about this, and to help you learn new skills that you can apply within your organization to become more productive, more versatile, and more valuable.

Do I Need to Start from Scratch?

Does going to the Web mean starting from scratch? Do you need to scrap what you have, and start over? By no means. Not only is this cost-prohibitive, but also foolish. Why not continue to use what you have, and learn some new tools to reach a broader audience or provide broader access to your applications? This allows you to retain much of your existing investment in complex business logic.

Does Web development mean new hardware? Not necessarily. Many of the tools we discuss can be used with a variety of platforms. Java technologies can be used on any platform that supports use of the Java Virtual Machine, commonly referred to as *JVM*. Often, a separate server is used for hosting sites. Is this necessary? No, not always; depending on the size of your servers, available capacity, security issues, and application workloads, you might be able to host your applications on existing servers. Since opening applications up to the Web often creates new security considerations, however, you might need separate servers, despite having sufficient capacity on existing servers.

Choosing Development Tools

Choosing the best technology for a development project is a complicated subject. There is a lot of debate on which tool is the best tool. Often, arguments seem biased based on the technology comfort zone of those providing opinions. The bias also lies in the thought that a single technology needs to be used. The further a business programmer delves into Web application development, the clearer it is that a wide variety of tools are available. All of these tools have positive features and functionality, as well as limitations.

If a business developer is looking for a quick way to generate dynamic Web content, PHP might be the right solution, as it is easy to learn, inexpensive, and available on many platforms. On the other hand, advocates of .NET technology are very pleased with their development tools and the resulting solutions, even though they are generally constrained to a Windows-based environment. Java-related technologies are very robust and are available for use on a wide variety of platforms and servers, but developers are often deterred because of the learning curve. CGI has been around a long time, but there seems to be a trend in replacing CGI with other easier, more flexible technologies.

Which is the right fit for your organization? It might well be a combination of these, or other, technologies.

A Word about Apostrophes

This might seem a little random, but we need to address the issue of that little apostrophe in "Bill's" as in "Bill's Barbeque Barn." For those of you who have an eye for such things, you will notice that we sometimes drop the apostrophe and refer to "Bills Barbeque Barn." Let us reassure you that we (as well as our editors) do know the difference between possessive and plural, but for the sake of simplicity, we have chosen to sometimes drop the apostrophe. That little character requires some extra code (as we will show you in Chapter 8), so rather than complicate the coding in the early chapters, we have dropped it when necessary. We hope you will forgive this sacrifice of editorial correctness for simplicity of code.

Summary

This book introduces HTML, covering the basics and enabling you to begin developing Web pages. Then, we add cascading style sheets, JavaScript, and form processing to these basic skills. Once we've covered the basics, we are ready to delve into the really fun stuff of applications development! We'll introduce technologies such as PHP, Java, ASP.NET, and CGI, which transform HTML into a useful business application development language.

Which of these is the correct choice for your needs? After reading this book, you might see that it takes a combination of languages and tools to satisfy your development requirements. After reading this book, you'll have enough knowledge to get down to business and start developing your own Web applications.

CHAPTER 1

An Introduction to Browser-Based Applications

This book is written for business programmers, by business programmers. Since HTML is the foundation language for all browser-based business applications, we'll start there. However, any browser-based application almost certainly involves languages or tools in addition to HTML. In later chapters, you'll see many examples of how those other languages and tools integrate with HTML.

What exactly is a browser-based application? Application development in the 21st century can be broken down into two categories: *legacy* and *modern*. (These terms are commonly used by business application developers, but they can be a bit misleading, as legacy applications are sometimes quite modern in their design, while some so-called modern applications have horribly archaic designs.) Modern application development splits further into two sub-categories: *browser-based* and *client-based*. Client-based applications are typically deployed as executable files loaded onto each computer that needs the application. This often involves one or more installation CDs or a lengthy download from a Web site. A browser-based application, the topic of this book, is quite different.

A Web browser is a program such as Microsoft's Internet Explorer or Mozilla's Firefox. It is designed as a generic Web page presenter, accepting complex streams of commands and data from remote Web servers and composing them into visually appealing Web pages. A browser can typically process instructions written in a number of different languages, but by far the most common is HTML, which stands for *HyperText Markup Language*.

HTML is one of many markup languages. All of them rely on small snippets of code called *tags* that are intermixed with the content being processed. In the case of HTML, a tag is recognized by the less-than and greater-than signs that surround it. For example, to create a large page heading, you might code **<h1>MY PAGE HEADING</h1>**. The **<h1>** tag signals the browser that the text that follows appears very large, as shown in Figure 1.1.

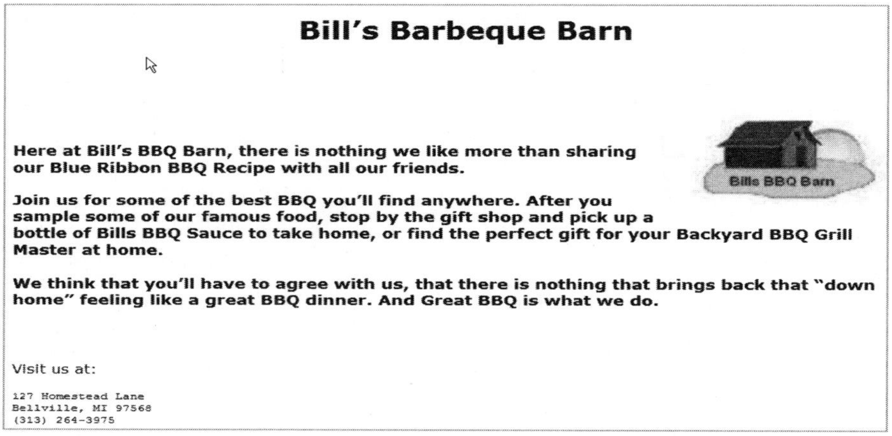

Figure 1.1: An example of an HTML page heading.

The **</h1>** tag is called an *end tag*. The slash indicates that this tag ends the previous heading tag. Any text processed after the end tag appears in the default size and style. Most, but not all, HTML tags have corresponding end tags.

HTML is a relatively simple language. While it does have some quirks, it should not intimidate anyone. Generally, the most complex aspects of Web page design come from integrating other languages into the HTML code, such as JavaScript and cascading style sheets.

What Additional Languages?

Initially, you'll learn how to incorporate JavaScript and cascading style sheets (CSS) into your Web pages. Then, you'll see how to combine those pages with other languages, such as JSP, PHP, ASP.NET, and CGI, to provide database integration.

Each language has its own strengths and weaknesses. JavaScript is a powerful Java-based language modeled on C++, but simpler and with key design changes to make it easier to deploy on a variety of computers. PHP is a popular scripting language designed specifically for database integration. This HTML preprocessor runs on a Web server and creates dynamic HTML content that is returned to the remote user via the browser. ASP.NET is similar in concept to PHP, but the syntax is similar to VB.NET, the version of Microsoft's Visual Basic (VB) implemented on its .NET Framework. CGI programming is not actually a language, but a technique that involves the *Common Gateway Interface* protocol. CGI defines a standard method for a Web browser to interact with custom-written application programs on remote Web servers. Both PHP and ASP.NET rely on specialized CGI programs. CGI programs can be written in many languages and provide a powerful and flexible method for developing dynamic Web pages.

Which language you choose is up to you, and will be the product of a decision with many factors, such as your current skill sets, your coworkers' skill sets, executive mandates, existing applications, and personal preference. Our goal is to provide complete, clear, and functional examples of browser-based applications written with each of these methods, enabling you to be productive immediately upon completion of this book.

What Is a Client?

The client is the hardware device that will be used to access the Web application. The client is probably a laptop or desktop computer, but it might be a handheld device such as a PDA or even a cell phone. The devices that your application will need to support usually depends on who your application users are and what devices they use to access the Internet. These devices will also likely use a variety of operating systems. While the most common operating system is Microsoft Windows, there are many other possibilities, including the Mac OS, Linux, and the Palm OS.

Even if all of your Web site's visitors will be using Windows on PCs, they might be using different screen sizes and resolutions, which will affect the appearance of the site and applications. There might or might not be an impact on how applications are coded. For example, if your visitors are going to be using handheld devices, your application might need to be designed and coded to easily fit displayed data on a smaller screen. If your application has a lot of graphics, the need to consider performance and appearance will be more important. (Considerations based on device types, operating systems, screen sizes, and resolution are discussed in more detail in chapter 13.)

What Is a Browser?

A browser is software that acts as an interface between the user client and the Web. The browser is also sometimes referred to as a *Web client*. The browser sends requests for information, receives that information, and displays it on a user client.

You are probably already familiar with some of the browsers available. They include, but are not limited to, Internet Explorer, Firefox, Opera, and Netscape. The browsers used to access applications can affect appearance and impose other considerations for Web development. Browsers are free of charge and change in popularity. If your application provides access to the general Internet community, many different browsers will probably be used to access your site and applications. (Browsers are discussed in more detail in chapter 13.)

What Is HTML?

If you are creating a Web application, you almost certainly will use HTML. HTML has been around quite a while and will certainly be used for a long time to come. It is the language of the Web, so you definitely need to have at least a basic understanding of it. HTML has changed since its initial inception to include functions and features to make it more flexible and easier to use for Web application development. You will be introduced to HTML in the following chapters.

A document in pure HTML is static, meaning it exists in a constant state. *Client-side scripting* can be embedded within HTML to make a Web application dynamic. Most often, the language used for client-side scripting is JavaScript. You'll learn about JavaScript and client-side scripting in chapter 8.

HTML forms are often used as the means to incorporate CGI within a Web application. As mentioned earlier, CGI is a protocol for interfacing with applications on a Web server. This involves *server-side scripting*. You will learn about CGI and server-side scripting in later chapters.

What Is a Web Server?

The term *Web server* can refer to the program that is responsible for communicating with client browsers. A Web server accepts HTTP requests from client browsers and serves HTTP responses, including optional data content, which is usually in the form of an HTML document and linked objects. The term *Web server* can also refer to the system that runs Web server programs. There are really two components of a Web server: hardware and software.

Writing Web applications doesn't necessarily mean that you'll need to purchase new hardware. Many platforms can be used to serve Web sites. Some are more compatible and better suited to Web development than others, but most can accommodate Web development. Your organization probably already has a system that can be used for serving a Web site and Web applications.

A decision will need to be made whether additional hardware is required to serve your site and Web applications. Additional hardware may add another layer of security. Data and applications can reside on the same system, or you might want to separate data to add yet another layer of security. On the other hand, having additional hardware requires additional support and administration. Using a Web hosting service should also be considered.

What Database(s) Are Used?

Nearly any database could have been used for the examples in this book. Web programming is generally very inclusive, and most databases are supported. The examples in this book use primarily Microsoft Access databases and MySQL databases, but chapter 7 includes a brief discussion on connecting to a Microsoft SQL Server database. Chapters 10 and 12 use a MySQL database and include several examples of connections that can be used to incorporate dynamic database content within your Web applications.

Where Can I Find Sample Code?

The examples used in this book are available on MC Press's Web site (*www.mcpressonline.com*). Go to the forums tab and select the MC Press Product Downloads and Reviews forum. There you will find a list of titles arranged alphabetically. Select HTML for the Business Developer to find the download files. Feel free to download and use the examples. We hope this book and the examples included will help you develop your own Web-based applications as quickly and easily as possible. Corresponding code files can be found for all of the code examples provided within this book.

The Development Process

The tools and techniques may be different for Web development than for traditional business programming, but the process is very similar. Developing applications still requires analysis, design, coding, testing, documentation, implementation, and support. Web development also requires looking at the application life cycle and building flexibility into the design so it can adapt to business process changes.

Your organization's development standards should be updated to provide developers a structure and process to follow as a standardized guide. Like development with legacy code, having predefined standards for Web development keeps code consistent, organized, easily maintained, and manageable.

All environments have their own unique challenges, just as all programmers have their own unique methods of coding. You can ask a number of programmers to code the same solution, and none of the applications will be coded exactly the same. Having a defined development process minimizes the effects of development differences. This holds true for Web applications as well as other applications. Organizations may also have internal requirements, such as Sarbanes-Oxley compliance, that cannot be overlooked and need to be accounted for in the development process. Web applications may add another twist, as additional hardware is often introduced into the mix. For example, application databases and some of the application code might reside on one system, and the browser-based components and server on another.

Take the time to consider how Web development fits into the process and have a defined process to follow. This will be time well spent. When learning a new language, developers will try to stick to a comfortable coding style. If a process is not predefined, developers will also define their own. Having a defined process and coding style will result in more consistent code and a more organized application. This kind of application is much easier to support in the long term, whether you or someone else has to go back and change, maintain, or debug code.

Once a decision has been made on the tools, technology, and hardware infrastructure that will be used for Web development, and prior to actual beginning development, consider the development process. This process should be revisited periodically. Changes will be made as a result of business requirements, business needs, and technology changes, among other reasons. The development process, like any other, can be defined, revisited, and enhanced to fit your organization's environment. How informal and flexible the process is depends on your environment's specifics.

IT Staff

As with legacy applications, development tasks for Web applications may be the responsibility of several groups or departments. This holds true especially in larger organizations. One group might be responsible for the application design and graphics, another for database support, another for administration, and another for business application logic and development. Responsibility might also be structured by platform, as Web applications often involve more than one platform. This does not mean that Web development requires more staff than legacy development, but it does mean you must consider the components, tasks, and IT staff structure. Staff structure will be based in part on resource skill sets and project requirements. In smaller organizations, the developer may also be responsible for configuration, Web design, and coding. However, you'll often find that experts in design or coding are not necessarily expert in configuration or hardware infrastructure. Therefore, tasks are often spread among different staff members and departments.

The size of the organization and the skill sets of resources can have a great impact on the structure of an IT staff. As shown in Table 1.1, small organizations require individuals with very diverse skill sets and an understanding of the complete realm of requirements. One of the interesting challenges of Web development is that it enables business developers to try their hand at design. Often, developers with strong analytical skills, who are able to tackle complex business requirements and turn them into well-functioning applications, aren't nearly as intuitive at designing the look of an application. This might mean stepping outside of a comfort zone, but it does not mean a business developer cannot fulfill this role within an IT staff structure.

Table 1.1: Size of Organization and IT Staff	
Organization Size	IT Staff Roles
Large	Often structured with multiple departments segmented by various roles required for Web development tasks. Departments may include, but are not limited to, management, project leaders, hardware and operations support, security and administration, design and graphics, database administration, and development. The size of Web projects tends to be large in regards to scope and timeline.
Medium	Often structured with multiple departments, but fewer than larger organizations. A combination of structuring is often based on staff skill sets.
Small	Often structured with few, if any, departments. Staff members fulfill many roles, as "jacks of all trades."

While this book focuses on business programming, it also includes other topics to provide insight into the many areas of Web development. Whether you will be responsible for many Web application tasks or programming only, an understanding of the related tasks will help you develop solid Web programming skills and make you better prepared to decide where you fit. Trying to be a jack of all trades may result in your being a master of none. Don't overwhelm yourself. We have intentionally focused on the business developer and on coding dynamic business applications so you will have an understanding of the technical skills required. You'll find, after gaining some experience, that there are often similarities in the languages and tools used for Web development. Learning HTML is valuable no matter what role you will fill as a developer. Learning common languages to create business applications is always beneficial.

So what does this mean to you as a developer? You can focus your effort on coding only, or you can decide to develop expanded Web skills to fulfill a role requiring a diverse skill set. Your personal goals, job status, and skill set will affect where you fit within your organization's IT staff structure. A developer with diverse skills will have more flexibility in the roles and organizations that are a good fit. If your desire is to learn other skills in addition to business application Web development, you might be more content within a small to medium organization. If you want to focus your skills on application coding and development, and not learn design, administration, or other related skills, a large organization will likely be a better fit.

Platforms

Creating Web applications does not necessarily mean an organization will need to change or add new platforms. Often, existing hardware can be used, if it is fit for Web development. Most organizations already have clients set up with Web browser support. Browser support is a necessity. The back-end hardware will probably not be the same as the client devices users have to access the Web. The configuration will also include a Web server. One of the most popular platforms for a Web server is a PC. This might be the same PC-based server used for the organization's intranet, or for security purposes, it might be a server dedicated to Web applications.

Legacy code may be reused with Web applications and will likely continue to reside on the legacy platform. Databases will also likely continue to reside on their current platform. So, will you need to learn new hardware operating systems? Probably not, unless the platforms currently used do not support Web applications.

If the decision is made to use Java-based technology, any platform that is a JVM (Java Virtual Machine) can be used. If the decision is made to use ASP.NET, a Microsoft server will probably be used. Some languages are better suited to specific hardware, but most languages used for Web development are supported by a variety of platforms. Web development is much more open than legacy application development. Its flexibility makes platform decisions easier.

Cost, resource skills, and staff knowledge will also be factors in deciding which platforms to use for Web development. Most organizations already have platform knowledge of PC-based client hardware with Web browser support, as well as platforms that are able to be used as a Web server.

Devices

Web applications open up the ability for additional devices to be supported. Any device that is able to connect to the Internet and provides a browser-based emulator can be used for Web applications. The decision to create and use Web applications enables you to provide user access through a variety of devices, including PDAs and cell phones.

The key to using nontraditional devices is application design. The design needs to accommodate the screen size, keyboard, and operating system of the devices to be used. With Wi-Fi making it possible for field staff or shop-floor staff to easily access and use applications, you can breathe new life into your old applications. (*Wi-Fi* is an abbreviation for *wireless fidelity*, a wireless technology often used for Internet connectivity.) An organization's sales staff could use their cell phones to determine inventory quantities. Shop-floor staff could use handheld devices to easily inquire on manufacturing requirements. While this book does not focus on building applications using unconventional devices, it does put you on the path to making these Web-based applications a reality.

Ajax

Web applications are fun to build. However, some Web applications are slow and sometimes frustrating for users. Because Web applications are made up of several components, even well-coded sites sometimes require the user to wait for data and pages to be loaded. You've probably seen the hourglass display at a Web site when, behind the scenes, the application goes through the processing steps to evaluate input, respond to the request, retrieve information, and format it for display through your Web browser.

Ajax (Asynchronous JavaScript and XML) is a buzzword, and for good reason. It is a way of programming for the Web that gets rid of the hourglass and slower response time. It is not new technology; it is a new way of looking at technology that is already mature and stable.

Ajax is a group of interrelated Web development techniques for creating dynamic, interactive Web applications. Using Ajax, data, content, and design are merged together. The primary advantage and reason for using Ajax is the increased responsiveness and interactivity of Web pages. The improvement is realized by exchanging small amounts of data with the server so that the entire Web page does not have to be reloaded each time the user performs an action. Because the Ajax engine is handling requests, the information can be held by the Ajax engine and allow interaction with the application and user to happen independently of any interaction with the

Web server. When a user clicks on something in an Ajax-driven application, very little response time is required. The page simply displays what the user is asking for. The result is speed, functionality, usability, and increased Web page interactivity.

Web applications are usually coded so the interaction between the user and the server are *synchronous*, meaning one step has to follow another. If a user clicks a link and initiates a request, the request is sent to the server, which then processes the request and returns the results back to the user's Web browser.

Ajax is *asynchronous*, in that extra data can be requested from a server and loaded in the background, without interfering with the display and behavior of the current Web page. JavaScript is usually the scripting language used for Ajax function calls. The JavaScript is loaded when the page loads and handles most of the basic tasks on the client side, including data validation, data manipulation, and data display, without a trip to the server. At the same time, the Ajax engine is sending data back and forth to the server. The data transfer does not depend on user actions and occurs concurrently. Data within an Ajax site is retrieved using the XMLHttpRequest object available to all scripting languages that are compatible with modern Web browsers. XML is often used with Ajax, but it is not a requirement that the asynchronous content be formatted in XML.

Ajax is a flexible technique based on cross-platform usability. It can be used with a variety of platforms, operating systems, and Web browsers. Ajax is based on open standards such as JavaScript and the DOM. While Ajax itself is beyond the scope of this book, you'll learn more about JavaScript and the DOM throughout this book. Free, open-source Ajax examples are available that are suitable for most Web-based application projects.

A great example of an Ajax site is Google Maps *(http://maps.google.com/)*. Visit the site and check it out. There really is very little wait time when maneuvering around the site and enlarging or moving around the maps.

SOA

Another hot technology today is *SOA, Service Oriented Architecture.* SOA defines how two or more entities interact in such a way as to enable one entity to perform a unit of work on behalf of the other. The unit of work is referred to as a *service*.

SOA is really a collection of services that communicate with one another. The communication can include services either simply passing data or coordinating some activity. The service interactions use a well-defined description language. SOA is an evolution of distributed computing based on the request-and-reply paradigm for asynchronous and synchronous applications.

Using SOA, an application's business logic or individual defined functions are modularized and presented as services for user applications. The key is each interaction is self-contained and has a loosely coupled nature. Each interaction remains independent of any other interaction. The service interface is independent of the implementation. Application developers can build applications by composing one or more services without knowing the service or the underlying implementations of the service. For example, a service can be implemented in .NET or Java on an NT server, and the application consuming the service could be in RPG running on an AS400.

SOAP-enabled Web services are the most common implementation of SOA. *SOAP*, or *Simple Object Access Protocol*, is a standard that defines the application-level structure for messages. For applications to integrate, they must agree on the message structure used. SOAP provides an application-level message structure for use over many communication protocols. Applications that speak SOAP can easily exchange information with each other, so SOAP facilitates integration between completely different systems.

The protocol independence of SOA means that different consumers can use a service by communicating with it in different ways. Service orientation is a method of architecting systems of autonomous services. Using SOA, services are built to be functional, flexible, reliable, and available. New service topologies may evolve over time, so systems using SOA are also built to accommodate changes.

This book does not focus on SOA, but it does introduce skills and tools that can be used to develop SOA applications.

Other Languages

This book starts with HTML and continues to introduce other programming languages used for Web development. Not all of the possible languages that may be used for Web development are introduced here. However, careful thought has been given to introduce some of the more common ones. You'll find many options and examples that can be used to create dynamic Web applications.

Although Web development has been around for quite a few years, it is still in its infancy compared to business application development. The growth has been like wildfire, and by no means is Web development for business applications a mature technology. Like any other growing technology, new languages and tools continue to be developed and introduced. There is a lot of debate on which are the best and what will be popular in the future.

Many languages and tools used for Web development are quite similar. Often, a combination of languages is used to create a Web application. Web development tends to be much more open than traditional development in regards to mixing things up. Traditionally, for example, RPG is used to code on an AS400, COBOL is used on a mainframe, and Visual Basic is used on a Microsoft server. Web development, on the other hand, typically does not lock an organization into a specific platform or a single language.

So, what are some of the languages that can be used for Web development? In addition to the tools covered in this book (HTML, CSS, JavaScript, CGI, PHP, ASP, and JSP), many other languages may be used for Web development, including A, ActionScript, Ada95, AppleScript, BEF, C, C++, CCI, CMM, Dylan, Eiffel, GEL, Glyphic Script, Guile, hyperTalk, Icon, Java, KQML, Linda, Lingo, Lisp, Logo, ML, Modula-3, NewtonScript, Obliq, Perl, Phantom, Python, REXX, Ruby, ScriptX, SDI, Self, SIMPLE, Sloth, Smalltalk, SMSL, Spynergy, Tcl, Telescript, Tycoon, UserTalk, Viola, VBScript, WebScript, VRML, XHTML, and XML. This is by no means a complete list, but gives it you an idea of the extent of tools available for Web development. All of the languages have their own unique features, advantages, and disadvantages. This book focuses on some of the most mature, proven, and popular tools for Web development.

Fear of Web Technology

Many business application developers who are experienced and comfortable with so-called legacy applications are a bit intimidated by the thought of coding an application using Web technology. Applications written in non-Web technology can also easily be written with Web technology. For intensive data-entry tasks, it may be argued that non-Web applications are best. This is very debatable, however; a well-designed and well-coded Web application can be a great fit for intensive data-entry needs. It is more likely the comfort level of a developer speaking rather than an unbiased opinion.

This doesn't necessarily mean you should rewrite all of your non-Web applications using Web technology. That isn't realistic or practical. For example, consider an organization that has a considerable investment in a non-Web-based ERP package with in-house add-on applications. It does not make sense to undertake rewriting the ERP package and its add-ons just for the sake of having a Web-based application. However, when you're already heavily enhancing or rewriting an application, or developing a new one, don't fear the Web. (We discuss reusing legacy applications in chapter 7.)

There are many practical reasons why Web technology should be considered and used. Business application development is changing, and may one day be dominated by Web applications. It may even be argued that Web applications have already established dominance within the business environment.

While those new to business application development are likely to be already using Web tools, those who have been staff developers for years might consider Web development outside their comfort zone. If that's you, it's time to step out of the box and expand your skills. Learning Web development isn't as scary as it might seem at first glance. Like any other technology, once you've learned it, used it, and have established a comfort and understanding of how it technically works, you're off to the races.

We've met many developers throughout the years who have been exposed to Web development in a variety of ways. A classic example of the wrong way is that a developer is tasked with creating a Web application and sent off to a Java class, with the expectation to return with the tools and knowledge needed to start pumping out code. This isn't realistic and can result in a fear of developing Web applications. Java in itself is not scary. It is a very robust, powerful, useful language. It is also, however, a complex language that does take time to learn.

We have taken care in this book not to focus on a single technology, but to introduce and provide examples of combinations of tools, so you can develop business applications upon completion of this book. If you are a bit afraid of Web development, upon finishing this book, you'll be over your fear and eager to use the tools you've learned.

Expanding Your Skill Set

With organizations becoming more global—expanding, merging, and changing—everyone needs to keep their skills updated. Should you be scared? Not at all. Being open to change is a fact of life.

As an experienced business developer, think about how technology has changed in regards to development. It's amazing what has been accomplished. Business thrives on technology. Technology provides a framework for the smooth operation of the business and the opportunity to improve the business. That opportunity can be in the form of resource savings or other cost savings. It can also be in the form of fulfilling basic business requirements and needs.

Not that long ago, it was possible to argue that the Web might be a phase and might not be here for the long term. Time has shown this is definitely not the case. The Web is here, it's bigger than ever, and it hasn't stopped growing. Similarly, not many years ago, it was unusual to have a PC at home connected to the Internet. Now, most households have some sort of Internet connectivity. Technology has changed rapidly, making it possible for almost anyone to have Internet access. As a business application developer, this means if you intend to continue to advance in your career, you will probably need to include Web technology as a part of your skill set.

Where do you learn Web skills? There are many sources and options for learning. Some options are less expensive and time-consuming than others. There are many books and classes available on a variety of Web topics. Our experience, however, has been that most education sources focus on a specific segment of Web development and are not always based on the viewpoint of the business developer. Care has been taken in writing this book to focus on you, the business developer. Upon completing this book, you will have the tools you need to start coding business Web applications.

The Job Market

Today's job market still provides a place for legacy coders, but more often than not it requires some sort of Web skills. Most businesses have evolved significantly. Buyouts, consolidations, and global business infrastructures are commonplace today. Change in business is a big factor. This has had a significant impact on today's business application developers. Change is a constant within the business infrastructure, but don't be misled into thinking it is such a moving target that you cannot safely determine where your time is best spent in developing your skill set.

The near future promises to be strong for IT job seekers with the right technical skill sets. Baby boomers are starting to reach retirement age. While the boomers are beginning to retire, the number of people entering the computer world is declining. According to the Education Research Institute at UCLA, interest among prospective students in computer science as a major has dropped 70 percent between 2001 and 2005. The decline in supply of future IT workers, combined with the aging IT population, might spell trouble for some organizations in regards to global competitiveness. The decline will be good news, however, for programmers who wish to move up within their IT departments or for those who are new to the job market. The supply is down and the demand continues to grow for IT workers.

In recent years, organizations have started to invest again in IT projects. The trends show a strong need for business analysts. According to a study from Foote Partners, companies are seeking and paying premiums for skills that help them adapt quickly to fast-changing business needs. The trend is to reward IT professionals based on the specific technical skills that fit into the organization's business needs. The demand for rapid development skills also reflects many organizations' intense focus on speed and agility. Organizations are spending more on training of their IT staffs. Developing and training existing staff is often easier and less costly than finding and hiring new talent.

Organizations are continuing to Web-enable their existing applications and to pursue Web-based solutions, making Web-based skills very hot. Business developers with Web skills including Ajax, Java, .NET, and PHP are in high demand. The growth of Java jobs has declined somewhat, but remains strong, while .NET jobs have skyrocketed in recent years. Currently, these two languages are neck-and-neck in terms of available job opportunities. Many believe this is due to Java being in the marketplace longer and the maturity of the .NET technology.

Business knowledge is important as organizations strive to align IT services with the businesses they support. Demand remains strong for application developers with business-specific knowledge and system analysis skills. Organizations also want developers who are familiar with the entire software development life cycle and are well rounded in terms of leadership and communication skills. Organizations are looking for individuals with broader sets of development skills.

Today's business market is global. The Web and technology has played an important role in global markets. Even small organizations are affected by the globalization of business. The Web has made it possible for both large and small businesses to expand their reach to a very distant base of clients.

Outsourcing

Outsourcing is a commonplace consideration today within the business environment. The intent of introducing this topic is not to debate the advantages and disadvantages of outsourcing. As a business developer, you should simply be aware of it.

Organizations look at outsourcing for several reasons. One reason might be budget considerations. Another reason might be because available in-house resources do not have the required skills to complete a project. When an organization makes the decision to take applications to the Web, if the necessary skills aren't available to the organization, outsourcing may well be considered. If you are an experienced staff business developer, contractor, or someone just getting your feet wet in business development, having the appropriate skills to fit business needs will improve your career. The fact that you are reading this book shows you have the desire to advance your skills.

There has been a lot of controversy over the topic of outsourcing. The claims that IT jobs are being shipped in droves offshore are usually exaggerated. The conclusion for most organizations that track such statistics is about five percent of all IT jobs have been displaced by foreign workers. Most of these are lower-level coding jobs, technical support positions, or call-center work. The jobs requiring more advanced skills are likely to remain within an organization. According to the September 2006 SIM report, only about 3.3 percent of 2007 corporate IT budgets have been allocated to offshore outsourcing programs. Skills that will be in declining demand in the near future are routine coding and systems testing, application maintenance, technical support, data continuity, and data recovery. These skills are among jobs that are being increasingly outsourced and offshored. IT jobs related to customer service and helping a business grow tend to remain within an organization. Organizations are coming to the realization that a lot of work has to take place in interfacing and managing projects to have outsourcing work effectively.

What does this mean to you as a business developer? It is important that your skill set is advanced and fits the industry's needs. This, of course, includes Web development skills.

Summary

We have covered a lot of information within this chapter. Hopefully, it has inspired you to think through some of the considerations that affect you as a business developer. You can do what you set your sights to do, if you really want to. The stronger the desire, the more successful you will likely be. Taking the first step is always significant. This book will help make the first step into Web development much easier. If you already have some Web development knowledge, you'll benefit from this book as well.

There are many choices on how to spend your time learning. We've made an effort to reduce the time you spend learning, and when you are done, you will be prepared to code a business Web application.

CHAPTER 2

An Introduction to HTML

Why should you, as a business programmer, take the time to learn HTML? What is it all about, anyway?

Why Learn HTML?

HTML is the *de facto* language for nearly every Web page that exists on the Internet. While it's true that other options are available for creating Web pages, many of those dynamically create HTML code as they execute, so knowledge of HTML is still required. It is almost inconceivable that any programmer could deploy a browser-based application without using HTML at some point in the process.

Programmers who do not continue to update their skills risk professional obsolescence. You have probably worked with someone who was either reluctant or unable to update his or her skill set. Eventually that person was out of a job, for one reason or another. Finding another job was difficult, if not impossible, with the skills he or she had to offer. After the fact, that person regretted not working harder at learning new skills.

Well, that answers half the question. Learning something is necessary, but why HTML? As mentioned, it's the most common language used in browser-based application development. In case you hadn't noticed, our industry is making a huge conversion. In the past, many business applications were written and customized to run on a particular platform, using the language most common to that platform: COBOL on mainframes, Visual Basic (VB) on Windows, C++ on Unix, and

RPG on IBM. All of these languages are optimized for the environments in which they run. By definition, however, they are tied to that specific environment. Porting one of these applications to another platform or deploying it in a different way is a serious challenge.

The idea of browser-based applications deployed over the Internet has its origins in the early 1990s. Tim Berners-Lee invented the term "World Wide Web" and the first Web browser, and went on to found the World Wide Web Consortium, also know as the *W3C*. Among other things, the W3C acts as a shepherd watching over the development of Web technologies. It provides guidelines, standards, recommendations, and education on many aspects of Web-related technology. You can find out more about the W3C at *www.w3c.org*.

Perhaps the most fundamental guideline that the W3C produces is the HTML specifications found at *www.w3.org/TR/1999/REC-html401-19991224/.* This document provides information on the HTML language and recommendations as to its correct usage. While these guidelines in no way prevent developers from coding any way they like, it is wise to be aware of them. As the language continues to evolve, changes could make the code obsolete in Web pages you have written. For example, the W3C guidelines indicate which HTML language elements are *deprecated*. Deprecated features remain in the standard, but with the understanding that they might be removed in the future. At the very least, their use is discouraged. Since many existing pages contain these deprecated elements, we'll cover them here. Review the W3C guidelines for clear documentation on this issue.

What Is HTML All About?

First, HTML stands for *Hypertext Markup Language*. It is a relatively simple language for defining the appearance of content displayed in a Web browser such as Microsoft's Internet Explorer. Developed in the early 1990s, HTML went through a rapid growth spurt as the Internet exploded into the public's consciousness. One after another, rapid and significant enhancements were released. Now, more than 20 years later, the pace of change has slowed. Throughout the rest of this chapter we'll explore the basics of HTML coding.

A Basic HTML Page

HTML coding is based on *tags*, recognized by the less-than and greater-than signs, <...>, that surround each instruction. For example, to create a minor heading, you might code **<h5>Contact us at:</h5>**. The **<h5>** tag signals the browser that the text that follows appears somewhat larger and darker than the default text, as shown here:

Contact us at:

The **</h5>** tag is called an *end tag*. The slash indicates that this tag ends the previous **<h5>** tag. Any text processed after the end tag appears in the default size and style. Most, but not all, HTML tags have corresponding end tags.

Consider the simple Web page shown in Figure 2.1, which was introduced in chapter 1.

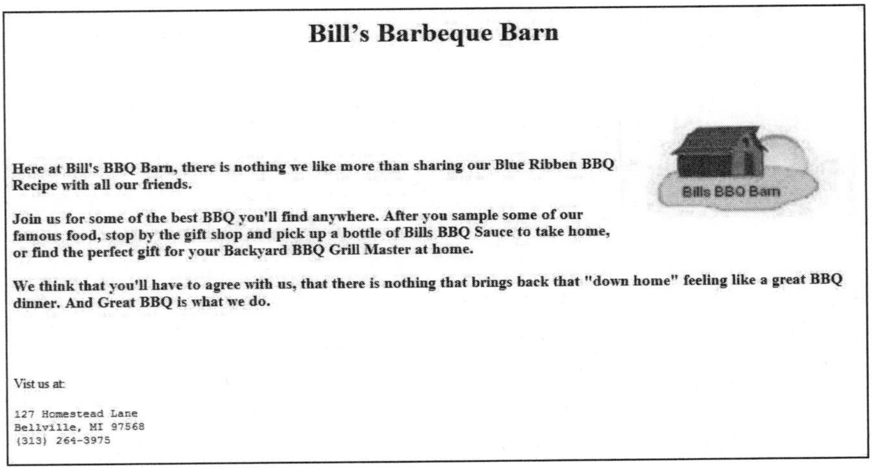

Figure 2.1: A simple Web page.

Any HTML novice could create this very simple Web page. Its code is shown in Figure 2.2. This is the complete source code to display the Web page. It's named "Barbeque Barn.html," but the file could have ended with ".htm" instead. Within the code, you can see a reference to the picture, "bbqbarn.jpg."

```
<html>
<body><center>
<h1>Bill's Barbeque Barn</h1>
</center>
<right><img src="bbqbarn.jpg" align="right"></right>
<br><br><br><br><br><br>
<left>
<h3>Here at Bill's BBQ Barn, there is nothing we like more than
sharing our Blue Ribbon BBQ Recipe with all our friends.
<br><br>
Join us for some of the best BBQ you'll find anywhere. After you
    sample some of our famous food, stop by the gift shop and pick
    up a bottle of Bills BBQ Sauce to take home, or find the perfect
    gift for your Backyard BBQ Grill Master at home.
<br><br>
We think that you'll have to agree with us, that there is nothing
    that brings back that "down home" feeling like a great BBQ
    dinner. And Great BBQ is what we do.
</h3>
<br><br><br>
Visit us at:
<pre>
127 Homestead Lane
Bellville, MI 97568
(313) 264-3975
</pre>
</left></body>
</html>
```

Figure 2.2: The HTML code for the page shown in Figure 2.1.

The first line of code in Figure 2.2 contains the **<html>** tag. This tag instructs the browser that the text after it is HTML code. Since browsers have to be able to process data written in many different languages,

Web pages typically identify their language at the beginning of the code. A matching **</html>** as the last line in Figure 2.2 ends the source code.

The **<body>** tag marks the beginning of the displayable content of the Web page. It includes a large number of optional attributes, discussed in the following paragraphs. The matching end **</body>** tag typically appears immediately before the **</html>** tag at the end of the source code.

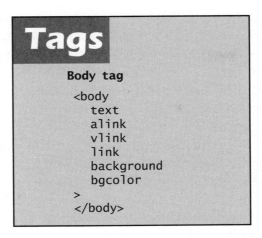

Tags

Body tag

```
<body
    text
    alink
    vlink
    link
    background
    bgcolor
>
</body>
```

Optional attributes appear inside the **<body>** tag with the format *attribute = value*. Separate the attributes in a tag with at least one space. One of the most common attributes for the **<body>** tag is **bgcolor**. Use this to set the background color for the entire Web page. For example, changing the **<body>** tag to **<body bgcolor="beige">** changes the background of the entire page to beige, as shown in Figure 2.3. The background of the image, however, is still white. Later, we will discuss options for dealing with the image.

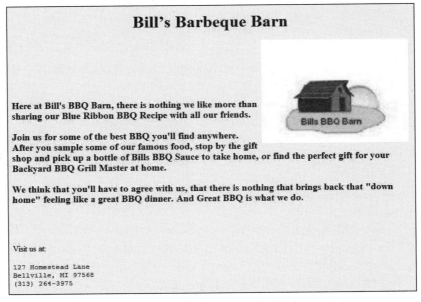

Figure 2.3: A sample Web page with a beige background.

The **text**, **alink**, **vlink**, and **link** attributes set the color for the text on the page. **Text** defines the default text color for the entire page. The others define the colors of hypertext links. **Alink** indicates the color of an active link, a link that is currently in use. **Vlink** indicates the color of previously visited links, and **link** sets the color for unvisited links. Browsers typically retain a history of links they have navigated to in the past, so it's possible that a site may show up as visited even if it has been months since it was used. Browsers also usually contain an option to clear this history, in which case no links will appear visited, unless they are visited again. These issues are discussed in more detail in chapter 4.

The **background** attribute identifies an image to use for a tiled background. Typically, these are referred to as "texture" images. These images are of relatively simple patterns that tile seamlessly, disguising the borders between tiles. This option does not support defining a single image as the page background, although chapter 3 discusses other methods for achieving this.

The **<center>** tag instructs the browser to center the contents of the page between the left and right margins. The browser centers all content until the **</center>** tag, or until another alignment command supersedes

Center tag

```
<center>
</center>
```

it. This command centers the heading "Bill's Barbeque Barn." Without it, the heading would be left justified by default.

The level-one heading defines the text within the tags as the heaviest weighted or largest heading. Each browser has some control over the actual size of text displayed, so that users with limited eyesight,

Heading 1 tag

```
<h1>
</h1>
```

for example, can define their preferred size of text. Web developers refer to a "logical" size of text. Rather than specifying an exact size, such as 12 pixels, the developer indicates a relative size, such as H1 (big), H3 (medium), or H6 (small).

The **<right>** tag instructs the browser to right-justify the contents of the page until the **</right>** tag, or until another alignment command supersedes it. You might think this command is used to right-justify the

bbqbarn.jpg image in Figure 2.3, but the image actually is not affected by it. Instead, the **align=right** attribute of the **<img>** tag forces the image to the right side of the page. The **<right>** command does not affect floating images.

The **<img>** tag places an image on the page. Its attributes modify the image as desired. The **align** attribute defines the flow of text around the image. There are five options for **align**:

- **Top** aligns the top of the image to the baseline.
- **Bottom** aligns the bottom of the image to the baseline.
- **Middle** aligns the middle of the image to the baseline.
- **Left** floats the image to the left margin.
- **Right** floats the image to the right margin.

Alt defines an alternate text displayed when a user hovers the mouse over the image. It is also used by page readers for the blind, and by

Web crawlers for search engines such as Google and Yahoo that catalog the content of a page. So, while this is an optional attribute, it is highly encouraged to provide assistance to the disabled and to assist your own page being placed correctly by search engines.

Border defines the width of an image border, in pixels. Obviously, a border will destroy any "seamlessness" between the images and the background of the page. However, for many pages, this might be perfectly fine.

Height and **width** define the size of a picture, in either pixels or percentages. Pixels are expressed as an integer, while percentages use the percent sign, %. If a percentage is used, it refers to the size of the entire page, so an image set to 50% height and width is half as tall as the page, and half as wide. When resizing an image, be aware of how the image will scale. Some images do not look good if their height-to-width ratios are changed. An image that is defined as 200x100 could be scaled to 300x300, but there is a good chance that it would look distorted. Scaling to 400x200 would probably look better. It is also true that many images look increasingly grainy as they are enlarged.

Hspace refers to the white space on the left and right sides of an image. **Vspace** refers to the white space above and below the image. **Src** defines the location of the image. This can be a physical location on the server, or a *URL* (*Universal Resource Locator*) to another location on the Internet. If no path is given before the image name (such as *c:* or *http:*), it is assumed the image is in the same location as the Web page. To indicate the image is stored in a folder one level up, use the syntax *../file-name*.

Ismap indicates that the image has a corresponding server-side image map. **Usemap** indicates a client-side server map. In general, an image map applies to an image that is used as a link. Rather than assigning a single target to the entire image, an image map allows different sections of an image to link to different locations. For example, if you had a picture of a car, you could define different links for the door, hood, engine, tires, interior, and trunk. These links could be to pages that further describe these areas. Image maps are discussed in more detail in chapter 3.

A commonly used attribute that is not included in the W3C standard is **lowsrc**. Some browsers, such as Microsoft's Internet Explorer, support this attribute. It defines a small image that will be preloaded and displayed before the primary image defined in the **src** attribute. When the primary image is very large and slow loading, the **lowsrc** image provides a "placeholder" image. The primary image overlays the **lowsrc** image once it is loaded. As the speed of desktop computers and Internet connections increase, this option becomes less useful.

To illustrate how the attributes of the image tag can affect the look of an image on a Web page, let's modify the image tag, as shown in Figure 2.4. As a result of this change in the code, the Web page changes significantly, as shown in Figure 2.5. The image is now on the left side, much larger, and with a border. The alternate text, not shown in this picture, appears when you place the mouse over the image.

```
<img src="bbqbarn.jpg" align="left" hspace="50"
vspace = "50" Border="3" height="400" width="552"
alt="Bill's Barn with Green Grass and Sun">
```

Figure 2.4: The HTML code for an image.

Figure 2.5: The Web page with a modified *<img>* tag.

OK, so Figure 2.5 is not the prettiest Web page. Remember, this is not a book about graphic design. It's about HTML and how it works. It's quite likely that you will need to place images of such things as facilities, products, and logos on your Web pages. It's also quite possible that you'll need to control the size, placement, borders, and other attributes of these images. So, while the example here might seem a bit silly, it illustrates the use of the **<img>** tag. We'll put the **<img>** tag back the way it was, though, because we do not want our page looking like this!

The break tag, **
**, has no end tag. It forces the browser to insert a line break at that location. By default, a browser compresses white space in the Web page and arranges content as the browser deems best.

Break tag

This can sometimes create discrepancies in how a Web page is displayed. The sample Web page uses many break tags to force blank lines between paragraphs. Other, more advanced methods for dealing with this are discussed later.

The **<left>** tag instructs the browser to left-justify the contents of the page until the end **</left>** tag, or until another alignment command supersedes it. This is the default behavior if no other alignment commands are in effect.

Left tag

The level-3 heading, **<h3>**, defines the text within the tags as a medium-weighted heading. Figure 2.6 shows the various heading levels, H1 through H6.

Heading 3 tag

<h3>
</h3>

H1...Bill's Barbeque Barn

H2...Bill's Barbeque Barn

H3...Bill's Barbeque Barn

H4...Bill's Barbeque Barn

H5...Bill's Barbeque Barn

H6...Bill's Barbeque Barn

Figure 2.6: Samples of the **<h1>** *through* **<h6>** *headings.*

Preformatted text is placed between the **<pre>** and **</pre>** tags. This tag overrides the browser's ability to compress white space and blank lines as it sees fit. Any white space and carriage returns included between the

Tags

Preformatted tag

```
<pre>
</pre>
```

tags are preserved by the browser when the Web page is displayed. For things such as addresses or sets of data that have specific formatting, the **<pre>** tag can be quite useful.

Additional HTML Tags

The **<pre>** tag is the last of the HTML tags used in our beginning Web page. There are quite a few more tags to discuss, though. Some are fairly simple and straightforward, while

others are much more complex. You'll see all of them in the remainder of this book, but this chapter focuses on the remaining simple HTML tags.

Comments are an important feature for any language, and HTML is no exception. You will frequently find that comments are particularly useful in clarifying the more complex, less intuitive portions of your Web pages.

The **<head>** tag must be placed after the **<html>** tag, and the end **</head>** tag must come before the **<body>** tag. The heading generally provides additional information about a Web page, not additional content to display on the page. Other tags, such as **<title>**, **<link>**, and **<meta>**, are included within the heading. The **<title>** tag is discussed below, while **<meta>** and **<link>** are discussed later in this chapter.

The text between the **<title>** and **</title>** tags are used as the title of the Web page. This title is displayed at the top of the window, and also on the minimized tab for the window. For example, if we add a title to our Web page,

the modified HTML code might look like Figure 2.7.

```
<html>
<head>
<title>Bill's BBQ Barn</title>
</head?
<body>
```

Figure 2.7: The HTML code to create a title.

Figure 2.8 shows the title in the title bar of the window containing the Web page. This is also the title of the tab when the window is minimized, as show in Figure 2.9.

Figure 2.8: An example of a title in a Web page's title bar.

Figure 2.9: An example of the title in a minimized Window tab.

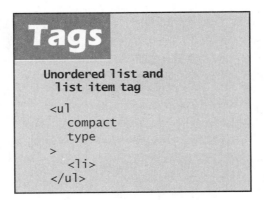

Unordered lists, which use the **<ul>** tag, are commonly referred to as bullets. The **compact** attribute is used by some browsers as a signal that the list should be displayed more densely than usual. The **type** attribute changes the look of the bullet itself. The possible values are **disk**, **square**, and **circle**. If we wanted to add a menu to our Web page, we might use an unordered list to make it stand out from the other text on the page. The HTML code shown in Figure 2.10 generates the catalog text shown in Figure 2.11.

```
<ul type=disc>
<li>Bill's Sweet BBQ Sauce</li>
<li>Grandma's Secret Hot Sauce</li>
<li>Bill's Country Cookbook</li>
<li>Bill's Babyback Ribs</li>
<li>Bill's Beef Ribs</li>
</ul>
```

Figure 2.10: The HTML code to create Figure 2.11.

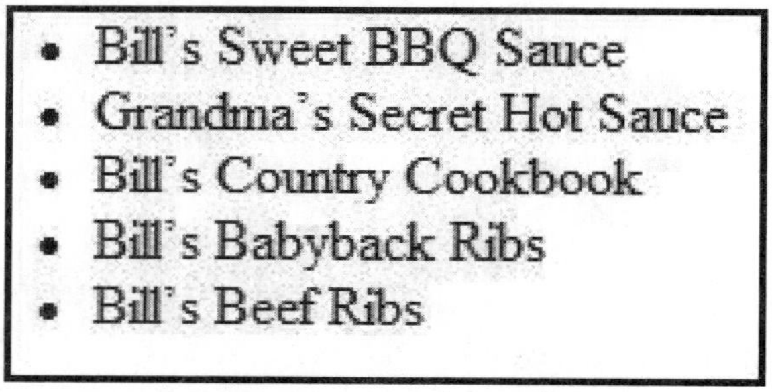

- Bill's Sweet BBQ Sauce
- Grandma's Secret Hot Sauce
- Bill's Country Cookbook
- Bill's Babyback Ribs
- Bill's Beef Ribs

Figure 2.11: An example of an unordered list.

Tags

Ordered list and list item tag

```
<ol
   compact
   type
   start
>
   <li
      value
   >
</ol>
```

Sometimes, bullets are not appropriate for the items you're listing. Yes, they worked fine for the catalog shown in Figure 2.11, but what if we had a series of instructions to follow in a specific sequence? That is where an ordered list shines. The valid values for the type attribute are **1**, **a**, **A**, **i**, and **I**. The **start** attribute sets the beginning value. This is always numeric, even if the **type** is not. For example, a value of **2** for **start** yields "b" for type **a**, and "ii" for type **i**.

Figure 2.12 shows an ordered list to add some instructions for cooking the perfect BBQ. The resulting instructions are shown in Figure 2.13.

```
<ol type=1>
<li>Start with Bill's Sweet BBQ Sauce</li>
<li>Follow a great recipe such as "Backyard BBQ Babyback Pork
   Ribs" found on Page 17 in Bill's Country Cookbook</li>
<li>Get the highest quality Babyback Pork Ribs you can. If you
   don't know where to get your ribs, stop by the barn and take some
   home to cook up yourself.</li>
</ol>
```

Figure 2.12: The HTML code to create Figure 2.13.

1. Start with Bill's Sweet BBQ Sauce
2. Follow a great recipe such as "Backyard BBQ Babyback Pork Ribs" found on Page 17 in Bill's Country Cookbook
3. Get the highest quality Babyback Pork Ribs you can. If you don't know where to get your ribs, stop by the barn and take some home to cook up yourself.

Figure 2.13: An example of an ordered list.

As you can see in this example, the list automatically starts at one and increments by one. There are only a few supported options. If you need something else, you can create it manually using the **value** attribute of the **<li>** tag. For example, to number the menu by tens (silly, but it's just an example), see Figure 2.14. The **value** attribute is similar to the **start** attribute, in that the number represents the sequence of a specific value in a list. In an alphabetical list, 10 represents "j," not the number 10.

```
<ol type=1>
<li value=10>Start with Bill's Sweet BBQ sauce</li>
<li value=20>Follow a great recipe such as "Backyard BBQ Babyback
   Pork Ribs" found on Page 17 in Bill's Country Cookbook</li>
<li value=30>Get the highest quality Babyback Pork Ribs you can.
   If you don't know where to get your ribs, stop by the barn and
   take some home to cook up yourself.</li>
</ol>
```

Figure 2.14: An ordered list with specific numeric values.

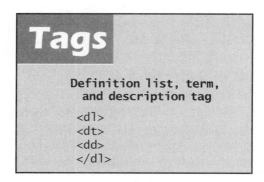

The third type of list is the definition list. It is designed for assigning a definition or description to a list of terms. Obviously, this is useful if you are publishing a dictionary, but where else does it work? In our example Web page, we might want to add a description of the various flavors of BBQ sauce offered. The code to do that is shown in Figure 2.15 and illustrated in Figure 2.16.

```
<dl>
<dt>Honey BBQ</dt>
<dd>Our favorite traditional sweet and tangy sauce</dd>
<dt>Sweet Honey BBQ</dt>
<dd>Like Honey BBQ, but with a bit less tang and lot more sweet!</dd>
<dt>Prairie Fire BBQ</dt>
<dd>Our secret spicy BBQ sauce guaranteed to Sizzle!</dd>
</dl>
```

Figure 2.15: The HTML code for a definition list.

Honey BBQ
     Our favorite traditional sweet and tangy sauce
Sweet Honey BBQ
     Like Honey BBQ, but with a bit less tang and lot more sweet!
Prairie Fire BBQ
     Our secret spicy BBQ sauce guaranteed to Sizzle!

Figure 2.16: An example of a definition list.

The browser aligns and positions text in lists as well as it can, depending on a variety of factors, such as screen resolution and window size. In a large window, the instructions shown in Figure 2.13 flow across the entire screen. If the window size shrinks, the browser will shorten the width of the page and add more lines if needed, as shown in Figure 2.17.

1. Start with Bill's Sweet BBQ Sauce
2. Follow a great recipe such as "Backyard BBQ Babyback Pork Ribs" found on Page 17 in Bill's Country Cookbook
3. Get the highest quality Babyback Pork Ribs you can. If you don't know where to get your ribs, stop by the barn and take some home to cook up yourself.

Figure 2.17: An ordered list in a narrow window.

Paragraph tags are not required, but are very valuable. If the browser can recognize a section of text as a paragraph, it can better render the text onto a page. Without paragraph tags, you must explicitly code line breaks between paragraphs. The **align** attribute sets the text to left, right, or centered. The code sample in Figure 2.18 shows text from the sample Web page rewritten to use paragraph tags.

```
<h3><p>Here at Bill's BBQ Barn, there is nothing we like more than
    sharing our Blue Ribbon BBQ Recipe with all our friends.
</p><p>
Join us for some of the best BBQ you'll find anywhere. After you
    sample some of our famous food, stop by the gift shop and pick
    up a bottle of Bills BBQ Sauce to take home, or find the perfect
    gift for your Backyard BBQ Grill Master at home.
</p><p>
We think that you'll have to agree with us, that there is nothing
    that brings back that "down home" feeling like a great BBQ dinner.
    And Great BBQ is what we do.
</p></h3>
```

Figure 2.18: HTML code for the sample page, with paragraph tags.

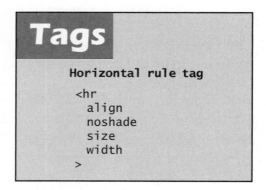

The **<hr>** tag simply draws a line across the Web page. The **width** attribute defines how far across the page the line should extend. The value for **width** can be expressed either in pixels or as a percentage of the page width. The **align** attribute determines if the line is centered, left-justified, or right-justified. The **size** attribute determines the line's thickness in pixels, and pixels only. The **noshade** attribute removes the 3D effect from the line, resulting in a "flatter" look. The code snippet in Figure 2.19 shows the HTML code needed to create the two horizontal lines shown in Figure 2.20.

```
<hr width = 80%>
<hr width = 50% size=4 noshade>
```

Figure 2.19: The HTML code to create two horizontal rules.

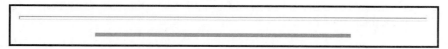

Figure 2.20: The horizontal rules.

You can use **<hr>** to add some structure to a Web page, by defining different sections.

The Updated Sample Page

Let's add the HTML code from many of the topics we've discussed to our Web page. The modified code shown in Figure 2.21 creates the updated Web page in Figure 2.22.

```
<html>
<body><center>
<h1>Bill's Barbeque Barn</h1>
</center>
<right><img src="bbqbarn.jpg" align="RIGHT"></right>
<br><br><br><br><br><br>
<left>
<h3><p>Here at Bill's BBQ Barn, there is nothing we like more than
  sharing our Blue Ribbon BBQ Recipe with all our friends.
</p><p>
Join us for some of the best BBQ you'll find anywhere. After you
  sample some of our famous food, stop by the gift shop and pick
  up a bottle of Bills BBQ Sauce to take home, or find the perfect
  gift for your Backyard BBQ Grill Master at home.
</p><p>
We think that you'll have to agree with us, that there is nothing
  that brings back that "down home" feeling like a great BBQ din-
  ner.  And Great BBQ is what we do.
</p></h3>
<br><br><br>
<hr size=4 width=80%>
<center><h4>Country Store</h4></center>
<ul type=disc>
<li>Bill's Sweet BBQ Sauce</li>
<li>Grandma's Secret Hot Sauce</li>
<li>Bill's Country Cookbook</li>
<li>Bill's Babyback Ribs</li>
<li>Bill's Beef Ribs</li>
</ul>
<hr size=4 width=80%>
<center><h4>BBQ Flavors</h4></center>
<dl>
<dt>Honey BBQ</dt>
<dd>Our favorite traditional sweet and tangy sauce</dd>
<dt>Sweet Honey BBQ</dt>
<dd>Like Honey BBQ, but with a bit less tang and lot more sweet!</
  dd>
<dt>Prairie Fire BBQ</dt>
<dd>Our secret spicy BBQ sauce guaranteed to Sizzle!</dd>
</dl>
<hr size=4 width=80%>
<center><h4>BBQ "How To"</h4></center>
<ol type=1>
<li>Start with Bill's Sweet BBQ sauce</li>
<li>Follow a great recipe such as "Backyard BBQ Babyback Pork
  Ribs" found on Page 17 in Bill's Country Cookbook</li>
<li>Get the highest quality Babyback Pork Ribs you can. If you
  don't know where to get your ribs, stop by the barn and take some
  home to cook up yourself.</li>
<hr size=4 width=80%>
<br>
```

Figure 2.21: The HTML code to create the Web page in Figure 2.22 (part 1 of 2).

```
Visit us at:
<pre>
127 Homestead Lane
Bellville, MI 97568
(313) 264-3975
</pre>
</left></body>
</html>
```

Figure 2.21: The HTML code to create the Web page in Figure 2.22 (part 2 of 2).

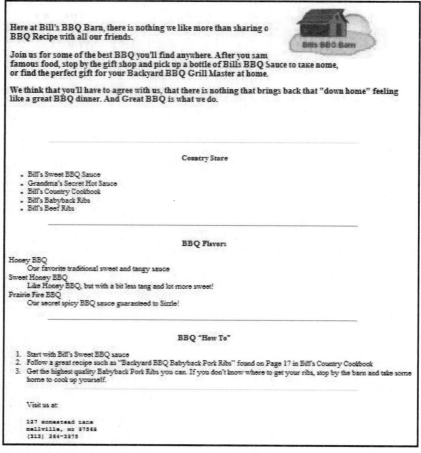

Figure 2.22: An updated Web page.

This page is probably too long to fit on a screen all at once, so the browser will add scroll bars as needed to allow you to view it. Generally, it is preferable to keep all of your Web content on the screen at the same time. Vertical scrolling is occasionally used, but horizontal scrolling is rare and should be avoided.

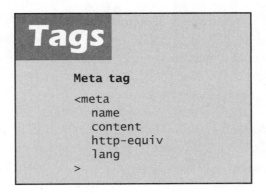

The **<meta>** tag provides information about the Web page to browsers and Web crawlers. A *crawler* is a tool used by search engines such as Yahoo and Google to systematically examine the content of Web pages on the Internet. Crawlers evaluate and catalog these Web pages for inclusion in search engines.

Crawlers are constantly trolling through the Internet, examining page after page. The **<meta>** tags in your Web page can affect your placement within these search engines. You can find out more about search engines in chapter 14. Just how useful these **<meta>** tags are is subject to change as the Internet continues to evolve. Tags that were useful last year might not be useful this year, and ones we don't use today might become useful next year. It's an area that needs periodic reevaluation. For our purposes, we'll stick to a few of the most common values for **<meta>** tags: **"description," "keywords," "robot," "content-type," "content-style-type,"** and **"content-language."** Figure 2.23 shows our Web page with sets of **<meta>** tags added.

```
<head>
<meta http-equiv="Content-Type"
 content="text/html; charset=ISO-8859-1">
<meta http-equiv="Content-Style-Type"
 content="text/css">
<meta name="Description"
 content="Bill's BBQ Barn.">
<meta name="keywords"
 content="Bill's, BBQ, Barbeque, Barn">
<meta name="robot"
 content="noindex, follow">
</head>
```

Figure 2.23: HTML *<meta>* tags.

Different tools use different tags. For example, some Web crawlers use the **keywords** value, but many do not, so the effect of this value depends on the browsers, tools, and search engines used. The **content-type** value identifies the character set being used. ISO-8859-1 is the typical character set used for a Web page. For best results, include this on all pages, and change the code if needed for other languages. The **content-style-type** value defines the method for encoding style information for the page. This is discussed further in chapter 5.

The **description** value provides succinct information about the content of the page. This is the text that most search engines, such as Google, display when presenting your page to searchers. In the past, the **keywords** value assisted search engines in evaluating which keyword searches applied to each Web page. Because some developers abused this value, it fell out of use. Some search engines do still look at it, and it's always possible that others might reconsider it in the future. For that reason, and the fact that it is easily implemented, we still find it useful.

The **robot** value provides instruction to Web crawlers that evaluate your Web page. **Noindex** indicates that the Web crawler should not include this Web page in its search-engine database. This can be set to **index**, which is the default. **Follow** instructs the crawler to follow links on this page to other pages. The alternative is to set that option to **nofollow**. By default, crawlers will follow the links on your page to other pages. While some Web crawlers honor the **robot** value, not all do. Often, a better approach to dealing with robots is to use the Robots Exclusion Protocol, as explained in Wikipedia at this URL:

http://en.wikipedia.org/wiki/Robots_Exclusion_Standard

The most important thing to remember about the **<meta>** tag is that it does not involve data or content. Rather, it provides information about the page.

Tags

Document type tag

`<!doctype>`

The **<!doctype>** tag provides additional information about the way in which the Web page is written. Three common options are used. The first, shown in Figure 2.24, defines the HTML code in use as "strict," preventing the use of deprecated tags.

```
<!doctype html public "-//W3C//DTD HTML 4.01//EN">
```

*Figure 2.24: An example of the HTML **<!doctype>** tag.*

For a looser set of rules on the coding of the Web page that does allow the use of deprecated tags, use the **<!doctype>** declaration in Figure 2.25.

```
<!doctype html public "-//W3C//DTD HTML 4.01 Transitional//EN">
```

*Figure 2.25: The HTML **<!doctype>** tag for transitional rules.*

If your Web page uses framesets (discussed in chapter 6), include the **<!doctype>** declaration shown in Figure 2.26. The **frameset** option is based on the transitional rules, and includes extensions for framesets. Be sure to code the **<!doctype>** tag as the first line of text in the HTML document, no matter which choice you make.

```
<!doctype html public "-//W3C//DTD HTML 4.01 Frameset//EN">
```

*Figure 2.26: The HTML **<!doctype>** tag for frameset rules.*

Tags

Big, small, and code tags

```
<big>
</big>
<small>
</small>
<code>
</code>
```

Many tags affect the general display of text on the screen. The **<big>** and **<small>** tags cause a section of text to display in larger or smaller size than normal, respectively. The **<blockquote>** tag defines and displays a section of text as a quote, giving it a markedly different appearance. The snippet of code in Figure 2.27 uses these three tags to create the output shown in Figure 2.28.

```
This is some normal text<br>
<big>This is some really BIG text</big><br>
<small>This is some small text</small><br>
<code>x = obj.x;
        y = obj.y;</code>
```

Figure 2.27: HTML code for various text styles.

This is some normal text
This is some really BIG text
This is some small text
x = obj.x; y = obj.y;

*Figure 2.28: A sample using the **<big>**, **<small>**, and **<code>** tags.*

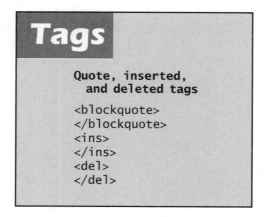

Tags

**Quote, inserted,
and deleted tags**

```
<blockquote>
</blockquote>
<ins>
</ins>
<del>
</del>
```

To define a section of text as a quote, use the **<blockquote>** tag. To mark text as either being inserted or deleted, use **<ins>** or **<del>**, respectively.

The code snippet in Figure 2.29 uses these tags to produce the output shown in Figure 2.30.

```
This is some <del>normal</del>
<ins>typical</ins> text<br>
<blockquote>And you can quote me on that!</blockquote>
```

Figure 2.29: HTML *<blockquote>* code.

This is some ~~normal~~ <u>typical</u> text

And you can quote me on that!

Figure 2.30: A sample using the *<blockquote>*, *<ins>*, and *<del>* tags.

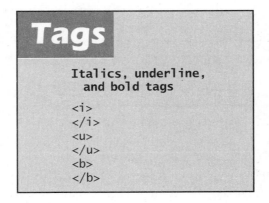

Tags

Italics, underline, and bold tags

```
<i>
</i>
<u>
</u>
<b>
</b>
```

Use **<i>**, **<u>**, and **<b>** to create text that is italicized, underlined, or bolded. These are common attributes used in many other languages and tools, so no more explanation of them should be needed here.

The subscript and superscript tags allow you to deal with things such as exponential notation and footnotes. The code snippet in Figure 2.31 shows how to use these tags to create the output in Figure 2.32.

```
Fore more information on HTML check out the 3WC<sub>1</sub>
<br>
This is will increase your skills by 10<sup>3</sup> times.
```

Figure 2.31: HTML code using the superscript and subscript tags.

Fore more information on HTML check out the $3WC_1$

This is will increase your skills by 10^3 times.

*Figure 2.32: The result of the **<sub>** and **<sup>** tags.*

Many of the tags discussed so far directly affect the appearance of the content on the Web page. This was fine in earlier days of HTML coding, but as mentioned earlier in this chapter, many of these HTML codes have been deprecated. Their use is discouraged, and they are not considered acceptable for HTML documents coded with the "strict" document type. Eventually, support for these tags may be dropped completely. However, many existing pages still use them, so some knowledge of them is essential.

Tags

Font tag

```
<font
    size
    face
    color
>
</font>
```

As we move forward, we'll review increasingly modern and sophisticated methods for controlling the appearance of text on a Web page. Inline fonts or style sheets, discussed in chapter 5, are the primary means to accomplish this task. Actually, the **<font>** tag is deprecated because style sheets are replacing it. However, **<font>** tags are still commonly found in existing code, as shown in Figure 2.33. The output from this code sample is shown in Figure 2.34.

```
<font size=4 face="Times" color="Blue">
Here is some Big Blue Text</Font><br>
<font size=-2 face="Verdana, Times" color="Red">
Here is some small red text</Font><br>
<font size=-1 face="Verdana, Times" color="Red">
Here is some bigger red text</Font><br>
And some normal sized text
```

Figure 2.33: The HTML **<font>** tag.

Here is some Big Blue Text
Here is some small red text
Here is some bigger red text
And some normal sized text

Figure 2.34: A sample of a page that uses the **<font>** tag.

In the code sample in Figure 2.34, the second and third lines are red text printed in either the Verdana or Times font. List the fonts in the order of preference, to instruct the browser to use the first one found on the remote user's computer. This allows the use of some less common fonts for better effect, while also providing a backup, in case the preferred font is not available. A font size may be entered as a specific numeric value, or as a variation from the default size, as in *-2*. Font colors can be listed as either their text names, or their hex code. For example, red could be coded as *#FF0000*.

The hex code represents the RGB (red, green, and blue) component of each color. The value is made up of three parts. Each part is made up of two hex digits (0 to 9 and A to F), indicating the amount of that component in the color. So, *00* indicates that there is none of that component in the color, while *FF* indicates the maximum amount of that component is included. See appendix E for a list of common colors.

It is important to note that not all colors appear the same when displayed by different browsers. There are, however, some consistently agreed-upon colors called *browser-safe* colors. Sticking to these colors will provide a more dependable presentation of your Web page on the many available browsers.

Special Characters

In addition to special codes for colors, there are special codes for characters. The previous examples have used fairly simple text. What if we wanted to include quote marks, greater than or less than symbols, or other special characters? Many of these characters are available through the use of *escape codes*. The snippet of code shown in Figure 2.35 uses escape codes to add quotation marks around text, as shown in Figure 2.36.

```
<blockquote>&ldquo;
And you can quote me on that!
&rdquo;</blockquote>
```

Figure 2.35: The HTML **<blockquote>** *tag with special characters for quotation marks.*

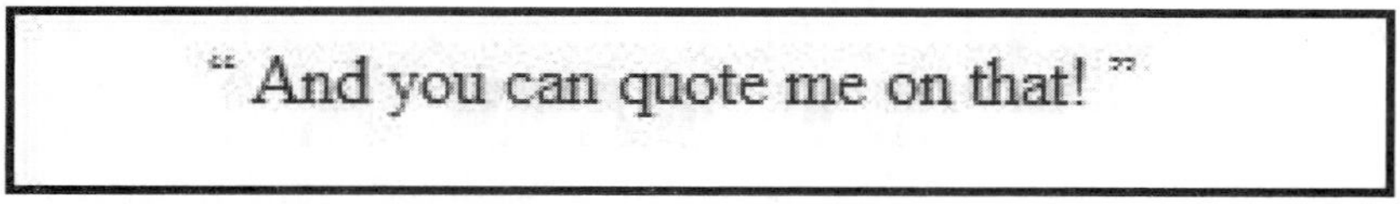

Figure 2.36: A sample of special characters.

The sample code uses **“** for the left double quote and **”** for the right double quote. For a complete list of special characters, see appendix B.

Another very important special character is the non-breakable space, ** **. This character appears as a blank on the screen, but unlike a typical blank, it does not allow the browser to break the line at that point. Remember that, as the browser displays your Web page on the user's screen, it has to adjust the flow of text based on font sizes, window sizes, and other factors. This might cause the browser to split a line of text at an awkward point. The code snippet in Figure 2.37 uses ** ** to prevent an awkward line break in the resulting output, shown in Figure 2.38.

```
Welcome to Bill's BBQ Barn, home of our world famous Baby Back
Ribs!
<br>
Welcome to Bill's BBQ Barn, home of our world famous
Baby Back Ribs!
```

Figure 2.37: HTML code with non-breakable spaces.

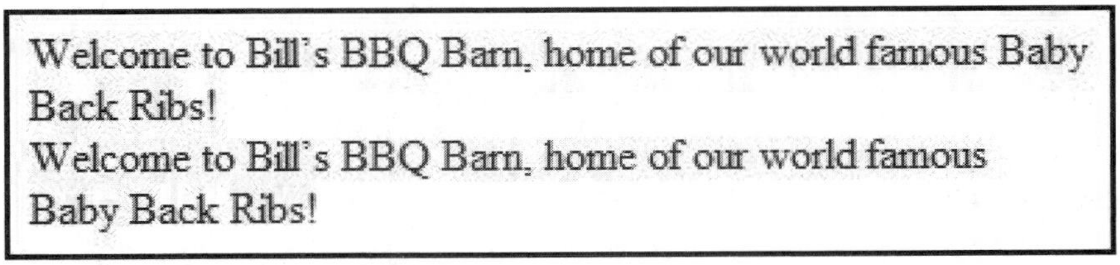

Welcome to Bill's BBQ Barn, home of our world famous Baby
Back Ribs!
Welcome to Bill's BBQ Barn, home of our world famous
Baby Back Ribs!

*Figure 2.38: An example of using ** **.*

If the browser window shrinks to just the right size, it looks like we have a "world famous baby" in the first line of text, instead of baby back ribs. The second line of text uses ** ** to separate those three words from one another, but prevents the browser from splitting the line between them.

A second function of ** ** controls the indention of text on a page. Normally, extra blanks in HTML code are simply ignored. However, the code snippet in Figure 2.39 shows how to use ** ** to indent the text a specific number of spaces, shown in Figure 2.40.

```
      
      
      Catalog
<ul type=disc>
<li>Bill's Sweet BBQ Sauce</li>
<li>Grandma's Secret Hot Sauce</li>
<li>Bill's Country Cookbook</li>
<li>Bill's Babyback Ribs</li>
<li>Bill's Beef Ribs</li>
</ul>
```

Figure 2.39: HTML code with non-breakable spaces as indention.

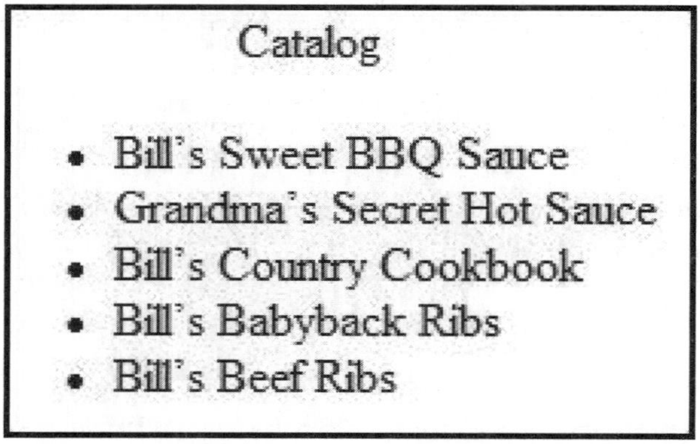

*Figure 2.40: An example of using ** ** to control spacing.*

Summary

Is this all there is to HTML? Certainly not! This is just the tip of the iceberg. We've covered many of the basic tags in HTML, but there are many more to discuss. Also, remember that some of the tags discussed here are considered deprecated by the 3WC, and may fall into disuse. However, you will still find them on many Web pages today, so some familiarity with them is necessary. Later in the book, you'll learn about alternatives to some of these deprecated options.

CHAPTER 3

Embedding Images in Web Pages

Graphics are a key form of Web page content. Browsers are inherently visual, so effective, clear graphics are critical for your Web page. Business applications often include images in product catalogs and other types of Web pages. What kinds of image files are there? How do we incorporate them into Web pages? What about video? What tools are there for working with images? What are the do's and don'ts of image processing? We'll answer these questions and more in this chapter.

Nearly since the moment of the PC's inception, the push began for better graphics. IBM's first graphics card for their new PC, the "Color/Graphics Monitor Adapter," or CGA, was a rather limited card that provided support for up to 16 colors and a 640x200 pixel screen resolution. This was supplanted in 1984 by an "Enhanced Graphics Adapter," or EGA. This graphics card supported up to 64 colors and a maximum resolution of 640x350 pixels. Although some third-party vendors offered additional options beyond EGA, it dominated the market until 1987, when IBM released the new "Video Graphics Adapter," or VGA, card.

VGA is a standard for graphics that is still in use today. Typically, all types of graphics hardware and software support VGA or better graphics modes. While VGA is not sufficient for most modern graphical applications, it does provide a safe "fall back" option for manufacturers and developers. VGA supports up to 256 colors and a maximum resolution of 640x480. It is important to note that to achieve maximum resolution, the number of colors must be reduced, and to display the maximum number of colors, the screen resolution must be reduced. Eventually, IBM replaced VGA with XGA, but that standard did not dominate the marketplace.

Both VGA and XGA were supplanted by SVGA, also know as "Super VGA," in 1989. Its maximum resolution started at 800x600 and soon increased to 1024x768 pixels. The number of supported colors became almost limitless, due to improved techniques. Enhancements and improvements in graphics cards continued after the development of SVGA, but the "name game" stalled, and manufacturers continued to refer the graphics standard as SVGA, simply rolling new capabilities into the old standard.

Types of Image Files

As confusing as the different video standards might be, the number of different image formats is even more staggering. Each format has its own strengths and weaknesses. Table 3.1 shows a list of common formats and their strengths and weaknesses.

Table 3.1: Image Format Strengths and Weaknesses			
Format	Name	Strengths	Weakness
FH	Freehand	Excellent for scaling and complex images	Not commonly used in Web sites, requires specific editors
SWF	Flash File	Excellent for animation	Owned by Adobe
GIF	Graphics Interchange Format	Common in Web sites and good choice for simple images	Lacks sharpness and clarity in complex images
JPG, JPEG	JPEG 2000	Provides more sophisticated progressive downloads than JPEG	Longer decompression times than JPEG, not an open standard
JP2, J20	JPEG 2000	Provides more sophisticated progressive downloads than JPEG	Longer decompression times than JPEG, not an open standard
PNG	Portable Network Graphics	Common in Web sites, provides enhanced transparency	File sizes larger than GIF or JPEG
PSD	Photoshop Document	Excellent editability	Owned by Adobe, generally only used in editing applications
PSP	Paintshop Pro	Excellent editability	Owned by Corel, generally only used in editing applications
TIFF	Tagged Image File Format	Often used in printing, better quality than JPEG. Excellent scalability	Larger size than JPEG
BMP	Windows Bitmap	Good quality	Large size, slow download

Compression describes how relatively small the files are. *Transparency* is a feature that allows one image to be superimposed on top of another. The background color of the transparent image is not displayed. *Scalability* reflects the ability of an image to retain its clarity as its size is increased.

For simple images, GIF has been the standard for many years. However, PNG provides better functionality, and you might find that PNG images perform better than GIFs. While it is true that GIF has been the most common format for animation in the past, more recently, it is often replaced by Flash image files.

For complex images and photographs, JPEG has been and remains the standard format of choice. TIFF files do provide a higher quality image than JPEG, particularly when imaged are being scaled up, but they are also dramatically larger, and so take longer to download. This slows down the display of your Web page and generally diminishes the perceived quality of your Web site. Also, some browsers might not have support for TIFF files by default. Still, for certain specific functions, particularly if the primary function of an image is downloading for printing, the extra download time of TIFFs might be warranted by the improved quality of the printed image.

Some browsers, particularly older ones, also do not have good support for PNG files. If that presents a problem, you might need to use GIFs instead. While PNGs are generally thought of as a replacement for GIFs, they can also replace JPEG images. In certain situations, the "lossless" compression of the PNG format provides significant improvement in quality over JPEG's "lossy" compression method, which can lose image data.

Incorporating Images into Web Pages

As you saw in the chapter 2, images can easily be inserted into HTML code with the **<img>** tag, as shown in Figure 3.1.

```
<img src="bbqbarn.jpg" align="left" hspace="50"
vspace = "50" Border="3" height="400" width="552"
alt="Bill's Barn with Green Grass and Sun">
```

Figure 3.1: The HTML image tag.

Remember that the **src** attribute sets the name and path of the image, and **align** controls the flow of text around the image. In this case, the image aligns to the left side of the page and the text flows around it to the right. **Hspace** and **vspace** define the white space on each side, above, and below the image. This controls how far from the image text is placed. **Border** determines whether a border is drawn around the image, and if so, how many pixels wide it is. Set the border to zero to prevent a border. **Height** and **width** specify the size of the image, in pixels. If the image was not originally saved in the size specified, it will be stretched or shrunk to fit. **Alt** provides an alternate text for the image. When the mouse hovers over the image, this text is displayed. The **alt** parameter is also used by browsers designed for the visually impaired, and by some search engines when evaluating a page's contents.

As mentioned, images can be resized from their original. For example, if you have an image of your product taken at 300x300, such as the charcoal grill shown in Figure 3.2, it could be placed on a Web page at various sizes.

Figure 3.2: An image of a charcoal grill at 300x300 resolution.

The sample Web page in Figure 3.3 redisplays the image from Figure 3.2 at 150x150, 50x100, and 100x50 pixels.

Figure 3.3: The charcoal grill image at various sizes.

The sample images in Figure 3.3 were created using the code in Figure 3.4.

```
<html>
<body>
      150x150<br>
<img src="Figure3.1.JPG" height=150 width = 150><br>
<br>
<img src="Figure3.1.JPG" height = 50 width = 100>
 
<img src="Figure3.1.JPG" height = 100 width = 50>
      <br>
50x100
      
      
100x50<br>
</body>
</html>
```

Figure 3.4: The HTML code to scale an image to various sizes.

As you can see, reformatting the image sizes with the **height** and **width** attributes is quite simple. The more difficult part is determining and managing the original resolution of the images. To find an images resolution in Windows File Explorer, right-click the image, select **Properties**, select the **Summary** tab, and finally click the **Advanced** button to display the properties, as shown in Figure 3.5. Armed with the knowledge of the original dimensions of an image, resizing is much easier.

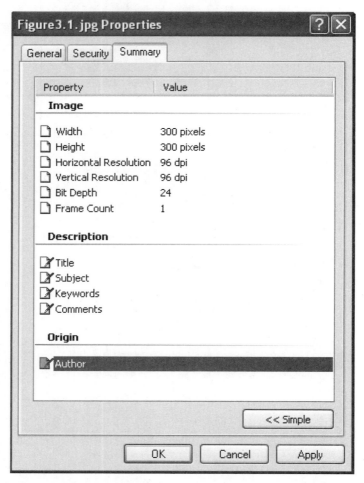

Figure 3.5: Image properties.

Once you know the resolution of an image, maintaining its proportions as you shrink or expand it is easy. Some applications might require images of specific sizes. Remember, as mentioned earlier, some image types scale better than others. Therefore, important images, such as those of products, are often best stored in exactly the same resolution and file type.

This will give a clean, consistent look on the Web page. Of course, if you are building pages specifically for certain items, the images can be managed independently.

The quality of an image is generally better preserved by shrinking it than expanding it. The results you get may vary widely, however, depending on factors such as the file format and the DPI (dots per inch) in which the image is stored.

How would we expand the use of images on our sample Web page? An obvious improvement is adding images to the catalog of items for sale. Figure 3.6 shows the Web page from chapter 2, including a catalog.

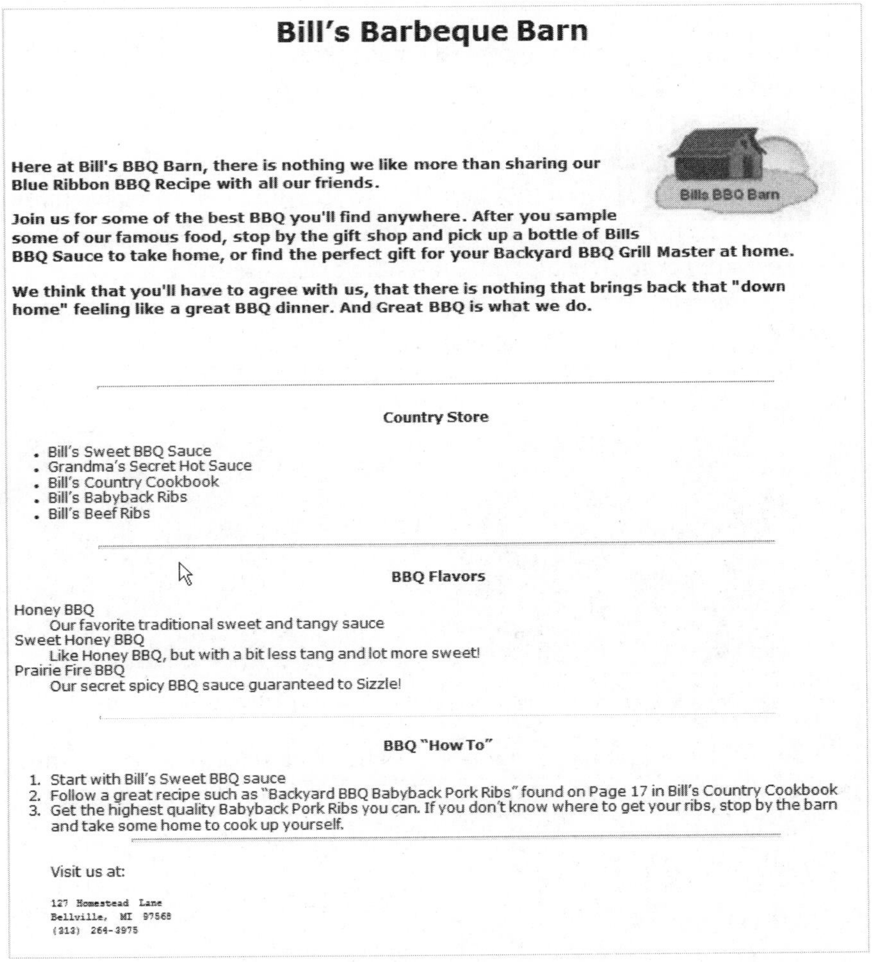

Figure 3.6: The updated sample Web page from chapter 2.

The HTML code for the "country store" catalog section of the Web page is shown in Figure 3.7.

```
<hr size=4 width=80%>
<center><h4>Country Store</h4></center>
<ul type=disc>
<li>Bill's Sweet BBQ Sauce</li>
<li>Grandma's Secret Hot Sauce</li>
<li>Bill's Country Cookbook</li>
<li>Bill's Babyback Ribs</li>
<li>Bill's Beef Ribs</li>
</ul>
<hr size=4 width=80%>
```

Figure 3.7: The HTML code for the catalog section.

Before we can add images to the page, we have to have image files to work with. For business purposes, images often come from marketing and design firms, although some companies might choose to handle their graphics in-house. In either case, the value of high-quality and well-coordinated graphics cannot be overestimated. Few programmers have the creative talent and skills to create beautiful images (although there are certainly exceptions). As the examples in Figure 3.8 clearly demonstrate, we are programmers, not graphic designers! So, please don't get distracted by the images themselves. Instead, focus on the coding techniques used to bring them into the Web page.

Figure 3.8: Pictures for the "country store" catalog.

To add the graphics in Figure 3.8 to the Web page, we insert **<img>** tags into the code, as shown in Figure 3.9. Note that we also remove the unordered list. Otherwise, the page looks a bit too "busy" with both images and bullets.

```
<center><h4>Country Store</h4></center>
<br>
<img src = "Bills_Sweet.jpg"> Bill's Sweet BBQ Sauce<br>
<img src = "Grandma_Spicy.jpg">Grandma's Secret Hot Sauce<br>
<img src = "Grandmas_Cookbook.jpg">Grandma's Country
   Cookbook<br>
<img src = "babybackribs.jpg">Bill's Babyback Ribs<br>
<img src = "Beef_Ribs.jpg">Bill's Beef Ribs<br>
<hr size=4 width=80%>
<center><h4>BBQ Flavors</h4></center>
```

Figure 3.9: The HTML code to show five images.

One problem remains, though. These images are quite large. At their
original sizes, each one nearly fills the screen. So, we need to reduce the
pictures to a more appropriate size for the catalog. The originals are all
formatted with a width of 354 pixels, and a height of 525 pixels. That's not
a very common size, but it should be fine for our purposes. The code in
Figure 3.10 shows how the images can be resized to fit better.

```
<hr size=4 width=80%>
<center><h4>Country Store</h4></center>
<br>
<img src = "Bills_Sweet.jpg" width = "35"
     Height = "52"> Bill's Sweet BBQ Sauce<br>
<img src = "Grandma_Spicy.jpg" width = "35"
     Height = "52">Grandma's Secret Hot Sauce<br>
<img src = "Grandmas_Cookbook.jpg" width = "35"
     Height = "52">Grandma's Country Cookbook<br>
<img src = "babybackribs.jpg" width = "35"
     Height = "52">Bill's Babyback Ribs<br>
<img src = "Beef_Ribs.jpg" width = "35"
     Height = "52">Bill's Beef Ribs<br>
<hr size=4 width=80%>
```

Figure 3.10: The HTML code with reduced image sizes.

These resized images fit much better on the newly updated page, shown
in Figure 3.11. However, you might notice that the size is small enough
that the clarity has suffered. We can resolve that by creating a link to a
larger image, most likely on another page, perhaps including additional
information about the item.

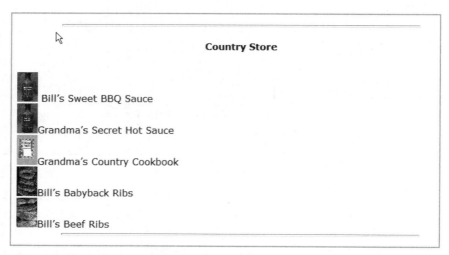

Figure 3.11: The catalog with five small images.

The new section, with its "snazzy" pictures of the various products, is a great step forward, but we're still missing a lot of detail. We don't know anything about product sizes, quantities, prices, availability, or anything else except their names and pictures. The following sections deal with adding links to the images so that prospective customers can get more information on the items they are interested in.

What Can We Do with Video Files?

Video files are often included in a Web page as either advertisements or promotional materials. Some Web pages automatically play video when the page is loaded, creating an "introduction" to the page. Many of these efforts are far closer to the interests of a Web designer than a programmer, at least as we see the distinction. So, we'll stick to some basic and practical uses for video that you might find in business today.

Our sample business, Bill's BBQ Barn, has the same issues that any business has. Whenever they hire someone, they need to train them to do their job the right way—their way. Rather than assigning a trainer to go over even the most basic parts of each new employee's job, Bill's BBQ Barn asks each new employee to review training videos that are made available over the Internet. The code in Figure 3.12 creates a Web page of these videos, as shown in Figure 3.13.

```
<html>
<body><center>
<h1>Bill's Barbeque Barn</h1>
</center>
<right><img src="bbqbarn.jpg" align="right"></right>
<br><br><br><br><br><br>
<left>
<h3><p>Here at Bill's BBQ Barn, we take pride in doing things
    right, and giving our customers the best in comfortable down
    home dining</p>

<p>Review the following Videos and learn how we do things at
    Bill's BBQ Barn.</p></h3>

<br><br><br>
<hr size=4 width=80%>
<center><h4>Training Videos</h4></center>
<ul>
<li><a href="BBQTrain1.wmv">BBQ'ing Basics</li><br>
<li><a href="BBQTrain2.wmv">Keeping it Clean</li><br>
<li><a href="BBQTrain3.wmv">Its all about Service</li><br>
</ul>
</left></body>
</html>
```

Figure 3.12: The HTML code to create a Web page of training videos.

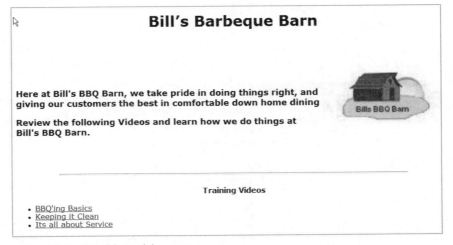

Figure 3.13: The video training page.

Clicking one of the links in Figure 3.13 will launch the interface shown in Figure 3.14, allowing you to either open a video and play it directly, or save it to disk. The exact behavior may change from browser to browser and depend on your specific settings. Depending on what format a video is in, you might also need to install additional software to play it.

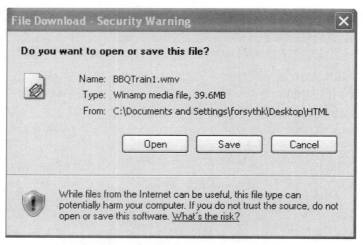

Figure 3.14: The open/save dialog box for handling a video file.

If you choose to open the video and play it immediately, you might experience slow or "laggy" playback if the download speed can't keep up with the speed at which the video is played. This will largely be determined by your connection speed and bandwidth.

Rather than providing a link to the video, it is possible to embed the video directly into the page itself. The **<embed>** tag in HTML allows you to "push" the content of the video and the video player into the surface of the Web page, making it feel much more integrated into the page.

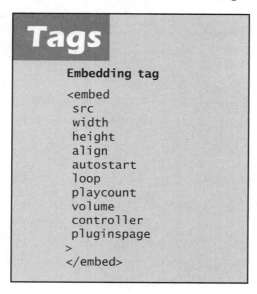

The code in Figure 3.15 shows how to embed the videos shown in Figure 3.16. This code sample uses a few of the attributes of the **<embed>** tag. **Src** identifies the location of the video file being played. **Height** and **width** perform as they do with other HTML tags, setting the size of the object. **Align** controls the flow of text around the video player. (See chapter 2 for more details on the **align** attribute.)

```
<hr size=4 width=80%>
<center><h4>Training Videos</h4>
<pre>       BBQ'ing Basics              Keeping it Clean              Its
  all about Service  </PRE>
<embed width ="250" height= "200" src="BBQTrain1.wmv"
      autostart = "false"></embed>
<embed width ="250" height= "200" src="BBQTrain3.wmv"
      autostart = "false"> </embed>
<embed width ="250" height= "200" src="BBQTrain3.wmv"
      autostart = "false"></embed>
</center>
```

Figure 3.15: The HTML code to embed videos.

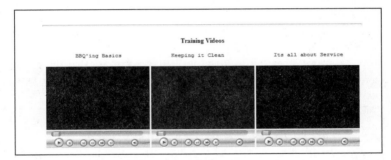

Figure 3.16: The embedded video files.

Autostart defaults to "true," but can be set to "false." This attribute controls whether an embedded video file should automatically begin playing when the page is displayed. **Loop** controls how many times the video will be played. It can be set to a specific number, "true," or "false." "False" is the default, meaning that the movie will play once and then stop. If set to "true," the video will loop continuously until stopped. **Playcount** also controls how many times a video will be played and takes precedence over the **loop** attribute.

Volume is set to a range from zero to 100, with 50 being the default. As you would expect, this controls the playback volume of the audio portion of the video file. Set the **controller** attribute to either "true" or "false" to indicate whether the controls for the video player should be displayed for the user. "True" is the default. If "false" is chosen, the user can still right-click the video player and use the control options included in the popup menu. If the user does not have the necessary player installed, the **pluginspage** attribute identifies the Web page where it can be found, providing the user with an easy mechanism for installing the needed player.

While certain video files, flash animations, and multimedia presentations typically fall under the responsibility of Web designers, those closely tied to products, human resources, and internal training often become the responsibility of programmers.

Using Images with Links

Previous examples showed how to embed an image directly into your Web page. The discussion on handling videos also showed how to create a link to a video file. Chapter 4 reviews linking in detail, but this section provides a brief overview of linking to an image.

Just as you saw with the video files, you can use the anchor tag, **<a>,** to create a simple link to an image. The code sample in Figure 3.17 shows how we might create a link to the full-sized images of the products in the "country store" catalog section. Figure 3.18 shows the resulting Web page.

```
<hr size=4 width=80%>
<center><h4>Country Store</h4></center>
<br>
<img src = "Bills_Sweet.jpg" width = "35"
     height = "52"> Bill's Sweet BBQ Sauce
     <a href="Bills_Sweet.jpg">(full size image)</a><br>
<img src = "Grandma_Spicy.jpg" width = "35"
     height = "52">Grandma's Secret Hot Sauce
     <a href="Grandma_Spicy.jpg">(full size image)</a><br>
<img src = "Grandmas_Cookbook.jpg" width = "35"
     height = "52">Grandma's Country Cookbook
     <a href="Grandmas_Cookbook.jpg">(full size image)</a><br>
<img src = "babybackribs.jpg" width = "35"
     height = "52">Bill's Babyback Ribs
     <a href="babybackribs.jpg">(full size image)</a><br>
<img src = "Beef_Ribs.jpg" width = "35"
     height = "52">Bill's Beef Ribs
     <a href="Beef_Ribs.jpg">(full size image)</a><br>

<hr size=4 width=80%>
```

Figure 3.17: The HTML code to link to images.

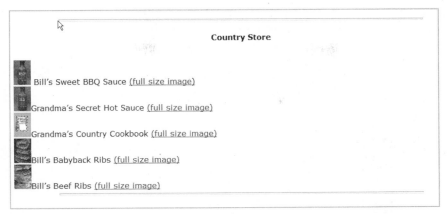

Figure 3.18: Links to full-sized images.

Figure 3.18 uses the text "(full size image)" as the anchor, but sometimes you either don't want to use text, or have a specific need to do something else. It's fairly common to make one image link to another, larger image. Figure 3.19 shows the HTML code to create such links with the catalog, so that the small images link to larger versions.

```
<hr size=4 width=80%>
<center><h4>Country Store</h4></center>
<br>
<a href="Bills_Sweet.jpg"><img src = "Bills_Sweet.jpg" width = "35"
    height = "52"></a>Bill's Sweet BBQ Sauce <br>
<a href="Grandma_Spicy.jpg"><img src = "Grandma_Spicy.jpg" Width = "35"
    Height = "52"></a>Grandma's Secret Hot Sauce <br>
<a href="Grandmas_Cookbook.jpg"><img src = "Grandmas_Cookbook.
  jpg"
    width = "35" Height = "52"></a>Grandma's Country Cookbook <br>
<a href="babybackribs.jpg"><img src = "babybackribs.jpg" width = "35"
    height = "52"></a>Bill's Babyback Ribs <br>
<a href="Beef_Ribs.jpg"><img src = "Beef_Ribs.jpg" width = "35"
    height = "52"></a>Bill's Beef Ribs <br>

<hr size=4 width=80%>
```

Figure 3.19: The HTML code for using images as links.

As you can see in Figure 3.20, each of the small images on the page is now outlined by a border. Although you can't seen it on a black-and-white page, each border is a color assigned in the **<body>** tag, discussed in chapter 2. The first image has a purple border, meaning its link has been visited. The other borders are all blue, meaning they have not been visited yet. This follows the same defaults for color-coding text when it's used as a link. The color-coding is a very useful tool, assisting users in keeping track of where they've been as they navigate through various pages.

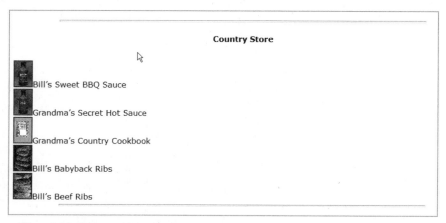

Figure 3.20: A page with images as links.

Image Maps

The previous example showed how to use an image as an anchor to another image or Web page. What if you had a large image with numerous features, each with its own associated target? That is an *image map*.

Consider, for example, a Web page about a car. It might have a picture of a car, and then allow the users to click on different parts of the car, such as its door, windows, lights, tires, and engine. Each click could act as a different link, taking the user to a Web page with details on that particular part of the car.

For our example Web page, the catalog section could have handled the images differently by presenting a single image of a table, nicely arranged with all of the items displayed. The user could then click on the product he or she was interested in, causing the larger image to display.

The image map, or *usemap*, identifies which parts of an image link to what pages or files. For simplicity's sake, and because we are not graphic designers, we'll use the simple image shown back in Figure 3.8. This rather inelegant image does contain each of the five products, so it makes a reasonable example of the image map.

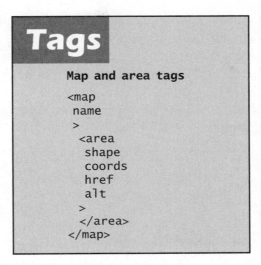

An image map requires two things:

- The **<img>** tag must include the **usemap** attribute, preceded by a pound sign (#), defining the image map to use.

- The **<map>** tag, along with its attributes, must define a series of areas within the image that are clickable links to other content.

The primary attribute of a map is its name. The name should match the one specified in the **usemap** attribute of the associated image. The **<area>** tag is subordinate to the **<map>** tag. Each **<area>** tag defines a clickable area that has a **shape**. Valid shapes are **rect** for rectangular shapes, **circle**, and **poly** for polygons. Depending on which shape is used, the coordinates in the **coords** attribute are specified differently.

For rectangles, the **coords** attribute needs four values, the x and y coordinates of the upper-left corner of the rectangle, and the x and y coordinates of the lower-right corner. These two points are all that is required to define the shape of the rectangle. For circles, only three coordinates are needed: the x and y coordinates of the center of the circle, and a third value to specify the radius of the circle. Polygons are more complex, as there can be any number of points defining the outside border of an area. The coordinates should be presented as a series of paired x and y coordinates.

The **href** attribute identifies the target of each clickable area, and the **alt** attribute provides alternate text associated with each clickable area. One benefit of the **alt** attribute that is particularly useful with image maps is that it will be displayed as the user moves the mouse over the image. If each clickable area has its own **alt** text, it is much easier to see where the boundaries between clickable areas are, and where they might lead.

The example in Figure 3.21 shows how an image map might be implemented with each of the area types.

```
<map name="mymap">
<area  shape=rect  coords="10,10,60,30"  href="first_image.jpg"
alt="Rectangle Image">
<area  shape=circle  coords="100,30,20"  href="second_image.jpg"
alt="Circle Image">
<area  shape=poly  coords="200,10,250,5,240,60,210,55,190,45"
href="third_image.jpg" alt="Polygon Image">
</map>

<img src="MyPicture.jpg" usemap="#mymap">
```

Figure 3.21: The HTML code to create a usemap.

Figure 3.22 shows how the image map defined in Figure 3.21 would mark specific areas of an image as clickable links to other images. The blue box represents the "MyPicture.jpg" image, with a size of 300x100. The three gray boxes represent the image map areas that can be clicked on. Virtually any shape can be represented with one or possibly more of these areas.

Figure 3.22: The layout of an image map.

One of the first questions programmers have about image maps is where to come up with the coordinates you need. Many Web-page authoring tools provide wizards to assist in creating image maps. Even with tools as simple as Microsoft's Paint, however, you can get what you need. Simply open an image in Paint, and as shown in Figure 3.23, the coordinates of the mouse pointer are displayed in the lower-right corner of the window. Simply hover the mouse over the key points of an image and record the coordinates for use in the image map. There is no need to be perfect; just be close enough that the user can identify what visual element in the picture distinguishes this area from the others.

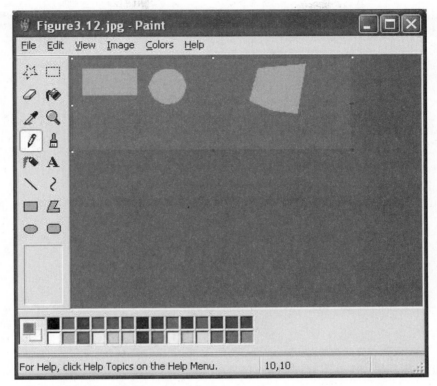

Figure 3.23: Using Paint to get coordinates.

Earlier, we talked about modifying the example application to include a single large image containing all of the products, rather than having individual images for each product. The code for the redefined page, including the usemap needed to handle the links for the various products, is shown in Figure 3.24.

```
<center>
<hr size=4 width=80%>
<h4>Country Store</h4>
<br>

<map name="mymap">
<area  shape=rect  coords="5,5,105,160"  href="Bills_Sweet.jpg"
alt="Bills Sweet BBQ Sauce">
<area  shape=rect  coords="120,5,220,160"  href="Grandmas_Spicy.
jpg" alt="Grandma's Spicy Sauce">
<area shape=rect coords="230,5,330,160" href="Grandmas_Cookbook.
jpg" alt="Grandma's CookBook">
<area shape=rect coords="340,5,440,160" href="Babybackribs.jpg"
alt="Baby Back Ribs">
<area  shape=rect  coords="455,5,555,160"  href="Beef_Ribs.jpg"
alt="Beef Ribs">
</map>

<img src="Figure3.5.jpg" usemap="#mymap">
</center>
<br>
<ul>
<li>Bill's Sweet BBQ Sauce</li>
<li>Grandma's Secret Hot Sauce </li>
<li>Grandma's Country Cookbook </li>
<li>Bill's Babyback Ribs </li>
<li>Bill's Beef Ribs </li>
</ul>
<hr size=4 width=80%>
```

Figure 3.24: The HTML code for an image with a usemap.

The coordinates used in this image map are quite simple, since each product occupies a very similar area, and all are evenly spaced and consistently sized. Had they been more irregular, we would have needed much more varied map areas. The coordinates for the usemap were easily determined using the readily available and attractively priced (free) Paint program.

Figure 3.25 shows the resulting catalog section of the Web page. There is nothing obvious about the image to suggest it has an associated image map until you hover the mouse over it. At that point, the mouse changes to a pointing finger and the alternate text is displayed.

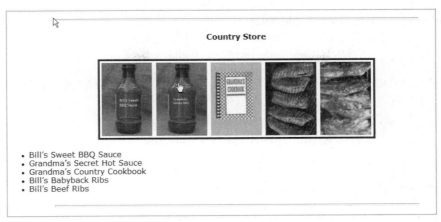

Figure 3.25: The catalog section using an image map.

Tools for Working with Images

A great variety of tools for working with images are available off the shelf or for download from the Internet. Here is a rundown of some of the more popular/useful tools in image handling:

- Photoshop CS3—Generally considered the king of photo editing software, this product is not cheap. But then, as they say, you get what you pay for.

- Photoshop Elements—This is a more moderately priced version of the popular Photoshop tool. While it might be missing some of the high-end options, it is still great for general editing.

- Photo Impact—At half the price of Photoshop, this feature-rich tool gives you a lot of value, but with less ease of use.

- Photosuite—This is one of the lowest-priced tools on the market, though it has far fewer features than the previously mentioned tools.

- Paint Shop Pro Photo—This is another tool with a price in the low to middle range, but with high-end capability.

- Gimp—Originally designed for Unix/Linux, this open-source free-ware tool for photo editing has been ported to Windows.

- Paint.net—Another open-source photo tool, this one was developed with help from Microsoft.

- Web design tools—If you use a Web page design tool, it might well include at least some basic photo editing capability. Some include GIF animation wizards and other such tools.

For typical business applications, you probably won't need extremely high-end photo editing software. If you're doing graphical design work or dealing with particularly demanding graphics-based applications, such as CAD, you might. If you're not sure what you need, start with some of the free/inexpensive options and then upgrade to something better if you need to.

The Do's and Don'ts of Working with Image Files

Here are some tips to keep in mind when working with image files:

- First, be sure you know the format(s) of the files you are working with and why each format was chosen. Don't assume that the image files you receive are always in the most appropriate formats for browser-based applications.

- Consider the sizes of the images. Bigger images generally take more time to load, although this can be mitigated to a great degree depending on which file format you are using. Should the images you're using be consistent with one another? Or can each one be uniquely sized?

- Generally avoid displaying bitmaps (BMP) and TIFF files on your Web pages. These are probably better handled by providing links to the images, and letting the users download them to their PCs and work with them locally.

- Remember that it's generally better to shrink a large image to a certain size rather than starting with small images and expanding them. Expanding images generally degrades their quality.

- Avoid placing a large number of images on one page. Reducing the number of images reduces page load time and makes the page generally easier to work with.

- Use transparency in images, so they appear better integrated with the Web page. If an image has a background different from the Web page's color, it typically results in an ugly square block around the image. This cheapens the feel of the application.

- For images requiring a large amount of scaling, the PNG format might work better than JPEG. Remember that JPEG uses a "lossy" scheme for encoding the image, meaning that it is subject to losing data as it changes, either by being saved again and again or by scaling. PNG images use a "lossless" scheme for encoding the data, which makes them a better choice when scaling.

What about Our Example Page?

Although we aren't graphic designers, it's time we update the look of our sample page. This is the perfect chapter to use as an excuse to replace that cartoonish barn picture with something a bit cooler looking. Figure 3.26 shows a new layout for our example page. It also illustrates that we are definitely not artistically talented!

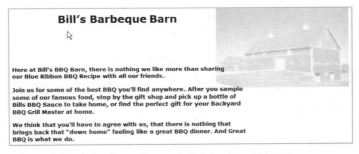

Figure 3.26: A new example page with a background photo.

The code in Figure 3.27 shows all of the HTML code for the final page shown in Figure 3.26.

```
<html>
<body background="barn4.jpg">

<h1>           
   nbsp; 
Bill's Barbeque Barn</h1>
<BR><BR><BR><BR><BR><BR>
<LEFT>
<H3><P>Here at Bill's BBQ Barn, there is nothing we like more than
   sharing<br>
 our Blue Ribbon BBQ Recipe with all our friends.
</P><P>
Join us for some of the best BBQ you'll find anywhere. After you
   sample<br>
 some of our famous food, stop by the gift shop and pick up a
   bottle of <br>
```

Figure 3.27: The HTML code for Figure 3.26 (part 1 of 2).

```
Bill's BBQ Sauce to take home, or find the perfect gift for your
   Backyard <br>
BBQ Grill Master at home.
</P><P>
We think that you'll have to agree with us, that there is nothing
   that <br> brings back that "down home" feeling like a great BBQ
   dinner. And Great BBQ is what we do.
</P></H3>
<BR><BR><BR>
<HR size=4 width=80%>
<CENTER><H4>Country Store</H4></CENTER>
<ul type=disc>
<li>Bill's Sweet BBQ Sauce</li>
<li>Grandma's Secret Hot Sauce</li>
<li>Bill's Country Cookbook</li>
<li>Bill's Babyback Ribs</li>
<li>Bill's Beef Ribs</li>
</ul>

<HR size=4 width=80%>
<CENTER><H4>BBQ Flavors</H4></CENTER>
<dl>
<dt>Honey BBQ</dt>
<dd>Our favorite traditional sweet and tangy sauce</dd>
<dt>Sweet Honey BBQ</dt>
<dd>Like Honey BBQ, but with a bit less tang and lot more sweet!</
   dd>
<dt>Prairie Fire BBQ</dt>
<dd>Our secret spicy BBQ sauce guaranteed to Sizzle!</dd>
</dl>
<HR size=4 width=80%>
<CENTER><H4>BBQ "How To"</H4></CENTER>
<ol type=1>
<li>Start with Bill's Sweet BBQ sauce</li>
<li>Follow a great recipe such as "Backyard BBQ Babyback Pork
   Ribs" found on Page 17 in Bill's Country Cookbook</li>
<li>Get the highest quality Babyback Pork Ribs you can. If you
   don't know where to get your ribs, stop by the barn and take some
   home to cook up yourself.</li>
<HR size=4 width=80%>
<br>
Visit us at:
<PRE>
127 Homestead Lane
Bellville, MI 97568
(313) 264-3975
</PRE>
</LEFT></body>
</html>
```

Figure 3.27: The HTML code for Figure 3.26 (part 2 of 2).

Summary

As you probably know, there is a lot more to image handling than we have covered here, but those more sophisticated aspects typically fall into the realm of designers. These are truly artistic professionals who make their careers out of working with photographic images and design tools, and incorporating the images into print media, video, and Web sites.

Most programmers, whose concerns and experiences revolve around data and business management, are not talented graphical artists. That's not to say they can't be, but most people would agree that artistically talented computer programmers are rare. So, this chapter has focused on the more practical and "data-centric" aspects of managing images in HTML. We are much more concerned with applications like online catalogs than in background images and the look and feel of a Web page.

We hope that this chapter has provided you with useful insights and tools for incorporating various kinds of images into your Web pages. Obviously, it's just the tip of the iceberg, but once you know enough to get started, it's relatively easy to move forward on your own.

4

Adding Links and Anchors

Links are an essential ingredient on any Web page. They provide a means by which users can easily navigate from one page to another with a simple click of the mouse. If moving between Web pages required constantly typing URLs, far fewer people would surf the Web.

Because links are so easy and intuitive to use, they have become a major tool for interacting with the public. For many Web pages, links have few requirements beyond being clear and simple to use. For businesses, however, the needs can be far more significant. Links between Web pages affect placement in Web search engines. (For more information on search engines, see chapter 14.) Linking to a Web page deep inside another Web site ("deep linking") might be attractive, but it has its pitfalls. The good use of anchors can dramatically improve navigation through a large Web page. These and other important topics are discussed throughout the remainder of this chapter.

How to Place a Link on a Page

The key to placing a link onto a Web page is the anchor tag. This tag defines a clickable link on your page, and then acts as an anchor for the user to return to when he or she is done viewing the linked-in page.

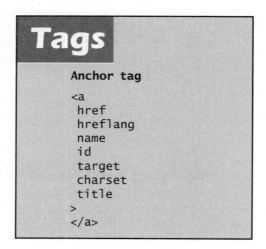

The anchor tag has many attributes. The **href** attribute is the most important one because it defines the target of the link. Typically, this is another Web page, but it could be a different place on the current page, or even a file of a different type. If your browser can render the file type, you can just click the link to process it through the browser. Files that your browser cannot render may still be right-clicked on and saved to your local PC.

The **hreflang** attribute sets the language ID for the Web page. For example, for American English, set this to "en-US." Use "en" for British English, and "ja" for Japanese.

Both the **name** and the **id** attributes provide a mechanism for naming the anchor. Within the anchor tag, **name** has been more commonly used than **id**, so it may be a better choice. However, in future versions of HTML, the **name** attribute may be replaced by **id**. Links in other documents or even at other locations within the same document may navigate directly to a named anchor, as discussed later in this chapter. **Target** controls the behavior of the link. The following list explains the options for the **target** attribute:

- _Self opens a link in the current frame.

- _Blank opens a link in a new window.

- _Parent opens a link in the frameset parent frame (discussed in chapter 7).

- _Top opens a link in the topmost window.

Title defines the popup tooltip text for the link, which will appear when the user's mouse hovers over it. **Charset** indicates which character set should be used. The most common character set is "ISO-8859-1," which is used for English and many European languages. A complete list can be found at *http://www.iana.org/assignments/character-sets*.

The code snippet in Figure 4.1 shows the HTML code to create a link to Google, as shown in Figure 4.2. This is one of the easiest and most basic links that can be created.

```
<a href="http://www.google.com" title="Go to Google">Google</a>
```

Figure 4.1: A basic example of the HTML anchor tag.

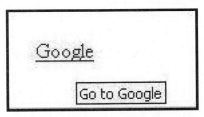

Figure 4.2: The link created from the code in Figure 4.1, showing tooltip text.

To change this link so that it opens in a separate windows, use the **target** parameter, as shown in Figure 4.3.

```
<a href="http://www.google.com" title="Go to Google"
target="_blank">Google</a>
```

Figure 4.3: A hypertext link to Google that opens in a new window.

The code snippet in Figure 4.3 shows the target entered in lowercase. This is important, as some browsers might not support this value in uppercase. If you're designing an application that opens a link in a new window, it might be useful to set the size of the window smaller than the original, so that it is clearly a "child" window displayed above its "parent." Chapter 8 includes some JavaScript that can be used to open a child window in a specific size.

How Links Affect Search Engines

Links do more than just provide connections to other documents. They can affect the placement of your Web page in search engines. In general, the inbound links to your site matter most, not the ones you write. So, one of the best things you can do to improve your Web page's placement in a search is to get other reputable sites to link to yours. Focus on getting sites in your industry to link to your site—perhaps business partners' sites, or those of clients or vendors. The anchor text in those links should relate to the keywords of your Web site.

The anchor text for your outbound links could also affect the apparent quality of your pages. Having valid links, with anchor text that includes relevant keywords pointing to reputable sites, might give your Web page a slight bump in its perceived quality.

It is also important to note that different search engines use different rules, and these rules are constantly evolving. Therefore, what works today might not work tomorrow.

Deep Linking

Deep linking refers to the practice of linking to a Web page or other document located well inside another Web site. This site might belong to a company that you do business with, or it might just be a site that provides useful information for the public. An example of a deep link appears in Figure 4.4.

```
<a href="http://www-03.ibm.com/systems/x/hardware/enterprise/
x3850m2/flash.html"
target="_blank">IBM Demo Video</a>
```

Figure 4.4: An example of deep linking.

This link is only good until IBM reorganizes its Web site or removes that file. Once the site is restructured, your link to its page will no longer work. Therefore, the safest way to link to another site is by linking to its home/main page. Your users can explore the site themselves to find the document they need. This might be easy for you as a developer, as well as safe, but it is hardly effective. You'd like your links to attach directly to relevant content. Typically, this is accomplished by contacting the owner of the Web site and discussing the matter with staff members. It's possible that they can provide you with a URL that is unlikely to change no matter what happens with their internal structure. However, it's more likely that they will allow you to link to their site while providing the warning that there is no guarantee that the link will continue to work for any period of time. If you do have deep links, test them periodically to ensure they continue to work correctly.

How to Use Anchors

So far in this chapter, you've seen how to use anchors as links. Now, let's discuss using them as… anchors! The key to making an anchor tag function as an anchor is the **name** attribute. As mentioned earlier, **id** also works, but **name** has traditionally been more commonly used for this task.

The code snippet in Figure 4.5 shows the HTML to define an anchor on a page. As you can see, this anchor tag does not contain an **href** attribute. Since it is not acting as a link, no such attribute is needed. There is also no anchor text between the begin and end tags(**<a>** and **</a>**). Since all we are doing is marking a section of the page, this is fine. Another Web page or even another section of the same Web page might link to this anchor to position the browser at that specific place in the Web page.

```
<a name="location"></a>
```

Figure 4.5: An anchor tag with the name attribute.

The code snippet in Figure 4.6 demonstrates how to link to a specific anchor on a page. This link opens the requested Web page in the current window and positions it at the anchor named "location." As you can see, the anchor name comes after the HTML file's name and is prefixed by a pound sign (#).

```
<a href="your-document.html#location">Anchor-Text</a>
```

Figure 4.6: A hypertext link to the anchor in Figure 4.5.

Links such as these are invaluable on long pages, which include features such as a table of contents or a "Frequently Asked Questions" (FAQ) section. In such cases, anchors mark specific sections of a page, and

a list of links at the top of the page points to the various anchors.
For example, the code in Figure 4.7 is for an FAQ page that answers
questions a new HTML programmer might have.

```html
<html>
<body><center><h1>HTML FAQ's</h1></center>

Questions?
<br>
<br>
<a href="#mean">What does HTML mean?</a><br>

<a href="#do">What does HTML Do?</a><br>

<a href="#style">What is a Style Sheet?</a><br>

<a href="#link">How do I link to another web page?</a><br>

<a href="#tool">What tool do we use to edit HTML?</a><br>
<br>

<a name="mean"></a>
What does HTML mean?
<p>HTML stands for Hyper Text Markup Language.
There are many markup languages, of which HTML is one.
The language is designed to send a mix of text content and
links to other content to the user's web browser.</p>

<a name="do"></a>
What does HTML Do?
<p> HTML defines the method in which text and images can be
integrated by a web browser. The browser is responsible for
interpreting the document correctly and displaying it in a
fashion that integrates text with other
content such as images.</p>

<a name="style"></a>
What is a Style Sheet?
<p>A stylesheet is a document containing one or more style
definitions. These definitions control the look of a web
page. The same style sheet can be linked to multiple
documents allowing a single point of control for the look
of your web page.</p>

<a name="link"></a>
How do I link to another web page?
<p>As discussed earlier in the chapter, the anchor tag (<a>)
provides the mechanism by which a web page makes clickable links
to other web pages. The href attribute is the key to defining
the link.</p>
```

Figure 4.7: HTML code to create the FAQ page shown in Figure 4.8 (part 1 of 2).

```
<a name="tool"></a>
What tool do we use to edit HTML?
<p>Numerous tools exist for editing web pages. You can use something
as simple at NOTEPAD from Microsoft to edit your web page, Microsoft's
Front Page, IBM's Websphere Studio, or Dreamweaver and Coldfusion
   from Adobe.</p>


</body>
</html>
```

Figure 4.7: HTML code to create the FAQ page shown in Figure 4.8 (part 2 of 2).

This HTML code creates the Web page shown in Figure 4.8. The questions near the top are displayed as anchors. Each one uses an anchor name to create a link to the specific section lower on the page that answers that question. Therefore, the **<a href="#style">** link connects to the **<a name="style">** anchor. Note that the anchors themselves are not displayed on the Web page, only the anchor text (or other content) coded between the **<a>** and **</a>** tags.

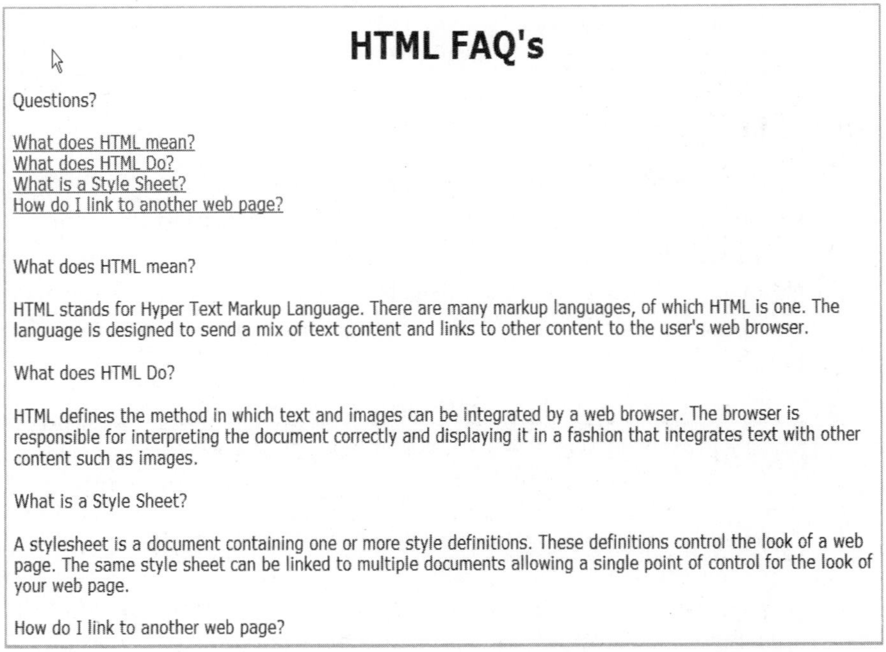

HTML FAQ's

Questions?

What does HTML mean?
What does HTML Do?
What is a Style Sheet?
How do I link to another web page?

What does HTML mean?

HTML stands for Hyper Text Markup Language. There are many markup languages, of which HTML is one. The language is designed to send a mix of text content and links to other content to the user's web browser.

What does HTML Do?

HTML defines the method in which text and images can be integrated by a web browser. The browser is responsible for interpreting the document correctly and displaying it in a fashion that integrates text with other content such as images.

What is a Style Sheet?

A stylesheet is a document containing one or more style definitions. These definitions control the look of a web page. The same style sheet can be linked to multiple documents allowing a single point of control for the look of your web page.

How do I link to another web page?

Figure 4.8: An FAQ page using named anchor tags.

Tips for Using Anchors

When linking to a subfolder, it's a good idea to end the URL with a slash (/), such as *href= "http://www.mycompany.com/download/"*. This simplifies the handling of the link for the server. Otherwise, it goes through a lot of processing to add the slash for you. Similarly, whenever linking to other files in the same folder, use a local reference, such as *href= "mywebpage. html"*, instead of *href= "http://www.mycompany.com/mywebpage.html"*. The local reference requires less work for the server and improves response time.

If you want to create links that do not have underlines, try adding the **style** attribute to the anchor tag, as shown in Figure 4.9.

```
<a href="http://www.mycompany.com" STYLE="text-decoration: none">
some-anchor-text</a>
```

Figure 4.9: A hypertext link without an underline.

Periodically test your links to ensure that they are still valid. Bad links will lower the quality of your Web page, both in the eyes of the viewers and the rankings of the search engines.

Other Kinds of Links

The previous examples have all worked with typical HTML files. The links simply move the browser through Web pages, or perhaps to an image file. There are other kinds of links, as well. One of the more common examples is the *mailto* link. If you want to provide a clickable link that opens a new email message and fills in some of the content, try the code shown in Figure 4.10.

```
<a href="mailto:kevin.forsythe@dmcconsulting.com?subject=HTML">
Send mail to Kevin</a>
```

Figure 4.10: Creating a link to the default mail client.

This sample creates the link shown in Figure 4.11. When the link is clicked, the opened email message has its destination address and subject already filled in.

Figure 4.11: The mailto link on a Web page.

If you had more than one recipient, all of the email addresses would be listed, with commas separating them, as shown in Figure 4.12.

```
<a href="mailto:user@whoknows.com,another@whoknows.com?cc=boss@
   yourcompany.com,secretary@yourcompany.com">Send Some Mail</a>
```

Figure 4.12: An example of a mailto link with additional data predefined.

A more sophisticated example loads all of the parts of the email that can be filled in. As shown in Figure 4.13, the link includes more email addresses for the CC (carbon copy) and BCC (blind carbon copy) sections, and even adds some text in the body of the email. The link created by this HTML code looks exactly the same as Figure 4.11, but its behavior after it is clicked is different. It simply fills in more fields than the first example.

```
<a href="mailto:kevin.forsythe@dmcconsulting.com?cc=sales@your-
   company.com&bcc=IT@yourcompany.com&subject=HTML%20Book&body=K
   evin,%0A%0AHello!">Send mail to Kevin</a>
```

Figure 4.13: An example of a mailto link with embedded blanks and new-line characters.

Notice the *%20* code. It is used to represent a blank. Actually coding a blank between *HTML* and *Book* would create an error in the mailto link, so the %20 escape character is used instead. It translates as a blank when it is displayed in the email's subject line. Similarly, the escape character %0A moves to the next line. Two together (%0A%0A) create a single blank line after other text.

Also notice that after the first email address, a series of parameters is passed. The first parameter is preceded by a question mark. The remaining parameters are preceded by ampersands. In more complex URLs, these codes are very important in allowing more flexible processing of Web content. The mailto link from Figure 4.13 creates an email message like the one in Figure 4.14.

Figure 4.14: A mailto email message.

Drawbacks to Using Mailto

The mailto link is a simple way to generate emails from a Web page, but it does have its drawbacks. First, the remote user must have a mail client installed. Without one, the mailto link will not know what program to execute to open a new email. This is out of our control, as Web developers.

A second drawback is that spammers scour the Internet looking for email addresses in mailto links to add to their directories. Some developers suggest using the escape sequence *@* in place of the "at" sign (@) in the email addresses. This will still render correctly in the email message, but (supposedly) will cause the address to not be read by spammer robots searching for new email addresses.

Finally, it's simply not as professional to use mailto as it is to use a form to create an email. (This is shown in chapter 10, on PHP programming.) So, using mailto might give some users the impression that you're new to HTML—which of course you are, but you might not want anyone else to know that!

Using an FTP Link

Another kind of link is an FTP link. This one replaces the *mailto* with *FTP*, as shown in Figure 4.15.

```
<a href="ftp://ftp.yoursite.com/yourfolder/yourfile.txt">
```

Figure 4.15: An example of an FTP link.

This type of link automates an FTP transfer of the specified file from the given Web site and downloads it to your system. The target Web site does not need to be the one that hosts your Web page.

Using Invisible Links

Another kind of link involves the **<link>** tag. Notice that there is no end tag for **<link>**. It simply defines the related documents, with no visible content to display.

```
Tags

        Link tag
        <link
         href
         hreflang
         rel
         rev
         target
         type
         media
         charset
         lang
          >
```

This tag can be used to define a variety of connections to other documents. For example, you can define the relative position of a document within a series of documents using the **<link>** tag's **rel** attribute, as shown in Figure 4.16.

```
<html>
<head>
<title>Second Page</title>
<link rel="prev" href="page1.html">
<link rel="next" href="page3.html">
</head>
```

Figure 4.16: An example of invisible links to other pages.

These links should be coded within the heading section of the document. Certain tools, such as book readers, may look for tags like these, allowing readers to easily navigate through a series of HTML documents that make up a larger document, such as a book.

Another use of the **<link>** tag that is very practical is defining a style sheet. Style sheets are discussed in detail in chapter 5. For now, Figure 4.17 shows a simple link to a style sheet. This link identifies the style sheet file as being a Cascading Style Sheet (CSS), which is in use for this Web page. In short, the style sheet contains a series of formatting definitions. These could be anything from the default font and size to the background color of the page, and more.

```
<head>
<link rel="stylesheet" type="text/css" href="stylesheet.css" />
</head>
```

Figure 4.17: A link to a Cascading Style Sheet.

It's also possible to define an alternate style sheet as in Figure 4.18, so users might someday be able to choose what format they'd like to see the page displayed in. For now, it is of little value, but as browsers constantly improve, it might become more useful.

```
<head>
<link rel="stylesheet" type="text/css" href="stylesheet.css" />
<link rel="alternate stylesheet" type="text/css"
     href="stylesheet2.css" />
</head>
```

Figure 4.18: A link to both a main style sheet and an alternate style sheet.

The **<link>** tag also lets you define alternate-language versions of a page. Simply add code such as Figure 4.19 to point to language-specific versions of your page.

```
<link rel="Alternate" HREF="page1.fr.html"
   hreflang="fr" title="Page1 - française">
<link rel="Alternate" href="page1.ja.html"
   hreflang="ja" charset="Shift_JIS"
   title="page1 - Japanese" lang="ja">
<link rel="Alternate" href="page1.pdf"
   type="application/pdf" media="print"
   title="page1 - PDF">
```

Figure 4.19: Linking to alternate HTML and PDF documents for printing in different languages.

The **rev** attribute defines the link from the document in the **href** to this document. In other words, it is the reverse of the **rel** attribute. The **rev** and **rel** attributes identify the link type being defined. Many of the choices for link type are defined in Table 4.1.

Table 4.1: Link Types	
Link Type	**Description**
Alternate	A replacement document for the one with the link
Stylesheet	A Cascading Style Sheet used by this document
Start	The first document in a series
Copyright	The copyright statement for a series of documents
Contents	The table of contents for a series of documents
Next	The next document in a series
Prev	The previous document in a series
Chapter	A chapter in a series of documents
Section	A section in a series of documents
Subsection	A subsection in a series of documents
Glossary	The glossary for a series of documents
Appendix	An appendix for a series of documents
Index	The index for a series of documents
Help	An additional information resource for this document
Bookmark	A bookmark to a specific part of a document

As cool as these all seem, remember that support for them is a bit thin. So, check the tools and browsers that you work with to see if there is any advantage to be gained from these options.

What about Our Example Page?

In chapter 3, we changed our example Web page to include a nicer photo of a barn, rather than the simple cartoon we used at first. How can we improve the site by adding links?

The page really isn't long enough to warrant using internal links to jump to various sections. Instead, let's move the content for the store, flavors, and "how to" into their own pages. The modified code for the main page is shown in Figure 4.20.

```
<html>
<body background="barn4.jpg">
<h1>>          
    ;  
Bill's Barbeque Barn</h1>
<br><br><br>
<left>
<h3><p>Here at Bill's BBQ Barn, there is nothing we like more than
    sharing<br>
 our Blue Ribbon BBQ Recipe with all our friends.
    </p><p>
Join us for some of the best BBQ you'll find anywhere. After you
    sample<br>
some of our famous food, stop by the gift shop and pick up a bottle
    of <br>
Bill's BBQ Sauce to take home, or find the perfect gift for your
    Backyard <br>
BBQ Grill Master at home.
    </p><p>
We think that you'll have to agree with us, that there is nothing
    that <br>
brings back that "down home" feeling like a great BBQ dinner. And
    Great BBQ is what we do.
</p></h3>
<br><br><br>
<hr size="4" width="80%">
Learn More about:<br>
      <a href="Barbeque Barna.
    html" target="_blank">Country Store</a> <br>
      <a href="Barbeque Barnb.
    html" target="_blank">BBQ Flavors</a> <br>
      <a href="Barbeque Barnc.
    html" target="_blank">"How To" BBQ</a> <br>
</left></body>
</html>
```

Figure 4.20: The HTML code for the sample main page, including links.

Notice that the targets of the links all reference "_blank". This causes each of the three sections to open in their own, new windows. Remember that the character string creates a blank space on the form. We make extensive use of that here, to indent some of the text.

The code for the country store page ("Barbeque Barna.html") is shown in Figure 4.21. Notice that there is no link back to the main page. Since this page is opened in a new window, the original page is still open. The user can return to it at any time by activating that window, or by closing this one.

```
<html>
<body>
<center><h1>Bill's Barbeque Barn</h1></center>
<br><br><br>
<left>
<h4>         
          
Country Store</h4>
<ul type="disc">
<li>Bill's Sweet BBQ Sauce</li>
<li>Grandma's Secret Hot Sauce</li>
<li>Bill's Country Cookbook</li>
<li>Bill's Babyback Ribs</li>
<li>Bill's Beef Ribs</li>
</ul>
<hr size="4" width="80%">
</left></body>
</html>
```

Figure 4.21: The HTML code for the country store page.

The code for the BBQ flavors page ("Barbeque Barnb.html") is listed in Figure 4.22. Notice that the codes are located inside the **<H4>** tag. If they were located outside, the browser would most likely move the heading to the next line rather than sliding it over as we want. Remember that subtle changes in coding like this can have a significant effect on the page.

```
<html>
<body>
<center><h1>Bill's Barbeque Barn</h1></center>
<br><br><br>
<left>
<h4>          
    ;     
BBQ Flavors</h4>
<dl>
<dt>Honey BBQ</dt>
<dd>Our favorite traditional sweet and tangy sauce</dd>
<dt>Sweet Honey BBQ</dt>
<dd>Like Honey BBQ, but with a bit less tang and lot more sweet!
    </dd>
<dt>Prairie Fire BBQ</dt>
<dd>Our secret spicy BBQ sauce guaranteed to Sizzle!</dd>
</dl>
<hr size="4" width="80%">
</left></body>
</html>
```

Figure 4.22: The HTML code for the BBQ flavors page.

The code for the how-to section ("Barbeque Barnc.html") appears in Figure 4.23.

```html
<html>
<body>
<center><h1>Bill's Barbeque Barn</h1></center>
<br><br><br>
<left>
<h4>          
   ;      
BBQ "How To"</H4>
<ol type="1">
<li>Start with Bill's Sweet BBQ sauce</li>
<li>Follow a great recipe such as "Backyard BBQ Babyback Pork
   Ribs" found on Page 17 in Bill's Country Cookbook</li>
<li>Get the highest quality Babyback Pork Ribs you can. If you
   don't know where to get your ribs, stop by the barn and take
   some home to cook up yourself.</li>
<hr size="4" width="80%">
<br>
</left></body>
</html>
```

Figure 4.23: The HTML code for the how-to page.

All four pages, or at least portions of them, can be viewed at once. Figure 4.24 shows what the Web site might look like with four open windows.

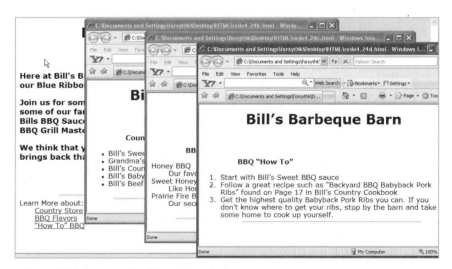

Figure 4.24: An example of four open windows.

For some applications, this might be fine, but you might prefer a smoother experience at the Web site. So, instead of opening new pages in separate windows, let's open them in the current window. However, doing this will require us to add a link back to the main page. Sure, we could expect the user to just hit the browser's "Back" button, but that might be a bad assumption.

The code for the links in the main page changes by removing the "_target" value. Remember that without this attribute, the links will automatically open in the current window. The code for the links in the main page is shown in Figure 4.25.

```
<hr size="4" width="80%">
Learn More about:<br>
      
   <a href="Barbeque Barn6a.html">Country Store</a> <br>
      
   <a href="Barbeque Barn6b.html">BBQ Flavors</a> <br>
      
   <a href="Barbeque Barn6c.html">"How To" BBQ</a> <br>
```

Figure 4.25: Hypertext links that open in the current window.

These changes will not create any apparent changes in the look of the page. Only the behavior changes, after the links are clicked. You can see what the new page looks like in Figure 4.26. The modified code for that page is shown in Figure 4.27.

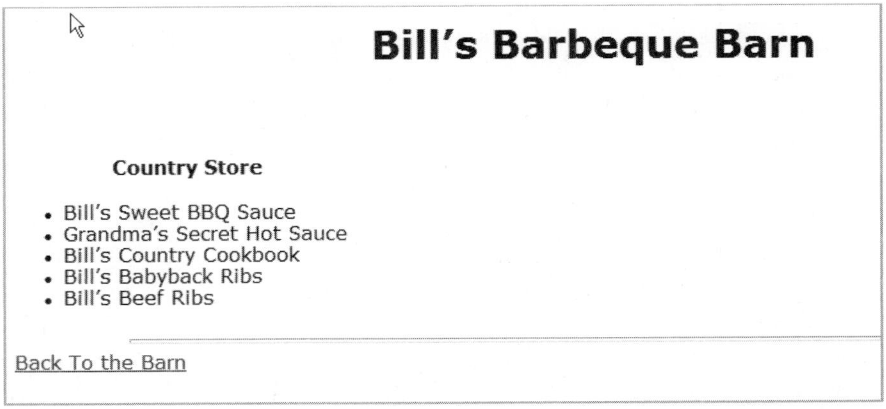

Bill's Barbeque Barn

Country Store

- Bill's Sweet BBQ Sauce
- Grandma's Secret Hot Sauce
- Bill's Country Cookbook
- Bill's Babyback Ribs
- Bill's Beef Ribs

Back To the Barn

Figure 4.26: The country store page with a link back to the main page.

```
<html>
<body>

<CENTER><h1>Bill's Barbeque Barn</h1></CENTER>
<BR><BR><BR>
<LEFT>
<H4>          
   ;     
Country Store</H4>
<ul type=disc>
<li>Bill's Sweet BBQ Sauce</li>
<li>Grandma's Secret Hot Sauce</li>
<li>Bill's Country Cookbook</li>
<li>Bill's Babyback Ribs</li>
<li>Bill's Beef Ribs</li>
</ul>

<HR size="4" width="80%">
<br>
<a href="Barbeque Barn6.html">Back to the Barn</a>
</LEFT></body>
</html>
```

Figure 4.27: The source code for Figure 4.26.

Summary

When creating links, keep in mind their purpose. Typically, people digest information better when it's given in small pieces. If you create a single, gigantic page with massive amounts of data, it might overwhelm and confuse users, or at least make finding any specific thing much more difficult. It might be better to create a smaller main page that has links to other pages, which provide additional information on specific topics. Each page should contain only about one screen's worth of data. Additional pages can be added to further break up the content into appropriately sized pages. An exception to this might be lists of data, where a larger number of rows of similarly formatted data is not terribly confusing.

Also, remember that no matter what tips and guidelines we or anyone else give you, you are responsible for managing your users' experience when they view your pages. Take the time to think about how they might use your site, what they might be looking for, and what they might be trying to accomplish. If you keep those thoughts in mind as you develop your Web pages, you will greatly enhance their effectiveness.

CHAPTER 5

Using Cascading Style Sheets

A cascading style sheet provides a great, flexible way for controlling the look or presentation of your Web pages. Small changes to this one document can dramatically change the appearance of many Web pages. This easy method for controlling the design of your pages allows you to rapidly implement changes to the look and feel of your Web site. Programmers appreciate this single point of control.

A cascading style sheet is a file that ends in the *.CSS* suffix. Developers often name their cascading style sheet *theme.css*. "Theme" is a good choice for the file name, since a style sheet can create the visual theme for a Web site. All you need to do is have all the pages in your Web site reference the same cascading style sheet. It's also possible to have multiple style sheets all in effect for the same HTML documents. We'll discuss how that is accomplished later in this chapter.

Creating a Cascading Style Sheet

You can attach a cascading style sheet to your Web page using the **<link>** tag. The code snippet in Figure 5.1 shows an example of such a link. When the HTML page is opened, the browser will search the theme.css style sheet to find rules for handling the content of the page.

```
<link href="theme.css" rel="stylesheet" type="text/css">
```

Figure 5.1: Linking to a cascading style sheet.

You can create the theme.css style sheet using a tool as simple as Notepad, by using a sophisticated tool in a Web design product. Figure 5.2 shows the code for a basic theme.css style sheet.

```
body {font-family : arial,courier new,times new roman;
}

h1 {font-family : times new roman;
}

h3 {font-family : times new roman;
}

P {font-family : courier new;
}
```

Figure 5.2: A basic style sheet for four HTML tags.

The styles in the theme.css code in Figure 5.2 are for the HTML **<body>** element, the **<h1>** and **<h3>** heading elements, and the paragraph element. One of the basic things you can do with style sheets is define a default style for each of the HTML elements. As the HTML document is rendered, the styles are read in from the style sheet and applied. There other ways to define styles, such as using style classes, discussed later in this chapter.

When defining the style for an element, the element's tag is listed without the angle brackets (<>) and followed by braces ({}). Within these braces, any available property can be defined. Each property is followed by a colon (:) and then by its associated value. Each value is followed by a semicolon (;). Additional properties may be listed as needed. Once all of the properties are listed, the ending brace is coded.

In theme.css, each of the four element styles sets the default font family for that element. In the **body** style, the font family is set to Arial. If Arial is not available on the user's computer, one of the alternate fonts listed will be used. Simply list all of the fonts in order of preference. The first one available on the user's computer will be used. If none of the listed fonts are available, the default font of the user's browser will be used. The **h1** and **h3** styles define the font family as Times New Roman. The fourth style is for the paragraph tag **<p>**. This style sets the default font to Courier New.

A wide variety of fonts are available. *Monospace* fonts such as Courier New use the exact same width for every letter. This makes them very attractive when you need to get text to line up a certain way.

Figure 5.3 shows the code for a sample Web page that links to the theme. css style sheet. The Web page is shown in Figure 5.4.

```
<html>
<head>
<link href="theme.css" rel="stylesheet" type="text/css">
</head>
<body>
This font is Arial
<h1>This font is Times New Roman</h1>
<h3><P>This font is Courier New</P></h3>
</body>
</html>
```

Figure 5.3: The HTML code for a Web page using a style sheet.

This font is Arial

This font is Times New Roman

`This font is Courier New`

Figure 5.4: Sample font families using a style sheet.

Notice in Figure 5.3 that within the second **<h3>** tag, there is also a **<p>** tag, so two of the styles from themes.css are in effect. In general, the innermost, or *child*, element will inherit properties from a parent element, but the child also has the option to override those properties. Both element styles attempt to change the font family, but the **<p>** tag takes precedence, since it is the innermost tag. Therefore, the text in the **<h3>** tag appears in Courier New instead of Times New Roman.

What Other Properties Do Fonts Have?

In addition to the **font-family** property, you can also set the font size, font style, or font weight. Alternatively, you can set the **font** property, which has several values, including style, variant, weight, size, and family.

```
Tags

{font-family:font1, font2,…

  font-size:size
  font-style:normal
    italic
    oblique
  font-weight:normal
    bold
    bolder
    lighter
    number
  font:style weight
    size family
}
```

Most of the properties have specific options to choose from. For example, **font-weight** can use relative terms such as **lighter**, **normal**, **bold**, or **bolder**. These choices are displayed here in **bold** text. Other properties allow more varied values. These are displayed here in ***bold italics***. For example, **font-weight** accepts a numeric value that is a multiple of 100, from 100 to 900. A value of 100 is the lightest (thinnest) font weight, while 900 is the heaviest (thickest).

The **font-size** property requires a value that may be followed by a code such as **12px**, which means 12 pixels wide. Here are the available size codes:

- **em**, the width of the letter *m* in the current font
- **ex**, the width of the letter *x* in the current font

- **cm**, centimeters

- **mm**, millimeters

- **pc**, picas (1 pica = 4.216 mm)

- **pt**, points (1 point = 1/12 pica)

- **in**, inches

- **px**, pixels

Using the **em** and **ex** sizes allows you to define the size of certain portions of text without needing to know the underlying size of the font. Specifying a value of *.5em*, for example, means you want the font to be 50% smaller than the current text size for the letter *m*. Similarly, to define a size 20% greater than the current text size of the letter *x*, use a value of *1.2ex*. Avoiding hardcoded font sizes provides better support for users who have adjusted their own font sizes.

Use the **font-style** to determine if the text should be printed in its normal form, italics, or as oblique text. (Oblique prints "slanted" text that, to the untrained eye, looks the same as italics.)

There are a number of other text properties not directly associated with a font. These include **color**, **direction**, **line-height**, **letter-spacing**, **text-align**, **text-decoration**,

Tags

```
{color:color
   rgb(r,g,b)
   #rrggbb
 direction:ltr
   rtl
 line-height:normal
     number
     percent
 letter-spacing:normal
     number
 text-align:left
   right
   center
   justify
 text-decoration:
   none
   underline
   overline
   line-through
   blink
 text-indent: number
     percent
 text-shadow: color
 horizontal-distance
 vertical-distance
 blur radius
 text-transform:none
     capitalize
     uppercase
     lowercase
 white-space: normal
   pre
   nowrap
 word-spacing:normal
   number
 Unicode-bidi:normal
     embed
     bidi-override
}
```

text-indent, text-shadow, text-transform, Unicode-bidi, white-space, and word-spacing.

Color may be coded as a specific name, such as *blue* or *red*, as an RGB hex value, or as RGB decimal values (rarely used). Color names are easy to use, but not all browsers present the colors in exactly the same way. The 16 standard HTML colors are shown in Table 5.1, together with their hex values. More colors can be found in appendix E.

Examples of hex values are #000000 (black), #c0c0c0 (silver), and #FFFFFF (white). Each hex code is made up of a pound sign (#) followed by three hex values (00 through FF), representing the red, green, and blue values of the color. Most programmers know that hex is a base-16 number system, where 0=0 and F=15. So, a hex code of #3366CC has 33 for the red value, 66 for the green, and CC for the blue, resulting in a medium grayish-blue.

Table 5.1: Standard Color Names and Hex Codes	
Color Name	Hex Code
Aqua	#00FFFF
Black	#000000
Blue	#0000FF
Fuchsia	#FF00FF
Gray	#808080
Green	#008000
Lime	#00FF00
Maroon	#800000
Navy	#000080
Olive	#808000
Purple	#800080
Red	#FF0000
Silver	#C0C0C0
Teal	#008080
Yellow	#FFFF00
White	#FFFFFF

The direction property can be set to left-to-right (ltr) which is the default, or right-to-left (rtl). Line-height can be set to normal, a specific number, or a percentage.

Letter-spacing controls the space between text characters. This property can be set to either **normal** or a specific number.

The **text-align** property can be set to **left**, **right**, **center**, or **justify**.

Text-decoration lets you add an underline or overline effect to the text. You can also cause the text to appear with a line through it. This is often used to represent deleted text. A blinking effect can also be added.

The **text-indent** property sets the amount of indention for the first line of text in the paragraph. It can be entered either as a fixed amount or as a percentage.

Text-shadow sets the color for a shadow effect added to the text. Horizontal and vertical distance properties indicate the offset distance of the shadow effect from the text. This property is not supported by many browsers at this time.

Use the **text-transform** option to force the text to appear in uppercase or lowercase, or to capitalize the first letter of every word.

White-space controls the way in which the browser handles the white space within the HTML text. Setting it to **pre** causes the text to be handled as if the HTML **<pre>** tag were specified. Using the **nowrap** value indicates that the text should never wrap down to the next line. It will continue on the same line until the end of the text or a line-break tag (**
**).

The **word-spacing** property sets the distance between each word in the text. Set this to a specific size.

If you use the **rtl** directional text, you can set the **Unicode-bidi** property to **bidi-override**, causing the first letter of text to be printed at the right margin, with each following character moving closer to the left margin. Otherwise, **rtl** will simply cause the text to be aligned on the right margin. For an example of this, consider the code in Figure 5.5. If the style sheet in Figure 5.6 is applied, the sentence is printed right to left, as shown in Figure 5.7. The text is aligned on the right margin by default.

```
<p>this text prints right to left</p>
```

Figure 5.5: The HTML code to print a line of text.

```
p {direction:rtl; unicode-bidi:bidi-override;
```

Figure 5.6: The style sheet code that controls the text in Figure 5.5.

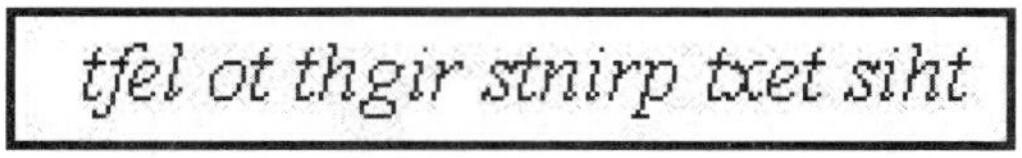

tfel ot thgir stnirp txet siht

Figure 5.7: Right-to-left text.

This example might be a bit silly, as it is rare that you would need to print text right to left. However, most of the other font properties, such as color assignment and weight, don't show up well in printed material.

What Properties Control the Arrangement of an Element?

Use the padding properties to control the spacing around an element.

Tags

```
{padding-bottom:size
        auto
padding-left: size
    auto
padding-right: size
    auto
padding-top: size
    auto
padding: top right
    bottom left
}
```

Typically, each element on a Web page is assigned a rectangular section or "box." Properties that affect the general positioning and arrangement of content on the page manipulate the format of these boxes. As a general rule, these boxes are not visible. *Padding* refers to the internal space between the content of an element and the element's border. You can control the padding values for each of the four sides of the element, or if you specify the **padding** property, you can set all four at once.

If **padding** contains just a single value, such as *{padding:3px;}*, that value applies to all four sides of the element. If two values are given, such as *{padding:3px 2px;}*, the first value is for the top and bottom, and the second value is for the left and right. When three values are given, the first is for the top, the second for the left and right, and the third for the bottom.

```
Tags

{height:size
      auto
width: size
      auto
 max-height: size
      auto
max-width: size
      auto
 min-height: size
      auto
min-width: size
      auto
}
```

The **height** and **width** properties refer to the size of the element itself. Use a size in one of the formats discussed earlier for the **font-weight** property. The **max-height** and **max-width** properties refer to the maximum size that an element can expand to. Rather than specifying an exact size, these properties set a limit on the element's size. The **min-height** and **min-width** properties control the minimum size the element can be shrunk to.

As the browser integrates a variety of elements on the same page, some will be placed beside others. If necessary, you can force the browser to leave either one side or both sides free of adjacent elements. You would set the **clear** property to **right**, for example, if you wanted to keep the right side clear.

The **bottom** property sets the distance that an element is above the bottom edge of its block area. **Left**, **right**, and **top** properties define the distance the element's content is from the edge of that block.

Use the **float** property to identify how the element should be arranged with other elements. Set it to **right** if it should float to the right, **left** to float left, or **none** to prevent it from floating at all.

Visibility controls whether an element can be seen or not. Set this to **visible** for elements that should be seen, **hidden** for ones that should remain in the background, and **collapse** if the element is to be hidden away from view, but available for quick display if needed.

Overflow determines how the browser handles content that will not fit in the defined space for the object. Set **overflow** to **visible** to guarantee that the content will be visible despite overflowing the element's maximum size. Use **hidden** to cause the overflow content to become invisible. Use **scroll** to indicate that scrollbars should be added to the element to allow access to its entire contents. **Clip** sets the size of the clipped

Tags

```
{clear: none
    both
    left
    right
bottom:number
    auto
float: left
  right
  none
visibility: visible
    hidden
      collapse
top: number
  auto
right: number
  auto
left: number
  auto
position: static
   relative
   fixed
   absolute
clip: auto
    rect(top,right,
    left,bottom)
overflow: visible
    hidden
    scroll
    auto
vertical-align:
   number
   baseline
   sub
   super
   top
   text-top
   middle
   bottom
   text-bottom
z-index: auto
    number
}
```

area of an element with overflow. It accepts four values, the top, right, left, and bottom positions, which identify the top right corner of the object, and the bottom left corner of the visible portion of the element.

Use the **position** property to control the way in which the browser places the element on the page. If the property is set to **absolute**, the element's position (top, right, left, and bottom) is relative to the page itself and independent of any parent elements on the page. If the position property is set to **relative**, the position of the element is adjusted from the location at which it would normally appear. So, an element that would normally appear 10 pixels from the top of the page and 20 pixels from the left, with position set to relative, and 5px for both the top and left properties, would appear 15 pixels from the top of the page, and 25 from the left.

Use **z-index** to define layers within the Web page. By default, all of the content is at the "0" index layer. Content placed at z-index 1 will overlay that, and content at z-index 2 will overlay the z-index 1 content. This provides an easy mechanism to overlay content. To avoid layering and keep all content at the same layer as the parent element, specify **auto** as the z-index.

The **vertical-align** property controls the alignment of elements in line with each other within a containing box. **Baseline** is the default value. It causes all the elements in the line to align with each other along the baseline of the containing box. **Sub** and **super** cause elements to align as if they were subscript and superscript, respectively. **Top**, **bottom**, and **middle** cause the elements to align along the top of the highest element, the bottom of the lowest element, or the middle of all the elements. With **text-bottom** or **text-top**, the elements are lined up with the bottom or top of the parent item's **font** property.

What Properties Control the Display of an Element?

The **cursor** and **display** properties provide the ability to customize the look of the cursor and the text of the page. The cursor can be modified to appear as a variety of pointers, arrows, or crosshairs. The **display** property affects text in numerous ways. For example, it can force text to appear in line with other text, or force the text to appear in vertical lists.

Reformatting the mouse pointer may be a useful tool for communicating with users. For example, you could use the cursor to indicate that a certain link provides help information. The **cursor** property sets the appearance of the mouse pointer. Set it to **crosshair** to change the mouse pointer into a targeting crosshair. Use **move** to create a mouse pointer that indicates the element can be moved. This looks similar to the crosshairs, but includes arrows on the end of each line.

The resize values of **cursor** switch the pointer to a sizing arrow that points in the given direction. So, the **e-resize** cursor is an arrow that points east-west, and the **nw-resize** cursor is an arrow that points northwest-southeast.

Use the **text** value of **cursor** to change the mouse pointer to the vertical line commonly used in text areas. **Wait** causes the cursor to change to an hourglass, and **help** changes it to a question mark.

Tags

```
{cursor: auto
    crosshair
    pointer
    default
    move
    e-resize
    ne-resize
    nw-resize
    n-resize
    se-resize
    sw-resize
    s-resize
    w-resize
    text
    wait
    help

display: none
    inline
    block
    list-item
    run-in
    compact
    marker
    table
    inline-table
    table-row-group
    table-header-group
    table-footer- group
    table-column-group
    table-row
    table-column
    table-cell
    table-caption
}
```

The **display** property has a wide range of options and an even wider range of support from the major browsers. Rather than going over all of these, we'll focus on a few of the more useful options. Set **display** to **none** to cause an element to not be displayed. This is different than the **hidden** value, which was discussed earlier. A hidden element occupies space on the page, and other elements will move as if it were there. **{Display:none}** causes the element to be ignored by the browser, so other elements on the page may be placed in the space that the non-displayed element would have occupied.

The **block** value essentially behaves like paragraphs have always behaved, advancing to a new line and avoiding placing other elements to its right or left. The **inline** option causes an element to display on the current line of the current block.

The code sample in Figure 5.8 creates a series of hypertext links. Figure 5.9 shows how they would normally appear in the browser. The links appear one after another until the right margin is reached, at which point the text moves down to the next line.

```
<a href="abc.html">Link to page 2</a>
<a href="def.html">Link to page 3</a>
<a href="ghi.html">Link to page 4</a>
```

Figure 5.8: HTML code to show three hypertext links.

<u>Link to page 2</u> <u>Link to page 3</u> <u>Link to page 4</u>

Figure 5.9: Links formatted inline with each other.

If you wanted each link to advance to the next line, similar to the way paragraphs behave, you could use the **display:block** property. To accomplish this, you could add the code in Figure 5.10 to a cascading style sheet. The output would change as shown in Figure 5.11.

```
a {display:block;
}
```

Figure 5.10: A cascading style sheet for block format.

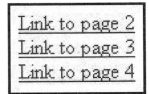

Figure 5.11: Links presented in block format.

Margins define the space between the border and the edge of a containing box.

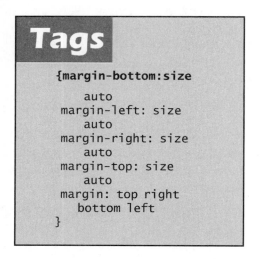

```
Tags

{margin-bottom:size
     auto
  margin-left: size
       auto
  margin-right: size
       auto
  margin-top: size
       auto
  margin: top right
     bottom left
}
```

Each margin can be set to a specific size, as for the **font-size** property described earlier. The **margin** property lets you set all four margins at once. If only one value is given, all four margins use that value. If two values are given, the top and bottom margins use the first value, and the right and left margins use the second. If three values are given, the first value is for the top margin, the second for the left and right, and the third for the bottom.

Use the **border** property to set the width, style, and color of the border. Set the width to a specific size, as for the **font-size** property. The style can be set to values such as **dashed**, **groove**, **inset**, or **outset**. The default border style is **none**. The color may be coded as a color name, a hex value, or an RGB value.

Tags

```
{border: width

    style
    color
border-color: color
    rgb
    hex
border-style: none
    hidden
    dotted
    dashed
    solid
    double
    groove
    ridge
    inset
    outset
border-width:size
    thin
    medium
    thick
border-top-color: as above
border-top-style: as above
border-top-width: as above
border-top: as above
border-bottom-color: as above
border-bottom-style: as above
border-bottom-width: as above
border-bottom: as above
border-left-color: as above
border-left-style: as above
border-left-width: as above
border-left: as above
border-right-color: as above
border-right-style: as above
border-right-width: as above
border-right: as above
}
```

By default, no border is shown for an element. Use **border-color** to set just the color property for the border. Similarly, the **border-width** property defines just the width of the element's border. The **border-style** property can be set to **none** to indicate that no border be displayed, or **hidden** to indicate that the border be rendered on the page, but invisibly.

The **dotted**, **dashed**, and **solid** values obviously describe the appearance of the border.

The **groove** border style appears like a channel cut into the surface of the Web page. **Ridge** creates a 3D raised border that surrounds the element. **Double** creates a border within a border. The **inset** border appears sunken into the surface of the Web page, while the **outset** value makes an element appear to be elevated, as if on top of a button.

Use **border-top**, **border-left**, **border-right**, and **border-bottom** to set the border properties for just that section of the element.

To make the links from Figure 5.11 more visually distinct, we could add a border. In this case, the code in Figure 5.12 adds an outset border to make them appear raised above the surface of the Web page, as shown in Figure 5.13.

```
a {display:block; border-style:outset;
    width:14ex;text-align:center;
}
```

Figure 5.12: The style sheet code for anchor tags with special borders.

The code in Figure 5.12 keeps the block attribute from the earlier example and adds the outset border. It also sets the width to **14ex** (fourteen *x*'s) so that the outset borders would not continue all the way to the right margin of the page. The text was also centered within the block so that it lined up nice and neat within the borders. This makes the links look like buttons.

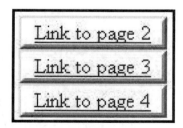

Figure 5.13: Centered links with outset borders of a specific width.

What Properties Control the Background of an Element?

Use the **background-image** property to indicate the URL of an image file you wish to use as the background of the element. When specifying the URL, be sure to code it within the **url('…')** wrapper, as shown in the syntax below.

Set the **background-attachment** property to **fixed** if you wish the background image to remain in exactly the same position within the viewable area of the Web page. If this property is set to **scroll**, the image will move with the content as the user scrolls through the element.

If you are not using a background image and would rather set the background to a solid color, use the **background-color** property. Set it to the desired color name, a hex code, or an RGB value.

Tags

```
{background-attachment: fixed
        scroll
background-color: color
        rgb(r,g,b)
        #(rr,gg,bb)
background-image:url('url')
background-position:
    x y
    top left
    top center
    top right
    center left
    center center
    center right
    bottom left
    bottom center
    bottom right
background-repeat: repeat
        repeat-x
        repeat-y
        no-repeat
background: color
    image
    repeat
    attachment
    position
}
```

If you want a background image to repeat (tile) to fill the element, set the **background-repeat** property. The property's default is **repeat**, which causes the image to tile as many times as needed to fill the available space. If it is set to **repeat-x**, the image repeats across the element horizontally, but only one row is tiled. If the property is set to **repeat-y**, the image repeats vertically, but only one column is tiled. To cause the image to only appear once, use the **no-repeat** value.

The **background-position** property identifies the starting position of the background image. Specify the *x* and *y* distances, where *x* is the offset distance from the left border, and *y* is the offset from the top border. Use the standard size values discussed earlier in this chapter. To avoid hardcoding a specific distance, you can specify one of the special values, such as **top left** or **center center**. As you would expect, the image is anchored to the element at the specified location. To set all the background image properties at once, use the **background** property and provide the values in the order shown.

To update the background of our sample Web page, we might remove all the background properties set in the **<body>** tag in the HTML code, and add the code in Figure 5.14 to the cascading style sheet.

```
body {background:url(barn5.jpg);background-repeat:no-repeat;
    background-position:top right;
}
```

Figure 5.14: The style sheet code for the body of a Web page.

This style defines the background as a single image (barn5.jpg), positioned in the upper-right corner of the page. This doesn't change the look of the page at all, but it does move the control of the background image into the cascading style sheet and out of the HTML code. There is another advantage to this that we'll discuss at the end of this chapter.

What Properties Control the Appearance of Elements?

The **list-style-type** property sets the specific symbol to use for ordered and unordered lists. The **disc**, **circle**, and **square** values create the standard symbols discussed in chapter 2. Set the type to **lower-roman** to use lowercase Roman numerals in an ordered list, or **upper-roman** for uppercase. **Upper-alpha** creates an ordered list with uppercase alphabetic characters, and **lower-alpha** uses lowercase. **List-style-position** has two values: **inside** indents the list items, while **outside** (the default) prints them aligned to the current text.

Tags

```
{list-style-type:

    disc
    circle
    square
    decimal
    decimal-leading-zero
    lower-roman
    upper-roman
    lower-alpha
    upper-alpha
    lower-greek
    lower-latin
    upper-latin
    Hebrew
    armenian
    georgian
    cjk-ideographic
    hiragana
    katakana
    hiragana-iroha
    katakana-iroha
list-style: type position image
list-style-position: inside
        outside
list-style-image: url(url)
marker-offset: length
    auto
}
```

If the standard symbols are not sufficient for you, use the **list-style-image** property to specify a URL containing an image file of a symbol. Be sure to wrap the URL with **url(...)**. Many people report having difficulty in getting **list-style-image** to work correctly and consistently in multiple browsers. If you have this problem, first try setting the position to **outside**. If that does not fix the problem, you might need to consider attaching a background image to the text instead of using an **<li>** tag.

The **marker-offset** property exists in the CSS definition from the W3C, but few, if any, browsers support it at this time.

To set the style, position and/or image at once, use the **list-style** property, and then provide a type, position, and URL. Any of these may be omitted, as needed.

The page properties affect the way an HTML document is printed. The two most common properties are **page-break-before** and **page-break-after**. Add one or the other of these to an element to control how it handles page breaks.

Tags

```
{marks: crop
       cross
orphans: number
page-break-after: auto
       always
       avoid
       left
       right
page-break-before: (as above)
page-break-inside: auto
       avoid
size: length width
   auto
   landscape
   portrait
widows: number
}
```

To force a page break before a given element prints, set its **page-break-before** property to **always**. This forces a page break no matter how far down the page it is. Set a **page-break-inside** property to prevent page breaks from occurring within a given element.

Use the **orphans** property to set the minimum number of lines that must print at the bottom of a page before advancing to the next page. Similarly, **widows** defines the minimum number of lines that may print on a new page after a page break occurs in the middle of an element.

Set the **marks** property to **crop** if you want to allow images to print all the way to the edge of the paper, ignoring margins. Set this property to **cross** if you want to print alignment crosses on the paper, which are special symbols used by certain printers to guarantee correct alignment.

You may define the basic layout of the page by setting the **size** property to either **landscape** or **portrait**. **Auto** uses the default page size. If you want to manually set the page size, simply provide the length and width sizes.

There are also specific CSS properties for working with tables. For example, **table-layout** can be set to **fixed** if you have consistent row and column sizes. The sizes of the cells in the first row of the table provide the template that all subsequent rows use. This can lead to a performance improvement when loading large tables, as the browser does not need to calculate the size of each cell as it is displayed.

Tags

```
{border-collapse: collapse
        separate
border-spacing: length
        horz vert
caption-side: bottom
        left
        right
        top
empty-cells: show
        hide
table-layout: auto
        fixed
}
```

Use the **empty-cells** property to control how empty table cells are handled. Set this to **hide** if you want empty cells to be hidden from view, or **show** (the default) to indicate that all cells should be visible.

The **border-collapse** property compresses two adjacent borders into a single border, creating a more compact table. Setting this value to **separate** (the default) displays the two adjacent borders with a small space between them. Use the **border-spacing** property to control the size of the space between the borders when they are separated. Set **border-spacing** to a single value, and that length will be used as the size for both the vertical and the horizontal borders. Alternatively, provide the horizontal and vertical border sizes separately. The **caption-side** property simply determines the side of the table on which the caption appears. This can be set to **top**, **right**, **left**, or **bottom**.

Defining Style Classes

So far, you have seen ways to change the properties of standard HTML elements. There is a far more powerful option within cascading style sheets, however. You can define something called a *class*, which is a set of properties that can be used by one or more types of elements. You can define a class as a subclass of a specific element, as shown in Figure 5.15.

```
P.question {font-weight:bold;
}
P.answer {font-weight:normal;
}
```

Figure 5.15: Examples of subclasses.

You can then write some HTML code that uses the style sheet, as in Figure 5.16. As you can see, the style sheet defines two types of paragraph tags: the question class and the answer class. Questions will be displayed in bold, while answers will be displayed in normal text.

```
<p class="question" >How do we define style classes?</p>
<p class="answer">Using the ".class-name" syntax in the style
    sheet</p>
```

Figure 5.16: HTML code controlled by subclasses.

The beauty of this method is that if you decide you want to display all questions in, say, blue, and the answers in green, you would only have to update the style sheet, and all pages that reference it would be updated. The HTML code references the class by adding the **class** property to a tag. If there is a paragraph class defined with that name, its properties will be used on this element.

You also have the option to define classes that are completely independent of all elements. The code for this is shown in Figure 5.17. As you can see, a class is defined with a period (.) as its first character.

```
.question {font-weight:bold;
}
.answer {font-weight:normal;
}
```

Figure 5.17: Examples of classes.

Since the question class in Figure 5.17 is not associated with a specific HTML tag, any tag could inherit its properties by simply referring to it. This allows multiple elements, such as paragraphs and headings, to acquire the same properties.

How Do Elements Inherit Properties from a Parent Element?

Elements inherit any properties they can from their parent. So, if the **<body>** tag has its **font-family** set to Arial, every element within the body that prints text will acquire that font property by default. However, any child element that defines its own **font-family** property supersedes the value in the **<body>** tag.

It's also possible to use classes in style sheets to define properties for child elements. For example, suppose you created a list of questions and answers using the definition-list HTML tags. You could use the style classes shown in Figure 5.18 to define the look of the definition terms and the definition descriptions. You could also provide a separate look for the major and minor questions.

```
.major {background:gray;font-size:120%; width=200px;
}
.minor {background:white; font-size 90%;
}
.question {color:blue;
}
.answer {color:black;
}
```

Figure 5.18: Styles for a question-and-answer page.

The styles in Figure 5.18 define the major topics as having a gray background and larger text, while the minor topics have a white background and smaller text. Each cell within the row will inherit these properties from its parent. They will also define their own class as being either a question, which is printed in blue, or an answer, which is printed in white. The code for an HTML table that uses these classes is given in Figure 5.19.

```
<dl class="major">
<dt class ="question">Question 1</dt>
<dd class ="answer">Answer for 1</dd>
<dl class="minor">
<dt class ="question">Question 1.a</dt>
<dd class ="answer">Answer for 1.a</dd>
<dt class ="question">Question 1.b</dt>
<dd class ="answer">Answer for 1.b</dd>
</dl>
<dt class="question">Question 2</dt>
<dd class ="answer">Answer for 2</dd>
<dl class="minor">
<dt class ="question">Question 2.a</dt>
<dd class ="answer">Answer for 2.a</dd>
<dt class ="question">Question 2.b</dt>
<dd class ="answer">Answer for 2.b</dd>
</dl>
</dl>
```

Figure 5.19: The HTML code for a question-and-answer page.

The **<dl>** tag defines the beginning of a new definition list. In this case, it also selects the class as being major or minor. The **<dt>** tag identifies a term, or in this case a question, and defines the class as being a question. The **<dd>**, or definition description, tag uses the answer class. The text that appears in the list acquires the properties of both the classes set in the **<dt>** and **<dd>** tags, as well as the class set in the **<dl>** tag. This is because the **<dt>** and **<dd>** tags are within the **<dl>**, making them child elements that inherit properties from their parent.

The code in Figure 5.19 creates the page shown in Figure 5.20. All of the questions appear in blue, while the answers are in black. The major questions appear in a larger text with a gray background. The **width** property in the major class limits the width of the element to 200 pixels. Without this, the gray background would extend all the way across the page.

You might be thinking that the list in Figure 5.20 is pretty ugly. While that's true, it provides a fairly simple way to illustrate the inheritance we're discussing, and that is our primary goal.

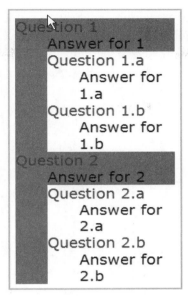

Figure 5.20: A question-and-answer
HTML page, showing definitions
with inheritance.

Rather than using inheritance to provide the flexibility needed in the
question-and-answer list, we could have assigned multiple classes to a
single element. The code for the cascading style sheet remains the same
as in Figure 5.18, but the HTML changes to that in Figure 5.21.

```
<dl>
<dt class ="question major">Question 1</dt>
<dd class ="answer major">Answer for 1</dd>
<dl class ="minor">
<dt class ="question minor">Question 1.a</dt>
<dd class ="answer minor">Answer for 1.a</dd>
<dt class ="question minor">Question 1.b</dt>
<dd class ="answer minor">Answer  for 1.b</dd>
</dl>
<dt class ="question major">Question 2</dt>
<dd class ="answer major">Answer for 2</dd>
<dl class ="minor">
<dt class ="question minor">Question 2.a</dt>
<dd class ="answer minor">Answer for 2.a</dd>
<dt class ="question minor">Question 2.b</dt>
<dd class ="answer minor">Answer for 2.b</dd>
</dl>
```

Figure 5.21: Alternative HTML code for the question-and-answer page.

In this version of the definition list, all of the decisions about question versus answer and major versus minor have been moved into the specific **<dt>** and **<dd>** tags. To improve the look of the list, we also included the minor class for the inner (minor) definition lists. As shown here, more than one class may be listed for the **class** property of an HTML tag. Simply list all of the relevant classes, with a space between each. The result of this modified code, shown in Figure 5.22, is noticeably different than the previous example.

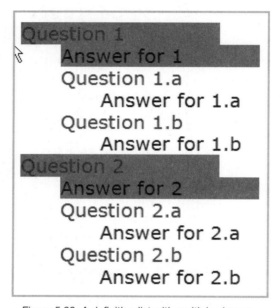

Figure 5.22: A definition list with multiple classes.

Since we moved the "major" class out of the **<dl>** tag and into the **<dt>** and **<dd>** tags, only those specific question-and-answer sections have a gray background. Since the answer is indented beneath the question, and both have a fixed length of 200 pixels, the gray shading for the answer boxes sticks out further than the questions. We might want to set a smaller width for the answer so that they align on the right side, but that is a cosmetic change that we don't need to worry about here. You can do it on your own, if you want.

It is also possible to define the style for elements that are the child of other specific elements. For example, you could define the look of the **<li>** tag when it is within an ordered list as being different from when it is within an unordered list. The CSS code might look like Figure 5.23.

```
UL LI {color:blue; font-size:120%;
}
OL LI {color:green; font-size:100%;
}
```

Figure 5.23: Styles for list items within unordered and ordered lists.

Using this style sheet, the sample HTML code shown in Figure 5.24 creates the output in Figure 5.25.

```
<ul>
<li>Major Topic A</li>
  <ol>
  <li>Minor topic a.1</li>
  <li>Minor topic a.2</li>
  </ol>
<li>Major Topic B</li>
  <ol>
  <li>Minor topic b.1</li>
  <li>Minor topic b.2</li>
  </ol>
</ul>
```

Figure 5.24: The HTML code to create the Web page in Figure 5.25.

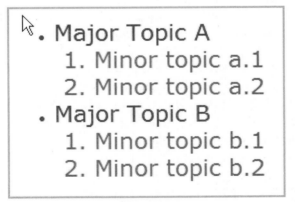

Figure 5.25: Nested lists with subclass styles.

Remember that in this example all six lines of code are generated within the **<li>** tag. The different behavior comes from the parent element, in this case, the **<ul>** or **<ol>** tag. This type of subclass is called a *child selector*.

Another type of a subclass is the *descendant selector*, which identifies an element that is descended from another element, but not necessarily an immediate descendant. For example if you added definition lists within the minor topics in the previous examples, you would have several layers of elements. You would have an **<ol>** containing a **<ul>** containing a **<dl>**. To assign a style to a definition list contained somewhere inside an ordered list, you would use the code shown in Figure 5.26.

```
OL>DL {color:green; font-size:100%;
}
```

Figure 5.26: The style for a definition list somewhere within an ordered list.

If you needed to define the style of a definition list that was the grandchild or later descendant of another element, you would use the code in Figure 5.27 in the CSS. In this example, if the definition list were immediately beneath the ordered list in the HTML code, this style would not apply. There would have to be at least one other element between them for this style to apply.

```
OL*DL {color:green; font-size:100%;
}
```

Figure 5.27: The style for a definition list that is at least a grandchild of an ordered list.

If you needed to identify sibling elements, such as a paragraph that immediately follows an **<h3>** tag, you could define a style sheet as shown in Figure 5.28. In this case, the plus sign indicates that the **<p>** tag must follow the **<h3>** tag. It is important to note that as opposed to the earlier examples, the **<p>** tag is not inside the **<h3>** tag, but adjacent to it, within a larger element such as the page body.

```
H3+P {color:blue; font-size:100%;
}
```

Figure 5.28: The style for a paragraph that immediately follows an *<h3>* tag.

Once you understand these basic methods of identifying various selectors based on their relationships, an even more complex method of identifying elements in relationships to one another is to string multiple dependent selectors together. For example, if you wanted to identify only those ordered lists that existed somewhere within a paragraph and immediately after an unordered list, you could write the CSS code shown in Figure 5.29.

```
P>UL+OL {color:blue; font-size:100%;
}
```

Figure 5.29: An example of nested subclasses.

This might seem at first like an odd and not terribly useful ability. However, what if you wanted to nest one unordered list inside another, such as shown in Figure 5.30?

```
<ul>
<li>Major Topic A</li>
  <ul>
  <li>Minor topic a.1</li>
  <li>Minor topic a.2</li>
    <ul>
    <li>Tertiary topic a.2.1</li>
    <li>Tertiary topic a.2.1</li>
    </ul>
  </ul>
</ul>
```

Figure 5.30: The HTML code for nested lists.

Normally, for nested lists like this, the browser will assign different symbols such as disk, circle, and square to the list items at each level. But what if you wanted to change more than the symbol? What if you wanted to change, say, the text color and size as well? You could use the CSS code in Figure 5.31 to define the behavior for each layer of nested, unordered lists.

```
ul {color:blue; font-size:120%;
}
ul ul {color:green; font-size:100%;
}
ul ul ul {color:Red; font-size:80%;
}
```

Figure 5.31: Styles for nested lists.

The first style is for the top-level unordered list. If you didn't code anything else, it would apply to all levels. The second style applies to the second level of nested unordered lists. The third style applies to all unordered lists that have been nested at least three levels deep. When this CSS code is combined with the previous HTML code, it generates the output shown in Figure 5.32. To continue defining different looks for deeper levels such as the fourth or fifth levels, simply add additional styles with either four or five **ul** identifiers at the beginning.

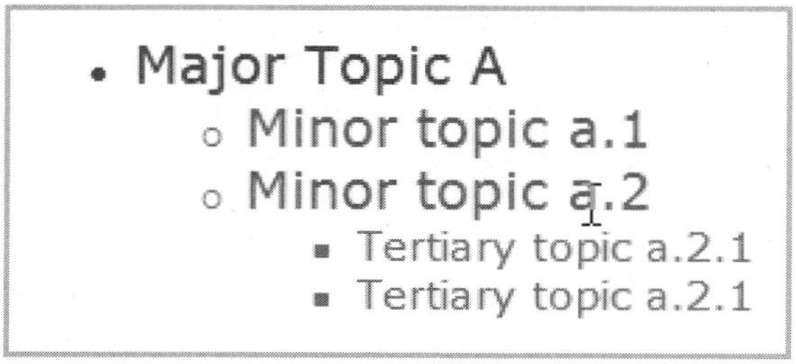

- Major Topic A
  - Minor topic a.1
  - Minor topic a.2
    - Tertiary topic a.2.1
    - Tertiary topic a.2.1

Figure 5.32: Three nested, unordered lists.

Whenever more than one selector applies to an element, the one that is most precise takes precedence. There is a formula for determining this, but it's a bit more complicated than we want to try to explain here, so the overly simplified rule is this:

The selector that refers to the most IDs (discussed next) takes precedence. If the selectors refer to the same number of IDs (or none), then the number of classes referenced determines the selector that takes precedence. If the selectors refer to the same number of classes (or none), then the number of HTML tags referenced determines the selector that takes precedence. If two selectors refer to the same number of HTML tags, then the one listed last in the style sheet takes precedence.

What Is an ID?

So far, we have been talking almost exclusively about classes. But there is another entity called an *ID*. Where classes are used to define styles for one or more HTML elements, IDs are exclusively designed to uniquely identify a single element. So, if a page had three paragraphs, you might assign the same class to all three, but also assign a unique ID to each one, as shown in Figure 5.33.

```
<p id="p1" class="notes">Some misc information</p>
<p id="p2" class="notes">More misc information</p>
<p id="p3" class="notes">The last misc information</p>
```

Figure 5.33: Paragraph tags with IDs.

Any attributes that are common to all three paragraphs can be assigned via the class's style. If you wanted only the second paragraph to print in italics, however, you might create CSS code such as that shown in Figure 5.34. The **.notes** entry defines the style for the notes class, which then applies to all three paragraphs. All ID tags referenced in a CSS precede the **id** identifier with a pound sign (#). So, the entry starting with **#p2** defines the style for the second paragraph. Because the HTML code has both a class and an ID, both styles apply. The entry for the **id** tag overrides any conflicting values from the notes class.

```
.notes {font-style:normal; width:60%;margin-left:20%;
}

#p2 {font-style:italic
}
```

Figure 5.34: The style for the notes class and the p2 ID.

The three paragraphs in Figure 5.33, with the CSS code in Figure 5.34, create the output in Figure 5.35. Remember that when you use an **id** tag, it should be unique within the HTML document.

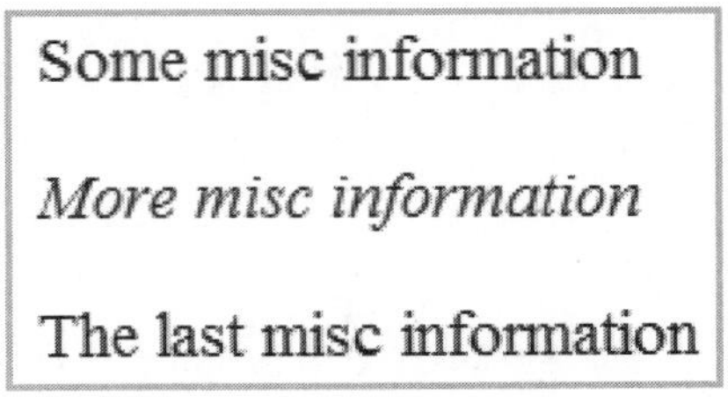

Some misc information

More misc information

The last misc information

Figure 5.35: Three paragraphs with classes and IDs.

What You Can Do with a Cascading Style Sheet

You can define style rules for virtually every HTML element, even if some are pointless, such as a font assignment for an embedded video file. All of the examples you've seen so far are fairly simple. This is appropriate, because you are just trying to figure out how these things work.

One of the main uses for style sheets is to control the arrangement of content on the page. By *arrangement*, we mean not just font sizes, colors, etc., but to actually move elements all over the page. One of the neat things you can do is create pages that can wildly change their looks and layouts, simply by changing the cascading style sheet they use. We'll discuss this further in chapter 6. For now, let's look at a revised version of our Web page that incorporates a cascading style sheet. We'll change the page to pull in the barn image as a background.

The modified HTML code is shown in Figure 5.36. Nearly all the line breaks, the width attributes, and even the background image have been removed. The previous background image was the size of the entire page, with white space to the left and bottom. By moving the background image's definition to a cascading style sheet, we have better tools for controlling its behavior, and we can eliminate the white space and use a smaller image that includes just the barn. Because it is smaller, the image will load faster than on the previous page. You will also notice the class definitions sprinkled throughout the code.

```
<html>
<head>
<link href="bbqtheme.css" rel="stylesheet" type="text/css">
</head>
<body>
<h1 class="heading1" >Bill's Barbeque Barn</h1>
<H3><P class="intro">Here at Bill's BBQ Barn, there is nothing
  we like more than sharing our Blue Ribbon BBQ Recipe with all
  our friends.
</P>
<P class ="intro">
Join us for some of the best BBQ you'll find anywhere. After you
  sample some of our famous food, stop by the gift shop and pick up
  a bottle of Bill's BBQ Sauce to take home, or find the perfect
  gift for your Backyard BBQ Grill Master at home.
</P>
<P class ="intro">
We think that you'll have to agree with us, that there is nothing that
brings back that "down home" feeling like a great BBQ dinner. And
  Great BBQ is what we do.
```

Figure 5.36: The modified HTML code for the BBQ Barn home page (part 1 of 2).

```
</P></H3>
<BR><BR><BR>
<HR>
Learn More about:<br>
<aclass="inset"href="BarbequeBarna.html"target="_blank">Country
   Store</a>
<aclass="inset" href="BarbequeBarnb.html" target="_blank">BBQ
   Flavors</a>
<aclass="inset"href="BarbequeBarnc.html"target="_blank">"How
   To" BBQ</a>
</body>
</html>
```

Figure 5.36: The modified HTML code for the BBQ Barn home page (part 2 of 2).

The new cascading style sheet for our home page is shown in Figure 5.37. This cascading style sheet defines the picture of the barn as the background for the page, positions it in the upper-right corner, and prevents it from repeating, so only one barn is shown.

```
body {background:url(barn5.jpg);background-repeat:no-repeat;
   background-position:top right;
}
.heading1 {width:70%; text-align:center; margin-bottom:40px;
}
.intro {width:60%;
}
hr {width=80%; text-align:center;height:2px;
}
.inset {margin-left:7em; width:80%;
}
a.block {display:block; border-style:outset;
    width:14ex;text-align:center; margin-left:7em;
}
```

Figure 5.37: The cascading style sheet for the BBQ Barn home page.

We've added a bottom margin to the first heading, so the text that follows appears farther down the page. The introductory section has its width defined as 60% of the page, so it won't overlap the background image. Virtually all of the properties of the horizontal rule, including its height, width, and alignment, are controlled in the cascading style sheet.

The **block** class defines the style for the hypertext links at the bottom of the page. It defines an indention, a width, a border style, and an alignment. As noted earlier in the chapter, the **display:block** property forces a new line after each link. The **outset** border makes the links appear like buttons on the page. The resulting Web page is shown in Figure 5.38.

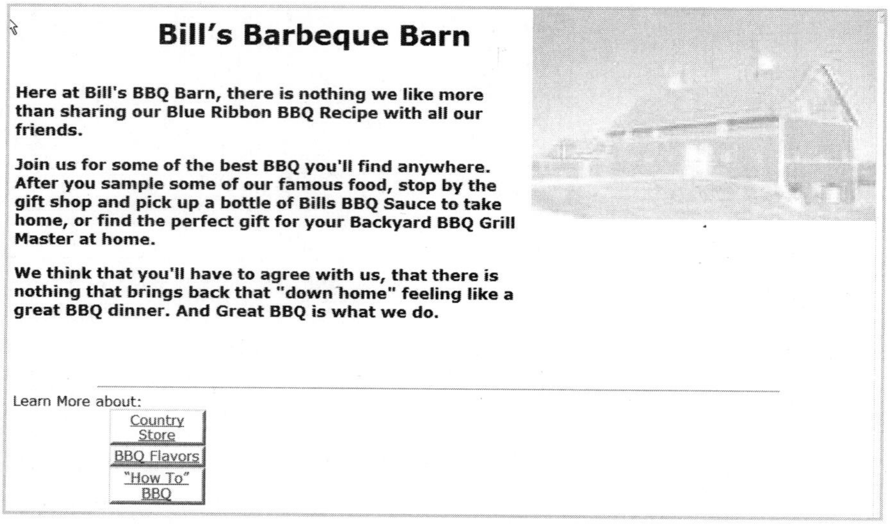

Figure 5.38: The updated Web page using a cascading style sheet.

Summary

Cascading style sheets provide a tremendous amount of flexibility and complexity to Web page design. Combining HTML with style sheets creates vastly more sophisticated Web pages, and the whole thing begins to feel more like programming.

Most programmers will, or at least should, partner with experienced Web designers to create the layout and look of their Web pages. If you don't have an experienced designer to learn from, there are countless online tutorials and books on cascading style sheets. With a little research and effort, you can build on this introduction to cascading style sheets, and you'll be on the road to becoming an experienced Web developer yourself!

6

Arranging Content

Now that you're armed with a fair command of HTML, and you've learned to incorporate cascading style sheets, you're ready to tackle the last major hurdle in Web page design: arranging the content of the page. This might seem simple and straightforward, but there are a number of subtle issues at work here. How easily maintained is your Web page? How smoothly will users be able to navigate through your Web site? Is the overall design of all the Web pages and their links clear and intuitive, so that untrained users can easily find what they need?

There are many methods for controlling the arrangement of content on our pages. You can use tables to align text and images into neat rows and columns. Historically (if we can use that word to describe something that didn't exist when we were born), tables have been used to control the overall framework of the entire page, but it's not now generally recommended.

Frames were designed specifically to control the overall framework of Web pages. They have some great features that are very useful for arranging content, but their use is diminishing in favor of other methods. We'll still discuss frames in this chapter, because you need to understand them to deal with the many Web sites that still do use them.

The **<div>** and **<span>** tags are the most up-to-date HTML tags for controlling the arrangement of content on your Web pages. Those tags, in conjunction with cascading style sheets, are currently the most accepted way to arrange the content of your Web pages.

The Purpose of Arranging Content

Before you can arrange the content of a Web page, you have to understand what the goal of your Web site is. What do you want the page to accomplish? Here are some of the goals you might have for the pages at your Web site:

- Tell potential customers about your company
- Generate sales leads
- Sell product
- Communicate with business partners
- Provide resources

Depending on what focus your Web site has, whether it is one of these, or something else, its requirements will change. So, before you worry about arranging the content on a page, consider what your ultimate goal is for the Web site. Keep that goal in mind as you design the site.

Tell Potential Customers about Your Company

Telling the public about your company is a relatively easy task. You can accomplish this with a static Web site that might be what is commonly referred to as "brochure-ware." Literally, you could take the artwork that you used in your company's print media, and incorporate that look into your Web site. This is useful in that it maintains a consistent look across all your marketing material. Basically, this treats the Web site as an extension of your marketing program.

Generate Sales Leads

Generating sales leads requires some form of two-way communication with the visitors to your site. It could be something as simple as an email link that lets visitors send a message to your sales department for follow-up. It could be an input form that allows visitors to provide information about their interests, and then sends that information to a CGI program (discussed later) on the server so that it can be entered directly into your database.

Sell Product

Selling product requires even more interaction with your users than generating leads. Not only do you need some kind of information from your visitors, but you also need to be able to provide a fair amount of detail on the products you have available. This might include prices, descriptions, and even pictures of the products. It's not practical to put that kind of dynamic information into a static Web page. How would you handle keeping the prices current and accurate? How would you handle adding new products, or removing obsolete ones?

Because of these kinds of issues, any Web site that needs this level of interaction needs to get data from a database. You probably already maintain up-to-date product information in a database, so there is minimal extra overhead there. There are many ways to deliver dynamic content from your database to a Web page. Among other ways, a CGI program, Java Server Page, PHP, or an Active Server Page could perform this task. These four common methods are discussed later in this book.

When you sell product via a Web site, your goals involve getting users to come to the site, optimizing its placement in search engines, generating a large number of hits, and keeping them on the site as long as possible.

Communicate with Business Partners

Communicating with business partners requires basically the same techniques as selling product. The focus changes, though, from presenting catalogs and taking orders to expanding your company's presence on the Internet. You will typically be presenting information from multiple databases through this kind of Web site. The information could be such things as order statuses, shipping schedules, and inventory levels.

Business partners need to come to your Web site to fulfill their own business requirements. You don't need to advertise or entice them to come to the site. In fact, you might very likely be concerned with preventing the public from getting to such a site, only allowing trusted business partners to gain access.

Provide Resources

Providing resources is almost as simple as producing brochure-ware. Resources are relatively static collections of information such as Frequently Asked Questions, user manuals, technical support documents, how-to videos, software downloads, and links to other useful Web sites. Rather than focusing on marketing, a resource site is more likely to feature a large number of links to documents and other Web sites.

As with sales sites, search-engine optimization would be very important for a resource site. However, the focus would be on delivering useful and easy-to-find content to your visitors, without concern for how often they visited or how long they stayed.

Tables

In business programming, we often need lists. We produce lists of items, orders, inventory, and more. Tables are a great tool for arranging lists of data. Therefore, it's likely that tables will become a common tool for you in developing Web pages.

Tags

Table tag

```
<table
    align
    bgcolor
    border
    cellspacing
    cellpadding
    frame
    rules
    summary
    width
>
</table>
```

Simply put, tables are just grids of data. You specify some number of rows and columns, perhaps defining a heading, a footer, and other properties, and the browser takes care of the rest. If you don't provide specific instructions to do otherwise, the browser will expand or contract the sizes of the rows and columns to fit the content within them. So, you can have some columns that contain very large text blocks or images, while other columns contain minimal info, like a yes/no flag (Y/N).

Even though browsers take care of a lot of formatting issues for us, there are still plenty of options for defining the specific behavior we want from tables. Therefore, the **<table>** tag has many properties. For example, you can define the alignment as left, center, or right. Use the **bgcolor** property to set the background color of the table, as either a color name or a hex code. The total width of the table is controlled by the **width** property, which can be set to a specific size in pixels, or a percentage of the page width. **Cellspacing** refers to the distance between cells in the table, while **cellpadding** refers to the distance between the border of a cell and its contents.

To show the borders between cells, set the **border** attribute to one or more pixels. When this is set to zero (the default), no border is shown. The **rules** attribute defines which borders/rules to show within the table. When **rules** is set to "none," only the outside border is shown. Alternatively, it can be set to "cols," indicating that only the vertical rules between the columns are shown, or "rows" to display only the horizontal rules between the rows.

The **frame** attribute defines the behavior of the outside border/frame. Set it to "void" to prevent the frame. If this attribute is set to "box" or "border," the frame on all four sides of the table is shown. Setting it to "lhs" or "rhs" displays the frames on the left side or the right side only, respectively. Use "hsides" to show only the top and bottom sides of the frame, or "vsides" to show only the right and left sides to display. Set the **frame** attribute to either "above" or "below" to show the top or bottom frames, respectively. The **summary** attribute provides a text description of the table for visually impaired users.

Even with all of these attributes, the **<table>** tag by itself is not enough to create a table. The simplest of tables will include tags for both rows and data. These tags define the rows and columns within the table. Other tags also affect the row and column definitions. We'll discuss these later in this chapter.

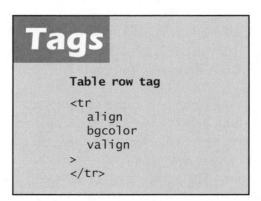

Tags

Table row tag

```
<tr
    align
    bgcolor
    valign
>
</tr>
```

The **<tr>** tag defines a row within a table. This tag should always be coded between the **<table>** and **</table>** tags. Its **align** and **bgcolor** attributes

provide the same options as those for the table itself. The **valign** attribute
lets you define the vertical alignment for the entire row. The options are
"top," "middle," and "bottom." Whichever is chosen, the content of each
cell in the row will be aligned to that point.

```
Table data tag

<td
   align
   bgcolor
   valign
   width
   height
   abbr
   scope
   nowrap
   colspan
   rowspan
>
</td>
```

The **<td>** tag defines each separate cell within the row. It has the same
align, **bgcolor**, and **valign** attributes as the **<tr>** tag. Use the **height** and
width properties to define the size of each cell. The **abbr** attribute provides
an abbreviated description of the contents of the cell. Use the **scope**
attribute to assign headings to cells for use in screen readers (discussed
later in this chapter). The **nowrap** attribute prevents the text within a cell
from automatically wrapping down to the next line. This can result in very
wide cells. The **colspan** and **rowspan** attributes are used to define how
many columns wide or rows high the cell is.

With these three tags, we can create a basic table. The code in Figure 6.1
creates a table that has one row and three columns. The total width of the
table is 200 pixels, and the second cell uses the **nowrap** attribute to force
its text to appear in a single line. The table also has its **border** property set
to 2 to create an obvious border around the table and between the cells.
The output from the code sample is shown in Figure 6.2.

```
<table width=200px border=2>
<tr>
<td>stuff 1 and stuff 2</td>
<td nowrap>stuff 3 and stuff 4</td>
<td>stuff 5 and stuff 6</td>
</tr>
</table>
```

Figure 6.1: The HTML code for a table.

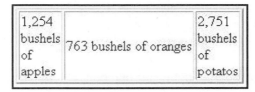

Figure 6.2: A simple table with one row.

This clearly shows the behavior of the **nowrap** attribute in the second cell. Remember, however, that managing the look of content such as this is best done with a style sheet, rather than with HTML itself. (Style sheets are discussed in chapter 5.)

Now let's add a couple of rows of data to the table, remove the **width** attribute of the **<table>** tag, and remove the **nowrap** attribute of the second **<td>** tag. The code for these changes is in Figure 6.3, and the output is shown in Figure 6.4.

```
<table border=2>
<tr>
<td>1,254 bushels of apples</td>
<td>763 bushels of oranges</td>
<td>2,751 bushels of potatoes</td>
</tr>
<tr>
<td>323 bushels of apples</td>
<td>982 bushels of oranges</td>
<td>1,200 bushels of potatoes</td>
</tr>
<tr>
<td>769 bushels of apples</td>
<td>255 bushels of oranges</td>
<td>3,100 bushels of potatoes</td>
</tr>
</table>
```

Figure 6.3: The HTML code for a multi-row table.

1,254 bushels of apples	763 bushels of oranges	2,751 bushels of potatoes
323 bushels of apples	982 bushels of oranges	1,200 bushels of potatoes
769 bushels of apples	255 bushels of oranges	3,100 bushels of potatoes

Figure 6.4: A table with three rows.

This example illustrates how the browser will adjust the size of each cell to fit its contents, and adjust the size of the table to fit all the cells. Sometimes this is fine, but often we need to control some aspect of the size of the table to better manage the way it is presented to users.

The table in Figure 6.4 is missing both column headings and row headings. There is a special tag just for column headings, and that is the table column heading (**<th>**) tag.

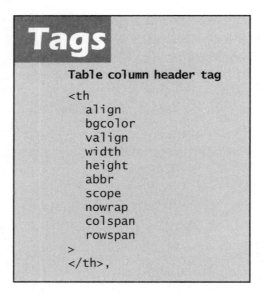

Table column header tag

```
<th
    align
    bgcolor
    valign
    width
    height
    abbr
    scope
    nowrap
    colspan
    rowspan
>
</th>,
```

The **<th>** tags create a row of cells specifically designed as headings for the other rows in the table. The modified code for a table with headings is shown in Figure 6.5. You can see the table it creates in Figure 6.6.

```
<table border=2>
<tr align=center>
<th>Apples</th>
<th>Oranges</th>
<th>Potatoes</th>
</tr>
<tr>
<td>1,254 bushels</td>
<td>763 bushels</td>
<td>2,751 bushels</td>
</tr>
<tr>
<td>323 bushels</td>
<td>982 bushels</td>
<td>1,200 bushels</td>
</tr>
<tr>
<td>769 bushels</td>
<td>255 bushels</td>
<td>3,100 bushels</td>
</tr>
</table>
```

Figure 6.5: The HTML code for the table in Figure 6.6.

Apples	Oranges	Potatoes
1,254 bushels	763 bushels	2,751 bushels
323 bushels	982 bushels	1,200 bushels
769 bushels	255 bushels	3,100 bushels

Figure 6.6: A table with column headings.

The headings in this table have been centered inside each cell. The browser is still automatically adjusting the size of the cells, rows, and the table itself. You can begin to see the table taking shape as we add more and more code to it. To make the cells a bit larger, giving the content more room, we could use the **cellpadding** attribute. We could also add additional column and row headings. The code sample in Figure 6.7 includes an enhanced version of the table, which is shown in Figure 6.8.

```
<table border=2>
<tr align=center bgcolor=gray>
<th colspan=4>Produce (in Bushels)</th>
</tr>
<tr align=center bgcolor=gray>
<th>Warehouse</th>
<th>Apples</th>
<th>Oranges</th>
<th>Potatoes</th>
</tr>
<tr>
<td bgcolor=gray>Toledo</td>
<td>1,254 bushels</td>
<td>763 bushels</td>
<td>2,751 bushels</td>
</tr>
<tr>
<td bgcolor=gray>Detroit</td>
<td>323 bushels</td>
<td>982 bushels</td>
<td>1,200 bushels</td>
</tr>
<tr>
<td bgcolor=gray>Chicago</td>
<td>769 bushels</td>
<td>255 bushels</td>
<td>3,100 bushels</td>
</tr>
</table>
```

Figure 6.7: The HTML code for the table in Figure 6.8.

Produce (in Bushels)			
Warehouse	Apples	Oranges	Potatoes
Toledo	1,254 bushels	763 bushels	2,751 bushels
Detroit	323 bushels	982 bushels	1,200 bushels
Chicago	769 bushels	255 bushels	3,100 bushels

Figure 6.8: A table with more complex headings.

As you can see in this example, the cells are a little less cramped, as there is now a little extra space between the content and the borders of the cells, and the headings are automatically emphasized in a darker print. We added a gray background to the two heading rows and the first cells in each of the data rows. The top cell uses the **colspan** attribute to extend itself four columns wide.

Now that we've removed the word *bushels* from the data cells, we can see that the left-aligned text doesn't work well for numbers. The bushel counts would look better if they were aligned to the right side of the cells. Since we only want to adjust the alignment of the data cells, and not the entire row, we'll add the alignment to the cells themselves. We can also add a column on the right side that contains some legend information for the table. Because we want this cell to extend down across all four rows, we'll use the **rowspan** attribute, and set it to five. The code in Figure 6.9 contains these changes, creating the table shown in Figure 6.10.

```
<table border=2 cellpadding=2>
<tr align=center bgcolor=gray>
<th colspan=4>Produce (in Bushels)</th>
<th rowspan=5 width=10px>2 0 0 7</th>
</tr>
<tr align=center bgcolor=gray>
<th>Warehouse</th>
<th>Apples</th>
<th>Oranges</th>
<th>Potatoes</th>
</tr>
<tr align=right>
<td bgcolor=gray align=left>Toledo</td>
<td>1,254</td>
<td>763</td>
<td>2,751</td>
</tr>
<tr align=right>
<td bgcolor=gray align=left>Detroit</td>
<td>323</td>
<td>982</td>
<td>1,200</td>
</tr>
<tr align=right>
<td bgcolor=gray align=left>Chicago</td>
<td>769</td>
<td>255</td>
<td>3,100</td>
</tr>
</table>
```

Figure 6.9: The HTML code for the table in Figure 6.10.

Produce (in Bushels)				2
Warehouse	Apples	Oranges	Potatoes	0
Toledo	1,254	763	2,751	0
Detroit	323	982	1,200	7
Chicago	769	255	3,100	

Figure 6.10: A table using the **align**, **rowspan**, and **colspan** attributes.

Notice in Figure 6.9 that the year is entered with a space between each number. This allows the browser to insert line breaks between each number, and the width of 10 pixels is too narrow to let more than one number in the year print on the same line. Making the alignment as easy to manage as possible, we added the **align=right** attribute to the **<tr>** tag beginning each data row. Then we added an **align=left** attribute to the warehouse city name cells.

Tables can be split into three sections: the header, the body, and the footer.

Tags

Table header tag

```
<thead
    align
    valign
>
</thead>
```

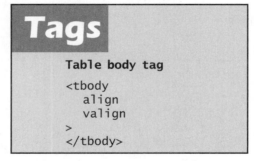

Tags

Table body tag

```
<tbody
    align
    valign
>
</tbody>
```

What this table needs now is a total line. This can be created using a table-footer section. Unlike the headings, which can be created with **<th>** cells, the footer cells must be defined using the **<tfooter>** tag, which defines the footer section of a table.

The code in Figure 6.11 modifies our table to take advantage of these sections. It creates the image shown in Figure 6.12.

```
<table border=2 cellpadding=2>
<thead>
<tr align=center bgcolor=gray>
<th colspan=5>Produce (in Bushels)</th>
</tr>
</thead>
<tbody>
<tr align=center bgcolor=gray>
<th>Warehouse</th>
<th>Apples</th>
<th>Oranges</th>
<th>Potatoes</th>
<th rowspan=4 width=10px>2 0 0 7</th>
</tr>
<tr align=right>
<td bgcolor=gray align=left>Toledo</td>
<td>1,254</td>
<td>763</td>
<td>2,751</td>
</tr>
<tr align=right>
<td bgcolor=gray align=left>Detroit</td>
<td>323</td>
<td>982</td>
<td>1,200</td>
</tr>
```

Figure 6.11: The HTML code for the table in Figure 6.12 (part 1 of 2).

```
<tr align=right>
<td bgcolor=gray align=left>Chicago</td>
<td>769</td>
<td>255</td>
<td>3,100</td>
</tr>
</tbody>
<tfoot>
<tr align=right>
<td bgcolor=gray align=left>Total</td>
<td>2,346</td>
<td>2,000</td>
<td>7,051</td>
<td bgcolor=white></td>
</tr>
</tfoot>
</table>
```

Figure 6.11: The HTML code for the table in Figure 6.12 (part 2 of 2).

Produce (in Bushels)			
Warehouse	Apples	Oranges	Potatoes
Toledo	1,254	763	2,751
Detroit	323	982	1,200
Chicago	769	255	3,100
Total	2,346	2,000	7,051

Figure 6.12: A table with a header and footer.

In the first section, **<th>** tags define the cells within the heading. In the footer section, the cells are defined using the standard **<td>** tags. To make the total even more visually distinct, we could choose to define the footer row with a different color of text or a background color. For our purposes, though, this is good enough.

Screen Readers

To improve the accessibility of Web pages for visually impaired users, HTML includes the ability to define supplemental information by a specialized type of software called a *screen reader*. Such software packages read the content of Web pages and provide an alternative presentation to the user. For example, they might magnify or speak the text.

Tags

Caption tag

```
<caption
  align
  >
  </caption>
```

To improve the accessibility of our table, we might make some changes such as replacing the top row with a caption, and providing an abbreviation to explain that the oddly formatted cell on the right side of the table is a year. We'll also change the city name cells to table headers and add the **scope** attribute to all of the table header cells. The sample code in Figure 6.13 shows the HTML for the table in Figure 6.14 with these modifications.

```
<table border=2 cellpadding=2>
<Caption>Produce (in Bushels)</caption>
<thead>
</thead>
<tbody>
<tr align=center bgcolor=gray>
<th scope=col>Warehouse</th>
<th scope=col>Apples</th>
<th scope=col>Oranges</th>
<th scope=col>Potatoes</th>
<th rowspan=4 width=10px abbr="Year 2007">2 0 0 7</th>
</tr>
<tr align=right>
<th bgcolor=gray align=left scope=row>Toledo</th>
<td>1,254</td>
<td>763</td>
<td>2,751</td>
</tr>
<tr align=right>
<th bgcolor=gray align=left scope=row>Detroit</th>
<td>323</td>
<td>982</td>
<td>1,200</td>
</tr>
```

Figure 6.13: The HTML code for the table in Figure 6.14 (part 1 of 2).

```
<tr align=right>
<th bgcolor=gray align=left scope=row>Chicago</th>
<td>769</td>
<td>255</td>
<td>3,100</td>
</tr>
</tbody>
<tfoot>
<tr align=right>
<th bgcolor=gray align=left scope=row>Total</th>
<td>2,346</td>
<td>2,000</td>
<td>7,051</td>
<td bgcolor=white></td>
</tr>
</tfoot>
</table>
```

Figure 6.13: The HTML code for the table in Figure 6.14 (part 2 of 2).

Produce (in Bushels)			
Warehouse	Apples	Oranges	Potatoes
Toledo	1,254	763	2,751
Detroit	323	982	1,200
Chicago	769	255	3,100
Total	2,346	2,000	7,051

Figure 6.14: A table with a caption and table headers.

The **scope** attribute used in the table headers is an important tool for screen readers. It helps to identify which pieces of data belong to what headings. Most of us are able to easily grasp that relationship visually, but when the table is being described verbally, it's much more challenging. Also notice that the **scope** was applied to both the columns and the rows. The caption, if one is provided, must immediately follow the **<table>** tag. With the exception of the caption, none of the changes made any difference in the way the table was displayed. Hopefully, though, these changes would improve the experience of visually impaired users.

Accessibility is a difficult issue to pin down. Different browsers support different tags, different readers use different tags, and different users have vastly different needs. We've tried to focus on practical examples in introducing this topic, but an in-depth review is beyond the scope of this book. If accessibility is a major issue for your organization, additional research in that area is required.

Columns and Column Groups

Earlier in this book, you saw how row groups (**<thead>**, **<tbody>**, and **<tfoot>**) can better define a table. Similarly, column groups can better define the columns in the table. There are two tags used to define columns: **<col>** and **<colgroup>**. Use **<col>** to define a single column, while **<colgroup>** defines multiple columns.

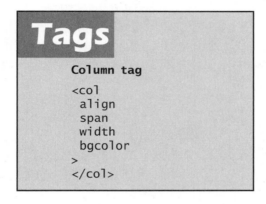

Tags

Column tag
```
<col
  align
  span
  width
  bgcolor
>
</col>
```

Tags

Column group tag
```
<colgroup
  align
  span
  width
  bgcolor
>
</colgroup>
```

The primary role of both these tags is to provide attributes for all the cells in their column(s), not the content. The updated table appears exactly as it did in Figure 6.14. However as the code in Figure 6.15 shows, the **<col>** and **<colgroup>** tags now contain most of the cell formatting attributes.

```
<table border=2 cellpadding=2>
<Caption>Produce (in Bushels)</caption>
<col bgcolor=gray align=left></col>
<colgroup span=3 align=right></colgroup>
<col width=4px></col>
<thead>
</thead>
<tbody>
<tr align=center bgcolor=gray>
<th scope=col>Warehouse</th>
<th scope=col>Apples</th>
<th scope=col>Oranges</th>
<th scope=col>Potatoes</th>
<th rowspan=4 abbr="Year 2007">2 0 0 7</th>
</tr>
<tr>
<th scope=row>Toledo</th>
<td>1,254</td>
<td>763</td>
<td>2,751</td>
</tr>
<tr>
<th scope=row>Detroit</th>
<td>323</td>
<td>982</td>
<td>1,200</td>
</tr>
<tr>
<th scope=row>Chicago</th>
<td>769</td>
<td>255</td>
<td>3,100</td>
</tr>
</tbody>
<tfoot>
<tr align=right>
<th scope=row>Total</th>
<td>2,346</td>
<td>2,000</td>
<td>7,051</td>
<td bgcolor=white></td>
</tr>
</tfoot>
</table>
```

Figure 6.15: The HTML code for a table with columns and column group definitions.

In this example, the first **<col>** tag defines the attributes of the first column, which holds the city name. The **<colgroup>** tag spans three columns, providing the alignment for all the data cells in the table. Some of the produce heading cells were also affected, but those will have their alignment corrected within the **<tr>** tag.

Nested Tables

Sometimes one table is just not enough, and you might find a need to nest one or more tables inside another table. Our example so far in this chapter lists produce inventory for various locations. What if each location stocked different produce? Sure, we could simply add more columns to the table, but then we wouldn't have an excuse to nest one table inside another.

Look at the table in Figure 6.16. It is actually two tables. The outer table contains a row for each location, and within the data cell for each location, another table lists that location's inventory. Review the code in Figure 6.17, which generates Figure 6.16.

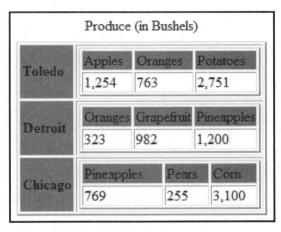

Figure 6.16: Nested tables.

```
<table border=2 cellpadding=2 margin-top=2px>
<Caption>Produce (in Bushels)</caption>
<col bgcolor=gray align=left></col>
<colgroup span=3 align=right></colgroup>
<col width=4px></col>
<thead>
</thead>
<tbody>
<tr>
<th scope=row>Toledo</th>
<td>
  <table border=2 width=100%>
  <tr bgcolor=gray>
  <td>Apples</td>
  <td>Oranges</td>
```

Figure 6.17: The HTML code for nested tables (part 1 of 2).

```
      <td>Potatoes</td>
      </tr>
      <tr>
      <td>1,254</td>
      <td>763</td>
      <td>2,751</td>
      </tr>
      </table>
  </td>
  </tr>
  <tr>
  <th scope=row>Detroit</th>
  <td>
    <table border=2 width=100%>
    <tr bgcolor=gray>
    <td>Oranges</td>
    <td>Grapefruit</td>
    <td>Pineapples</td>
    </tr>
    <tr>
    <td>323</td>
    <td>982</td>
    <td>1,200</td>
    </tr>
    </table>
  </td>
  </tr>
  <tr>
  <th scope=row>Chicago</th>
  <td>
    <table border=2 width=100%>
    <tr bgcolor=gray>
    <td>Pineapples</td>
    <td>Pears</td>
    <td>Corn</td>
    </tr>
    <tr>
    <td>769</td>
    <td>255</td>
    <td>3,100</td>
    </tr>
    </table>
  </td>
  </tr>
  </tbody>
  </table>
```

Figure 6.17: The HTML code for nested tables (part 2 of 2).

As you can see, there are a lot of options for working with tables. You can define columns and rows, format the cells, and even nest one table inside another. The code given here should provide good examples for the majority of tables you're likely to create.

Anywhere that you need to organize content into clearly defined rows and columns, columns are likely to be useful. Remember, though, to avoid using tables to define the layout of your entire Web page. This is better handled with **<div>** and **<span>** tags, discussed later in this chapter.

Frames

Frames are vaguely similar to tables. They define blocks of content that can be organized into rows and columns, if desired. However, frames, or *framesets* as they are sometimes called, were specifically designed to control the layout of Web pages, as opposed to tables, which should not be used for that task.

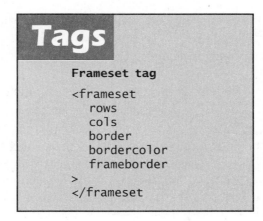

Tags

Frameset tag

```
<frameset
    rows
    cols
    border
    bordercolor
    frameborder
>
</frameset
```

Tags

Frame tag

```
<frame-, end tag
   name
   src
   scrolling
   noresize
   bordercolor
   frameborder
   marginwidth
   marginheight
>
</frame>
```

Even though frames were designed to control page layout, there are a number of controversial issues with them. Rather than go into that debate here, we'll leave it to you to dig into that topic on your own, if you wish. We'll focus instead on showing you how framesets work, so you can use them if you need to. Then, later in the chapter we'll review the best methods for arranging content on your Web pages.

A simple frameset might include two frames. One might be a small frame along the left side displaying a series of links, sometimes called an *index*, while the larger frame on the right side displays the selected content. Each frame in the frameset references the URL of the content that should fill that frame. The code sample in Figure 6.18 shows a simple example of such a two-frame frameset, illustrated in Figure 6.19.

```
<html>
<frameset border=2 cols="30%,*">
<frame src="index.html">
<frame src="main.html">
<noframes>Frames not working</noframes>
</frameset>
</html>
```

Figure 6.18: The HTML code for a page with framesets.

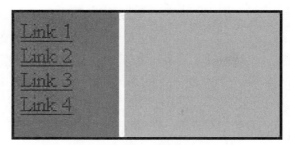

Figure 6.19: A two-frame frameset.

This example uses the **border** attribute of the **<frameset>** tag to define a border between the frames that is two pixels wide. The **framespacing** attribute does the same thing, but it is not as intuitive, so it wasn't included here. The **cols** attribute indicates that the first frame's width is 30% of the page width and is the left frame in a pair. The second frame will fill the rest of the page. (The asterisk, *, means to use what's left.) If we had used the **rows** attribute, the frames would be split horizontally. We could have used the **bordercolor** attribute to define a colored border, and the **frameborder** attribute can be set to "yes" or "no," indicating if a 3D border effect should be used.

The frames may be resized manually by the user, by clicking and dragging the border between the frames, unless the **noresize** attribute is set. By default, scrollbars will appear if needed, but you can force the scrollbars not to appear by setting the **scrolling** attribute to "no." To control the margins within the frame, use the **marginwidth** and **marginheight** attributes.

Targets of Links in Frames

One of the key tricks for working with frames is controlling which window the links are loaded into. In our two-frame frameset, the links were in the left pane. By default, the links in that frame will change the HTML shown in the left pane, but what we'd really like to do is load the new page in the right pane, which we might call the "content pane." To control the frame in which the linked documents load name the frames and use the **target** attribute in the links. To modify the links in our two-frame example, we would first use the **name** attribute as shown in Figure 6.20.

```
<html>
<frameset border=2 rows="30%,*" cols="30%,*">
<frame src="index.html" name="index">
<frame src="main.html" name="content">
<noframes>Frames not working</noframes>
</frameset>
</html>
```

Figure 6.20: The HTML code framesets with named frames.

In this case, we've labeled the frames as "index" and "content." Figure 6.21 shows the line of code that will cause the target of a link in one frame to load in a different frame. The result is shown in Figure 6.22.

```
<a href="barbeque barn.html" target="content">Link 1</a>
```

Figure 6.21: A hypertext link that opens in the Content frame.

Figure 6.22: A two-frame frameset with targeted links.

There are other targets you can specify for a link. The following are special targets that have a specific meaning:

- **Target = "_blank"** opens the link in a new window.
- **Target = "_self"** opens the link in the current window.
- **Target = "_parent"** opens the link in this frame's parent frame.
- **Target = "_top"** opens the link in the topmost window frame.
- **Target = "_search"** opens the link in search pane.

Inline Frames

The framesets we've discussed so far are rigid and fixed in their structure. A more flexible type of frame is the *inline frame*. It is called an inline frame because the frame and its contents are placed on the Web page as if they were an inline element, such as an image. This enables you to pull content from other pages into frames placed on the current page. You might do this if you have a common document that contains information that you want to present on multiple pages. Each of those pages might include an inline frame that displays the same information. The advantage of this is that the information is stored in a single document, so it is more easily maintained. Otherwise, keeping the same information consistent across multiple changes is difficult and time-consuming.

Tags

Inline frame tag

```
<iframe-, end tag
   name
   src
   scrolling
   width
   height
   align
   frameborder
   marginwidth
   marginheight
>
</iframe>
```

The attributes of the inline frame are similar to those for the **<frame>** and **<frameset>** tags. The **src** attribute identifies the document being displayed within the frame, while the other attributes control various aspects of how it is displayed.

Figure 6.23 shows the code for a simple example of an inline frame. Figure 6.24 shows the resulting Web page.

```
<html>
<body>
<p>This is just some text for paragraph one.
We need to make this long enough so that it looks like it
might be a real paragraph.  How much more text
do we need to add?  What do you think?</p>
<p>Then we might start another
<iframe src="barbeque barn.html" width=45%>
if you see this, your browser does not support iframes
</iframe>
</p>
</body>
</html>
```

Figure 6.23: The HTML code for an inline frame.

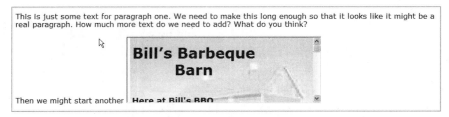

Figure 6.24: A Web page with an inline frame.

As you can see, the inline frame is placed in the middle of the second paragraph, with a width of 45% of the page. Because the HTML document is too long to fit in the area for the inline frame, a scrollbar is added. Also notice, in Figure 6.23, the text between the **<iframe>** and **</iframe>** tags. The sentence "if you see this, your browser does not support iframes" should only display if the user's browser does not support inline frames.

The <div> and <span> Tags

The last, and perhaps most important, tags for controlling the arrangement of content on a Web page are **<div>** and **<span>**. These two tags perform similar tasks, marking a section of content and provide the ability to control the presentation of that content through cascading style sheets. Both **<div>** and **<span>** have very few attributes that can be set.

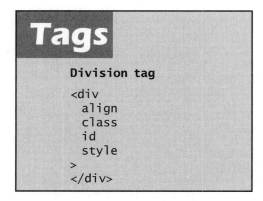

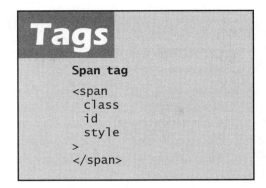

The **<div>** tag supports the **align** attribute, but the use of that attribute is discouraged because its functionality can be handled through cascading style sheets instead. The one difference between these two tags is that **<span>** is an inline element that appears exactly where you code it, much like an inline frame, while **<div>** is a block element that performs a line break before its contents are displayed.

The simple code sample in Figure 6.25 uses **<div>** and **<span>** to create the Web page shown in Figure 6.26.

```
<html>
<body>
<p>This is just some text for paragraph one.
We need to make this long enough so that it looks like it
might be a real paragraph.  How much more text
do we need to add?  What do you think?</p>
<p>Then we might start another
<span>XXXXXXXXXXX</span>
paragraph
</p>
<p>After that we could add a third
<div>YYYYYYYYYYYYY</div>
paragraph
</p>
</body>
</html>
```

*Figure 6.25: HTML code with **<div>** and **<span>** tags.*

This is just some text for paragraph one. We need to make this long enough so that it looks like it might be a real paragraph. How much more text do we need to add? What do you think?

Then we might start another XXXXXXXXXXXX paragraph

After that we could add a third
YYYYYYYYYYYYYY
paragraph

Figure 6.26: A Web page using ***\<div>*** *and* ***\<span>*** *tags.*

The sample in Figure 6.23 shows that the *X*s in the **\<span>** tag are included inline within the paragraph, while the **\<div>** tag forces a line break before and after the *Y*s. The **\<div>** tag is meant to define large sections of the page, while the **\<span>** tag is intended for smaller sections of content.

To see **\<div>** and **\<span>** working as intended, you must incorporate cascading style sheets into your Web page. By assigning class names to the **\<div>** and **\<span>** tags, you can assign positioning, alignment, and other formatting properties to these tags.

You can use the **\<div>** and **\<span>** tags to provide page formatting similar to what you've seen with tables and frames. The Web page shown in Figure 6.27 includes an index section on the left, and a content pane on the right. The style for the index is positioned absolutely at the top left corner of the page, with a width that is 20% of the page size. The content pane is defined as 80% of the page size and positioned at the top right corner of that page.

Figure 6.27: A Web page created using ***\<div>***, ***\<iframe>***,
and a cascading style sheet.

The code for the cascading style sheet is shown in Figure 6.28.

```
.index {width:20%; position:absolute; top:0; left:0;
}

.content {width:80%; position:absolute; top:0; right:0;
}
```

Figure 6.28: A cascading style sheet for use with the HTML in Figure 6.29.

The code for the Web page, shown in Figure 6.29, uses the **<link>** tag to identify the style sheet to use. It includes two **<div>** tags, each with an **<iframe>** tag inside that loads content from either the "index.html" or "barbeque barn.html" documents.

```
<html>
<head>
<link rel="stylesheet" type="text/css" href="TESTcss.css">
<body>
<div class="index">
<iframe src="index.html">
Your browser does not support frames
</iframe>
</div>
<div class="content">
<iframe src="barbeque barn.html">
Your browser does not support frames
</iframe>
</div>
</body>
</html>
```

*Figure 6.29: The HTML code for a page created with the **<div>** and **<iframe>** tags, and a style sheet.*

Summary

We've kept the examples pretty basic in this chapter. Of all the tags we discussed, tables are probably the most universally useful, since virtually all business applications need to display content in neatly defined rows and columns. Framesets and inline frames provide additional capabilities to blend content from various documents into a single Web page. Using these tags to control the presentation of content is discouraged, however, in favor of the **<div>** and **<span>** tags.

Keep in mind the ultimate purpose of your Web page, and arrange your content in a way that supports that purpose.

Web Application Overview

Up to this point, we've talked almost exclusively about HTML. Now that we have a foundation in place, and an understanding of how to use HTML to develop Web pages, it's time to move on to using Web pages in actual business applications. Developing business applications introduces new considerations and components.

Traditional business applications typically use a single system and an emulator for access to that system. Web applications open up the use of your systems and software to more users and often involve multiple servers. These servers may be nearby, across the country, or even in another country. Users will be connecting and accessing the applications using Web browsers. The applications will serve up dynamic Web pages using one or more additional tools, such as Active Server Pages, PHP, Java Server Pages, or Common Gateway Interface (CGI) programs.

Before diving into some of these tools, let's take a closer look at the components of a Web application. Applications used only by internal staff will typically be less complex than those open to the general Web community. In either case, a Web application may contain a number of confusing components. Remember, though, that a business application developer might only be responsible for part of the system. Especially within midsize and large organizations, there will probably be a separation of responsibility, with a Webmaster or systems staff responsible for system configuration, security, and performance, and another group responsible for developing applications.

For experienced business developers, this isn't anything new. It's similar to the separation of responsibilities in traditional applications. While a business developer might not need to be an expert on configuration, performance, or security, a basic understanding is helpful. A better understanding of the system components and requirements improves application design and results in improved applications.

Components of a Web Application System

A business Web application system consists of hardware and software components, as shown in Figure 7.1. This diagram provides a basic understanding of the components required, but there might be additional components, depending on the complexity of an organization's specific environment. You probably already have an understanding of the basic components, but to fill in any blanks, we will review them.

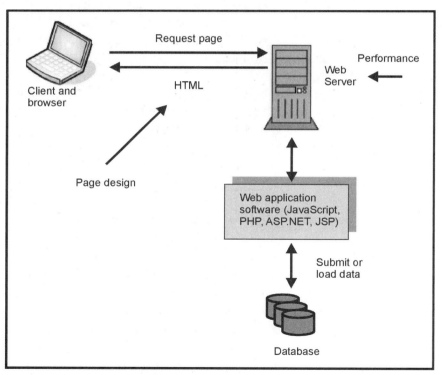

Figure 7.1: A Web application system.

The Client

The client is the hardware device that will be used to access the Web application. It is probably a laptop or desktop computer, but it might be a handheld device such as a PDA, PalmPilot, or cell phone. Consider carefully what types of devices your application should support. This usually depends on who your application users are and what devices they use to access the Internet.

The client devices will probably use a variety of operating systems. The most common operating system, of course, is Microsoft Windows. Even if all of your site visitors are using Windows on PCs, they might be using different screen sizes and resolutions. The screen size and resolution settings will affect the appearance of the site and applications.

All of these factors can have an impact on how applications are coded. For example, if your users access your site through handheld devices, your application might require special design and coding techniques to easily fit data on a smaller screen. If your application has a lot of graphics, such as product pictures or logos, the need to consider performance and appearance will be even more important. Client device types, operating systems, screen sizes, and resolutions are discussed in more detail in chapter 13.

The Browser

A browser is software that acts as an interface between the client and the Worldwide Web. The browser is also referred to as a *Web client*. The browser sends requests for information, receives the information, and displays it on the client. You are probably already familiar with the browsers available, such as Internet Explorer, Firefox, Opera, and Netscape. Browsers are usually free and change in popularity.

A browser can affect an application's appearance and may also impose other considerations for Web development. If your application is used by the general Web community, your site will very likely need to support many different browsers. Browsers are discussed in more detail in chapter 13.

HTML

As we've mentioned in previous chapters, HTML is the language of the Web, and if you are creating a Web application, it will almost certainly be used. HTML has been around for quite a while and will certainly be used for a long time to come. It has changed, however, since its initial inception, to include functions and features that make it more flexible and easier to use for developing Web applications. HTML has been controlled by standards greatly influencing compatibility and making it a universal standard on the Web.

An HTML document is *static*, meaning it exists in a constant state. To make a Web application dynamic, you can add client-side scripting to the HTML. Most often, the language used for client-side scripting is JavaScript. JavaScript code is embedded within the HTML. You'll learn about JavaScript and client-side scripting in chapter 8. Another option for adding interactivity to HTML is to use forms that incorporate CGI. You will learn about CGI in chapter 9.

The Web Server

There are really two components of a Web server: hardware and software. So, the term *Web server* can mean either the hardware or the program that is responsible for communicating with client browsers. A Web server accepts HTTP requests from client Web browsers and serves HTTP responses, including data content, usually in the form of an HTML document and linked objects.

Writing Web applications doesn't necessarily mean that you'll need to purchase new hardware. Many platforms can be used to serve Web sites, although some are more compatible and better suited to Web development than others. Your organization probably already has a system that can be used for serving a Web site and Web applications. However, additional hardware might be helpful to serve your site and Web applications, and as a means of including another layer of security. On the other hand, having additional hardware requires additional support and administration. Therefore, you might want to consider using a Web hosting service, discussed later in this chapter.

In terms of Web server software, many different products are available, but some are much more popular than others. Table 7.1 lists the top Web server software vendors, as published in a Netcraft survey in September 2007. (Netcraft is an Internet monitoring company based in England.)

Table 7.1: Netcraft Survey, September 2007, Top Web Server Software		
Adabas D	Product	Product
Apache	Apache	67,898,632
Microsoft	IIS	47,226,195
Google	GWS	6,616,713
Sun Microsystems	Sun ONE Web Server	1,997,150
Oversee	Oversee	1,601,209
Lighttpd	Lighttpd	1,515,963
Others	-	8,296,292
Total	-	**135,152,154**

While Table 7.1 lists the top six software titles, being included on the list does not mean a particular server software product will best fit your needs. There are hundreds of Web server programs available. Many have been created for specialized purposes. Servers are chosen for many different needs and requirements. Table 7.2 is a more complete list of Web server software currently available.

Table 7.2: Expanded List of Web Server Software				
Abyss Web Server	Apache	Bad Blue	Eagle	Elemenope
Google Web Server (GWS)	Httperf	IBM Lotus Domino	IBM Websphere Application Server	In-kernel Web Server
Internet Information Services (IIS)	Jaminid	Kerio WebSTAR	Koala	LiteSpeed Web Server (Lighttpd)
MacHTTP	Macromedia JRun	Merak Mail Server	Mod wsgi	NetDynamics Application Server
Netscape Enterprise Server	Oversee	Oracle Application Server	Oracle HTTP Server	Personal Web Server
PoorMan	SAP Web Application Server	Server2Go	Stronghold	Sun Java System Web Server
Sun One Web Server	TV's server	UltiDev Cassini Web Server	WebLogic	WebSitePro
Windows Personal Web Server	Zeus Web Server			

How do you choose Web server software? Consider your needs and determine requirements. Research is the key. Consider and compare server software that meets your requirements and expectations. Here are some of the considerations that should be used for evaluation and comparison:

- Features provided

- Functionality provided

- Operating system support

- Cost

- Creator

- Open source

- Software license

- Dynamic content support

- Scripting languages supported

- Databases supported

- Platform compatibility

- Security provided

- Administration and support requirements

- Performance and response time

- Reliability

The Application Servers

Application servers are different than Web servers. A Web server provides client-side dynamic content and serving of the static components of a Web site. Application servers provide server-side dynamic content and integration with database engines. Usually, the application server is used for the business logic and data access of a Web application. Most Web servers are also capable of being application servers.

Application server software is usually bundled with middleware to enable applications to communicate with dependent applications, including Web servers and database management systems. Some application servers also include an API, making them operating-system independent. *Portals* are common application server mechanisms by which a single point of entry can be provided for multiple device types. Table 7.3 shows some of the reasons for incorporating an application server into your application design.

Table 7.3: Web Application Server Advantages	
Advantage	**Description**
Data and code integrity	By centralizing business logic on an individual or a small number of server machines, updates and upgrades to the application for all users can be guaranteed. There is no risk of old versions of the application accessing or manipulating data in an older, incompatible manner.
Security	Managing access to data and portions of the application through a central point provides a security benefit. Using an application server moves responsibility for authentication away from the potentially insecure client layer without exposing the database layer.
Centralized configuration	Changes to the application configuration, such as a move of the database server or new system settings, can be done centrally.
Performance	The client-server model improves the performance of large applications in heavy usage environments.
Total cost of ownership	Using an application server can save an organization money through the benefits provided when developing business applications.

Business Web Application Software

Adding dynamic capability to a static Web site is what Web development is all about. The programming tools used to add that capability are very important. It is not just a matter of learning HTML. You'll be using a combination of tools to create your Web applications. Some form of HTML will be part of the framework for embedding and executing application logic, while the actual programming code may execute on the client or on the server side.

Client-side Programming and Scripting

On the client side, dynamic content is generated on the client system. The Web server retrieves HTML pages with code embedded in them and sends them to the client. The Web browser on the client then processes the code embedded in the page. Client-side code can be used for such things as changing content, input validation, identifying environmental conditions, or triggering action events. Often, the script language embedded in an HTML page is JavaScript.

Operations performed on the client side of a client-server relationship require access to information or functionality that is available on the client, but not the server. The client is a dedicated user resource, so client-side processing can provide quick response times when designed and coded properly. Completing processing on the client side may also reduce security risks.

Programmers have a variety of tools available for use in client-side coding. JavaScript (discussed in chapter 8) is the most common tool. Another option is a combination of JavaScript and XML called Ajax. Still other options include Python, VBScript, and Perl.

Java is not a scripting language, but it can also be used for client-side applications. Java is an object-oriented, platform-independent language whose roots are in C and C++. Any hardware that has a Java Virtual Machine (JVM) can be used with Java. Java, however, is more complex and has a longer learning curve than the true scripting languages. Java is a compiled language. The source is compiled into byte code, which is actually what is used for program execution. Java may also be used for server-side Web application development.

Most Web server software packages also have scripting gateways used to create dynamic content. Scripting gateways are used within Web applications to provide the gateway to connect the client and server. Consider two fields with a gated fence between them. The fields are the client and the server, and the gateway is the gate that connects them. CGI hooks are the most commonly used gateway to allow developers to create entire pages and graphics under program control. The CGI hooks are initiated within HTML pages on the client side. Chapter 9 introduces Web development with CGI.

Users' browser settings determine how client-side code embedded in HTML will be handled. Most, but not all, browsers and devices currently support JavaScript. However, users can disable this functionality. The argument might be made that mission-critical programming and scripting should reside on the server side for universal accessibility.

Server-side Programming and Scripting

Server-side programming and scripting provides another way to add dynamics to your Web site. Figure 7.2 provides a high-level summary of server-side application execution. As you can see, server-side scripts or programs are executed when called upon from the client via an HTTP request. The HTTP protocol has been in use since 1990. Server-side dynamic page creation was made possible through CGI around 1993. Shortly after, Server-Side Includes (SSI) were introduced, with a more direct way to include server-side scripting.

Some of the uses for server-side programming and scripting include the following:

- Process users, queries, retrieving and returning select data.

- Add, change, or delete Web page content.

- Access data or databases to retrieve, add, change, or delete data

- Create applications to process information.

- Develop applications based on business logic.

- Provide security and access control.

- Validate data or input.

- Tailor output for different browser types.

- Access files.

- Customize Web pages to make them user-friendly.

- Improve application performance.

- Translate or transform data formats.

- Interface to other applications or systems.

Basically, server-side development is used for all the same tasks as traditional programming languages.

Unlike client-side scripts, server-side scripting does not allow the user to view the source code. Client-side scripts have greater access to information and functions on the user's computer. Server-side scripts require the language interpreter to be installed on the server and produce the same results regardless of the client browser or operating system used. Client-side scripts need to be written in a language that is supported by the browsers used by the majority of the site users.

A large number of application development tools are available for server-side Web application creation. In addition to SSI, tools include ASP, ASP.NET, APIs, CGI, Java, Java Servlets, JavaServer Pages (JSP), Perl, PHP, Python, Ruby, Ruby on Rails, and Visual Basic. Choosing the right tools might seem like a daunting task, but learning about the tools available and how they work is the first step. You might already be familiar with some of the tools, or a decision on what tools fit within your existing standards might already have been made. Some of the tools are relatively quick to learn, like Visual Basic and PHP, while others, like Java, take longer to learn and master. The most commonly used tools (ASP.NET, CGI programming, Java, JSP, and PHP) are discussed in later chapters.

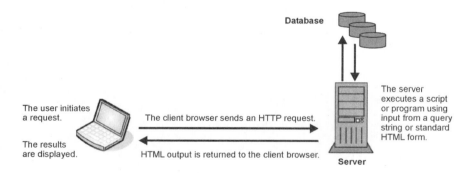

Figure 7.2: Server-side application execution.

Another option for server-side Web development is using *Rapid Application Development* (*RAD*) tools. RAD is a methodology that enables applications to be developed faster. Other potential benefits of RAD include the convenience of providing developers of any skill level the ability to create Web applications, and the usefulness of providing the developer access to support resources.

Many RAD tools are available for use with Web application development. RAD tools are purchased software. They come with support resources that developers may access as a part of the license agreement. Not all RAD tools are alike. Some are platform-specific, while others are portable or even platform-independent. Comparing RAD tools can be important to your success and satisfaction with a tool. Some of the RAD tools currently available include PlanetJ's WOW (Web Object Wizard), BCD Web Smart, IBM Rational Developer, NetBeans, Lazarus, LANSA, Boa Constructor, NetBeans, and RadRails.

There is no single best tool for server-side application development. Many factors should be considered to determine what is best for your needs. These factors include the task at hand, security considerations, developer skill levels, organizational policies, procedures, and standards. To code Web applications, a developer should have a variety of tools available. With experience, a developer will learn how to choose the best tool for the task at hand.

Compatibility

Review the components of your system for compatibility. Research and test all of the connection and interaction points within your system to be sure the components chosen work well together and are compatible. For sites and applications where it is critical to have quick performance, or for sites that have heavy traffic, it is a good idea to retrieve and log environment information, including the browser used. This information can help you better understand what configurations your users have, for the purposes of analysis and testing.

Using Proven, Established Technology

Don't risk using unproven technology just for the sake of being on the cutting edge. Make sure the tools are stable and have a performance record that meets your requirements. Choose technology that has a support system in place. This support system can be a phone number you can call, a Web user community, or known resources with technology knowledge. If you choose common, well-established technology, and you have a performance issue related to that technology, others have probably already had the same experience and are willing to share a solution.

Often, performance errors are the result of improper coding techniques or using the technology in combination with incompatible components. Before using the tools in a production environment, be sure to gain knowledge and a clear understanding of how they work. Like any technology, applications developed using Web development tools should be thoroughly tested.

Testing Devices, Browsers, Operating Systems, and Connections

When developing applications, it is easy to lose sight of the fact that end users will probably not have the same combination of device, browser, operating system, and connection you're using. For example, if you are using a high-speed connection, your response will not be the same as an end user who has a dial-up connection.

Applications should be tested using different browsers and different versions of browsers. The browser being used can have a noticeable impact on performance. Often, developers have newer devices that use a newer version of a common operating system. If your end users will potentially be using different devices with different operating systems, your application needs to address any differences.

A good Web application test plan will include testing using different combinations of devices, browsers, operating systems, and connections. Consider who your audience is and what the ultimate objective is for your application. This will help to determine what to use for testing.

The Database

A database is a structured collection of information, an electronic filing system consisting of files, records, and fields. A *database management system* (*DBMS*) or *relational database management system* (*RDMS*) is a software application used to manage, query, and update that data. The DBMS or RDMS you are using for traditional applications can probably also be used for your Web applications, although some databases are better suited than others for Web applications.

When choosing programming tools, Web servers, and Web application servers, consider their compatibility with your existing database and DBMS or RDMS. Alternatively, you might choose to have Web application data reside on a different system, for security purposes. If your data already resides in different locations, or more than one DBMS or RDMS is being used, choosing the right tools for compatibility and security is important.

Accessing Data Using SQL

In the 1960s, database software required the use of complex mainframes that were difficult to maintain and run, and often required tremendous resources to support. Each mainframe ran different software from different manufacturers. SQL (Structured Query Language) was created in the 1970s as a new standard for any database program. It quickly gained international popularity because it bridged the barriers between mainframes and allowed large corporations to network their efforts.

Today, SQL is both an ANSI and ISO standard. It is an interactive programming language for retrieving and updating data in RDMSs. SQL forms the backbone of most modern database systems. It is compatible with most databases and database engines, including SQL Server, DB2, Oracle, Sybase, MySQL, dBase, Unix, Linux, and Access. Many other products support SQL with proprietary extensions to the standard language.

SQL knowledge is invaluable for storing or retrieving data from a database. If you're not already familiar with SQL, you'll want to seriously consider developing SQL skills.

Database Triggers

Database triggers are user-written programs that are activated by the DBMS when a data change is performed in a database. The change might be adding, changing, or deleting a record.

The main purpose of a trigger is to monitor database changes and provide a tool to initiate an action. Triggers are application-independent, meaning a trigger is automatically activated regardless of the source of the database change. When a trigger is activated, the control shifts from the application program to the database system. The trigger program then performs the action you have designated to take place. Once the trigger action is complete, the control returns back to the application that initiated the trigger. The action performed may include executing a program. Figure 7.3 shows how a database trigger might be used within a Web application to reuse legacy code. (Reusing legacy code is discussed in more detail later in this chapter.)

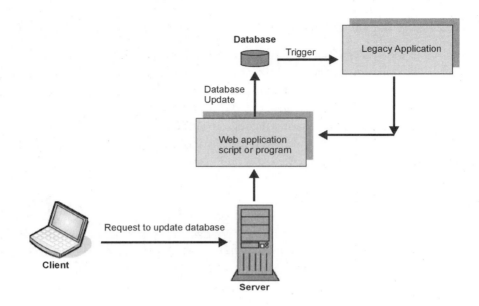

Figure 7.3: A database trigger making use of legacy code.

Not all DBMS or RDMS applications can use triggers. Those that do might have slightly different capabilities and will have different syntax and methods for creating the trigger. You'll need to investigate whether or not the DBMS or RDMS you are using allows database trigger functionality. Most systems that use SQL as the backbone can use triggers.

Web Site Design

The focus of this book is not on a Web site's appearance, but rather on the business applications that must be created to fulfill system requirements. Sometimes, a programmer will be responsible for graphics and appearance, but more often, a design or marketing group will be responsible for graphics and design. Even if you won't be responsible for Web site design, however, there are some site design considerations to keep in mind while developing a Web application, as listed in Table 7.4.

Table 7.4: Design Considerations	
Design Consideration	**Description**
Existing standards compliance	The design should be compatible with existing standards.
Development practices	Development practices currently used within the Web development community and industry best practices should be taken into consideration.
Device support	Device support and device independence should be considered.
Ease of use	Design and programming tools should be easy to use and avoid unnecessary complexity. Applications should be easy to use by developers, allow for effective usability and accessibility, and provide robust interoperability. The end result will be easy-to-use applications for end users.
Security	Security should not be overlooked. The design must incorporate security for end users as well as developers.
Internationalization and localization	Internationalization and localization guidelines should be followed and current practical internationalization solutions should be considered.
Development space	Web application development space on both the client and server sides should be considered. Reducing fragmentation gives authors a common implementation framework, making it easier to develop, package, and deploy Web applications.
Web delivery	The design should focus on Web delivery and deployment.

Page Content

Providing too much information on a Web page negatively affects the user's experience. If you think a user will take the time to read every word on such a Web page, you're mistaken. To be sure a user reads particular text, make it the very first sentence or very close to the top of the page. If there is a lot you need to share with users, logically break up the content and use multiple pages.

Sometimes less is more. Don't fill up pages with unneeded text. The same applies to images. Sometimes images pack a lot of punch and can add great value to a page, but too many images are distracting for users. Also, when using graphics, consider performance, as discussed in chapter 3. Loading images takes resources. How and when images are loaded should be considered. Simple and logically organized pages are most effective.

Search engines may also have a big impact on the content of your Web application page. Search engines are discussed later in this book.

Navigation

How users maneuver on a Web page is important. Again, keep it simple and logically organized. Try to create a common navigational structure for all the pages of an application. This will make the user's experience more intuitive.

Logically organize tasks and links to other pages. Keep the use of hyperlinks inside text paragraphs to a minimum. Having lots of hyperlinks inside text paragraphs destroys the feeling of a consistent navigational structure. Links and navigation to site pages should be mapped out, grouping like functions together. When hyperlinks to other pages are needed, add them to the bottom of a paragraph or to the navigational menus on your page.

Figures 7.4 and 7.5 are examples of sites that are simple, easy to understand, and easy to maneuver. In these examples, the menu buttons are placed at the top of the page and navigation capability is also provided through the menu list on the left side of the Web page. The verbiage used is simple, and the pages are not cluttered with too much information. The same visual look, menus, and buttons are used consistently throughout these Web sites to enhance the user's experience.

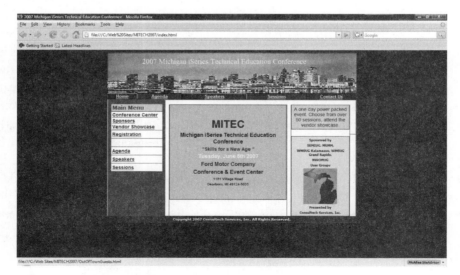

Figure 7.4: An example of an uncluttered Web page.

Figure 7.5: A Web page with simple, clear navigation tools.

Standards

Standards are an effective and useful mechanism for simplifying Web application development. Standards make it much easier for different developers to modify and support the Web application. In this respect, Web application development is no different than traditional application development.

Standards should include documentation, the location of code, technology used, Web site design, functions, features, and testing. Some developers might think that standards are restrictions, but they should understand that standards make the tasks of coding and debugging much easier. Coding errors, which are the most common source of application problems, can be minimized by using standards. Web standards also help ensure that all site users have access to the same information and have the same experience while using a Web application.

Choose your standard tools wisely. As mentioned earlier, there are many options available to for Web application programming. Be sure to choose tools that are stable, reliable, proven, and appropriate for the platform used for the Web site. Several tools are introduced in this book. An understanding of the tools available and how they work will help in making a decision on which to include as standards.

Other Considerations

Include in your site design a means for user feedback. Make it simple to use and easy to understand because feedback, whether positive or negative, can help improve your applications. Web visitors aren't usually shy about sharing insights on what you could have done better or how you can improve your site.

Unless the nature of your site dictates otherwise, make sure to provide appropriate contact information that is easy to find. There isn't anything more frustrating than visiting a Web site to find an organization's address or phone number and not being able to easily find this information.

Consider who your audience is and what the ultimate objective is for your application. This will help to determine what types of devices, operating systems and browsers should be used for testing.

Performance

Performance is a serious subject in developing any system or application, but it is especially important on the Web. Web servers are intended to receive and respond to user requests quickly. Slow applications quickly result in discontented end users.

Many things can affect performance. Depending on the purpose of the site, some pages may have more activity or heavier traffic than others. On an informational or query page, you'll quickly lose users' interest if they have to wait for responses or for pages to load. If your site is intended to sell a product or service, this will probably result in a potential customer moving on to another site that responds quicker. Within this section, we will review some of the opportunities to improve and control site performance.

Web Application Design

We've already discussed some of the factors that should be considered while designing a Web site and Web applications. The design will have an impact on performance. Jam-packed pages bogged down with too many images, in formats that make the files large, and with unnecessary content and poor design, all add up to slow loading. Design isn't limited to static content, but also the dynamic components. Unnecessary complexity or poor coding, such as multiple interactions with the database instead of just one, can result in performance issues.

Offloading Tasks to the Client

The client is a dedicated resource for a user. The server, on the other hand, is a shared resource. Applications can be designed to offload some tasks, like up-front validation or scripting logic, to minimize the server load. Client-side scripting isn't always the answer, but obviously as a dedicated user resource, it should be considered to minimize the performance impact of processing user requests and responses.

Configuration

A properly configured Web server and system will result in improved performance. Once a server is selected, the server's administrator should develop a thorough understanding of how it works and how it should be configured. The same applies to other hardware, as well as the database being used.

Develop benchmark testing scripts to test server configuration. It is a good idea to test using real applications, taking into consideration the hardware devices and operating systems being used to access your Web site. Often, configuration provides a number of variables that control how the system performs. Make sure there is a clear understanding of the configuration impact of these variable settings.

Response Standards

Develop response standards. To start, estimate the potential maximum number of users who will access your site and applications concurrently. Take into consideration the code that will need to execute and whether the applications will be accessing, retrieving, and updating data. Based on this information, define an acceptable user response time. The standards developed should be used in coordination with application testing and for choosing hardware and software.

Web Server Performance

Key performance factors for the Web server include the following:

- Number of requests per second
- Throughput in bytes per second
- Concurrency level supported
- Latency response time in milliseconds for each new connection request

A Web server has defined load limits based on the number of concurrent client connections and a maximum number of requests it can serve per second. The load limits are determined by configuration, the HTTP request type, whether page content is static or dynamic, whether server content is cached, hardware limits, and the software limits of the operating system being used. When a server reaches its limits, it becomes overloaded and unresponsive.

A server can become overloaded for a number of reasons, including the following:

- Too much user traffic
- Viruses
- Worms
- Distributed denial of service attacks
- Internet network slowdowns
- Server downtime

HTTP Traffic Managers

HTTP traffic managers are available for monitoring and classifying bandwidth usage. This provides system administrators with live readings and long-term usage trends for their network devices. The most common usage is bandwidth management, but you can also monitor many other aspects of your network, such as memory and CPU utilization.

Traffic Load

Firewalls can be used to block unwanted traffic coming in from select IP sources or to create specific patterns to reduce server traffic. HTTP traffic managers are available to drop, redirect, or rewrite requests using specific patterns that are identified as unwanted. Traffic managers are also used to smooth peaks in network usage. Web caching techniques can also be used to reduce traffic.

Another possibility is using different domain names to serve static and dynamic content, or to separate big files from small and medium-sized files. The idea is to fully cache small and medium-sized files while efficiently serving big files by using a different configuration. Multiple servers may also be used to reduce traffic for a single server and to balance the server load. Of course, increasing RAM and processor capacity is an option. If the server isn't right-sized to your needs, this might be necessary.

Coding Techniques

Coding techniques should be used to minimize resource requirements and programming bugs. Establishing standards, as mentioned earlier, will help ensure applications are developed to perform well and are easier to support. The design of Web applications is no different than traditional application development. Keep it simple. Use coding techniques to avoid unnecessary code from being executed and unnecessary request and response interactions. Learning and understanding the language is the first step. Using caching and programming to prevent buffer overload are useful ways to improve performance.

Performance Monitoring and Logging Tools

Web server software often includes or has available for purchase performance monitoring and logging tools. These tools provide collection information for analysis to determine if your system is operating at peak performance. They will also tell you if the components you are using fall short of meeting users' needs. It is worth spending the time to learn what is available and to make use of these tools.

Reusing Legacy Code

Making the decision to include Web applications as part of your business systems doesn't mean you have to scrap the applications already in use. It might make sense to leave some of these applications as they are, and only deploy select applications on the Web. Many organizations already have existing applications in place that they have invested considerable resource, time, and money on. Many of these applications are stable and still well suited to the business requirements. There is no reason to rewrite all of your applications unless a business need requires a change.

Consideration should be given to the reuse of legacy code. It might well affect the design, choice of tools, and framework for Web application development. It isn't always feasible to rewrite legacy code or maintain two different versions of programs that do the same thing. If you have existing applications that include detailed and complicated logic, it is possible to include these applications without a complete rewrite. There are many ways you can reuse legacy code. A few options are discussed in the following pages.

APIs

An Application Program Interface (API) enables one program to communicate with another. For example, an API can be used from within a PHP, JSP, or ASP. NET application program to execute and share data with a legacy application. APIs were developed in response to the need to exchange information between two or more different software applications. APIs have been around for a long time, and most systems can use them. Stored procedures and user-defined functions are two types of APIs.

Stored Procedures

A stored procedure is a subroutine available to applications that make use of a relational database system. Stored procedures are typically used for data validation, access control, or to trigger execution of a legacy application. Stored procedures are used to consolidate and centralize logic that was originally implemented in applications. Stored procedures must be invoked using a call statement (unlike user-defined functions, which can be used like any other expression within SQL statements). Here is an example of a call statement:

```
CALL procedurename(parm1, parm2)
```

Stored procedures can be used to return data result sets or may be used as a method to initiate another application to execute. Stored procedures may also receive and return variables, making it possible to pass parameters between the Web application and the stored procedure. While the call to the stored procedure is quite simple, you need information specific to your platform and DBMS to create the stored procedure.

On most platforms, a stored procedure can only be used to execute SQL statements and directives. Stored procedures are cataloged in the SQL system catalog using the CREATEPROCEDURE statement. On a i5, however, the rules for stored procedure are relatively relaxed; the stored procedure can be written in several languages, including RPG, COBOL, FORTRAN, PL/I, REXX, CL, and C. Stored procedures written in a language other than SQL are usually referred to as *external stored procedures*. External stored procedures do not necessarily have to include embedded SQL statements, and they do not need to be cataloged. Other platforms provide similar functionality. You will need to verify the platform that you are using provides this functionality.

One example of how a stored procedure can make reuse of legacy code is to create a stored procedure that executes a legacy application. Pass required parameters within the stored procedure call within the Web application. This enables you to access and use the complicated code or extensive business logic of the legacy application without a rewrite.

Figure 7.6 is an example of creating a stored procedure using SQL on a System i to initiate running an RPGLE program. In this example, a stored procedure named MYSTRPRC is created in library MYLIB. The procedure created references the RPG program named MYRPGPGM in the library MYLIBRARY. In this example, no parameters are passed.

```
Step 1:  Create the stored procedure on the System i

CREATE PROCEDURE MYLIB/MYSTRPRC ( )
            DYNAMIC RESULT SETS 1
            LANGUAGE RPGLE
            SPECIFIC MYLIB/MYSTRPRC
            NOT DETERMINISTIC
            MODIFIES SQL DATA
            CALLED ON NULL INPUT
            EXTERNAL NAME 'MYLIBRARY/MYRPGPGM'
            PARAMETER STYLE GENERAL;

Step 2:  Call the stored procedure from a Web application

CallableStatement cstmt = connection.prepareCall("CALL MYLIBRARY.
   MYSTOREDRPROC");
```

Figure 7.6: Using a stored procedure to call an iSeries RPGLE program.

Figure 7.7 is another example of creating a stored procedure using SQL on an i5 to run a CL program. This example is very similar to the one in Figure 7.6, except it calls a CLP rather than an RPGLE program. Also, two parameters are passed: PARMIN and PARMOUT. The call statement is from a Java program.

```
Step 1: Create Stored Procedure

CREATE  PROCEDURE  LUBELHOR/HITACHICLP  (IN  PARMIN  CHAR(120),
PARMOUT CHAR(120))
LANGUAGE CL
SPECIFIC LUBELHOR/HITACHICLP
NOT DETERMINISTIC
MODIFIES SQL DATA
CALL ON NULL INPUT
EXTERNAL NAME LUBELHOR/HITACHICLP
PARAMETER STYLE GENERAL

Step 2: Call Stored Procedure

CallableStatement cstmt = connection.prepareCall("CALL LUBELHOR/
  HITACHICLP (?, ?)");
```

Figure 7.7: Using a stored procedure to call an iSeries CL program.

User-defined Functions

User-defined functions (UDFs) are another possible option to reuse legacy code with minimal or no changes to the code. Most database management applications with SQL roots allow the use of UDFs. Calling legacy code is not the sole purpose of UDFs, but it is one of the possible uses.

Like a stored procedure, a UDF is executed by a call statement. The main difference between stored procedures and UDFs is that a stored procedure must be invoked using a call statement, while a UDF can be used like any other expression within a SQL statement.

Figure 7.8 is an example of how to create a DB2 UDF on a System i for referencing an RPGLE program. (The syntax for other database systems and platforms will vary slightly.) In the example, an integer variable is passed and will return a 15,0 decimal value. Once created, this function can be executed within PHP, JSP, or ASP.NET.

```
CREATE FUNCTION MYLIBRARY/MYFUNCTION(INTEGER)
 RETURNS DECIMAL(15,0)
 SPECIFIC MYUDFD1
 DETERMINISTIC
 LANGUAGE RPGLE
 NO SQL
 NO EXTERNAL ACTION
 RETURNS NULL ON NULL INPUT
 SCRATCHPAD
 FINAL CALL
 ALLOW PARALLEL
 EXTERNAL NAME 'MYLIBRARY/MYUDFPROGRAM(MYPARM)'
 PARAMETER STYLE DB2SQL;
```

Figure 7.8: Creating a UDF.

While stored procedures can have input and output parameters, UDFs have only input parameters. An output parameter must be returned as a return value. Just because UDFs return a single value does not mean they can't include applications with complex logic, however.

Some database management systems with roots in SQL may allow use of user-defined table function (UDTFs). A UDTF is a UDF that returns a virtual table instead of a single value. Using a UDTF, you can return a set of values. Like a stored procedure, a UDTF allows code reuse with minimal changes, enabling you to use legacy applications in coordination with Web applications.

The create function statement in Figure 7.9 identifies the function name in this example, MYFUNCTION, within the library MYLIBRARY. The external name keyword specifies the ILE CL program the function calls. In this example, it is MYUDTFPGM, found in the library MYLIBRARY. The example uses two parameters: PARM1 is a character value and PARM2 is a decimal value.

```
CREATE FUNCTION  MYLIBRAY/MYFUNCITON ()
RETURNS TABLE (
  PARM1     CHAR   (10)
, PARM2     DECIMAL (5, 0)
)
LANGUAGE CLLE
PARAMETER STYLE DB2SQL
NOT DETERMINISTIC
NO SQL
CALLED ON NULL INPUT
NO DBINFO
NO EXTERNAL ACTION
NOT FENCED
NO FINAL CALL
DISALLOW PARALLEL
SCRATCHPAD
EXTERNAL NAME MYLIBRARY/MYUDTFPGM
CARDINALITY 1
```

Figure 7.9: Creating a UDFT.

If you want to reuse legacy code within Web applications, research the possibility of a UDF or UDTF. The syntax is usually pretty similar from platform to platform. The answer to the question "how to" likely can be found within your DBMS documentation. Which one you use is best answered after thoroughly reviewing the documentation specific to your platform. The Web is another good source for research. UDFs have been used in many organizations for legacy code reuse. If the DBMS you are using provides for UDFs or UDTFs, you'll easily be able to find examples of them on the Web.

Conversion Tools

Many platforms provide software applications that can be used to convert legacy programs from one language to another. Sometimes, the conversion tools are referred to as *migration tools*. On some platforms, the tools may be provided for free to encourage the use of newer technology. In other instances, the tools must be purchased. If you'd like to keep legacy code but don't want to rewrite applications, it is worth researching conversion tools. The work required to complete the conversion may be done by in-house staff or by an outside service organization. Conversion may also be used to move software from one platform to another in a format that can be used on the new platform.

Conversion likely will not be worthwhile if you only need to reuse a select few applications. If you need to reuse a large system or all of your applications, however, a conversion tool might well be the right solution.

Security

Opening up your applications to the Web introduces new security considerations. If your site and applications will be used by a few users with controlled access, the security requirements will be far less complicated. On the other hand, if your site and applications will be used by a large number of users, security will be more complex. Haphazard user sloppiness and intentional attempts to damage or misuse your system both create security risks that must be prevented or at least minimized. This book isn't focused on security, and we realize developers don't shoulder all of the responsibility for it. However, developers do have an impact and should understand security considerations and prevention measures. Within this section, we review security and consider some of the opportunities to provide a secure Web application.

Table 7.5 lists some of the potential security risks that should be considered. This list is pretty intimidating, and it continues to grow as unethical users invent new ways to attack systems. With consideration and action, however, your system can be protected from security threats.

Table 7.5: Potential Security Threats	
Security Threat	**Description**
Adware	Adware is software installed on your computer to show you advertisements. It can slow your system by using RAM and CPU cycles. It can also slow your Internet connection by using bandwidth to retrieve advertisements. In addition, adware can increase the instability of your system because many adware applications are not programmed well. Finally, adware can annoy you and waste huge amounts of your time by popping unwanted ads onto your screen, which require you to close them before you can get back to using your PC.
DDOS	In a DDOS (distributed denial of service) Internet attack, multiple external sources attack a single target system, with the goal being denial of service for its users. DDOS attacks flood the target system with incoming messages at a rate much higher than it can process, slowing it down to a level where it is rendered useless.
Hacking	Hacking refers to attempts to gain unauthorized access to network and systems.
Interception of network data	Messages can be sent from the browser to the server or vice versa via network eavesdropping. Eavesdroppers can operate from any point on the pathway between the browser and the server.
Keystroke logging	Keystroke logging involves installing hardware on a computer that captures information typed into it. This is often used to capture personal details, including passwords.

Table 7.5: Potential Security Threats (Continued)	
Security Threat	**Description**
Phishing	Phishing refers to an attempt to criminally and fraudulently acquire sensitive information by masquerading as an authorized entity. It is typically carried out by email or instant messaging, and often directs users to enter personal details at a Web site.
Smurf attack	The smurf attack is a way of generating a lot of computer network traffic to a victim site. That is, it is a type of denial of service attack that floods a target system via spoofed broadcast ping messages.
Spam	Spam is flooding the Internet with many copies of the same message, in an attempt to force the message on people who would not otherwise choose to receive it. Most spam is commercial advertising, often for dubious products, get-rich-quick schemes, or quasi-legal services.
Spyware	Spyware is software that secretly gathers information about a user while the user navigates the Internet. This information is normally used for advertising purposes. Spyware can also gather information about email addresses and even passwords and credit card numbers.
Trinoo	Trinoo is a set of computer programs to conduct a DDOS attack. It is believed that trinoo networks have been set up on thousands of systems on the Internet that have been compromised by remote buffer overrun exploit. Trinoo is famous for allowing attackers to leave a message in a folder called "cry baby." The file is self-replicating and modified on a regular basis as long as port 80 is active.
Trojan horses	A Trojan horse is a program that disguises itself as another program. Similar to viruses, these programs are hidden and cause unwanted effects. They differ from viruses because they are normally not designed to replicate.
Unauthorized access	Unauthorized access in an attempt to steal confidential information, execute commands on a system to modify the system, gather information about a system, or launch a denial of services attack to render the machine temporarily unusable.
Viruses	Computer viruses are small software programs that are designed to spread from one computer to another and to interfere with computer operation. A virus might corrupt or delete data on your computer, use your email program to spread itself to other computers, or even erase everything on your hard disk. Viruses are most easily spread by attachments in email messages or instant messaging. That is why it is essential that you never open an email attachment unless you know who it's from and you are expecting it. Viruses can be disguised as attachments of funny images, greeting cards, or audio and video files. Viruses also spread through downloads from the Internet. They can be hidden in illicit software or other files or programs you might download.
Worms	A worm is a self-replicating virus that does not alter files, but resides in active memory and duplicates itself. Worms use parts of an operating system that are automatic and usually invisible to the user. It is common for worms to be noticed only when their uncontrolled replication consumes system resources, slowing or halting other tasks.

Security Practices

Here are some security practices that can help reduce risks:

- Limit the number of log-in accounts available on the machine. Delete inactive users.

- Make sure that people with log-in privileges choose good passwords. The Crack program will help you detect poorly chosen passwords.

- Turn off unused services. For example, if you don't need to run FTP on the Web server host, get rid of the software. The same applies to sendmail, gopher, NIS (Network Information Services) clients, NFS (Networked File System), finger, and systat. Deactivate any that you don't use.

- Remove shells and interpreters that you don't absolutely need. For example, if you don't run any Perl-based CGI scripts, remove the Perl interpreter.

- Check both the system and Web logs regularly for suspicious activity.

- Scan security logs for suspicious activity.

- Use Internet security scanning software and review the information provided.

- Make sure that permissions are set correctly on system files, to discourage tampering.

- Create and use firewalls. A *firewall* is a security scheme that prevents unauthorized users from gaining access to a computer network or that monitors transfers of information between the network and the client.

- Configure routers to provide additional security.

- Don't open all ports on your system.

- Create Secure Socket Layers (SSL). SSL is a protocol that provides a high level of security for communication over the Internet.

- Use anti-spyware software. Anti-spyware software protects your client and server devices and helps keep personal details secure.

- Use anti-virus software to detect viruses and prevent them from infecting your system.

Coding for Security

Developers have a lot of control over the security measures built into applications. Many of the same security concepts used within traditional application development apply to Web development. Table 7.6 lists some of the techniques that can be used to reduce security risks.

Table 7.6: Security Coding Techniques	
Technique	**Description**
Avoid hardcoding.	Avoid hardcoding user IDs and passwords, as well as sensitive information.
Use CGI scripts with care.	CGI is not inherently insecure. However, CGI scripts must be written with just as much care as the server itself because CGI provides a gateway and connection between the client and the server.
Use SSI with care.	Server-Side Includes, snippets of server directives embedded in HTML documents, are another potential hole. A subset of the directives available in SSI instructs the server to execute arbitrary system commands and CGI scripts. Unless the author is aware of the potential problems, it's easy to introduce unintentional side effects. Unfortunately, HTML files containing dangerous SSI directives are seductively easy to write.
Test the application.	Within your application test plan, be sure to include security testing. Create and use a list of valid security risks for testing. The extra time spent catching security holes during testing provides a high return on the resource investment. Security risks should be found during testing, not when the application is implemented and in production.
Limit updates.	Build into the application limitations on the amount of data that can be updated within the appropriate logic for the application. Don't rely on defaults or ignore setting limits. Track how many update attempts are received per session, and don't allow users to add, change, or delete numerous records when it is not appropriate.
Require log-ins.	Require a user log-in and password when it is appropriate.
Authenticate.	Build in user authentication when appropriate.
Be aware of client-side information visibility.	Do not use client-side scripting tools when the information should not be shared. Parameters passed and source code are easily viewed when embedded within HTML.
Validate input.	Validate input from all untrusted data sources. Incorporating well-designed input validation can eliminate the majority of software vulnerabilities. Validate external data sources, including command-line arguments, network interfaces, environmental variables, and user-controlled files.
Keep it simple.	Keep the design as simple and small as possible. Complex designs increase the likelihood that errors will occur during configuration, implementation, and ongoing use. The effort required to code and support an application will increase as the security design becomes more complex.

Table 7.6: Security Coding Techniques (Continued)	
Technique	**Description**
Define security requirements.	Identify and document security requirements early in the development lifecycle. Revisit the security requirements periodically to reflect environment and application changes. The security of a system cannot easily be evaluated if you don't have defined security requirements. Security requirements need to include the established organization requirements, such as those for ISO or Sarbanes-Oxley.
Model threats.	Use threat modeling to anticipate the threats to which the application might be subjected. Threat modeling includes identifying key assets, decomposing the application, identifying and categorizing the threats to each asset or component, rating the threats based on a risk ranking, and then developing threat mitigation strategies that are implemented in designs, code, and test cases.
Default to deny.	Base access decisions on permission rather than exclusion. This means that, by default, access is denied, and the design identifies conditions under which access is permitted.
Design for security policies.	Create a software architecture that fits your security policies. Design your applications to implement and enforce security policies.
Use compiler warnings.	Compile code using the highest warning level available for your compiler, and eliminate warnings by modifying the code. Ignoring warnings is risky.
Adopt a secure coding standard.	Develop and use secure coding standards for the languages and platforms that will be used. Be sure to understand your system architecture's security capabilities and limitations.
Use the principle of least privilege.	Processing should execute with the least level of authority necessary to complete the job. Any additional authority should be held for a minimum time. This approach reduces the opportunities an attacker has to execute arbitrary code and access your system with a higher level of authority.
Use effective quality assurance techniques.	Using well-defined quality assurance techniques can be effective in identifying and eliminating security risks. Quality assurance techniques should include penetration testing, fuzz testing, and source code audits. External testers will bring an independent perspective and should be able to complete quality testing without biases or assumptions.
Sanitize data sent to other systems.	Sanitize data passed to complex subsystems such as command shells, relational databases, and commercial off-the-shelf components. Attackers may be able to invoke unused functionality in these components through the use of SQL, command, or other injection attacks.
Build in layers of defense.	Build your security defense in layers. Don't rely on a single defensive strategy. Make sure to have additional layers to catch any breaches that slip through a layer.

Security Policy

If you are a Webmaster, system administrator, or otherwise involved with the administration of a network, the single most important step you can take to increase your site's security is to create a written security policy. This security policy should clearly define your organization's rules with regard to the following:

- Determine who is allowed to use the system.

- Determine when they are allowed to use it.

- Determine what they are allowed to do. (Different groups may be granted different levels of access.)

- Define procedures for granting access to the system.

- Define procedures for revoking access, for example, when an employee changes position or leaves.

- Define what constitutes acceptable use of the system.

- Determine remote and local log-in methods.

- Define system monitoring procedures.

- Identify protocols for responding to suspected security breaches.

- Identify a course of action for a breach of security.

The policy needs to be clearly defined, communicated, implemented, and followed.

Security is vital to your system. Put together a security plan and incorporate it within your design, development, and testing standards. Revisit the plan periodically to include changes in the application environment and to address new security risks that arise. Evaluate the components of your Web application periodically and test how secure your system is. For more information on Web application security, visit the Web site *http://www.w3.org/Security/Faq/*.

Password Protection

Adding a prompt for a user ID and password is an easy way to allow only intended users access to a system, Web page, or Web application. Of course, users often aren't fond of being prompted for a user ID and password. (How often have you heard, "I've already logged on to the network. Why do I have to log on again?") However, user IDs and passwords are effective in reducing security risks.

Password protection should be thought out carefully. Static content doesn't usually require this kind of security (although it might, in some circumstances). A site that includes dynamic content is more likely to require a user ID and password. Similarly, there are probably pages on your site intended for the general public that can be unprotected, while other pages need password protection because they're intended for only specific users.

The password field type on an HTML form automatically makes the password unreadable by anyone who might be in sight of a user's screen. An example of a password field in use can be found in chapter 9, in the "Forms" section.

Securing Data

Access to data on your system increases the likelihood security measures will need to be implemented. Prompting for a user ID and password is one way to help protect data. If you deal with sensitive data such as bank account numbers, Social Security numbers, or financial information, you need to make sure this information isn't shared with everyone on the Web. Encryption can help secure sensitive data. It transforms and stores plain text data to make it unreadable to anyone except those possessing the encryption key.

Your applications published on the Web should have layers of security to protect from unwanted users accessing data and also from potentially corrupting or damaging data. For example, a malicious user might update your database with erroneous data, deleting data or adding large amounts of data to intentionally fill your server. Read-only access should be the default. Only provide the ability to update database when it is authorized. Data validation and logic to limit the size of transactions should be included in your application design when database update capability is provided. All databases provide some measure of securing data. Be sure security is understood and implemented where needed. Don't leave your data unprotected.

Server Security

When choosing a server, make sure to consider the security protection provided. Servers usually come with a complete range of password protection, authentication, and user-management solutions. Here are some of the capabilities provided through server administration software:

- Password protection
- Authentication
- User management solutions
- Grant or deny any users/groups on a per-resource basis
- Capability to set user start and expiration dates
- User email authority control
- Audit logging
- Web site file protection, including images, databases, HTML, scripts, and programs
- Directory security
- Concurrent user log-in protection
- Limits on user ID and password attempts
- Features to protect against hacking, worms, phishing, spam protection, viruses, Trojan horses, spyware, adware, keystroke logging, DDOS, smurf attack, trinoo, and other security risks
- Active directory authentication
- Built-in firewall capabilities
- Built-in proxy capabilities
- Internal user access scheme
- LDAP authentication
- Other system authentication
- Secure Socket Layer (SSL) hardware
- SSL software

As you can see, server administration software provides a means to protect and provide security for your systems. Be sure to make use of the tools provided to protect your server(s).

Web Hosting

You might decide to forgo hosting your own Web site in favor of subscribing to a Web hosting service. Web-hosting services provide a variety of solutions, from free, small-scale hosting, where files can be uploaded through FTP or a Web interface, to *colocation*, in which a host provides connectivity to the Internet for servers it does not own, but which are located in its data center. Table 7.7 shows some of the wide variety of services provided.

Table 7.7: Types of Web Hosting Services	
Service	**Description**
Free Web site hosting	Hosting is offered for free, with limited features and functionality, usually in return for allowing advertisement on your site.
Shared Web hosting	Hosting is on a server shared with other sites, ranging from a few to many. The servers are configured to share server resources, including RAM and CPU.
Reseller Web hosting	This type of hosting allows clients to become Web hosts. The allotted hard drive space and bandwidth can be used to host third-party Web sites for a profit.
Virtual dedicated server	This hosting allows complete control over the server, similar to renting a server. The least expensive dedicated plans are usually those that are self-managed or unmanaged. In this case, the client has full administrative access to the server and is responsible for security and maintenance.
Managed hosting service	A dedicated server is provided, and you're allowed to manage data via FTP or other remote management tools. However, full control is not allowed because the hosting service guarantees the quality of service provided and assumes responsibility for modifications, configuration, and support.
Colocation Web hosting service	With this service, you own the server, and the hosting company physically houses and supports it. This is the most expensive option provided. Usually, with this service, you would have your own administrator who would visit the hosting center to complete hardware upgrades or changes.
Clustered hosting	Multiple servers are used for hosting the same content, for better resource utilization.
Grid hosting	Grid hosting is relatively new. The service provides a server cluster that acts like a grid and is composed of multiple nodes. The grid configuration makes this option very fault-tolerant and stable.
File hosting system	This service provides server space for files.

Table 7.7: Types of Web Hosting Services (Continued)	
Service	**Description**
Image hosting service	This service provides server space for images.
Video hosting service	This service provides space for video.
Blog hosting service	This service provides space for blogs.
One-click hosting	This service allows Internet users to easily upload one or more files from their hard drives onto one-click host servers free of charge.
Shopping cart service	This service provides a secure and protected shopping-cart capability.

Hosting services are commonly used by larger organizations to outsource network infrastructure. How do you choose a hosting service? The best way is to consider your organization's Web site and Web application needs. There is an endless list of hosting service providers. Information about these organizations and their services is easily obtained on the Web. Do your research, and keep in mind your goals and expectations. Here are some of the considerations that should be used for evaluation and comparison:

- Services provided
- Email services provided
- Scripting software supported
- Operating system support
- Compatibility
- Database support
- Application development options
- Security
- Interface provided
- Host's specialty
- E-commerce
- Length of time in business
- Pricing
- Hosting reliability and uptime
- Service Level Agreements
- Network performance and response time

Summary

Since its inception, the Worldwide Web has changed drastically. Not that long ago, creating business Web applications wasn't a common consideration. Today, it is commonplace. The Web has grown from displaying static content to including sites with dynamic content. There is a shift within organizations to create new applications as Web applications and to move existing applications to the Web. Doing so opens the applications to worldwide access. The browsers, Web servers, Web application servers, and programming technology available will continue to change.

Making the leap to the Web might seem like a daunting task, but like any other change, once accomplished, and used a feeling of comfort will settle in. Fortunately, groups like the Worldwide Web Consortium (W3C) are dedicated to developing standards. These standards have a significant impact on what developers do.

Real Web applications require more than just HTML. While HTML is the foundation upon which everything else is built, once you have mastered HTML, you need to start acquiring the other skills needed to develop Web applications.

This chapter paints the big picture, showing you how HTML fits into that picture. To move forward, you'll need to know more about languages such as PHP, Java, and VB.NET. The following chapters introduce you to some of these languages and show you how they integrate with HTML to develop truly dynamic business Web applications.

As you go through the following chapters, keep the big picture in mind. Remember the many issues raised in this chapter, such as performance, security, database access, and integration with legacy applications. The information we've shared with you here should help shorten your learning curve and save you from some of the pitfalls we've encountered along the way.

CHAPTER 8

Incorporating JavaScript

Previous chapters discussed how to create static documents using HTML. The next step is to incorporate automation to make Web pages dynamic. Many tools can be used to do this. This chapter introduces JavaScript, one of the most popular tools. JavaScript is a fairly simple but very powerful programming language. It is usually used along with other Web development tools to create dynamic Web applications.

In this chapter, you will learn the basics of JavaScript by example, to see how JavaScript is used within Web applications. The examples in this chapter are based on the most current version of JavaScript used in common browsers such as Internet Explorer, Firefox, and Netscape. This chapter assumes a basic understanding of HTML. If necessary, review the earlier chapters on HTML before proceeding.

Introduction to JavaScript

HTML and JavaScript are two different Web tools. HTML is used to create static Web page content, while JavaScript is designed for performing dynamic tasks. Java, Java Server Pages (JSP), and JavaScript are not the same. They are completely different programming languages.

A JavaScript program consists of lines of executable computer code that can be embedded directly into HTML pages. JavaScript is an *interpreted* language, meaning the script will execute without preliminary compilation. JavaScript does not require a purchase or a license, nor does it require a special editor. To code in JavaScript, you can use anything from a simple text editor like Notepad to a Web development tool such as WDSc, Eclipse, or Dreamweaver.

JavaScript is currently the most popular scripting language on the Web. It is the only language supported by all Web browsers that support client-side scripting. (Most browsers do.) Alternatives to JavaScript on the client side include VB Script and Perl. Other alternatives for some programming tasks are server-side languages like PHP, JSP, .NET or Java. Which language you use should be based on when you want the code to be run and what tasks are required. If your application requires the code to be run before the Web page loads, you will want to use a server-side language. If the code needs to run after the page is loaded, JavaScript is a good choice. Because JavaScript code runs on the client rather than on the server, it can respond to user actions quickly, making an application feel more responsive to users. JavaScript is not intended for stored data retrieval or update.

Although JavaScript can be embedded directly into your HTML pages, if the code will be reused on multiple pages, it should be put into a separate file. The file's *.js* extension identifies it as JavaScript. The script file is linked with an HTML page by inserting a **<script>** tag.

For JavaScript to work properly, it must be enabled within the user's browser settings. On newer browsers, JavaScript scripts are run in a restricted "sandbox" environment that isolates them from the rest of the operating system. Scripts are permitted access only to data in the current document or documents from the same site. No access is granted to the local file system, the memory space of other programs running, or the operating system's networking layer. Containment of this kind is designed to prevent malfunctioning or malicious scripts from running in the user's environment.

JavaScript Compared to Other Tools

Since JavaScript is not the only language that can be used to make your Web applications more dynamic, how does it compare to other tools?

JavaScript Versus Server-side Scripting

Compared to using server-side scripting such as CGI to collect and validate data entered on a form, JavaScript is much easier to learn and to code. As you will soon see, JavaScript is not a difficult language to learn and can easily be placed within HTML pages. Use of a CGI script requires placing a hook for the CGI within the HTML, as well as writing the CGI script or program.

JavaScript provides quick response times because its validation takes place on the client side using a dedicated resource, rather than on the server. Using a server-side script, the information must be collected from an entry form sent to the server, processed, and then returned to the browser as an HTML-based Web page. This must happen every time the user makes a change to an entry form. This results in slower response times for users.

JavaScript is compatible with any browser that supports client-side scripting; it is not platform-dependent like some server-side scripting languages. Therefore, JavaScript code can be written once and will work on any system using a browser that supports scripting. On the other hand, server-side scripting can be used to update databases, while JavaScript is not intended for data update.

JavaScript is a lightweight language intended for form processing and some other tasks to make a Web page more dynamic. Server-side scripting provides a gateway to access scripts and programs that may be used for incorporating intricate logic. You will probably find good uses for both JavaScript and server-side scripting languages like CGI and JavaScript within your Web applications.

JavaScript Versus VB Script

Like JavaScript, VB Script allows for embedding commands into an HTML document. VB Script is also an interpreted language that executes on the client side rather than on the server. In fact, JavaScript and VB Script are quite similar in functionality. VB Script, like JavaScript, is often used for collecting data from a form, validating it for completeness and correctness, and sending it off to a server-side application to update a database.

The most significant difference between JavaScript and VB Script is the language syntax. VB Script is a fast and flexible subset of the Microsoft Visual Basic language. JavaScript, on the other hand, is rooted in C, C++, and Java.

While VB Script may be an excellent choice if you are already familiar with Visual Basic, JavaScript is currently more widely used. More developers are familiar with the JavaScript language than with VB Script, and it appears this trend will not change soon. Those supporting the use of VB Script would argue this point, but it is easy to do the research to support this conclusion.

The preference for JavaScript over VB Script probably goes back to the roots of the languages. VB Script is rooted in Microsoft-specific tools and platforms, while JavaScript has roots that are not platform-specific. That's not to say using VB Script isn't a good fit for certain tasks. In fact, you could use both VB Script and JavaScript in the same HTML page, although this is uncommon. Choose the tools you are most comfortable with and that fit within your organization's standards.

JavaScript's Advantages and Disadvantages

Like any other tool, JavaScript has advantages and disadvantages. We will highlight some of each.

Here are some of the advantages of JavaScript:

- Easy to learn

- Interpreted language, resulting in a fast response time

- Uses client-side resources rather than server-side shared resources

- Runs on any browser allowing client-side scripting

- Most popular scripting language; many resources available

- Easily embedded within HTML

- No additional cost to use

- Platform independent

- Can easily be integrated for use with other languages

Here are some of JavaScript's disadvantages:

- Dependent on browser support

- Dependent on user's browser settings to allow scripts to run

- Source code viewable by users

- Does not allow for data update

What Can JavaScript Do?

JavaScript is a lightweight and very useful tool for a Web business application developer. Many developers know JavaScript, and there is a large community of JavaScript developers. You can do many things with JavaScript. Some of the common things JavaScript is used for include the following:

- *React to events*—JavaScript can be used to have your HTML react to events. Clicking the mouse, moving the mouse cursor over a hotspot, loading a page or image, selecting an input box on a form, submitting a form, or entering a keystroke can trigger some JavaScript code to be invoked.

- *Detect browser types*—JavaScript can be used to detect the type of browser being used by the client accessing the Web page. After determining the type of browser, JavaScript can be further used to determine what code should be executed. This enables you to accommodate browser differences, as described in chapter 13.

- *Make dynamic Web pages*—JavaScript can be used to make your Web pages dynamic. JavaScript can enhance static HTML pages through special effects, control of page behavior, animations, and inclusion of dynamic text.

- *Validate data*—JavaScript can be used to validate data. For example, suppose a user is required to fill out an online form. JavaScript checks the format and content of the data on the form before it is submitted. If the input is not valid, it prevents the form from being submitted and tells the user what needs to be corrected. Note that this validation is completed before the data is sent to the server. This eliminates the need for server-side validation processing, provides quick responses for application users, and reduces server-side processing activity.

- *Read and write HTML elements*—Because JavaScript is intended for client-side interaction, it can be used to read and change the content of an HTML element.

- *Display forms and pop-up windows*—JavaScript can be used to display forms and pop-up windows for data entry and validation. For example, it might be used to prompt for a user ID and password, and then display a welcome window after the user enters the correct log-in information.

- *Create cookies*—JavaScript can be used to create cookies, which are used to retrieve and store information on the site visitor's computer.

Syntax

JavaScript was modeled on Java syntax. Java syntax, in turn, was modeled on C and C++ syntax. JavaScript was created to be easier for non-programmers to work with than C, C++, or Java. Programmers who have used C, C++, or Java will find that JavaScript syntax is comfortably familiar.

Case-sensitivity

JavaScript is a case-sensitive language. All keywords are in lowercase. All variables, function names, and other identifiers must be typed with consistent capitalization.

Comments

JavaScript supports both C and C++ comments. Text on one or more lines between the special characters "/*" and "*/" is a comment and is ignored by JavaScript. Also, any text between "//" and the end of the current line is a single-line comment and is ignored by JavaScript.

Figure 8.1 shows examples of JavaScript comments. The first comment is a single-line, C++ style comment that begins with "//". The second comment is a multi-line, C-style comment that begins with "/*" and ends with "*/".

```
// Bill's Barbeque Barn - single line comment

/* Date: June 29, 2007
   Author: Laura A. Ubelhor
   Purpose: Script to prompt forUser id and password
   multiple line comment
*/
```

Figure 8.1: JavaScript comment styles.

Identifiers

Variable, functions, and label names are JavaScript identifiers. Identifiers are made up of any number of letters and digits, along with the underscore character (_) and dollar sign ($). The first character of an identifier must not be a digit. Avoid creating variables that have the same names as global properties and methods. Figure 8.2 provides examples of legal identifiers.

```
x
X
Total_amount
total_amount
TotalAmount
Amount$
amount$
Amount123
amount123
```

Figure 8.2: Examples of legal identifiers.

Keywords

Keywords, listed in Table 8.1, have special meaning to the JavaScript interpreter and cannot be used as identifiers. JavaScript also has some words that are reserved for future extensions of the language. These reserved words, shown in Table 8.2, cannot be used as identifiers.

Table 8.1: JavaScript Keywords					
break	case	catch	continue	default	delete
do	else	false	finally	for	function
if	in	instanceof	new	null	return
switch	this	throw	true	try	typeof
var	void	while	with		

Table 8.2: JavaScript Reserved Words				
abstract	Boolean	byte	Char	class
const	debugger	double	Enum	export
extends	final	float	Goto	implements
import	int	interface	Long	native
package	private	protected	Public	short
static	super	synchronized	Throws	Transient
volatile				

Semicolons

JavaScript statements are terminated by semicolons. When a statement is followed by a new line, the terminating semicolon may be omitted. Note that this places a restriction on where you may legally break lines in your JavaScript programs. A statement may not be spread across two lines when the first line can be a complete, legal statement on its own.

With programming languages like Java and C++, each code statement must end with a semicolon. In JavaScript, on the other hand, the semicolon is generally optional. Still, many programmers use a semicolon as a standard to easily identify the end of a statement.

White Space

JavaScript ignores white space between tokens. White space is empty space with no character representation. White space characters include space characters, tabs, and line-break characters. You may use spaces, tabs, and new lines to format or indent your code to make it more readable. Therefore, all three of the following JavaScript statements will be interpreted the same way:

```
TotalAmount  =  Quantity * Price;
TotalAmount  =  Quantity * Price;
TotalAmount  =  Quantity * Price;
```

Because white space is ignored within JavaScript, you can make the code more readable and understandable.

How to Put JavaScript into an HTML Page

To insert JavaScript into an HTML page, use the **<script>** tag and the **type** attribute, as shown in Figure 8.3.

```
<html>
<body>
<script type="text/javascript">
// JS0804 - JavaScript Within HTML Example
document.write ("Welcome to Bills Barbeque Barn Product Page")
</script>
</body>
</html>
```

Figure 8.3: Inserting JavaScript into an HTML page to display the message "Welcome to Bills Barbeque Barn Product Page" in the browser.

The **<script type="text/javascript">** tag tells where the JavaScript starts. The **</script>** tag tells where the JavaScript ends. The **document.write** command is a JavaScript command used for writing output to a page. Because **document.write** is between the start and end JavaScript tags, the browser recognizes the command as JavaScript and will execute the line of code.

JavaScript Code Placement

Because JavaScript is executed without any preliminary compilation, it will be executed while the page loads in the browser unless it is specially designed to be executed when an event occurs or the script is called. Scripts to be executed when a page loads go in the body section of the HTML. Scripts to be executed when explicitly called or triggered go in the head section of the HTML. Multiple scripts may be placed within the HTML, and scripts can be placed within both the head and body sections.

In the previous example, the JavaScript was in the body, so it executed as the page loaded. Figure 8.4 shows JavaScript in both the body and head sections of an HTML page. When the button in Figure 8.5 is clicked, the script in the head executes, resulting in the message, "Welcome to Bills Barbeque Barn!"

```
<html>
<head>
<script type="text/javascript">
// JS0811 - JavaScript in HTML Head and Body Section Example
function welcome()
{
document.write ("Welcome to Bills Barbeque Barn!")
}
</script>
</head>
<body>
<input type="button" value="View Welcome Message" onClick="welcome
    ()" />
<script type="text/javascript">
document.write ("The Best Barbeque You'll Find Any Where!")
</script>
</body>
</html>
```

Figure 8.4: JavaScript in the head and body of an HTML page.

Figure 8.5: The initial results from Figure 8.4.

Using an External JavaScript

When a script will be used on multiple pages or multiple Web sites, it is practical to store it in an external file. The file is saved with a *.js* extension to indicate a JavaScript file type. To use an external JavaScript file, refer to it in the **src** attribute of the **<script>** tag. Be sure to use meaningful script file names, to make it easy to identify the script files. (The examples provided in this book use names to make it easier for you to cross-reference code files.)

Figure 8.6 calls the script file name *JS0815.js*, in the *js scripts* folder. The file's code is shown in Figure 8.7. It is a good practice to place your script files in a separate folder to make them easier to find.

```
<html>
<body>
<script type="text/javascript" src="js scripts/JS0815.js">
// JS0814 - Using An External File Script Example
</script>
</body>
</html>
```

Figure 8.6: Calling an external JavaScript file from a Web page.

```
// JS0815 - JavaScript in HTML Head and Body Section Example
// Author Laura A. Ubelhor July 29, 2007
document.write ("Welcome to Bills Barbeque Barn Product Page!")
```

Figure 8.7: The JS0815.js file, which will display "Welcome to Bills Barbeque Barn Product Page!" in the browser.

Breaking up a Text String

A long text string in a code line can be broken up by using a backslash. A code line cannot be broken up outside of the text string's quotation marks, however. The backslash does not affect the output; it's just for readability in the code. For example, the output from Figure 8.8 would still display "Welcome To Bills Barbeque Barn!" all on the same browser line, as in the previous examples.

```
document.write("Welcome To Bills \
Barbeque Barn!")
```

Figure 8.8: Breaking up a text string with a backslash.

Variables

Variables are used to store data. Variables are normally declared and initialized with the **var** statement. Although this is optional, it is a recommended practice to make it easier to identify variables quickly.

A variable must begin with a letter or with the underscore character (_). JavaScript is a case-sensitive language, so the variable *employee* is not the same as the variable *EMPLOYEE*.

Variables can contain values of any data type. The value of a variable can change during the script. By referring to the variable by name, the variable can be displayed or changed.

When you declare a variable within a function, it can only be accessed within that function. It no longer exists after you leave the function. This type of variable is called a *local variable*. The same variable names can be used in different functions because they are only recognized within the function they are declared in. Local variables are found within functions and are implemented as properties of the argument object for that function. Objects will be discussed later in this chapter.

If a variable is defined outside of a function, it is a global variable and can be accessed by all of the functions on the page. Global variables in JavaScript are implemented as properties of a global object. Unlike C, C++, and Java, JavaScript does not have blocked-level scope. Variables declared within the curly braces of a compound statement are not restricted to that block and are visible outside of it.

The lifetime of a global variable starts when you open your page and ends when the page is closed. Here are some examples of variables:

```
var employeenumber = 105
employeenumber = 105
var employeelastname = "Forsythe"
employeelastname = "Forsythe"
```

The variable name is on the left side of the equal sign, and the value you want to assign to the variable is on the right. Multiple variables can be defined on the same line by using a comma to separate the variables, like this:

```
Var employeenumber = 10005, employeelastname = "Forsythe"
```

Data Types

Javascript supports several value data types, including Booleans, numbers, and strings, as shown in Table 8.3.

Table 8.3: JavaScript Value Data Types		
Type	Description	Example
String	A series of characters within quotation marks	"Welcome To Bills Product Page"
Number	Any number not within quotation marks	7.13
Boolean	Logical true or false	True
Null	Devoid of any value	True
Object	Properties and methods belonging to the object or array	
Function	Function definition	

Booleans

The Boolean type has two possible values: true or false. The values are represented by the JavaScript keywords **true** and **false**. Boolean values include truth or falsehood, yes or no, on or off, and any other value that can be represented with one bit of information.

Numbers

Numbers in JavaScript are represented in 64-bit floating-point format. JavaScript makes no distinction between integers and floating-point numbers. Numeric literals appear in JavaScript programs using the syntax of a sequence of digits with an optional decimal point and an optional exponent. All of the following are valid numbers in JavaScript:

```
17
29.62
158.2345092
000013
5.02e23
```

Strings

A string is a sequence of letters, digits, and other characters from the 16-bit Unicode character set. String literals appear in JavaScript programs between single or double quotes. Single and double quotes can be nested within each other. Here are some examples of strings:

```
'barbeque'
"9.99"
"Barbeque Barn"
```

Special escape characters can be used within a string to insert quotes, an apostrophe, a carriage return, or other special characters. As shown in Table 8.4, the backslash character begins the special escape sequence, and can be placed anywhere within the string.

Table 8.4: JavaScript String Escape Characters	
Character	Description
\\	Single backslash (\).
\"	Double quote (").
\'	Single quote (').
\b	Backspace.
\f	Form feed.
\n	New line.
\r	Carriage return.
\t	Tab.

Table 8.4: JavaScript String Escape Characters (Continued)	
Character	Description
\ddd	An octal number between 0 and 377 representing the Latin-1 character equivalent. For example, the octal code for the copyright symbol is \251.
\xXX	A hexadecimal number between 00 and FF representing the Latin-1 character equivalent. For example, the hexadecimal code for the copyright symbol is /xA9.
\uXXXX	A hexadecimal number between 00 and FF representing the Unicode character equivalent. For example, the hexadecimal code for the Unicode copyright symbol is \u00A9.

Figure 8.9 is an example of using the single-quote escape character to create the effect of an apostrophe in the message, "Welcome to Bill's Barbeque Barn Product Page!"

```
<html>
<body>
<script type="text/javascript">
// JS0822 - String Escape Characters Example
document.write ("Welcome to Bill\'s Barbeque Barn Product  Page!")
</script>
</body>
</html>
```

Figure 8.9: Using a string escape character to produce a single quote.

String values are *immutable* in JavaScript, which means their value cannot be modified. *Methods* may be used to operate on strings. A method is all about action related to an object like the string object. A method either does something to the object or with the object that affects other parts of a script or document. Methods can copy the value of a string and return the copied value, but cannot modify the value of a string. The string class includes many methods that can be used to manipulate strings.

Operators

Tables 8.5 through 8.8 list the operators supported by JavaScript. Arithmetic operators used within Javascript are very similar to those used within other scripting and programming languages.

Operator	Description	Example	Result
+	Addition	x=5, y=7, x+y	12
-	Subtraction	x=3, y=1, x-y	2
*	Multiplication	x=2, y=4, x*y	8
/	Division	x=4, y=2, x/y	2
%	Modulus (division remainder)	x=5, y=2, x%y	1 (remainder of 5/2)
++	Increment	x=2, x++	3
--	Decrement	x=2, x--	1

Table 8.5: Arithmetic Operators

In addition to arithmetic operators assignment operators are also provided. An assignment operator assigns a value to its left operand based on the value of its right operand. The basic assignment operator is the equal sign, which assigns the value of its right operand to its left operand. That is, $x = y$ assigns the value of y to x. The other assignment operators are usually shorthand for standard operations.

Operator	Description	Example	Result	Is the Same As
=	Assignment	y=2, x=y	x=2	x=y
+=	Increment assignment	x=2, y=3, x+=y–	x=5	x=x+y
-=	Decrement assignment	x=5, y=3, x-=y	x=2	x=x-y
*=	Multiplication assignment	x=5, y=3, x*=y	x=15	x=x*y
/=	Division assignment	x=6, y=2, x/=y	x=3	x=x/y
%=	Modulus assignment	x=6, y=5, x%=y	x=1	x=x%y

Table 8.6: Assignment Operators

Comparison operators are used in logical statements to determine equality or difference between variables or values. The comparison operator is use to get a Boolean value indicating the result of the comparison.

Table 8.7: Comparison Operators			
Operator	Description	Example	Result
==	Is equal to	x=5, y=5, z=7 x==y x==z	 True False
!=	Is not equal to	x=5, y=5, z=7 x!=y x!=z	 False True
>	Is greater than	x=5, y=6, z=3 x>y x>z	 False True
<	Is less than	x=5, y=6, z=3 x<y x<z	 True False
>=	Is greater than or equal to	x=5, y=6, z=3 x>=y x>=z	 False True
<=	Is less than or equal to	x=5, y=6, z=3 x<=y x<=z	 True False

Logical operators are typically used with Boolean values. When logical operators are used with Boolean values, they return a Boolean value. However, the *&&* and *//* operators actually return the value of one of the specified operands. If logical operators *&&* and */ /* are used with non-Boolean values, they may return a non-Boolean value.

Table 8.8: Logical Operators			
Operator	Description	Example	Result
&&	And	x=5 x==5 && x<3 x>3 && x==5	 False True
||	Or	x=5 x>3 || x>6 x==4 || x==3	 True False
!	Not	X=5 !(x==5)	 False
		!(x==4)	True

Operator Precedence

Operator precedence determines the order in which operators are evaluated when combined within a statement. Operators with higher precedence are evaluated first. Associatively, left-to-right or right-to-left determines the order in which operators of the same precedence are processed. Table 8.9 is ordered from highest precedence (1) to lowest precedence (17).

Table 8.9: Operator Precedence				
Precedence	Associativity	Operator	Operator Type	Operation Peformed
1	left to right	[]	MemberExp Expression	Member
1	left to right	.	MemberExp Identifier	Member
1	right to left	New	MemberExp Arguments	New
2	left to right	( )	CallExpression Arguments	Function call
2	left to right	[]	CallExpression Expression	Function call
2	left to right	.	CallExpression Identifier	Function call
3	n/a	++	LeftHand SideExp	Postfix increment
3	n/a	--	LeftHand SideExp	Postfix decrement
4	right to left	!	UnaryExp	Logical not
4	right to left	~	UnaryExp	Bitwise not
4	right to left	+	UnaryExp	Unary plus
4	right to left	-	UnaryExp	Unary minus
4	right to left	Typeof	UnaryExp	Return type of object
4	right to left	Void	UnaryExp	Eval and return undefined
4	right to left	delete	UnaryExp	Call delete method
5	left to right	*	MultExp UnaryExp	Multiplication
5	left to right	/	MultExp UnaryExp	Division
5	left to right	%	MultExp UnaryExp	Remainder
6	left to right	+	AddExp MultExp	Addition
6	left to right	-	AddExp MultExp	Subtraction
7	left to right	<<	ShiftExp AddExp	Bitwise left shift
7	left to right	>>	ShiftExp AddExp	Signed right shift
7	left to right	>>>	ShiftExp AddExp	Unsigned right shift
8	left to right	<	RelExp ShiftExp	Less than
8	left to right	<=	RelExp ShiftExp	Less than or equal to
8	left to right	>	RelExp ShiftExp	Greater than

Precedence	Associativity	Operator	Operator Type	Operation Peformed
colspan header				
8	left to right	>=	RelExp ShiftExp	Greater than or equal to
8	left to right	In	RelExp ShiftExp	Call has property method
8	left to right	instanceof	RelExp ShiftExp	Call has instance method
9	left to right	==	EqualExp RelExp	Is equal to
9	left to right	!=	EqualExp RelExp	Is not equal to
9	left to right	===	EqualExp RelExp	Is strictly equal to
9	left to right	!==	EqualExp RelExp	Is strictly not equal to
10	left to right	&	BitwiseAndExp EqualExp	Bitwise and
11	left to right	^	BitwiseOrExp EqualExp	Bitwise xor
12	left to right	|	BitwiseOrExp EqualExp	Bitwise or
13	left to right	&&	LogicalAndExp BitwiseOrExp	Logical and
14	left to right	||	LogicalOrExp LogicalAndExp	Logical or
15	right to left	?:	LogicalOrExp AssignExp	Conditional expression
16	right to left	=	LeftHandSide-Exp AssignExp	Assignment expression
16	right to left	+=	LeftHandSide-Exp AssignExp	Assignment with addition
16	right to left	-=	LeftHandSide-Exp AssignExp	Assignment with subtraction
16	right to left	*=	LeftHandSide-Exp AssignExp	Assignment with multiplication
16	right to left	/=	LeftHandSide-Exp AssignExp	Assignment with division
16	right to left	%=	LeftHandSide-Exp AssignExp	Assignment with remainder
16	right to left	<<=	LeftHandSide-Exp AssignExp	Assignment with bitwise left shift
16	right to left	>>=	LeftHandSide-Exp AssignExp	Assignment with bitwise right shift
16	right to left	>>>=	LeftHandSide-Exp AssignExp	Assignment with unsigned right shift
16	right to left	&=	LeftHandSide-Exp AssignExp	Assignment with bitwise and

Table 8.9: Operator Precedence (Continued)

Table 8.9: Operator Precedence (Continued)				
Precedence	Associativity	Operator	Operator Type	Operation Peformed
16	right to left	^=	LeftHandSide- Exp AssignExp	Assignment with bitwise or
16	right to left	|=	LeftHandSide- Exp AssignExp	Assignment with logical not
17	left to right	,	Expression AssignExp	Sequential evaluation

Parentheses are used to alter precedence. The expression within parentheses is fully evaluated before the expression's value is used in the statement. An operator with higher precedence is evaluated before one with lower precedence. For example, consider the following:

$$\text{OrderTotal\$} = 9.99 * (2 + 3 + 4 - 1)$$

There are six operators in this expression: =, *, (), +, +, and -. Based on precedence, they are evaluated in this order: (),+, +, -, *, =. Evaluation of the expression in parentheses is from left to right, $2 + 3 + 4 - 1$, resulting in the value 8. Multiplication is next, so 9.99 multiplied by 8, resulting in the value 79.92. The assignment operator is last. The value 79.92 is assigned to OrderTotal$.

The equality operator, ==, can be used to compare two strings to determine if they include exactly the same sequence of characters, as shown in Figure 8.10.

```
var LastName = "UBELHOR"
LastName    == "Ubelhor"  // result is false because UBELHOR is
    not the same as Ubelhor
```

Figure 8.10: JavaScript code using the equality operator.

The inequality operator, !=, can be used to compare strings to determine if they are *not* exactly the same sequence of characters, as shown in Figure 8.11.

```
var LastName = "UBELHOR"
LastName    != "Ubelhor" // result is true because UBELHOR is not
    the same as Ubelhor
```

Figure 8.11: The inequality operator.

The addition operator, +, can be used to concatenate strings and variables, as shown in Figure 8.12.

```
<html>
<body>
<script type="text/javascript">
// JS0827 - Addition Operator Used to Concatenate Data Example
var UserName = "Joe Walsh"
document.write ("Welcome to Bill\'s Barbeque Barn Product Page "
   + UserName)
</script>
</body>
</html>
```

Figure 8.12: This code will display "Welcome to Bill's Barbeque Barn Product Page Joe Walsh" in the browser.

The relational operators (greater than, less than, greater than or equal to, and less than or equal to) can be used to compare strings using alphabetical order, as shown in Figure 8.13.

```
<html>
<body>
<script type="text/javascript">
// JS0829 - Relational Operator Compare Strings Using Alphabetical
   Order Example
var City1 = "Ubly"
var City2 = "Lakeville"
if (City1 > City2)
{
document.write (City1 + " Comes After " + City2 + "Alphabetically")
}
</script>
</body>
</html>
```

Figure 8.13: The relational operators compare strings to produce "Ubly Comes After Lakeville Alphabetically" in the browser.

Statements

JavaScript programs are made up of statements. Most of the statements used with JavaScript have the same syntax as C, C++, and Java statements.

Conditional Statements

Conditional statements perform actions based on whether a condition is true or false. When you want to perform different actions for different decisions, use a conditional statement. Conditional statements are case-sensitive and must be written in lowercase, as shown in Table 8.10.

Table 8.10: Conditional Statements	
Statement	**Description**
if	Code is executed only if a specified condition is true
if else	Code is executed if the condition is true and another group of code if the condition is false
if else if else	One of multiple blocks of code is executed when the condition used in the block of code is true
Switch	One of multiple blocks of code is executed when the condition used in the block of code is true

If Statements

The **if** statement is used when code is to be executed when a single condition is true.

> **if (*condition*)**
> **{**
> ***code to execute if condition is true***
> **}**

The code in Figure 8.14 displays a welcome message and prompts the site user for a password. If the password entered is "BBQEmployee," the condition is true and an additional welcome greeting is displayed, as shown in Figure 8.15.

```
<html>
<body>
<script type language="javascript">
// JS0832 - If Statement Example
document.write("Welcome to Bills Barbeque Barn Employee Page" +
    ".<BR>");
var passWord=prompt("Please Enter your Pass Word:","")
if (passWord =="BBQEmployee")
{
```

Figure 8.14: An example of the if statement (part 1 of 2).

```
document.write("Welcome to the Employee Work Schedule Page" +
    ".<BR>");
}
</script>
</body>
</html>
```

Figure 8.14: An example of the if statement (part 2 of 2).

Password entered "BBQEmployee"

Welcome to Bills Barbeque Barn Employee Page.
Welcome to the Employee Work Schedule Page.

*Figure 8.15: The results when the **if** statement in Figure 8.14 is true.*

The **if else** statement is used when code is to be executed when a single condition is false.

```
if (condition)
{
code to execute if condition is true
}
else
{
code to execute if condition is false
}
```

Figure 8.16 is very similar to Figure 8.14, but we have added additional code to include an **else** statement. With this change, if any value other than a valid user password is entered, a message will be displayed informing the site user the password is invalid, as shown in Figure 8.17.

```
<html>
<body>
<script type language="javascript">
// JS0835 - If Else Statement Example
document.write("Welcome to Bills Barbeque Barn Employee Page" +
    ".<BR>");
var passWord=prompt("Please Enter your Pass Word:","")
if (passWord=="BBQEmployee")
{
document.write("Welcome to the Employee Work Schedule Page" +
    ".<BR>");
```

*Figure 8.16: An example of the **if else** statement (part 1 of 2).*

```
}
else
{
document.write("The Password Entered is Invalid");
}
</script>
</body>
</html>
```

*Figure 8.16: An example of the **if else** statement (part 2 of 2).*

Password entered is not = "BBQEmployee"

Welcome to Bills Barbeque Barn Employee Page.
The Password Entered is Invalid

---

*Figure 8.17: The results when the **if** statement in Figure 8.16 is false.*

The **if else if else** statement is used when multiple conditions are tested and, when true, control execution of a block of code. The final **else** is used to execute code when all conditions are false.

```
if (condition1)
{
code to execute if condition is true
}
else if (condition2)
{
Code to execute if condition2 is true
}
else
{
Code to execute if condition1 and 2 are false
}
```

The code in Figure 8.18 is very similar to Figure 8.16. However, another **if else** has been added.

```
<html>
<body>
<script type language="javascript">
// JS0838 - If Else If Else Statement Example
document.write("Welcome to Bills Barbeque Barn Employee Page" +
    ".<BR>");
```

*Figure 8.18: An example of the **if else if else** statement (part 1 of 2).*

```
var passWord=prompt("Please Enter your Pass Word:","")
if (passWord=="BBQEmployee")
{
document.write("Welcome to the Employee Work Schedule Page" +
   ".<BR>");
}
else if (passWord=="BBQManager")
{
document.write("Welcome to the Managers Work Schedule Page" +
   ".<BR>");
}
else
{
document.write("The Password Entered is Invalid");
}
</script>
</body>
</html>
```

*Figure 8.18: An example of the **if else if else** statement (part 2 of 2).*

In this example, illustrated in Figure 8.19, if the user enters "BBQEmployee" as the password, the message "Welcome to the Employee Schedule Page" will be displayed. If the user enters "BBQManager," the message "Welcome to the Managers Work Schedule Page" will be displayed. If any other password is entered, a message stating the password is invalid will be displayed. Also notice the use of the break tag, **
**, ensuring that the next text displayed will be on a new line.

Password entered = "BBQManager"

Welcome to Bills Barbeque Barn Employee Page.
Welcome to the Managers Work Schedule Page.

Password entered = "BBQEmployee"

Welcome to Bills Barbeque Barn Employee Page.
Welcome to the Employee Work Schedule Page.

Password entered anything other than "BBQEmployee" or "BBQManager"

Welcome to Bills Barbeque Barn Employee Page.
The Password Entered is Invalid

Figure 8.19: The results from the code in Figure 8.17.

The Switch Statement

The **switch** statement is used to execute one of multiple blocks of code.

```
switch(expression)
{
case 1:
   execute code block 1
   break
case 2:
   execute code block 2
 default:
   execute code block when case 1 and case 2 are false
}
```

The case and **default** keywords are often used with the **switch** statement. These keywords are not JavaScript statements. Instead, they are labels. The **break** keyword may be used to end execution of the statement when a condition is true.

The code in Figure 8.20 uses **switch** to evaluate the password entered by a user. The value of the password is compared with the values for each case. If "BBQEmployee" is entered, there is a case match, and the alert "Welcome Employee!" is displayed. If "BBQManager" is entered as the password, there is a case match, and the alert "Welcome Manager!" is displayed. If a case match is made, **break** terminates the execution of the remaining code within the statement. If a case match is not made, the default statement executes the alert "Password Is Invalid," as shown in Figure 8.21.

```
html>
<body>
<script type language="javascript">
// JS0841 Switch Statement Example
document.write("Welcome to Bills Barbeque Barn Employee Page" +
   ".<BR>");
var passWord=prompt("Please Enter your Pass Word:","");
switch (passWord){
case "BBQEmployee":
alert("Welcome Employee!")
break;
case "BBQManager":
alert("Welcome Manager")
break;
default :
alert("Password Is Invalid");
}
</script>
</body>
</html>
```

Figure 8.20: An example of the **switch** *statement.*

Figure 8.21: The result when an invalid password is entered.

Expression Statements

Every expression used with JavaScript can stand alone as a JavaScript statement. Value assignments, math expressions, and method calls are all examples of JavaScript statements. Here are some examples of JavaScript expressions:

```
x++;
y--;
OrderTotal$ = LineTotal1$ + LineTotal2$ + LineTotal3$ +Tax$
Greeting = "Welcome to Bills Barbeque Barn";
```

Compound Statements

When a sequence of JavaScript statements is enclosed within curly braces, { }, it counts as a single compound statement. Multiple statements enclosed with curly braces are considered compound statements. For example, the body of a **while** loop consists of a single statement. If you want the loop to execute more than one statement, a compound statement is needed. Compound statements are commonly used with **if**, **if else**, **if else if else**, **for**, and **switch** statements. Figure 8.22 is an example of a compound statement.

```
If (x == 1)
{
      If (y == 2)
         a = 5;
}
else
         a = 4;
```

Figure 8.22: A compound statement.

The Empty Statement

The empty statement is simply a semicolon by itself. Although it does nothing, it might be used for coding empty loop bodies. Empty statements should be used cautiously, however. Some editors identify the empty statement with a warning.

Labeled statements

A labeled statement provides an identifier that can be used with the **break** or the **continue** statement. In a labeled statement, **break** or **continue** must be followed with a label. Any type of statements can be used with a labeled statement. The labeled statement will be in the format *label: statement*.

The example in Figure 8.23 uses two labels, *labelxy* and *labely*. The script prompts for the value of x to be entered, asking for a number between zero and 10. It then prompts for the value of y to be entered, again between zero and 10. When the value of x is 10, the code found within *labely* will be executed. If the value of y is five, the code execution will break out of the code within *labely* and continue at the statement following the *labely* loop. The code to write a line will only be executed in this example when x = 10. Figure 8.24 shows the output for various inputs.

```
<html>
<body>
<script type="text/javascript">
// JS0845 Labeled Statement Example
var x=prompt("Enter a number value between 0 and 10 for x:","")
var y=prompt("Enter a number value between 0 and 10 for y:","")
labelxy :
        if (10==x) {
                document.write("You've entered " + x + ".<BR>");
                labely :
                        if (5==y) {
                        document.write("You've entered " + y +
                            ".<BR>");
                        break labely;
                                document.write("The  sum  is  " +
                                    (x+y) + ".<BR>");
                                }
                        document.write(x + "-" + y + "=" + (x-y) +
                            ".<BR>");
                }
</script>
</body>
</html>
```

Figure 8.23: An example of labeled statements.

You've entered 10.
10-4=6.

You've entered 10.
You've entered 5.

10-5=5.

Figure 8.24: The results when x=10 and y=4, and then when x = 10 and y = 5.

The Break Statement

The **break** statement can be used in a **while**, **for**, or labeled statement. In a **while** or **for** loop, **break** will terminate the current loop and transfer control to the statement following the terminated loop. In a labeled statement, **break** will be followed by a label that identifies the statement and will transfer control to the statement following the terminated statement. Figure 8.25 is an example of **break** used in a labeled statement. The **break** and **continue** statements will only be used within a JavaScript loop.

```
<html>
<body>
<script type="text/javascript">
// JS0848 Break Statement Example
var x=0
for (x=0;x<=20;x++)
{
if (x==5){break}
document.write("Number " + x)
document.write("<br />")
}
</script>
</body>
</html>
```

*Figure 8.25: An example of the **break** statement.*

In the example in Figure 8.25, **break** will execute when x is equal to five. When **break** is encountered, control will be transferred and the loop will end. The result of the loop is shown in Figure 8.26.

```
Number 0
Number 1
Number 2
Number 3
Number 4
```

Figure 8.26: The results from the code in Figure 8.25.

The Continue Statement

The **continue** statement can be used with a **while**, **for**, or labeled statement. It will break a current loop and continue with the next statement outside of the current loop. In a **while** or **for** loop, **continue** will terminate execution of the current loop with the next iteration of the loop. Unlike the **break** statement, **continue** does not terminate execution of the loop. In a **while** loop, execution will return to the increment expression. In a labeled statement, **continue** is followed by a label that identifies the labeled statement. The **continue** statement will terminate execution of the labeled statement and continue execution of the code within the labeled statement.

In the example in Figure 8.27, a prompt to enter the value of y is displayed. When the value of y is equal to three, the statements within the loop will be executed and execution will be returned to the next iteration of the *labely* loop. The results for y=3 and y=2 are shown in Figure 8.28.

```html
<html>
<body>
<script type="text/javascript">
// JS0850 Continue Labeled Statement Example
var y=prompt("Enter a number value between 0 and 5 for y:","")
labely :
        while (y < 5) {
                y++
          document.write("labely Loop y value is " + y +
             ".<BR>");
                  if (3==y) {
                          document.write("y is equal to 3!"
                          + ".<BR>");
                          continue labely;
                          }
              }
</script>
</body>
</html>
```

*Figure 8.27: An example of **continue** with a labeled statement.*

labely Loop y value is 4.
labely Loop y value is 5.

labely Loop y value is 3.
y is equal to 3!.
labely Loop y value is 4.
labely Loop y value is 5.

Figure 8.28: The results from Figure 8.27 when the value 3 is entered for y, and then when 2 is entered for y.

In Figure 8.29, the code will be executed until x = 6. When x = 5, the **continue** statement will direct execution to continue at the beginning of the loop, bypassing statements following **continue**. The results are shown in Figure 8.30.

```
<html>
<body>
<script type="text/javascript">
// JS0853 Continue Statement Example
var x=0
for (x=0;x<=6;x++)
{
if (x==5){continue}
document.write("Number " + x)
document.write("<br />")
}
</script>
</body>
</html>
```

*Figure 8.29: A **continue** statement in a loop.*

Number 0
Number 1
Number 2
Number 3
Number 4

Number 6

Figure 8.30: The results of Figure 8.29.

Loops

JavaScript has two kinds of loops: **for** and **while**.

While Loops

The **while** loop is used to repeat a block of code while a condition is true.

```
while(condition)
{
statement1;
statement2;
}
```

The **while** loop in Figure 8.31 defines a loop that will execute multiple statements under the condition that variable x is less than five, resulting in the output in Figure 8.32. The statement $x=x+1$ increments the value of x by one each time the loop is executed.

```
<html>
<body>
<script type="text/javascript">
// FS0857 While Loop Example
var x=0
while (x<5)
{
document.write("BBQ Line " + x)
document.write("<br />")
x=x+1
}
</script>
</body>
</html>
```

Figure 8.31: An example of a ***while*** *loop.*

```
BBQ Line 0
BBQ Line 1
BBQ Line 2
BBQ Line 3
BBQ Line 4
```

Figure 8.32: The results of executing the loop.

The **do while** loop is a variation of the **while** loop in which the loop will always execute a block of code once, and then it will repeat the loop as long as the condition is true. The loop will always execute once because the loop statements are executed before the condition is tested.

```
do
{
statement1;
statement2;
}
while (var<=endvalue)
```

Remember that the curly braces are used to execute multiple statements. They are not required if a single statement will be executed.

The **do while** loop in Figure 8.33 will execute at least once and will continue to execute while x is less than zero. The variable x is incremented by one each time the loop is executed. The result will be the single line "BBQ Line 0" because as soon as the condition is tested, it is found to be false.

```
<html>
<body>
<script type="text/javascript">
// JS0860 Do While Loop Example
var x=0
do
{
document.write("BBQ Line " + x)
document.write("<br />")
x=x+1
}
while (x<0)
</script>
</body>
</html>
```

*Figure 8.33: An example of a **do while** loop.*

For Loops

The **for** loop repeats the specified condition until the condition is false. A **for** loop usually begins with an expression to initialize counters. Next, the condition of the expression is evaluated. If the condition is false, the loop terminates. If the condition is true, the loop statements execute. Multiple statements can be included using curly brackets and semicolons.

After statement execution, there is usually an expression to increment the counters, and control returns to the condition of the expression.

```
var = value
for condition; increment expression
{
statement1;
statement2;
}
```

The example in Figure 8.34 begins with variable x being initialized to zero. The loop will continue to run as long as x is less than or equal to four, producing the results in Figure 8.35.

```
<html>
<body>
<script type="text/javascript">
// JS0863 For Loop Example
var x=0
for (x=0;x<=4;x++)
{
document.write("BBQ Line " + x)
document.write("<br />")
}
</script>
</body>
</html>
```

*Figure 8.34: An example of a **for** loop.*

```
BBQ Line 0
BBQ Line 1
BBQ Line 2
BBQ Line 3
BBQ Line 4
```

Figure 8.35: The results of executing the loop in Figure 8.34.

The **for in** loop is a variation of the **for** loop. It is used to loop through elements of an array. The loop is executed once for each array.

```
for (variable in object)
{
statement1;
statement2;
}
```

The example in Figure 8.36 executes the **document.write** and **
** for each element within the array, resulting in Figure 8.37.

```
<html>
<body>
<script type="text/javascript">
// JS0866 For In Loop Example
var x
var BBQSauce = new Array()
BBQSauce[0] = "Traditional."
BBQSauce[1] = "Sweet and Mild."
BBQSauce[2] = "Honey Mustard."
BBQSauce[3] = "Tangy Twist."
BBQSauce[4] = "Hot and Spicy."
BBQSauce[5] = "Flaming Hot"
for (x in BBQSauce)
{
document.write(BBQSauce[x] + "<br />")
}
</script>
</body>
</html>
```

*Figure 8.36: An example of a **for in** loop.*

```
Traditional.
Sweet and Mild.
Honey Mustard.
Tangy Twist.
Hot and Spicy.
Flaming Hot.
```

Figure 8.37 The results of the loop in Figure 8.36.

Functions

A JavaScript function is used to group and isolate code that will be executed by an event occurrence or by a call to the function, not simply executed when the page loads. A function can be called from anywhere within the page. If the function is saved in an external .js file, it can also be used from other pages.

Functions can be defined in the **<head>** or **<body>** section of an HTML document. If you would like a function to be loaded before being called, place it in the **<head>** section.

Defined Functions

Back in Figure 8.4, the JavaScript in the **<head>** section of the HTML document is actually an example of a defined function. The new function is named "welcome." Because it is placed in the **<head>** section, it will be loaded prior to being initiated when the button "View Welcome Message" is clicked.

```
function functionname(var1, var2,...varx)
{
statement1;
statement2;
}
```

Parentheses are required within a defined function, even when variables are not used, so you can have a function like *functionname()*. The curly brackets define the start and the end of the function.

The JavaScript example in Figure 8.4 is triggered by the event **onClick**. A function may also be called, as in Figure 8.38. In this example, a new function named **bbqSauces** is defined. The function is called, passing the **sauces** array values as parameters. When the function is executed, the list of sauces is displayed, as shown in Figure 8.39.

```
<html>
<head>
<script language="javascript">
// JS0869 Called Function Example
function bbqSauces(bbqSauce)
{
document.write("<UL>\n")
for (i = 0;i < bbqSauce.length;i++)
{
document.write("<LI>" + bbqSauce[i] + "\n")
}
document.write("</UL>\n")
}
</script>
</head>
<body>
<script language="javascript">
sauces = new
Array("Traditional","Zesty","Spicy","Sweet","Honey","Hot",
    "Flaming")
bbqSauces(sauces)
</script>
</body>
</html>
```

Figure 8.38: An example of a called function.

- Traditional

- Zesty

- Spicy

- Sweet

- Honey

- Hot

- Flaming

Figure 8.39: The results from the called function in Figure 8.38.

Predefined Functions

JavaScript has a number of predefined functions available for use, listed in Table 8.11. The list provided here is not all-inclusive, but it gives you an idea of what predefined functions are available.

Table 8.11: JavaScript Predefined Functions		
Function	**Description**	**Use**
eval(*expr*)	This function evaluates a string of JavaScript code without reference to a particular object.	*Expr* is a string to be evaluated. If the string represents an expression, **eval** evaluates the expression. If the argument represents one or more JavaScript statements, **eval** performs the statements. Do not call this function to evaluate an arithmetic expression; JavaScript evaluates arithmetic expressions automatically.
isFinite(*number*)	This function evaluates an argument to determine whether it is a finite number.	*Number* is the number to evaluate. If the argument is not a number, or is positive or negative infinity, this method returns false. Otherwise, it returns true. For example, the following code checks client input to determine whether it is a finite number: **if(isFinite(ClientInput) == true)** **{** **/* take specific steps */** **}**
isNaN(*testValue*)	This function evaluates an argument to determine if it is not a number (NaN).	*TestValue* is the value you want to evaluate.

Function	Description	Use
| | | The **parseFloat** and **parseInt** functions return "NaN" when they evaluate a value that is not a number. The **isNaN** function returns true if passed "NaN," and false otherwise. The following code evaluates the floatValue variable to determine if it is a number, and then calls a procedure accordingly:<br><br>```
floatValue=parseFloat(toFloat)
if (isNaN(floatValue)) {
   notFloat()
} else {
   isFloat()
}
``` |
parseInt(*str* [, *radix*])	These functions return a numeric value when given a string as an argument.	The **parseInt** function parses its first argument, the string *str*, and attempts to return an integer of the specified radix (base), indicated by the second, optional argument, radix. For example, a radix of 10 means to convert to a decimal number, eight means octal, 16 hexadecimal, and so on. For radixes above 10, the letters of the alphabet indicate numerals. For example, for hexadecimal numbers (base 16), A through F are used. If **parseInt** encounters a character that is not a numeral in the specified radix, it ignores it and all succeeding characters and returns the integer value parsed up to that point. If the first character cannot be converted to a number in the specified radix, it returns "NaN." The **parseInt** function truncates the string to integer values.
parseFloat(*str*)		The **parseFloat** function parses its argument, the string *str*, and attempts to return a floating-point number. If it encounters a character other than a sign (+ or -), a numeral (0-9), a decimal point, or an exponent, it returns the value up to that point and ignores that character and all succeeding characters. If the first character cannot be converted to a number, it returns "NaN" (not a number).
Number(*objRef*)	This function converts an object to a number.	*ObjRef* is an object reference.
| String(*objRef*) | This function converts an object to a string. | *ObjRef* is an object reference. The following example converts the Date object to a readable string:<br><br>```
D = new Date (430054663215)
// The following returns
// "Thu Aug 18 04:37:43 GMT-0700 (Pacific
Daylight Time) 1983"
x = String(D)
``` |

Table 8.11: JavaScript Predefined Functions (Continued)

Table 8.11: JavaScript Predefined Functions (Continued)		
Function	Description	Use
escape(*string*)	This function returns the hexadecimal encoding of an argument in the ISO Latin character set.	These functions are used primarily with server-side JavaScript to encode and decode name/value pairs in URLs. The **escape** and **unescape** functions do not work properly for non-ASCII characters and have been deprecated.
unescape(*string*)	This function returns the ASCII string for the specified hexadecimal encoding value.	

In addition to the predefined functions in Table 8.11, there are also special message functions, including **alert**, **confirm**, and **prompt**. These functions provide a means of displaying user messages, alerts, and confirmation prompts in dialog boxes. How often have you needed this functionality within an application? With JavaScript's predefined functions, it takes very little code. There are endless possibilities for using the message functions in your applications.

alert(*message*)

The alert dialog box function displays an alert box with a message defined by the string message. For example, the function in Figure 8.40 displays the dialog box in Figure 8.41.

```
<html>
<body>
<script language="javascript">
// JS0871 Alert Example
var Error1="Yes"
if (Error1="Yes") {
alert("An error Occurred!  Press OK to Continue.")
}
</script>
</body>
</html>
```

*Figure 8.40: An example of the **alert** function.*

Figure 8.41: The dialog box displayed from the code in
Figure 8.40.

confirm(*message*)

The **confirm** function displays a message and two buttons, *OK* and *Cancel*.
If the user clicks the OK button, a value of true is returned. If the user
clicks Cancel, a value of false is returned. Figure 8.42 uses **confirm** to
create the dialog box in Figure 8.43. If the user clicks OK, the message
"OK Pressed Continuing!" is displayed. If the user clicks Cancel, the
message "Operation Cancelled!" is displayed.

```
<html>
<body>
<script language="javascript">
// JS0873 Confirm Example
if (confirm("Press OK to Continue, or Press Cancel to Cancel
  the Operation"))
{
  document.write("OK Pressed Continuing!")
}
else
{
  document.write("Operation Cancelled!")
}
</script>
</body>
<html>
```

Figure 8.42 An example of the **confirm** function.

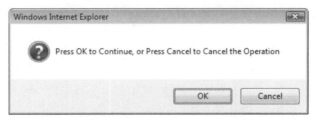

Figure 8.43: The dialog box displayed from the code in Figure 8.42.

prompt(*message*)

The **prompt** function displays a dialog box with a message that prompts the user to enter text in a field and click OK or Cancel. If the user clicks Cancel, a null value is returned. If the user clicks OK, the string value entered in the field is returned. The **prompt** function in Figure 8.44 creates the dialog box in Figure 8.45. It was also used in the examples earlier in this chapter in which the user was prompted for a password.

```
<html>
<html>
<body>
<script language="javascript">
// JS0876 Prompt Message Example
document.write("Welcome to Bills Barbeque Barn Employee Page" +
  ".<BR>");
var productSelection=prompt("Please Enter Your Product Selection","")
if (productSelection != null)
{
document.write("You have Selected " + productSelection);
}
</script>
</body>
</html>
```

*Figure 8.44: An example of the **prompt** function.*

Explorer User Prompt	
Script Prompt:	OK
Please Enter Your Product Selection	Cancel

Figure 8.45: The dialog box displayed from the code in Figure 8.44.

Figure 8.46 shows the message that is displayed if the user enters "Hot and Spicy BBQ Sauce" in the dialog box.

Welcome to Bills Barbeque Barn Employee Page.
You have Selected Hot and Spicy BBQ Sauce

Figure 8.46: The results from the prompt dialog box in Figure 8.45.

The Return Statement

The **return** statement is used with a function to return a value from that function. Use a meaningful name with **return** so you can easily identify what the value is for. For example, the code in Figure 8.47 defines the function **calculatePrice**. When passed the quantity and unit price, the function calculates the extended price and returns the value **extendedCost**. Given the quantity and unit price in the sample HTML, the message "Extended Cost = 39.75" will be displayed when the function executes.

```
<html>
<head>
<script language="javascript">
// JSP0879 Function With Return Statement Example
function calculatePrice(quantity,unitPrice)
{
extendedCost=quantity*unitPrice
return extendedCost
}
</script>
</head>
<body>
<script language="javascript">
quantity = 5;
unitPrice = 7.95;
extendedCost = calculatePrice(quantity, unitPrice);
document.write("Extended Cost = " + extendedCost);
</script>
</body>
</html>
```

*Figure 8.47: An example of a **return** statement.*

Catching Errors

When a browser encounters an error at a site, it will usually display an alert box stating the error and asking if the user wishes to debug. To prevent errors from being handled this way, you can use special JavaScript statements to trap and react to them. Errors can be handled using **try catch**

throw statements or the **onerror** event. The **onerror** event is described later in this chapter. **Try catch throw** is covered in this section.

> **try** {
> *execute this block*
> } **catch** (*error*) {
> *execute this block if there is an error*
> }

The **try** and **catch** statements can be used without **throw** to test a block of code for errors. **Try** is used to identify errors and **catch** contains code to be executed if an error occurs. The **throw** statement allows the creation of an exception. In combination, these statements can be used for data validation or capturing errors and controlling the response when errors occur.

Figure 8.48 is an example of using **try** and **catch** without **throw**. It has an intentional bug in the code ("document.writ"), so that clicking the Display Error Message button results in the dialog box in Figure 8.49. If you correct the error in the code from *document.writ* to *document.write*, the corrected page will display "Welcome to Bills Barbeque Barn!"

```html
<html>
<head>
<script type="text/javascript">
// JS0882 Try Catch Example

var messageText=""
function message()
{
try
  {
  document.writ ("Welcome To Bills Barbeque Barn!")
  }
catch(error)
  {
  messageText="An error was encountered on this page.\n\n"
  messageText+="Description: " + error.description + "\n\n"
  messageText+="Click OK to continue.\n\n"
  alert(messageText)
  }
}
</script>
</head>
<body>
<inputtype="button"value="DisplayErrorMessage"onclick="message()"
  />
</body>
</html>
```

*Figure 8.48: An example of **try catch**.*

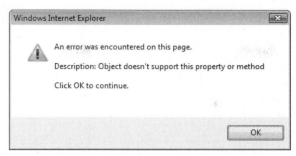

Figure 8.49: The dialog box displayed when an error occurs in the JavaScript code.

The **try catch throw** statements can be used with **if else** statements to provide multiple criteria checks for errors. This enables you to display different messages when different error conditions are true. The code in Figure 8.50 prompts the user to enter an item number, using the dialog box in Figure 8.51. The item number is then evaluated. If it is greater than 10 or less than one, the **throw** statement is used to send the error to the **catch** statement, which displays the appropriate message.

```
<html>
<body>
<script type="text/javascript">
// JS0885  Try Catch Throw Example
var item=prompt("Enter a item number between 1 and 10:","");
document.write("You entered item number " + item + ".<br>");
try
{
if(item>10)
throw "Error1"
else if(item<1)
throw "Error2"
}
catch(er)
{
if(er=="Error1")
alert("The item number entered is greater than 10.")
if(er == "Error2")
alert("The item number entered is less than 1.")
}
</script>
</body>
</html>
```

*Figure 8.50: An example of **try catch throw**.*

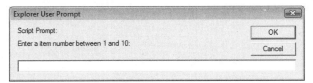

Figure 8.51: The dialog box created from the code in
Figure 8.50.

Suppose the user enters a zero. The error will be handled as shown in Figure
8.52. In this example, when the user enters a number less than one, a message
will be displayed stating the item number entered is less than one. If, on the
other hand, the user enters 11, the error message in Figure 8.53 is displayed.

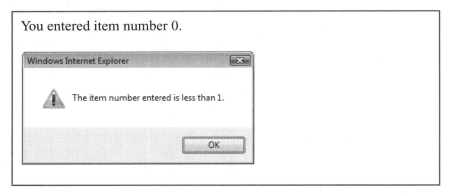

Figure 8.52: An error message for item numbers less than one.

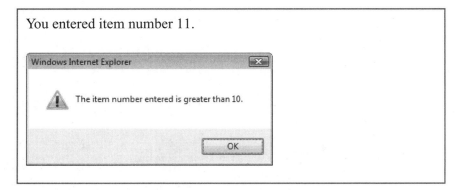

Figure 8.53: An error message for item numbers greater than 10.

The **try catch throw** statements have very practical uses in business
applications, to display more meaningful messages when errors are
encountered.

Objects

JavaScript, like Java and C++, is an *object-oriented programming* (*OOP*) language. An OOP language allows you to define your own objects and also create variable types. (Object and variable-type creation is an advanced feature not to be covered in this chapter.) Objects are a special kind of data. An object has *properties* and *methods*. Properties are the values associated with the object. Methods are the actions that can be performed on the object. This chapter shows you how some of the built-in objects provided in JavaScript can be used.

In JavaScript, everything you interact with is an object of some kind; from the strings, numbers, and arrays used in the script, to the functions that are executed. This is more than just a vague notion of objectness. In JavaScript, everything is an object. The JavaScript Object class is automatically inherited by every other object. This means that the methods and properties of the Object class are supported and implemented by all objects within JavaScript.

The first object to consider is the string object, which is used to manipulate a stored piece of text. It has two properties:

- The **length** property returns the number of characters in a string.

- The **prototype** property allow you to add properties and methods to an object.

In Figure 8.54, for example, the **length** property of the string object is used to determine the number of characters in the variable **welcomeGreeting**. The contents of the variable is "Welcome To Bills Barbeque Barn!", so the message "31" will be displayed when the code runs.

```
<html>
<body>
<script type="text/javascript">
// JS0890 Length Properties String Object Example
var welcomeGreeting="Welcome To Bills Barbeque Barn!";
document.write(welcomeGreeting.length)
</script>
</body>
<html>
```

*Figure 8.54: An example of the **length** property.*

The predefined string objects listed in Table 8.12 extend the JavaScript language extensively. The format is the same for all predefined objects, so once you've understood the examples in the following pages, it will be easy for you to use any of the objects from the predefined list.

Table 8.12: Predefined Methods of String Objects	
Method	**Description**
anchor()	Creates an HTML anchor
big()	Displays a string in a big font
blink()	Displays a blinking string
bold()	Displays a bold string
charAt()	Returns a character at a specified position
charCodeAt()	Returns the Unicode value of a character at a specified position
concat()	Joins multiple strings together
fixed()	Displays a string as "teletype" text
fontcolor()	Displays a string in a designated font color
fontsize()	Displays a string in a designated font size
fromCharCode()	Translates a Unicode value into a string
indexOf()	Returns the position of the first occurrence of a designated string value in a string
italics()	Displays a string in italics
lastIndexOf()	Returns the position of the last occurrence of a designated string value, searching from left to right from the designated position
link()	Displays a string as a hyperlink
match()	Searches for a designated value in a string
replace()	Replaces some characters with other characters in a string
search()	Searches a string for a specified value
slice()	Extracts part of a string and returns the extracted value in another string
small()	Displays a string in a small font
split()	Splits a string into an array of strings
strike()	Displays a string with a "strikethrough" effect
sub()	Displays a string as a subscript
substr()	Extracts a specified number of characters in a string from a start index
substring()	Extracts the characters in a string between a start and end position
sup()	Displays a string in superscript
toLowerCase()	Displays a string in all lowercase
toUpperCase()	Displays a string in all uppercase

The format of the statement is ***stringObject.property*()** or ***stringObject.method*()**. The *stringObject* part of this reference can be any expression that evaluates to a string, including string literals, variables containing strings, or other object properties. The parentheses are used for any parameters. Parameters can include characters within quotes or one or more integers separated by commas, depending on what is appropriate. If no parameter is passed, the character being converted by default is the first character of the string.

Figure 8.55 is an example of the **toUpperCase** method, which requires no parameters. This example will convert the string "welcome to bills barbeque barn!" to "WELCOME TO BILLS BARBEQUE BARN!"

```
<html>
<body>
<script type="text/javascript">
var WelcomeMessage ="welcome to bills barbeque barn!"
// JS0892  To Upper Case Example
document.write(WelcomeMessage.toUpperCase())</script>
</body>
</html>
```

Figure 8.55: An example of the ***toUpperCase*** method of the string object.

Figure 8.56 is another example of a string method. In this case, the **concat** method does require a parameter in parentheses to concatenate with the rest of the string. The result will display "Laura Ubelhor."

```
<html>
<body>
<script type="text/javascript">
// JS0894 concat Method Example
var fullName="Laura ".concat("Ubelhor");
document.write(fullName);
</script>
</body>
</html>
```

Figure 8.56: An example of the ***concat*** method.

Date Objects

A browser that supports scripts contains a date object that is always present and ready to be used. Date object methods, listed in Table 8.13, can be used to retrieve or set date and time values.

Table 8.13: Date Object Methods		
Method	**Value Range**	**Description**
Date()		Today's date and time
getTime()	0-.....	Milliseconds since 1/1/70 00:00:00 GMT
getYear()	70-...	Specified year minus 1900; four-digit year for 2000+
getMonth()	0 – 11	Month within the year (January = 0)
getFullYear()		Four-digit year
getDate()	1 – 31	Date within the month
getDay()	0 – 6	Day of the week (Sunday = 0)
getHours()	0 – 23	Hour of the day, in 24-hour time
getMinutes()	0 – 59	Minute of the specified hour
getSeconds	0 – 59	Second within the specified minute
setTime()	0-.....	Milliseconds since 1/1/70 00:00:00 GMT
setYear()	70-...	Set specified year minus 1900; four-digit year for 2000+
setFullYear)		Set four-digit year; optionally, can set month and day
setMonth()	0 – 11	Set month within the year (January = 0)
setDate()	1 – 31	Set date within the month
setDay()	0 – 6	Set day of the week (Sunday = 0)
setHours()	0 – 23	Set hour of the day, in 24-hour time
setMinutes()	0 – 59	Set minute of the specified hour
setSeconds	0 – 59	Set second within the specified minute

A date object always returns the current date unless parameters are specified with the date object's method. The example in Figure 8.57 retrieves the current date, uses it with various date object methods, and displays the results in the browser, as shown in Figure 8.58.

```
<html>
<body>
<script type="text/javascript">
// JS0896 Date Object Examples
var today=new Date();
var time1=today.getTime();
var year1=today.getYear();
var month1=today.getMonth();
var date1=today.getDate();
var day1=today.getDay();
var hours1=today.getHours();
var minutes1=today.getMinutes();
var seconds1=today.getSeconds();
```

Figure 8.57: Examples of date object "get" methods (part 1 of 2).

```
var time1=today.getTime();
document.write("The Date is " + today +  ".<BR>");
document.write("The Time is " + time1 +  ".<BR>");
document.write("The Year is " + year1 +  ".<BR>");
document.write("The Month is " + month1 +  ".<BR>");
document.write("The Date is " + date1 +  ".<BR>");
document.write("The Day is " + day1 +  ".<BR>");
document.write("The Hour is " + hours1 +  ".<BR>");
document.write("The Time is " + minutes1 +  ".<BR>");
</script>
</body>
</html>
```

Figure 8.57: Examples of date object "get" methods (part 2 of 2).

The Date is Wed Aug 15 02:42:39 EDT 2007.

The Time is 1187160159374.

The Year is 2007.

The Month is 7.

The Date is 15.

The Day is 3.

The Hour is 2.

The Time is 42.

Figure 8.58: The results from Figure 8.57.

The code in Figure 8.57 uses the current date defined as the variable **today**. The values returned from using the "get" methods and the date object are stored in variables defined within the script. Figure 8.59 shows similar examples, using the "set" methods. The results are displayed in Figure 8.60.

```
<html>
<body>
<script type="text/javascript">
/* JS0898 Set Date Examples */

var today = new Date();
document.write("The current date is" + today + ".<br>");
var y = new Date();
```

Figure 8.59: Examples of date object "get" methods (part 1 of 2).

```
var t = new Date();
t.setTime(9999999999999);
document.write("Example 9999999999999 since 1/1/70 00:00 GMT" +
    ".<br>")
document.write(t + ".<br>") ;

y.setYear(1891);
document.write("Example setting current date year to 1891" +
    ".<br>");
document.write(y + ".<br>") ;

var m = new Date();
m.setMonth(1);
document.write("Example setting current date month to 1" +
    ".<br>");
document.write(m + ".<br>");

var d = new Date();
d.setDate(1);
document.write("Example setting date within the month" +
    ".<br>");
document.write(d + ".<br>");

</script>
</body>
</html>
```

Figure 8.59: Examples of date object "get" methods (part 2 of 2).

The current date isWed Aug 15 17:10:39 EDT 2007.
Example 9999999999999 since 1/1/70 00:00 GMT.
Sat Nov 20 12:46:39 EST 2286.
Example setting current date year to 1891.
Sat Aug 15 17:10:39 EDT 1891.
Example setting current date month to 1.
Thu Feb 15 17:10:39 EST 2007.
Example setting date within the month.
Wed Aug 1 17:10:39 EDT 2007.

Figure 8.60: The results from Figure 8.59.

The date class is very useful for comparing dates, which is often needed in business applications. For example, Figure 8.61 compares the ship date to the current date. If the ship date is less than or equal to the current date, the user is alerted that the order is on its way, as shown in Figure 8.62. If the ship date is greater than the current date, the user is given the date.

```html
<html>
<body>
<script type="text/javascript">
/* JS08100 Comparing Dates Example */
var shipDate=new Date()
shipDate.setFullYear(2007,7,12)
var today = new Date()
if (shipDate>today)
  alert("Your Order will ship on " + shipDate) ;
else
  alert("Your Order shipped on " + shipDate + "and is on its way") ;
</script>
</body>
</html>
```

Figure 8.61: Comparing dates in an application.

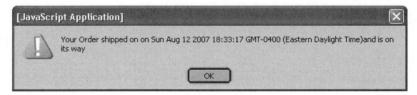

Figure 8.62: A dialog box produced from the code in Figure 8.61.

In the example in Figure 8.63, the delivery date is calculated as four days from the ship date. A message is displayed providing both the ship date and the arrival date, like this:

> **Your order is scheduled to ship on Mon Aug 20 19:09:15 EDT 2007.**
> **Your order will arrive by Fri Aug 24 19:09:15 EDT 2007.**

```html
<html>
<body>
<script type="text/javascript">
/* JS08102 Example To Calculate Delivery Date */
var shipDate=new Date();
```

Figure 8.63: Calculating a delivery date (part 1 of 2).

```
shipDate.setFullYear(2007,7,20);
var deliveryDate=new Date();
deliveryDate.setDate(shipDate.getDate()+4);
document.write("Your order is scheduled to ship on " +shipDate +
    ".<br>");
document.write("Your order will arrive by " +deliveryDate +
    ".<br>");
</script>
</body>
</html>
```

Figure 8.63: Calculating a delivery date (part 2 of 2).

The Boolean Object

A Boolean object is useful in applications where you need the results of conditional tests. It has two possible values: true and false. These values can represent truth or falsehood, on or off, yes or no, or anything else that can be stored in one bit. The Boolean object is used to convert a non-Boolean value to a value of true or false. It is defined using the **Boolean()** keyword, like this:

var booleanTest=new Boolean()

If the Boolean object has no initial value, or if it is 0, -0, null, blank, false, undefined, or NaN (not a number), it is set to false. If it is not one of these values, it is true. Boolean objects have the methods shown in Table 8.14.

Table 8.14: Boolean Object Methods	
Method	**Description**
toSource()	Used to represent the source of an object
toString()	Used to convert the result of a Boolean test and return the result as a string
valueOf()	Used to return the primitive value of a Boolean object

Math Objects

The Math object enables you to perform common mathematical tasks. This object is most likely to be used when more than simple arithmetic is required for the coding solution. The Math object's properties, listed in Table 8.15, represent certain constant values needed in arithmetic.

Table 8.15: Math Object Properties	
Property	**Description**
Math.E	Euler's constant
Math.LN2	Natural log of 2
Math.LN10	Natural log of 10
Math.LOG2E	Log base-2 of E
Math.LOG10E	Log base-10 of E
Math.PI	Pi
Math.SQRT1_2	Square root of 0.5
Math.SQRT2	Square root of 2

These properties can be used in regular mathematical expressions. For example, the following statement obtains the circumference of a variable named **diameter**:

Circumference = diameter * Math.PI

The Math object also includes methods, listed in Table 8.16. With the exception of the **Math.random()** method, all Math object methods take one or more values as parameters.

Table 8.16: Math Object Methods	
Method(parms)	**Description**
Math.abs(*n*)	Absolute value of n
Math.acos(*n*)	Arc cosine in radians of n
Math.asin(*n*)	Arc sine in radians of n
Math.atan(*n*)	Arc tangent in radians of n
Math.atan2(*n1,n2*)	Angle of polar coordinates n1 and n2
Math.ceil(*n*)	Next integer greater than or equal to n
Math.cos(*n*)	Cosine of n
Math.exp(*n*)	Euler's constant to the power of n
Math.floor(*n*)	Next integer less than or equal to n
Math.log(*n*)	Natural logarithm base E of n
Math.max(*n1,n2*)	The greater of n1 or n2
Math.min(*n1,n2*)	The lesser of n1 or n2
Math.pow(*n1,n2*)	n1 to the n2 power

Table 8.16: Math Object Methods (Continued)	
Method(parms)	**Description**
Math.random()	Random number between zero and one
Math.round(*n*)	Rounds to the next integer
Math.sin(*n*)	Sine in radians of n
Math.sqrt(*n*)	Square root of n
Math.tran(*n*)	Tangent in radians of n

The code in Figure 8.64 shows some uses of the Math object's methods. The results of this code are shown in Figure 8.65.

```html
<html>
<body>
<script type="text/javascript">
// JS08106 Math Object Properties Examples
document.write("Absolute value of 133.17 is " + Math.abs(133.17)
   + "<br/>")
document.write("Absolute value of -133.17 is " +Math.abs(-133.17)
   + "<br/>")
document.write("Absolute value of 133.17 minus 225.17 is " +Math.
   abs(133.17 - 225.17) + "<br/>")
document.write("Display a Random Number " + Math.random() +
   "<br/>")
document.write("Display Another Random Number " + Math.random()
   + "<br/>")
document.write("The Square Root of 10 is "+ Math.sqrt(10) +
   "<br/>")
document.write("The Square Root of 121 is "+ Math.sqrt(121) +
   "<br/>")
</script>
</body>
</html>
```

Figure 8.64: Using Math object methods.

Absolute value of 133.17 is 133.17

Absolute value of -133.17 is 133.17

Absolute value of 133.17 minus 225.17 is 92

Display a Random Number 0.6953919309453365

Display Another Random Number 0.6771415344548015

The Square Root of 10 is 3.1622776601683795

The Square Root of 121 is 11

Figure 8.65: The results from the code in Figure 8.64.

JavaScript Arrays

An array is a structure for storing and manipulating ordered collections of data. As a business application programmer, you are probably already familiar with arrays, but we will provide a brief review here.

An array can be visualized as a table, like a spreadsheet. In JavaScript, an array is limited to a one-column table, with as many rows as needed. Dimensional arrays can be created using an array of objects. That is beyond the scope of this chapter, but it is important to understand that the capability exists.

Previous code samples in this chapter have used arrays. For example, Figure 8.66 repeats the code from Figure 8.36, showing an example of a **for** loop. This example defines an array using the following statement:

Var BBQSauce = new Array()

```
<html>
<body>
<script type="text/javascript">
// JS08108 Simple Array Example
var x
var BBQSauce = new Array()
BBQSauce[0] = "Traditional."
BBQSauce[1] = "Sweet and Mild."
BBQSauce[2] = "Honey Mustard."
BBQSauce[3] = "Tangy Twist."
BBQSauce[4] = "Hot and Spicy."
BBQSauce[5] = "Flaming Hot"
for (x in BBQSauce)
{
document.write(BBQSauce[x] + "<br />")
}
</script>
</body>
</html>
```

Figure 8.66: A simple array example.

The array is defined as a new variable named **BBQSauce**. Values are *populated* (loaded) into the array using square brackets to designate the array index. The example array is populated with values as follows:

BBQSauce[0] = "Traditional."
BBQSauce[1] = "Sweet and Mild."
BBQSauce[2] = "Honey Mustard."
BBQSauce[3] = "Tangy Twist."
BBQSauce[4] = "Hot and Spicy."
BBQSauce[5] = "Flaming Hot"

Finally, the **for** loop cycles through the array elements and prints their contents, as shown in Figure 8.67.

Traditional.

Sweet and Mild.

Honey Mustard.

Tangy Twist.

Hot and Spicy.

Flaming Hot

Figure 8.67: The results from Figure 8.66.

Array Methods

Table 8.17 lists JavaScript array object methods.

Table 8.17: Array Object Methods	
Method	Description
array.concat()	Joins multiple arrays and returns the result.
array.join()	A string of entries from the array, delimited by the separatorString value. The join method is used to join all the elements of an array into a single string, separated by a specified string separator. If no separator is specified, the default is a comma.
array.pop()	Removes and returns the last element of an array.
array.push()	Adds one or more elements to the end of an array and returns the new length.
arrayreverse()	Returns an array of entries in the opposite order.
array.shift([,])	Removes and returns the first element of an array.
array.slice()	Returns selected elements from an existing array.
array.sort()	Sorts the elements of an array.
array.splice()	Removes and adds new elements to an array.
array.toSource()	Represents the source code of an object.

Table 8.17: Array Object Methods (Continued)	
Method	**Description**
array.toString()	Converts an array to a string and returns the result.
array.unshift()	Adds one or multiple elements to the beginning of an array and returns the new length.
array.valueOf()	Returns the primitive value of the array object.

The example in Figure 8.68 puts the array object method **sort** to use.
Figure 8.68 uses the same array as the previous example, but the array
is populated a little differently. The array's elements are all listed on the
variable definition line, separated by commas. This example also creates
two new functions, **OrdA** and **OrdD**, to define the sort order as descending
or ascending. As shown in Figure 8.69, the contents of the array are
displayed first in their original order, then in ascending order, and then in
descending order.

```html
<html>
<head>
<script type="text/javascript">
// JS08113 Array Object Method Sort Example
function OrdA(a, b){ return (a-b); }
function OrdD(a, b){ return (b-a); }
</script>
</head>
<body>
<script type="text/javascript">
var x
var BBQSauce = new Array("Traditional", "Sweet and Mild", "Honey
   Mustard", "Tangy Twist", "Hot and Spicy", "Flaming Hot");

for (x in BBQSauce)
{
document.write(BBQSauce[x] + "<br />")
}

BBQSauce.sort( OrdA );
document.write('Ascending : ' + BBQSauce + '<br />');
BBQSauce.sort( OrdD );
document.write('Descending : ' + BBQSauce + '<br />');

</script>
</body>
</html>
```

*Figure 8.68: An example of the **sort** array object method.*

Traditional

Sweet and Mild

Honey Mustard

Tangy Twist

Hot and Spicy

Flaming Hot

Ascending : Honey Mustard,Sweet and Mild,Tangy Twist,Hot and Spicy,Traditional,Flaming Hot

Descending : Tangy Twist,Sweet and Mild,Hot and Spicy,Traditional,Honey Mustard,Flaming Hot

Figure 8.69: An array unsorted, sorted ascending, and sorted descending.

At this point, you have seen several of the JavaScript objects available for use. This chapter does not include a complete list of objects available, but you have seen enough to know how powerful they are and how easy it is to use predefined objects.

Events

Events are actions that can be used within JavaScript. They are a significant component of JavaScript, providing a means to make use of the objects available, based on a user's action. Events enable you to create dynamic Web pages. Many Web-page elements have events associated with them that can trigger functions to execute an action.

Event Handlers

One way to embed client-side JavaScript into HTML documents is to use the event-handler attributes of HTML tags. Event handlers were a new addition to HTML in HTML 4.0. The current versions of the more popular browsers, including Firefox, Internet Explorer, and Netscape, all support event handlers. Table 8.18 lists some common event handlers that can be used in HTML tags.

Table 8.18: Some Common Event Handlers	
Handler	Event Triggered By
onabort	Image load aborted
onblur	Window or element loses keyboard focus
onchange	Displayed value changes
onclick	Mouse click and release
ondblclick	Mouse double-click
onerror	Image or document loading fails
onfocus	Window or element gets keyboard focus
onkeydown	Key pressed
onkeypress	Key pressed and released
onkeyup	Key released
onload	Document, image, or object loaded
onmousedown	Mouse button pressed
onmousemove	Mouse moved
onmouseout	Mouse moves off element
onmouseover	Mouse moves over element
onmouseup	Mouse button released
onreset	Form reset requested
onresize	Window size changes
onselect	Text selected
onsubmit	Form submission requested
onunload	Document unloaded

Event handlers are quite easy to use, and their possibilities in connection with JavaScript functions are endless. For example, within a business application, a click of a button might display an order's status. A double-click on a product image might trigger the display of the product's details and price. A mouse-over on a location name might trigger the address of the location to be displayed. The following pages show examples of some common event handlers.

Onclick

The **onclick** event handler is triggered when the mouse button is pressed and released. The example in Figure 8.70 uses **onclick** to display an order's status when the button in Figure 8.71 is clicked.

```
<html>
<head>
<script type="text/javascript">
/* JS08116 Event handler onclick Example */
function orderStatus()
{
/* Example to calculate delivery date */
var shipDate=new Date();
shipDate.setFullYear(2007,7,20);
var deliveryDate=new Date();
deliveryDate.setDate(shipDate.getDate()+4);
document.write("Your order is scheduled to ship on " +shipDate +
    ".<br>");
document.write("Your order will arrive by " +deliveryDate +
    ".<br>");
}
</script>
</head>
<body>
<input type="button" value="Display Order Status" onclick="orderStatus
    ()" />
</body>
</html>
```

Figure 8.70: An example of the **onclick** event handler.

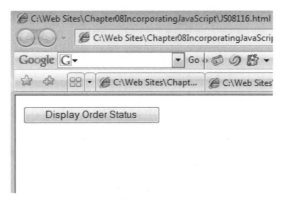

Figure 8.71: The button that will trigger the
orderStatus function when clicked.

The result of the event is the following messages:

Your order is scheduled to ship on Mon Aug 20 00:54:01 EDT 2007.
Your order will arrive by Fri Aug 24 00:54:01 EDT 2007.

Onmousedown

In the example in Figure 8.72, when the mouse button is pressed down while on the image in Figure 8.73, the "Barbeque Barn" address will be displayed. If you click anywhere else on the screen, no action is triggered. The **onmousedown** event does not gurantee that an **onclick** event will occur on the same target. For example, if you mouse over a link and then press and hold the click button, and then move off the link and release the button, the link will not be clicked.

```
<html>
<head>
<script type="text/javascript">
/* JS08118 Event handler onmousedown Example */
function displayAddress()
{
document.write("Bills Barbeque Barn " + ".<br>");
document.write("127 Homestead Lane " + ".<br>");
document.write("Bellville, MI 97568 " + ".<br>");
document.write("(313) 264-3975 " + ".<br>");
}
</script>
</head>
<body>
<img src="images/bbqbarn.JPG" width="276" height="200"
onmousedown="displayAddress()">
</body>
</html>
```

Figure 8.72: An example of the **onmousedown** event handler.

Figure 8.73: This image is replaced with an address
when the **onmousedown** event occurs.

Onerror

Earlier in this chapter, you saw how **try catch throw** can be used to control responses when errors are encountered on a Web page. The **onerror** event can also be used to control errors. This event is triggered when an error is encountered on a page.

To use **onerror,** a function must be created to handle the errors. The function is called with the following arguments:

- **msg**—The error message

- **url**—The URL of the page that caused the error

- **line**—The line where the error occurred

The value returned by **onerror** determines the error message. If it returns false, the browser displays the standard error message in the JavaScript console. If it returns true, the browser does not display the standard error message.

In the example in Figure 8.74, a button is displayed (shown in Figure 8.75), prompting the user to display a welcome message. When the button is pressed, an error is encountered because within the code, **adalert** is spelled incorrectly as *aaaaaddddlert*. When the error is encountered, the **onerror** event is triggered. It calls a function to display a message with the error, URL address, and line number of the error, as shown in Figure 8.76. The error message prompts the user to click OK to continue.

```
<html>
<head>
<script type="text/javascript">
/* JS08121 Event Handler onerror Example */
onerror=handleErr
var messageTxt=""
function handleErr(msg,url,l)
{
messageTxt="There was an error on this page.\n\n"
messageTxt+="Error: " + msg + "\n"
messageTxt+="URL: " + url + "\n"
messageTxt+="Line: " + l + "\n\n"
messageTxt+="Click OK to continue.\n\n"
alert(messageTxt)
return true
}
function message()
{
```

*Figure 8.74: An example of the **onerror** event handler (part 1 of 2).*

```
aaaaaddddlert("Welcome to Bills Barbeque Barn!")
}
</script>
</head>
<body>
<input type="button" value="Display Welcome Message"
   onclick="message()" />
</body>
</html>
```

*Figure 8.74: An example of the **onerror** event handler (part 2 of 2).*

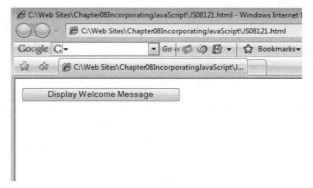

Figure 8.75: The initial result of the code in Figure 8.74.

Figure 8.76: The error message displayed when the button is clicked.

Events used to trigger actions make your Web application more dynamic and user-friendly.

Cookies

A cookie is a variable that is stored on the visitor's computer by a Web page. Each time the same computer requests the page with a browser, it sends the cookie, too. With JavaScript, you can both create and retrieve cookie values.

Cookies can be used for a variety of reasons. A cookie might be used to control the message displayed when the user visits a site, to retain a password so a returning user won't be required to enter it, or to store the date so the user can see the last time he or she visited the site.

In the cookie example in Figure 8.77, the first time a user visits the Web site, a prompt is displayed, requesting the user's name. The next time the user visits the site, he or she will not be prompted for a name. Instead, a "welcome back" message will be displayed.

To accomplish this, a cookie stores the user's name on the user's client computer. In this example, the cookie is set to expire after 30 days. When the cookie expires, the next time the user visits, he or she will again be prompted for a name, and that new name will be stored in the cookie. The cookie requires three functions: one to check to see if the cookie exists for

```
<html>
<head>
<script type="text/javascript">
/* JS08124 Cookie Example
/* function to check to see if cookie exists for the user */
/* the cookies are stored in the document cookie object */
/* if a cookie is found the value will be returned or if not found
   an empty */
/* string will be returned */
function retreiveCookie(cookie_name)
{
if (document.cookie.length>0)
  {
  cookid_start=document.cookie.indexOf(cookie_name + "=")
  if (cookid_start!=-1)
    {
    cookid_start=cookid_start + cookie_name.length+1
```

Figure 8.77: An example of creating and using a cookie (part 1 of 2).

```
     cookid_end=document.cookie.indexOf(";",cookid_start)
     if (cookid_end==-1) cookid_end=document.cookie.length
     return unescape(document.cookie.substring(cookid_start,cookid_
        end))
    }
  }
return ""
}
/* function that stores the name of a cookie in a variable*/
/* the parameters of the function hold the name of the cookie,
   the value */
/* of the cookie and the number of days until the cookie expires */

function storeCookie(cookie_name,value,expiredays)
{
var exdate=new Date()
exdate.setDate(exdate.getDate()+expiredays)
document.cookie=cookie_name+ "=" +escape(value)+
((expiredays==null) ? "" : ";expires="+exdate.toGMTString())
}
/* if the cookie user name exists a welcome back message will be */
/* displayed if not the user will be prompted to enter their user */
/* name and the store cookie function will be called */
function checkCookie()
{
username=retreiveCookie('username')
if (username!=null && username!="")
  {alert('Welcome back to Bills Barbeque Barn '+username+'!')}
else
  {
  username=prompt('Please enter your user name:',"")
  if (username!=null && username!="")
    {
    storeCookie('username',username,30)
    }
  }
}
</script>
</head>
<body onLoad="checkCookie()">
</body>
</html>
```

Figure 8.77: An example of creating and using a cookie (part 2 of 2).

this user, the second to store the name of the user if a cookie does not exist, and the third to display the user-name prompt or "welcome back" message.

The first time the user runs the application, the screen shown in Figure 8.78 is displayed. The next time the same user accesses the application, the screen in Figure 8.79 is displayed (as long as the cookie hasn't expired).

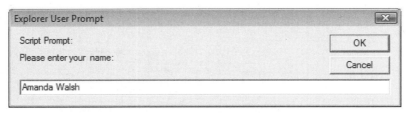

Figure 8.78: The cookie requesting the user's name the first time the page loads.

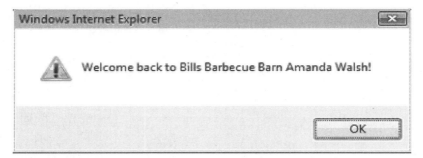

Figure 8.79: The cookie displaying the welcome screen on subsequent page loads.

Cookies can be used within business applications to display and use user-specific information, just like that information is used in traditional applications.

JavaScript Form Validation

Form validation is the process of checking that a form is filled out as expected. For example, an email address or phone number can be validated for the correct format, or required fields can be validated to ensure the user does not leave them blank. JavaScript can be used to validate data in an HTML form before sending that data to a server. Validation using JavaScript happens instantly because it takes place on the client rather than on the server.

Because form validation is one of the most valuable uses of JavaScript for the business application developer, the example in this section is a little more detailed and complex than most of the examples in this chapter. It uses a basic HTML form, shown in Figure 8.80, along with a number of functions to perform various form-validation tasks. The form requests a first name, last name, email address, phone number, message, and response. All of the fields are required. The email address must be in a valid format, the phone number must be numeric, and the response field must be chosen from a pull-down list. Review the form before reviewing the code.

Figure 8.80: The customer service form to be validated.

Defining the form is a pretty easy task using standard HTML tags. Figure 8.81 has the code for the page, as well as a reference to the JavaScript file *JS08129.js*, which contains the functions that will be used to validate the form data. (Coding forms in HTML is covered in more detail in chapter 9.)

```
<html>
<head>
<script language="JavaScript" src="js scripts/JS08129.js" type="text/
   javascript">
//JS08128 Form Validation Example
</script>
</head>
<body>
<p>Welcome to Bills Barbeque Barn Customer Service Page.</p>
<p> Please enter your message and press the submit button.
</p>
<form action="" name="myform" >
```

Figure 8.81: The code that creates the customer service form (part 1 of 3).

```
<table cellspacing="2" cellpadding="2" border="0">
<tr>
   <td align="right">First Name</td>
   <td><input type="text" name="FirstName"></td>
</tr>
<tr>
   <td align="right">Last Name</td>
   <td><input type="text" name="LastName"></td>
</tr>
<tr>
   <td align="right">Email Address</td>
   <td><input type="text" name="Email"></td>
</tr>
<tr>
   <td align="right">Phone #</td>
   <td><input type="text" name="Phone"></td>
</tr>
<tr>
   <td align="right">Message</td>
   <td><textarea cols="20" rows="5" name="Message"></textarea>
      </td>
</tr>
<tr>
   <td align="right">Response</td>
   <td>
         <SELECT name="Response">
             <option value="" selected>[please choose]
             <option value="001">No Response
             <option value="002">Phone Call
             <option value="003">Email Reply
      </SELECT>
         </td>
</tr>
<tr>
   <td align="right"></td>
   <td><input type="submit" value="Submit"></td>
</tr>
</table>
</form>
<script language="JavaScript" type="text/javascript">
  var frmvalidator = new Validator("myform");
    frmvalidator.addValidation("FirstName","req","Please  enter
      your First Name");
    frmvalidator.addValidation("FirstName","maxlen=20",
      "Max length for FirstName is 20");
    frmvalidator.addValidation("FirstName","alpha");
    frmvalidator.addValidation("LastName","req");
    frmvalidator.addValidation("LastName","maxlen=20");
    frmvalidator.addValidation("Email","maxlen=50");
    frmvalidator.addValidation("Email","req");
    frmvalidator.addValidation("Email","email");
```

Figure 8.81: The code that creates the customer service form (part 2 of 3).

```
    frmvalidator.addValidation("Phone","maxlen=25");
    frmvalidator.addValidation("Phone","req");
    frmvalidator.addValidation("Message","maxlen=150");
    frmvalidator.addValidation("Message","req");
    frmvalidator.addValidation("Response","dontselect=0");
</script>
</body>
</html>
```

Figure 8.81: The code that creates the customer service form (part 3 of 3).

Validation can be done in many ways. This example uses a JavaScript class to make form validation easier. Figure 8.82 is the code for the JavaScript class, stored in the *JS08129.js* file. Functions have been created to complete various validation tasks, and a set of validation descriptors is associated with each of the form-field elements. The validation descriptors are strings specifying the type of validation to be performed. Each of the fields on the form has multiple validations.

```
/* JS08129 Form validation functions */
function Validator(frmname)
{   this.formobj=document.forms[frmname];
        if(this.formobj.onsubmit)
        {   this.formobj.old_onsubmit = this.formobj.onsubmit;
            this.formobj.onsubmit=null;
        }
        else
        {       this.formobj.old_onsubmit = null;
        }
                this.formobj.onsubmit=form_submit_handler;
                this.addValidation = add_validation;
                this.setAddnlValidationFunction=set_addnl_
                    vfunction;
                this.clearAllValidations = clear_all_validations;
}

/* Additional Validation Function */
function set_addnl_vfunction(functionname)
{ this.formobj.addnlvalidation = functionname;
}
/* Clear all validations function */
function clear_all_validations()
{   for(var itr=0;itr < this.formobj.elements.length;itr++)
        {   this.formobj.elements[itr].validationset = null;
        }
}
/* form submit handler function */
```

Figure 8.82: The JavaScript functions to validate the form (part 1 of 5).

```
function form_submit_handler()
{   for(var itr=0;itr < this.elements.length;itr++)
        {   if(this.elements[itr].validationset &&
            !this.elements[itr].validationset.validate())
                { return false;
                }
        }
        if(this.addnlvalidation)
        { str =" var ret = "+this.addnlvalidation+"()";
            eval(str);
    if(!ret) return ret;
        }
        return true;
}

/* add validation function */
function add_validation(itemname,descriptor,errstr)
{ if(!this.formobj)
        {
            alert("ERROR: the form object is not set properly");
                return;
        }// end if
        var itemobj = this.formobj[itemname];
    if(!itemobj)
        { alert("ERROR: Could not get the input object named:
            "+itemname);
                return;
        }
        if(!itemobj.validationset)
        { itemobj.validationset = new ValidationSet(itemobj);
        }
    itemobj.validationset.add(descriptor,errstr);
}
/* Validation descriptuon function */
function ValidationDesc(inputitem,desc,error)
{   this.desc=desc;
        this.error=error;
        this.itemobj = inputitem;
        this.validate=vdesc_validate;
}
/* Vdesc validate function  */
function vdesc_validate()
{ if(!V2validateData(this.desc,this.itemobj,this.error))
    {     this.itemobj.focus();
                return false;
    }
    return true;
}
/* Validation set function */
function ValidationSet(inputitem)
{   this.vSet=new Array();
```

Figure 8.82: The JavaScript functions to validate the form (part 2 of 5).

```
        this.add= add_validationdesc;
        this.validate= vset_validate;
        this.itemobj = inputitem;
}
/* Add validation description */
function add_validationdesc(desc,error)
{    this.vSet[this.vSet.length]=
        new ValidationDesc(this.itemobj,desc,error);
}
/* Vset validate function */
function vset_validate()
{   for(var itr=0;itr<this.vSet.length;itr++)
        {    if(!this.vSet[itr].validate())
                { return false;
                }
        }
        return true;
}
/* Email validation function */
function validateEmailv2(email)
{
    if(email.length <= 0)
        { return true;
        }
    var splitted = email.match("^(.+)@(.+)$");
    if(splitted == null) return false;
    if(splitted[1] != null )
  { var regexp_user=/^\"?[\w-_\.]*\"?$/;
      if(splitted[1].match(regexp_user) == null) return false;
    }
      if(splitted[2] != null)
      { var regexp_domain=/^[\w-\.]*\.[A-Za-z]{2,4}$/;
      if(splitted[2].match(regexp_domain) == null)
          { var  regexp_ip =/^\[\d{1,3}\.\d{1,3}\.\d{1,3}\.\
              d{1,3}\]$/;
              if(splitted[2].match(regexp_ip) == null) return
                false;
    }// if
    return true;
    }
return false;
}
/* Validate data function */
function V2validateData(strValidateStr,objValue,strError)
{   var epos = strValidateStr.search("=");
    var command = "";
    var cmdvalue = "";
    if(epos >= 0)
    { command  = strValidateStr.substring(0,epos);
     cmdvalue = strValidateStr.substr(epos+1);
    }
```

Figure 8.82: The JavaScript functions to validate the form (part 3 of 5).

```
else
{ command = strValidateStr;
}
switch(command)
{ case "req":
    {
      if(eval(objValue.value.length) == 0)
      {
        if(!strError || strError.length ==0)
          {
            strError = objValue.name + " : Required Field";
        }//end if
        alert(strError);
        return false;
      }//end if
      break;
    }//case required
  case "maxlen":
    { if(eval(objValue.value.length) > eval(cmdvalue))
      { if(!strError || strError.length ==0)
        {
            strError = objValue.name + " : "+cmdvalue+"
              characters maximum ";
        }//end if
        alert(strError + "\n[Current length = " + objValue.
          value.length + " ]");               return false;
      }//end if
      break;
    }//case maxlen
  case "alpha":
    { var charpos = objValue.value.search("[^A-Za-z]");
      if(objValue.value.length > 0 &&  charpos >= 0)
      {   if(!strError || strError.length ==0)
          {   strError = objValue.name+": Only alphabetic
              characters allowed ";
        }
            alert(strError + "\n [Error: character pos "
              + eval(charpos+1)+"]");
        return false;
      }
      break;
    }//alpha
  case "email":
    {   if(!validateEmailv2(objValue.value))
      { if(!strError || strError.length ==0)
        { strError = objValue.name+": Enter a valid Email
            address ";
        }
        alert(strError);
        return false;
      }
```

Figure 8.82: The JavaScript functions to validate the form (part 4 of 5).

```
            break;
        }//case email
    case "dontselect":
    {  if(objValue.selectedIndex == null)
            { alert("ERROR: dontselect command for non-select
                Item");
         return false;
        }
        if(objValue.selectedIndex == eval(cmdvalue))
        { if(!strError || strError.length ==0)
        {
        strError = objValue.name+": Please Select a response ";
        }//end if
        alert(strError);
        return false;
        }
        break;
    }//case dontselect
  }//switch
  return true;
}
```

Figure 8.82: The JavaScript functions to validate the form (part 5 of 5).

This example uses a lot of the JavaScript functionality described in this chapter. Let's look closer at the application. The code in Figure 8.81 includes a reference to the external JavaScript file in Figure 8.82 with the following tag:

<script language="JavaScript" src="js scripts/JS08129.js" type="text/javascript">

Referencing the external file is like including the additional code within the **<head>** section of the HTML page. Having the code in a separate file enables it to be reused by any application within the site. (In a real-world situation, a more meaningful name would be used for the file, such as "formfieldvalidation.js.")

If no information is entered within the form and the user clicks the Submit button, the message in Figure 8.83 is displayed. The FirstName field is defined on the form within the HTML page with the code snippet in Figure 8.84.

Figure 8.83: The validation message for a missing first name.

```
<tr>
    <td align="right">First Name</td>
    <td><input type="text" name="FirstName"></td>
</tr>
```

Figure 8.84: The FirstName form field definition.

The action begins when the user clicks the Submit button, causing the script code in Figure 8.85 to be executed. This code first defines a variable named **frmvalidator**, which is the validator object that will be used for form-field validation. This variable is passed the name of the form, "myform." Next, validations are added, such as the validations for the FirstName field shown in Figure 8.85.

```
var frmvalidator  = new Validator("myform");
    frmvalidator.addValidation("FirstName","req","Please    enter
        your First Name");
    frmvalidator.addValidation("FirstName","maxlen=20",
        "Max length for FirstName is 20");
    frmvalidator.addValidation("FirstName","alpha");
```

Figure 8.85: The JavaScript to validate the first name.

The first argument is the name of the field, "FirstName." The second argument is the validation descriptor used to specify the type of validation to be performed. The third argument is the message that will be displayed if the field value does not pass validation. Using this technique requires that the validators be defined within the HTML page after the **</form>** end tag. The form-validation function code is executed. If the validation is false, the message will be displayed.

Suppose you entered a first name longer than the maximum allowed length of 20 characters. Because of the data validation, the message in Figure 8.86

would be displayed, indicating the maximum length allowed and the length of the value entered.

Figure 8.86: The validation message displayed when the first name exceeds the maximum length.

As you continue testing each of the field validations on the form page, note that the "Response" form field has been defined as a list of values, as shown in Figure 8.87.

```
<SELECT name="Response">
            <option value="" selected>[please choose]
            <option value="001">No Response
            <option value="002">Phone Call
            <option value="003">Email Reply
    </SELECT>
```

Figure 8.87: The creation of the "Response" form field.

When the user clicks the pull-down tab, the list of values for the response are displayed, as shown in Figure 8.88. The user would select a response from the list.

Figure 8.88: The pull-down list.

Notice also the "Message" field, which is defined as a text area with 20 columns and 5 rows. The code in Figure 8.89 validates that the field is not left blank and doesn't exceed the maximum of 150 characters.

```
frmvalidator.addValidation("Message","maxlen=150");
frmvalidator.addValidation("Message","req");
```

Figure 8.89: The validators for the "Message" field.

The data-validation example in this section uses just a few of the validation descriptors available. Table 8.19 provides a more complete list of the descriptors available.

Table 8.19: Validation Descriptors	
Descriptor	**Description**
alpha alphabetic	The value entered must be alphabetic data.
alnum alphanumeric	The value entered can only contain numbers and characters.
dontselect=99	This validator is used for input items in list boxes, when a selection is required. Usually, the index value 0 is associated with the default value of the list. The number referenced will correspond with the default value. In the example in Figure 8.81, the index is zero for the default value, [please choose].
Email	The field value entered must be a valid email address.
gt=999 greaterthan=999	The value entered is greater than the value passed. This validator is only for use with numeric fields.
lt=999 lessthan=999	The value entered is less than the value passed. This validator is only for use with numeric fields.
num numeric	The value entered must be numeric data.
maxlen=999 maxlength=999	The value entered is no longer in characters than the maximum value passed.
min=999 minlength=999	The value entered is at least the same length in characters as the minimum value passed.
regexp=	The value is validated with a regular expression, which is a series of characters that defines a pattern. The value entered needs to match the pattern of the regular expression. For example, to validate for positive or negative number, you could use regexp=^-{0,1}\d*\.{0,1}\d+$. To ensure that a password was at least six symbols, you could use regexp=^.{6,}$
req required	The field value cannot be empty.

Summary

We have covered a lot of ground in this chapter, but we have barely scratched the surface of what can be done with JavaScript. Clearly, JavaScript is an essential tool for Web application development. It is easy to learn and browser-friendly. It can be used in coordination with other tools, including server-side programming languages.

JavaScript is often used for form validation. Forms are discussed in more detail in chapter 9. Forms are also included in the examples of Web development with PHP, ASP.NET, and Java Server Pages in chapters 10, 11, and 12.

After reading this chapter, you should understand the basic syntax of JavaScript, understand some of the tasks for which the language is suited, and have some experience working through the examples provided. After working through the examples, you will be ready to begin incorporating JavaScript into your Web business applications. When you are ready to go further, there are many great Web sites that provide advanced code examples and forums for JavaScript developers to share ideas, experiences, and code.

CHAPTER 9

Web Development with CGI

CGI, the Common Gateway Interface, defines a standard for how external gateway programs and scripts communicate with a Web server. CGI is not a programming language; it is the interface between the Web page or browser and the Web server that runs a program. You might sometimes hear that CGI is old, outdated technology. This is not true. The languages used for CGI programs and scripts range from those that have been around a long time to recently created languages.

CGI is commonly used within Web applications to provide the gateway to connect the client and server. Consider two fields with a gated fence between them. The fields are the client and the server, and CGI is the gate that connects them.

When the Worldwide Web started, there was only one Web server and one Web client. The HTTPd Web server was developed by the Centre d'Etudes et des Recherche Nucléaires, or CERN, in Geneva, Switzerland. *HTTPd* has become the generic name of the binary executable of many Web servers. When CERN stopped funding the development of HTTPd, it was taken over by the Software Development Group of the National Center for Supercomputing Applications, or the NCSA. The NCSA produced the first Web browser, called Mosaic, and later went on to write the Netscape client browser. Mosaic could fetch and view static HTML documents and images served by the HTTPd server.

As the Web grew, search engines were developed to help Web users find what they were looking for. Search engines needed to be able to process user-entered data and quickly return the content Web users were looking for. Early search engines were implemented by extending the Web server and directly modifying the Web server's code. However, it was not practical to rewrite the source, so the NCSA developed the CGI specification. CGI quickly became a standard for interfacing with external server-based applications and providing dynamic content on the Web. Use of CGI has provided tremendous capability and is often used within Web-based business applications.

An HTML document is static. It is a text file that does not change from a constant state. CGI allows content for a Web page to come from a program or script rather than just from the static HTML. Using CGI programs and scripts, Web applications can become dynamic. CGI is executed in real-time and can output dynamic content within Web applications.

In chapter 8, you learned how JavaScript can provide dynamic content on the client side. CGI, on the other hand, makes use of programs and scripts executed on the server side. CGI programs or scripts can be written in almost any language that can read from standard input (*stdin*), write to standard output (*stdout*), and run on a Web server. Stdin refers to input via a keyboard or file that a program has accessed. Stdout refers to the browser screen.

CGI allows a Web application to run a program on the site's Web server, so it is often used for handling form input, database updates, or database queries. These are all critical tasks for business applications. Because CGI runs on the Web server, security should be considered when using it. Access to CGI scripts and programs should be controlled with restrictions as a precaution to prevent site users from creating CGI programs. CGI programs and scripts usually reside in a special directory, under the direct control of someone on the IT staff, probably the Webmaster.

CGI's Uses

There are many uses for CGI, as listed in Table 9.1. One of the most common uses is with forms. A Web page containing a form will require a CGI script or program to process the information entered. CGI may also be used to connect a Web page to a database so users can query the data. To connect to the database, a CGI program or script will be executed by the Web daemon to transmit information to the database engine and receive the results to be displayed. A *daemon* is a program that executes in the background, ready to perform an operation when required. A daemon functions like an extension to the operating system and is usually an unattended process that is initiated at startup.

Table 9.1: Typical Uses of CGI	
Use	**Example**
Form processing	Process data entered within an HTML form.
Sending an email message	Send an email message to the user or a specified email address when the Submit button is clicked.
Database queries	Connect to a database, retrieve and display content.
Displaying an HTML document	Display a screen after a user submits a request for the script file. This could be a message or displaying data entered or a page with another form that points to a different script file.
Informational interaction with site users, counters, and cookies	Use CGI counters for cookies, or to determine a user's browser and operating system. CGI might also be used to determine the number of times a page has been accessed or to monitor Web traffic.
Updating a database	Update a database either using data entered in a form or programming logic that includes logic based on input from a user.
Decoding form contents	Use form content to trigger application logic to execute.

CGI Compared to Other Tools

There are many ways to create dynamic Web content. When is CGI the correct choice? To decide, keep in mind that CGI is not a programming or scripting language, but an interface. The uses of CGI can be duplicated by other technology, such as JavaScript and ActiveX. However, some end users' firewalls may prevent technologies like JavaScript or ActiveX because of bandwidth or security issues. Unlike JavaScript or ActiveX, CGI does not require browser settings to be enabled. Therefore, CGI might make sense if you need to ensure that all users have access to your applications.

CGI Versus Java and JavaScript

Java includes standard APIs in the form of servlets that can be used for some of the same purposes as CGI scripts and programs. However, CGI and Java are fundamentally different and are not always interchangeable within applications.

CGI applications are executed on the server side, while Java or JavaScript programs may be executed on the client side. In general, applications requiring a lot of processing on a server, such as accessing or controlling databases, gateways, or other Internet services or protocols, are better developed with CGI applications. On the other hand, if you want to add dynamic features such as animations on Web pages, you will probably be better served by Java and possibly JavaScript. Because CGI applications are executed on the server side, they put some extra load on a Web server, while client-side Java and JavaScript do not.

Due to CGI's architecture and available system tools, a CGI application can easily use the hard disk of a server or initiate network connections on the Internet. Java programs are not able to directly access the server's disk or easily initiate network connections. (JavaScript cannot do this at all.) CGI applications are not limited to one programming language. They are limited only by the CGI specifications, which are general enough to allow the use of C, Perl, C++, and many other languages. CGI opens the gateway to the functionality provided by these languages.

Most often, developers decide to use either CGI or Java, but it is also possible to use both technologies as complementary tools. For example, a CGI application may call a Java application, a Java application may use CGI, or Java code may even be used as a CGI program.

CGI Versus SSI, PHP, or ASP

CGI and SSI (Server-Side Includes) are interchangeable for many purposes. Often, personal preference determines which is used. CGI is a common standard, agreed upon and supported by all major HTTPds. SSI is not a common standard, but an innovation of the NCSA's HTTPd, which has been widely adopted in later servers. CGI has the greatest portability, but if the requirement is so simple that it can be done without invoking an exec, SSI will probably be more efficient.

Typical SSI applications would be to include standard footers, identify when a document was last modified, display a page counter, or embedded CSS stylesheets. For more complex applications, like processing a form, CGI is usually the best choice. If a transaction returns a response that is not an HTML page, SSI is not an option at all. Many more variants on the theme of SSI are now available; probably the best known are PHP and ASP.

PHP embeds server-side scripting in a pre-HTML page. ASP is Microsoft's version of a similar interface.

CGI Versus APIs

APIs are proprietary programming interfaces supported by particular platforms. By using an API, you may lose all portability. If you know your application will only ever run on one platform, operating system, and HTTPd, and a suitable API exists, go ahead and use it. Otherwise, stick to CGI.

CGI's Advantages and Disadvantages

Like any other tool, CGI also has advantages and disadvantages. Here are some of its advantages:

- Provides a common gateway using most any language
- Not platform-specific
- Not dependent on client settings; provides access regardless of browser, settings, or operating system
- Easily combined with other tools
- Provides simple server access
- Easily passes variables between pages and applications

Here is a summary of CGI's disadvantages:

- Not high-performance
- Dependent on server support
- Misperception of being old technology
- Requires security consideration

CGI's Compatibility

Before including CGI within a Web application, it is important to make sure the server being used for the Web site can run CGI scripts or programs. Any program or script that will run on the Web server can be used as a CGI application. Often, an HTTP server is used as the gateway between a legacy information system and the Web server. CGI is an agreement between HTTP server implementers and is all about how to integrate the use of CGI scripts and programs. CGI specifications are currently maintained by the NCSA's Software Development Group.

A CGI program can be written in virtually any programming or scripting language that can read from standard input (stdin) and write to standard output (stdout). This includes interpreted languages, compiled languages, or a combination of both.

Some of the languages that CGI scripts and programs can be written in include the following:

- ASP.NET
- Basic
- C or C++
- Fortran
- Java
- JSP
- Pascal
- Perl
- PHP
- RPG
- Unix Shell
- Visual Basic

Scripts can be coded using more than one language, and more than one language may be used within a Web site containing CGI. So how do you choose which languages to use for CGI? The platform used for your applications will probably have an impact on your decision. Performance, security, reliability, maintainability, compatibility, and portability should also be considered. It is best to decide what factors are most important for your specific requirements, and choose languages that are available on your system and that you are comfortable with. The most common languages for CGI coding are C, C++, Perl, and UNIX Shell.

The first CGI programs were written in C and required compilation into binary executables. The compiled CGI programs were executed from a directory named *cgi-bin*, and the source-file directory was named *cgi-src*. Most servers today come with a preconfigured cgi-bin directory used to store CGI programs and scripts, but CGI programs do not have to use this directory. Sites are often designed to use different directory structures for CGI-executed programs and scripts.

The use of CGI is fairly straightforward for an experienced developer. To get started, verify that your server is already configured to run CGI applications. Look for the manuals, Readme files, ISP Web pages, and FAQs for your Web server. A number of sites on the Web provide a variety of free CGI applications that might already do what you are trying to do. You might find that these applications can be copied and modified to fit your specific needs. Information on the CGI specification and CGI application development can also be found on the NCSA site, *http://hoohoo.ncsa.uiuc.edu/cgi/interface.hmtl*.

CGI Specifications

There are four main ways in which CGI applications communicate with a server: environment variables, the command line, stdin, and stdout.

Environment Variables

Environment variables can be used as a method for the Web server to pass information to a CGI script. The environment variables are created and assigned values. The environment variables listed in Table 9.2 are used to pass data about the information request from the server to the CGI script or program. The variables are set when the server executes the CGI application. The table includes both non-request-specific and request-specific variables, with descriptions of each of the variables.

Table 9.2: CGI Environment Variables	
Variable	Description
Not Request-Specific:	
SERVER_SOFTWARE Format: name/version	The name and version of the information server software answering the request (and running the gateway).
SERVER_NAME	The server's hostname, DNS alias, or IP address as it would appear in self-referencing URLs.
GATEWAY_INTERFACE Format: CGI/revision	The revision of the CGI specification to which this server complies.

Table 9.2: CGI Environment Variables (Continued)	
Variable	**Description**
Request Specific:	
SERVER_PROTOCOL Format: protocol/revision	The name and revision of the information protocol this request came in with.
SERVER_PORT	The port number to which the request was sent.
REQUEST_METHOD	The method with which the request was made. For HTTP, this is "GET", "HEAD", "POST", etc.
PATH_INFO	The extra path information, as given by the client. In other words, scripts can be accessed by their virtual pathname, followed by extra information at the end of this path. The extra information is sent as PATH_INFO. This information should be decoded by the server if it comes from a URL before it is passed to the CGI script. The server provides translated version of PATH_INFO, which takes the path and does any virtual-to-physical mapping to it.
PATH_TRANSLATED	The server provides a translated version of PATH_INFO, which takes the path and does any virtual-to-physical mapping to it.
SCRIPT_NAME	A virtual path to the script being executed, used for self-referencing URLs.
QUERY_STRING	The information which follows the question mark in the URL that referenced this script. This is the query information. It should not be decoded in any fashion. This variable should always be set when there is query information, regardless of command-line decoding.
REMOTE_HOST	The hostname making the request. If the server does not have this information, it should set REMOTE_ADDR and leave this unset.
REMOTE_ADDR	The IP address of the remote host making the request.
AUTH_TYPE	If the server supports user authentication, and the script is protected, this is the protocol-specific authentication method used to validate the user.
REMOTE_USER	If the server supports user authentication, and the script is protected, this is the username the user has authenticated as.
REMOTE_IDENT	If the HTTP server supports RFC 931 identification, this variable will be set to the remote user name retrieved from the server. Usage of this variable should be limited to logging only.
CONTENT_TYPE	For queries that have attached information, such as HTTP POST and PUT, this is the content type of the data.
CONTENT_LENGTH	The length of the content, as given by the client.
HTTP_ACCEPT Format: type/subtype, type/subtype	The MIME types the client will accept, as given by HTTP headers. Other protocols may need to get this information from elsewhere. Each item in this list should be separated by commas according to the HTTP spec.
HTTP_USER_AGENT General format: software/ version, library/version	The browser the client is using to send the request

In addition to the CGI environment variables defined in Table 9.2, there are header lines received from the client. If any of the header lines are placed into the environment, the prefix *HTTP_* is followed by the header name. Any dash characters (-) in the header name are changed to underscores (_). The server may exclude any headers that it has already processed, such as the Authorization, Content-type, and Content-length. When necessary, the server may choose to exclude any or all of these headers if including them would exceed any system-environment limits.

The Command Line

The CGI command line is used with an ISINDEX query, a special query that uses the **<ISINDEX>** tag and the **<BASE HREF="*scriptname...*">** tag. The data entered by the user is sent to the CGI program using the command line. More than one parameter can be passed to the CGI program or script command line because the server replaces any plus sign (+) sent from the client with a space.

Standard Input

For requests that have information attached after the header, such as HTTP POST or PUT, the information will be sent to the script on stdin.

Standard Output

The script sends its output to stdout. This output can either be a document generated by the script, or instructions to the server for retrieving the desired output.

Security

As mentioned earlier, using CGI does create security risks because it probably opens up access to server locations where data and applications reside. Therefore, an organization's critical data and systems can potentially be exposed. A lot can be done to minimize this risk, however. The CGI protocol is not inherently insecure; it is the CGI scripts and programs that are the major source of security holes. CGI applications must be written with just as much care as the server or any other application that provides access to an organization's data. An understanding of good programming techniques, as well as the security features, configuration, and environment of the system being used as a server, can reduce or eliminate security issues.

It could be argued that a program in a compiled language is inherently more secure than one in an interpreted language, since the compiled program is a binary file while an interpreted one is stored in a readable format. Interpreted scripts also require an interpreter program, which might have potential bugs or security risks. Compiled languages aren't risk free, however, and may have security issues of their own. For example, compiled languages like C and C++ use a buffer overflow that might enable a clever hacker to attack your system. This can be avoided by using coding techniques to limit the buffer size. Another example is a program that is used to update your database. A hacker might find a hole to write endless entries to the database, filling your disk space. Again, there are relatively easy fixes, such as limiting the file sizes and limiting the size of a single update entry.

Any language has potential security risks. You can reduce problems by focusing on good coding techniques to prevent logical errors and bugs. A properly configured Web server and proper database administration can also reduce security risks. Developers need a solid understanding of the language and environment they are working in, including security considerations.

If the information processed by your application is confidential or private, you'll want to build in extra security. Consider placing data in another location with limited access, encrypting the data, and requiring a user ID and password before allowing access to the data. Again, understanding your database administration, server security, and programming tools is key. Developers who understand these elements are better equipped to prevent potential security issues.

Server Side Includes are another potential security hole. These server directives embedded in HTML documents can direct the server to execute system commands and CGI applications. If a developer is unaware of the potential risks, it would be easy to create code with security holes or unexpected side effects. Security configuration should be thoroughly reviewed to determine controls and recommendations to prevent security risks. Apache, NCSA, and some other servers allow the server administrator to selectively disable the types of includes that can be used to execute arbitrary commands.

For more information regarding CGI security, visit the Web site
http://www.w3.org/Security/Faq/www-security-faq.html.

Forms

One of the most common uses of CGI is for dealing with forms in Web
applications. Forms for gathering information from users were introduced
in chapter 8. Let's take a closer look at them now.

Forms can be used for such things as making selections from criteria,
entering information to update a database, creating a menu of options,
or prompting for a user ID and password prompt. When a form's Submit
button is clicked, the information on the form is transferred to the Web
server. When the Web server receives that information, it can run a
CGI script to process it. The CGI program or script controls how the
information will be handled.

The first thing you need to do is create the form. Once created, additional
information can be added to the form. The form is created using HTML
tags. In the examples used, a form will be created for Bill's Barbeque
Barn to allow customers to sign up for the company mailing list. The
information will be used to illustrate how forms are created using HTML.
The form may just as well be a product order form, inventory update
form, human resource form to enter employee information, an accounts
payable entry form, or any other type of form that might be used within a
business application.

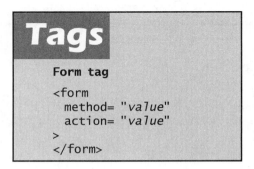

Tags

Form tag
```
<form
  method= "value"
  action= "value"
>
</form>
```

The **<form>** and **</form>** tags define the start and end of a form. The
form will be included within the body of the HTML page, as shown in
Figure 9.1.

```
<html>
<head>
</head>
<body>
<!--CGI0901 - Form Example -->
<h1><center>Bills  Barbeque  Barn  Customer  Mailing  List  Form
    </center></h1>
<p align=center>Please Sign Up For Our Customer Mailing List.</p>
<form method=post action="/cgi-bin/mailing.php">
</form>
</body>
</html>
```

Figure 9.1: An example of a simple HTML page with an empty form.

The tag **<form method=post action="cgi-bin/mailing.php">** in Figure 9.1 begins the form and designates the CGI script on your Web server that will be used to process information submitted through the form. The page is displayed as shown in Figure 9.2.

Figure 9.2: The Web page resulting from Figure 9.1.

Input Elements

Before going further, let's review HTML form input elements. Table 9.3 lists some of the possible input elements that can be used on an HTML form.

Table 9.3: HTML Form Input Elements	
Input Element	**Description**
Text	A single-line, text input field.
Password	Like a text field, but with the input rendered in such a way to hide characters. It is used for sensitive data like passwords or social security numbers.
Checkbox	A graphic checkbox for user selection.
Radio	A graphic radio button for user selection.
Submit	A graphic button to initiate action.
Reset	A graphic button to clear entered field values.
File	An element that provides the ability to attach a file. Its "value" attribute is used to designate the file name.
Hidden	A hidden input element, which may be used for passing values to a CGI application.
Image	Creates a graphical element that works like a button. The value of its "src" attribute designates the URI of the image that will be used for the button. When the user clicks the image, it will act like the Submit button, but will also pass the location coordinates of the image on the page. These coordinates may then be used to trigger actions within a CGI application.
Button	A graphic button.
Textarea	A multiple-line text input control. A user can enter an unlimited number of characters of text in the textarea.
Drop down box	A selectable list.

Table 9.4 lists some of the possible attributes for an HTML form's input elements. The attributes can be inserted into the HTML form element's tags to define event actions.

Table 9.4: Input Element Attributes	
Input Attribute	**Description**
Type	Indicates the type of input element: button, checkbox, file, hidden, image, password, radio, reset, submit, or text.
Name	Assigns the input element's name.
Value	Specifies the initial value of the input element. This is a required attribute for radio and checkbox elements. It is optional for all other input elements.
Checked	For a radio or checkbox element, this Boolean attribute specifies whether the button is on.
Disabled	Used to disable an input element.
Readonly	For a text or password element, this attribute designates the input value as read-only.

Table 9.4: Input Element Attributes (Continued)	
Input Attribute	**Description**
Size	Defines the initial width of the input element.
Maxlength	Sets the maximum length of the input element.
Src	Used with the image input element to designate the image location.
Alt	Alternate text.
Usemap	Used for client-side image maps.
Ismap	Used for server-side image maps.
Tabindex	Used for tabbing navigation.
Accesskey	Used for accessibility key characters.
Intrinsic events	Used to trigger activity based on even occurrence. Intrinsic events include onfocus, onblur, onselect, onchange, onclick, ondblclick, onmousedown, onmouseup, onmouseover, onmousemove, onmouseout, onkeypress, onkeydown, and onkeyup.
Accept	Indicates the legal content types for a server.

In the following sections, examples will demonstrate how some of the various input elements are defined on HTML forms.

Text Fields

The next step is to add information to the form. Text boxes can be defined to allow users to enter text into a form. In the example in Figure 9.3, text boxes have been added for the fields CustomerName, AddressLine1, AddressLine2, City, State, ZipCode, Phone, and EmailAddress. The text boxes have been added as input fields in between the **<form>** and **</form>** tags. The text boxes are defined using the **<input type="text">** tags. The field names are defined using the **name** attribute. The field sizes are defined using **size** attribute, which defines the width that will be used on the form, in characters. The maximum length of the fields is defined using the **maxlength** attribute. This designates the maximum number of characters that can be entered for the field. Notice also the **
** tag, which displays the fields on separate lines.

```
<html>
<head>
</head>
<body>
<!--CGI0903 - Form With Text Fields Example -->
```

Figure 9.3: Creating text boxes in an HTML form (part 1 of 2).

```
<h1><center>Bills Barbeque Barn Customer Mailing List Form</
   center></h1>
<p align=center>Please Sign Up For Our Customer Mailing List.</p>
<form method=post action="/cgi-bin/mailing.php">
<br>NAME........<input type = "text" name="CustomerName" size="50"
   maxlength="45">
<br>ADDRESS. <input type = "text" name="AddressLine1" size="50"
   maxlength="45">
<br>ADDRESS. <input type = "text" name="AddressLine2" size="50"
   maxlength="45">
<br>CITY........ <input type = "text" name="City" size="30"
   maxlength="25">
<br>STATE...... <input type = "text" name="State" size="30"
   maxlength="25">
<br>ZIP CODE <input type = "text" name="ZipCode" size="20"
   maxlength="15">
<br>PHONE NUMBER <input type = "text" name="Phone" size="25"
   maxlength="20">
<br>EMAIL ADDRESS <input type = "text" name="EmailAddress" size="25"
   maxlength="25">
</form>
</body>
</html>
```

Figure 9.3: Creating text boxes in an HTML form (part 2 of 2).

The user can position the cursor in a text box and type in the requested information, as shown in Figure 9.4.

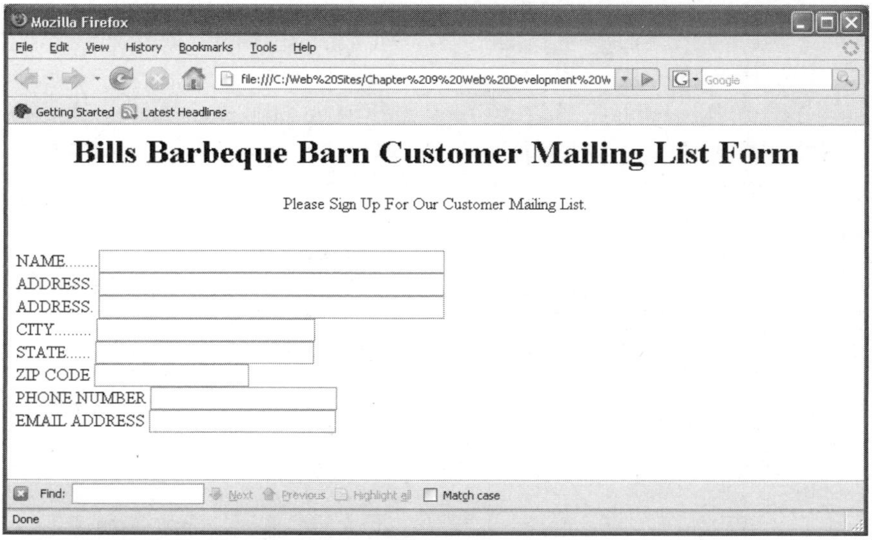

Figure 9.4: An HTML form with text boxes.

Password Fields

A password field allows users to enter confidential information such as a log-in ID, credit card number, bank account number, or tax ID number. It is defined as shown in Figure 9.5. The password field protects others from viewing confidential information while the user enters it, but does not protect the information as it is transferred over the Internet. To protect the data as it travels, the Web server must be secure. For sensitive information like passwords, encryption may be used to further protect the data. Encryption converts entered data from its original form into a format that can only be read by someone or an application that has a key to decrypt the data, so it prevents unauthorized reading of data.

```
<html>
<head>
</head>
<body>
<!--CGI0905 - Form Password Example -->
<form method=post action="/cgi-bin/mailing.php">
<br>Your Email Address Will Be Used As Your User Id.  Please Enter
   Your Password.
<br>Password...<input type = "password" name="PassWord" size="25"
   maxlength="15">
</form>
</body>
</html>
```

Figure 9.5: Creating a password field in an HTML form.

Figure 9.6 displays the resulting screen from the HTML in Figure 9.5. Note the asterisk displayed for each character the user types, preventing others from seeing the value of the field.

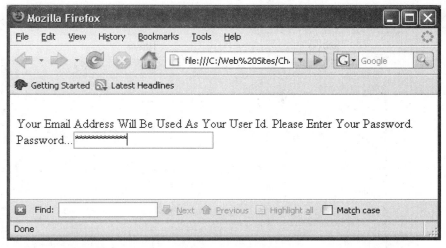

Figure 9.6: An HTML form with a password field.

Radio Buttons

We've all seen radio buttons in Web applications. The values associated with the radio buttons can trigger application actions. In the example in Figure 9.7, the radio buttons have different names. This way, a user can select one or more radio buttons to trigger application events.

```
<html>
<head>
</head>
<body>
<!--CGI0907 - Form Radio Button Example -->
<form method=post action="/cgi-bin/mailing.php">
<br>Select The Type of Customer Contact You Would Like To Receive.
<br><input type = "radio" name="EmailMethod" value="Email"> Email
<input type = "radio" name="MailMethod" value=" Traditional Mail">
  Traditional Mail
<input type = "radio" name="PhoneMethod" value=" Phone"> Phone
</form>
</body>
</html>
```

Figure 9.7: Creating radio buttons.

As shown in Figure 9.8, the user is prompted to select the preferred type of customer contact. The user may select any or all of the contact types. A validation might be added to the application, requiring the user to select at least one of the choices. A check box may also be used for this type of application. Prior to coding, some thought should be given to the form elements used for user response.

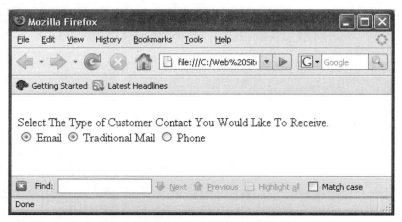

Figure 9.8: An HTML form with three different radio buttons.

Radio buttons may also share the same control name, as shown in Figure 9.9. In this example, all the radio buttons are named AgeGroup. When radio buttons share a name, they are mutually exclusive. When the user clicks one, the others will be turned off. Validation can be added to require at least one of the buttons is clicked. If it makes sense, one of the buttons can be the default by initially turning it on with the **checked** attribute of the **<input>** element.

```
<html>
<head>
</head>
<body>
<!--CGI0909 - Form Radio Button Example -->
<form method=post action="/cgi-bin/mailing.php">
<br>Please Select An Age Group.
<br><input type = "radio" name="AgeGroup" value="Under21"> Under 21
<input type = "radio" name="AgeGroup" value="Age21To39"> 21-39
<input type = "radio" name="AgeGroup" value="Age40To64"> 40-64
<input type = "radio" name="AgeGroup" value="65AndOver"> 65 and Over
</form>
</body>
</html>
```

Figure 9.9: HTML for radio buttons that share a name.

As shown in Figure 9.10, the user is prompted to select an age group. Because we would like the user to choose only one group, a shared control name fits our application objective.

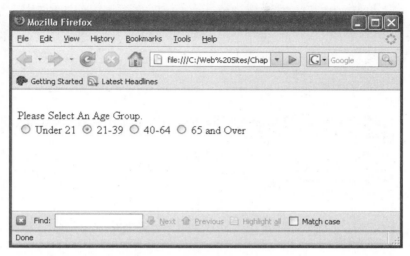

Figure 9.10: Mutually exclusive radio buttons.

Check Boxes

Like radio buttons, check boxes are used as on/off switches that can be toggled by the user's mouse click. The switch is on when the control element's checked attribute is set.

In the code in Figure 9.11, the check boxes share the control name FollowUpCall. Even when check boxes share a control name, they are not mutually exclusive like radio buttons are, so it would be necessary to add validation requiring the user to select one or the other. Radio buttons with a shared control would be a better fit because they would automatically be mutually exclusive. This example has been included to show how check boxes and radio buttons work differently.

```
<html>
<head>
</head>
<body>
<!--CGI0911 - Form Check Box Example -->
<form method=post action="/cgi-bin/mailing.php">
```

Figure 9.11: HTML for check boxes that share a name (part 1 of 2).

```
<br>Would You Like A Follow Up Phone Call Describing Customer
  Mailing List Program.
<br><inputtype="checkbox"name="FollowUpCall"value="FollowUpYes">
  Yes
<input type = "checkbox" name="FollowUpCall" value="FollowUpNo">
  No
</form>
</body>
</html>
```

Figure 9.11: HTML for check boxes that share a name (part 2 of 2).

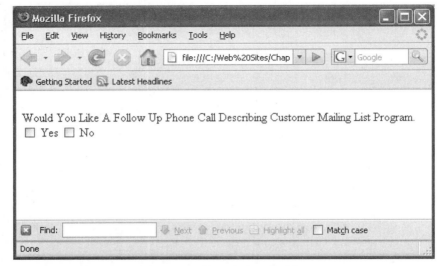

Figure 9.12: An attempt to have mutually exclusive check boxes.

The code in Figure 9.13 prompts users to select the items they would like to receive information about. As shown in Figure 9.14, a user may select none, one, or more than one item. This is an appropriate use for check boxes.

```
<html>
<head>
</head>
<body>
<!--CGI0913 - Form Check Box Example -->
<form method=post action="/cgi-bin/mailing.php">
<br>Select the Items You Would Like To Receive Information
  About.
```

Figure 9.13: Creating check boxes in an HTML form (part 1 of 2).

```
<br><input type = "checkbox" name="Coupons" value="Coupons">
  Coupons
<input type = "checkbox" name="News Letter" value="NewsLetter">
  Newsletter
<inputtype="checkbox"name="SpecialEvents"value="SpecialEvents">
  Special Events
<inputtype="checkbox"name="ProductSpecials"value="ProductSpecials">
  Product Specials
</form>
</body>
</html>
```

Figure 9.13: Creating check boxes in an HTML form (part 2 of 2).

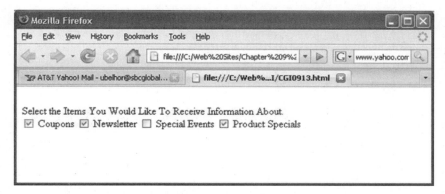

Figure 9.14: A form with more than one check box selected.

Check boxes and radio buttons are both useful tools for passing information to the CGI application. The results can be incorporated in the programming logic to trigger specific events and actions.

Menu/List

The **<select>** form element provides the capability to create a menu of options to choose from. The capability can be used as a pull-down menu or as a list. The selection of individual items from the menu could trigger routing to different Web pages or other events. The example in Figure 9.15 asks the user to identify how they found out about Bill's Barbeque Barn, based on the items listed. When the user clicks the pull-down button, the list of items is displayed, as shown in Figure 9.16.

```
<html>
<head>
</head>
<body>
<!--CGI0915 - Form List Example -->
<form method=post action="/cgi-bin/mailing.php">
<br>How Did You Find Out About Bills Barbeque Barn?
<select name="Source">
<option value="" selected>[please choose]
<option value="Radio">Radio
<option value="Television">Television
<option value="Internet">Internet
<option value="Advertisement">Advertisement
<option value="Referral">Referred By Someone
<option value="Other">Other
</select>
</form>
</body>
</html>
```

Figure 9.15: Creating a pull-down menu in an HTML form.

Figure 9.16: A form with a pull-down menu.

The number of options listed on the HTML page when the menu is closed defaults to one. The default is for the first item to be displayed, *[please choose]* in this example. By designating a size within the **<select>** tag, the number of items the user will be able to see without having to scroll can be changed. For example, if the tag **<select name="Source">** is changed to

\<select name="Source" size="7">, all of the items listed will be displayed as a list on the HTML page. Change the code this way yourself, and see what happens.

Large Text Area

A text area in an HTML form allows multiple-line input. To define a text area, you must designate its number of rows and columns, as shown in Figure 9.17. The text area in this example consists of five rows that are 50 columns each, for a total area of 250 characters, as shown in Figure 9.18.

```
<html>
<head>
</head>
<body>
<!--CGI0918 - Form Text Area Example -->
<form method=post action="/cgi-bin/mailing.php">
<br>Please Enter Comments and Suggestions
<br><textarea name="commentsbox" rows="5" cols="50" wrap>
</textarea>
</form>
</body>
</html>
```

Figure 9.17: Creating a text area in an HTML form.

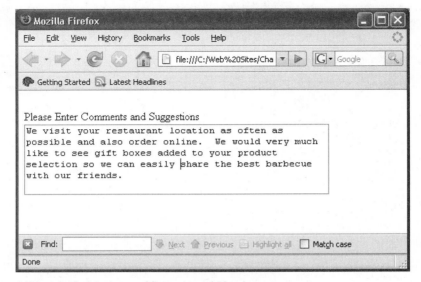

Figure 9.18: A text area of five rows and 50 columns.

An initial value for the text area can be defaulted by entering text in the code between the **<textarea>** and **</textarea>** tags, as shown in Figure 9.19.

```
<br><textarea name="commentsbox" rows="5" cols="50" wrap>
Enter default text here
</textarea>
```

Figure 9.19: The code to create a text area with default text.

Reset Button

Figure 9.20 shows an HTML form that includes a Reset button to clear the information entered on the form.. The **type="reset"** parameter defines the Reset button. The **value** parameter specifies the text that appears on the button. In this example, it is "Clear Entries," as shown in Figure 9.21.

```
<html>
<head>
</head>
<body>
<!--CGI0921 - Form Reset Example -->
<h1><center>Bills Barbeque Barn Customer Mailing List Form</center>
  </h1>
<p align=center>Please Sign Up For Our Customer Mailing List.</p>
<form method=post action="/cgi-bin/mailing.php">
<br>NAME........<input type = "text" name="CustomerName" size="50"
  maxlength="45">
<br> <input type="reset" value="Clear Entries">
</form>
</body>
</html>
```

Figure 9.20: Creating a form with a Reset button.

Figure 9.21: The "Clear Entries" button resets the data in the form.

Try the example. Enter some text in the Name field and then click the "Clear Entries" button. The button clears the form and resets any form fields to their initial values.

Submit Button

The Submit button is a very important element on an HTML form. When clicked, this button sends the information entered on the form to the Web server.

As with the Reset button, the text you would like displayed on the Submit button is defined using the **value** parameter. The code in Figure 9.22, for example, will display the word "Submit" on the button, as shown in Figure 9.23.

```
<html>
<head>
</head>
<body>
<!--CGI0923 - Form Submit Example -->
<h1><center>Bills Barbeque Barn Customer Mailing List Form</center>
  </h1>
```

Figure 9.22: Adding a Submit button to an HTML form (part 1 of 2).

```
<p align=center>Please Sign Up For Our Customer Mailing List.</p>
<form method=post action="/cgi-bin/mailing.php">
<br>NAME........<input type = "text" name="CustomerName" size="50"
  maxlength="45">
<br> <input type="reset" value="Clear Entries">
<input type="submit" value="Submit">
</form>
</body>
</html>
```

Figure 9.22: Adding a Submit button to an HTML form (part 2 of 2).

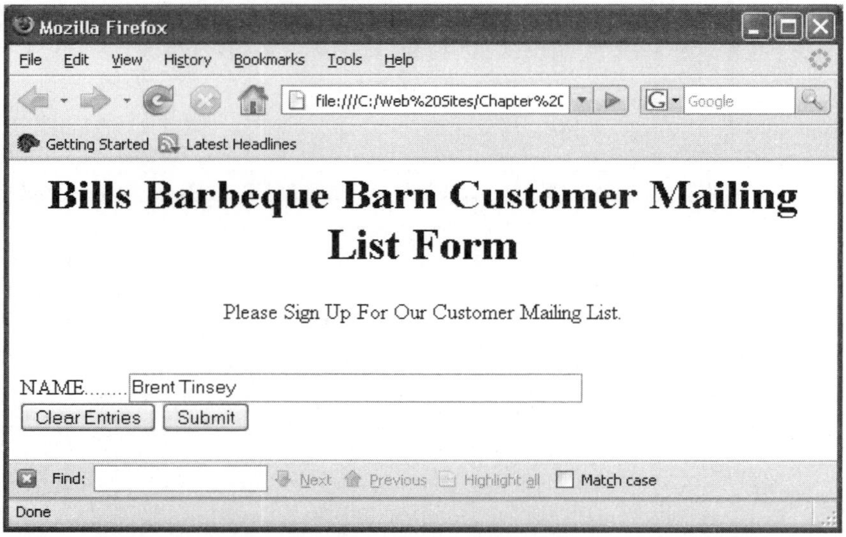

Figure 9.23: An HTML form with Reset and Submit buttons.

The **method** attribute of the **form** tag specifies the HTTP method used to send the form to the server for processing. The **method** attribute may take one of two values: **get** or **post**. The difference between **method=get** and **method=post** is defined in terms of form data encoding. The **get** method should be used when form processing is *idempotent*, meaning there are no side effects. Many databases queries have no effect on the data in the database, so they are ideal applications for **get**. If processing the form potentially causes side effects such as modifications to a database, **post** should be used. There can be problems related to long URLs and non-ASCII characters, however, that make it necessary to use **post** even for idempotent processing.

Putting It All Together

The HTML page in Figure 9.24 gathers all of the form elements covered in the previous examples into one mailing list form for Bill's Barbeque Barn. In this example, the data entered in the form should be retained, so we use the **post** method. The CGI application designated in /cgi-bin/mailing. php will be used to process the information and store it in a database. This application is a PHP script, but as described earlier in this chapter, it could be coded in any one of the many languages that can be used with CGI. We cover the specifics of several of the languages that can be used for CGI scripting, including PHP, in other chapters within this book. In this example, the mailing.php script is used to store the entered information. The script may also include edit checks to validate the entered data.

```html
<html>
<head>
</head>
<body>
<!--CGI0925 - Form With Input Fields Example -->
<h1><center>Bills Barbeque Barn Customer Mailing List Form</
    center></h1>
<p align=center>Please Sign Up For Our Customer Mailing List.</p>
<form method=post action="/cgi-bin/mailing.php">
<br>NAME........<input type = "text" name="CustomerName" size="50"
    maxlength="45">
<br>ADDRESS. <input type = "text" name="AddressLine1" size="50"
    maxlength="45">
<br>ADDRESS. <input type = "text" name="AddressLine2" size="50"
    maxlength="45">
<br>CITY........ <input type = "text" name="City" size="30"
    maxlength="25">
<br>STATE...... <input type = "text" name="State" size="30"
    maxlength="25">
<br>ZIP CODE <input type = "text" name="ZipCode" size="20"
    maxlength="15">
<br>PHONE NUMBER <input type = "text" name="PhoneNumber" size="25"
    maxlength="20">
<br>EMAIL ADDRESS <input type = "text" name="EmailAddress" size="25"
    maxlength="25">
<br>Your Email Address Will Be Used As Your User Id.  Please Enter
    Your Password.
<br>PASSWORD...<input type = "password" name="PassWord" size="25"
    maxlength="15">
<br>Select The Type of Customer Contact You Would Like To Receive.
<br><input type = "radio" name="EmailMethod" value="Email"> Email
<input type = "radio" name="MailMethod" value=" Traditional Mail">
    Traditional Mail
```

Figure 9.24: Creating a mailing list using HTML form elements (part 1 of 2).

```
<input type = "radio" name="PhoneMethod" value=" Phone"> Phone
<br>Please Select An Age Group.
<br><input type = "radio" name="AgeGroup" value="Under21"> Under 21
<input type = "radio" name="AgeGroup" value="Age21To39"> 21-39
<input type = "radio" name="AgeGroup" value="Age40To64"> 40-64
<input type = "radio" name="AgeGroup" value="65AndOver"> 65 and Over
<br>Would You Like A Follow Up Phone Call Describing Customer Mailing
   List Program.
<br><inputtype="checkbox"name="FollowUpCall"value="FollowUpYes">
   Yes
<input type = "checkbox" name="FollowUpCall" value="FollowUpNo">
   No
<br>Select  the  Items  You  Would  Like  To  Receive  Information
   About.
<br><input  type = "checkbox"  name="Coupons"  value="Coupons">
   Coupons
<input type = "checkbox" name="News Letter" value="NewsLetter">
   Newsletter
<inputtype="checkbox"name="SpecialEvents"value="SpecialEvents">
   Special Events
<input type = "checkbox" name="Product Specials" value="Product
   Specials"> Product Specials
<br>How Did You Find Out About Bills Barbeque Barn?
<select name="Source">
<option value="" selected>[please choose]
<option value="Radio">Radio
<option value="Television">Television
<option value="Internet">Internet
<option value="Advertisement">Advertisement
<option value="Referral">Referred By Someone
<option value="Other">Other
</select>
<br>Please Enter Comments and Suggestions
<br><textarea name="commentsbox" rows="5" cols="50" wrap>
</textarea>
<br> <input type="reset" value="Clear Entries">
<input type="submit" value="Submit">
</form>
</body>
</html>
```

Figure 9.24: Creating a mailing list using HTML form elements (part 2 of 2).

The form that will be displayed when this example is loaded in a browser is shown in Figure 9.25. This example uses many of the features available with forms.

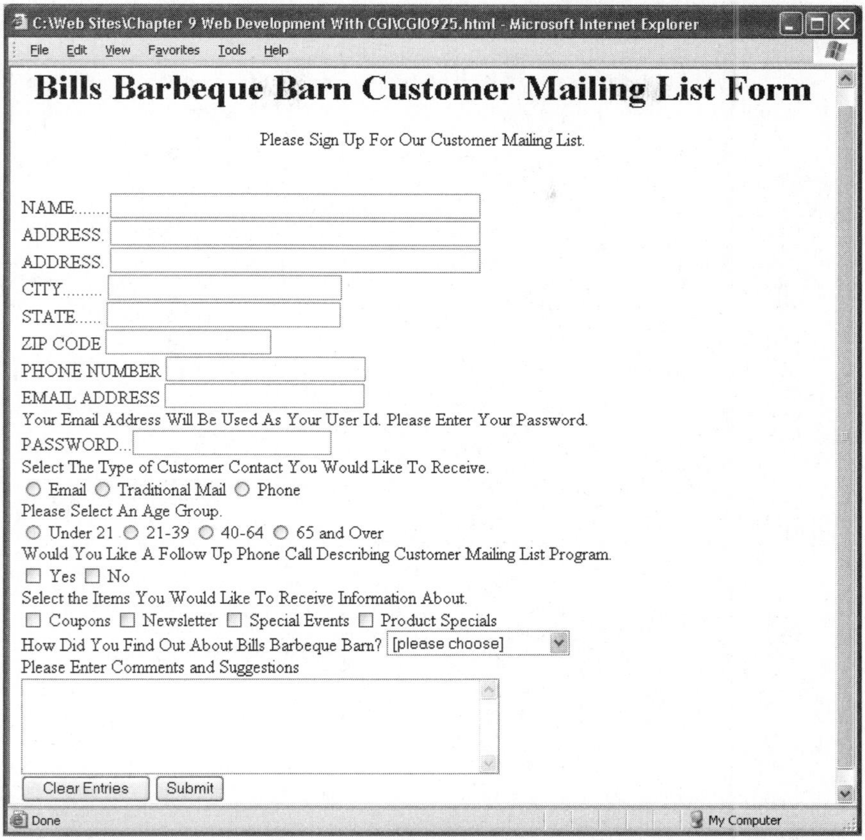

Figure 9.25: A form to gather information for a mailing list.

Summary

CGI may well be a good choice for Web application development when the users of your application might have firewalls or browser settings that preclude other technologies. It is also a good choice if you are already very familiar with a language used for CGI and are not able to spend the time or money to learn other tools. Chapters 10, 11, and 12 include CGI examples in PHP, ASP.NET, and Java Server Pages. Application examples for simple queries using **get** and updating database content using **post** are also included.

CHAPTER **10**

Web Development with PHP

In the discussion of CGI in chapter 9, you learned that many languages can be used for server-side programming, including Java, JSP, .NET, and PHP. This chapter introduces PHP, which stands for *PHP: Hypertext Preprocessor*. It is a scripting language embedded within HTML. Much of PHP's syntax is extracted from C, Java, and Perl, with some unique PHP-specific features. The goal of the language is to allow Web developers to write dynamically generated pages quickly. While PHP is mainly used for server-side scripting, it can also be used from a command-line interface or in stand-alone GUI (graphical user interface) applications. In this chapter, the focus is on server-side scripting with the business application developer in mind.

PHP can be used to do anything any other CGI programs can do, including retrieving and using input data, generating dynamic page content, and updating server-stored data. One of the most significant features of PHP is its support for a wide range of databases. Writing a dynamic Web application that is able to retrieve and store data is very easy to do with PHP. Currently, PHP supports the databases listed in Table 10.1.

Table 10.1: PHP Supported Databases			
Adabas D	dBase	Direct MS-SQL	Empress
FilePro (read-only)	FrontBase	Hyperwave	IBM DB2
Informix	Ingres	Interbase	mSQL
MySQL	ODBC	Oracle (OCI7 OCI8)	Ovrimos
PostgreSQL	SQLite	Solid	Sybase
Velocis	Unix dbm		

PHP's support of ODBC, the Open Database Connection standard, means it can be used to connect to any database that supports ODBC, including both Access and SQL Server. Also, in addition to the databases listed in Table 10.1, PHP can use a PDO extension, allowing use of any database supported by the PDO extension.

PHP may be used to solve business application needs, jazz up existing applications, create user interfaces, or make applications easily accessible for remote users without requiring additional software or hardware. You will learn the basics of PHP by reviewing examples in this chapter that show how to use it within Web business applications. Some knowledge of HTML will be helpful to understand these examples. If necessary, review the earlier chapters on HTML before proceeding.

PHP Compared to Other Tools

There are, of course, many tools that can be chosen for Web development. Choosing the best technologies for a development project is a complicated subject. How do you decide whether to learn PHP, and what to use it for? Comparing PHP to other tools will help you decide whether or not to include it in your toolkit.

PHP Versus JavaScript

PHP and JavaScript are technically quite different languages. As discussed in chapter 8, JavaScript is intended for client-side computing; its code is executed locally at the browser on whatever device is being used. PHP, on the other hand, can be executed on the server. PHP is much more robust than JavaScript and is intended for tasks that cannot be done with JavaScript. For example, PHP easily interacts with a wide variety of databases and other server-side applications. JavaScript requires other tools to interact with a database.

Both PHP and JavaScript share roots in C and Java, so their syntax and statements are quite similar. Both languages are also embedded within HTML. Whether to use PHP or JavaScript will depend on your need for client-side versus server-side functionality. It might make sense to use PHP and JavaScript together in an application.

PHP Versus ASP.NET

ASP.NET is not really a language. ASP is an acronym for *Active Server Pages*, and .NET refers to Microsoft's .NET Framework. The language used to program ASP.NET is VB Script. The biggest drawback of ASP. NET is that it is a proprietary system natively used only with Microsoft Internet Information Server (IIS), although efforts are under way to expand it's portability.

PHP, in contrast, is open source and quite portable. *Open source* refers to a program in which the source code is available to the general public for use and/or modification from its original design, free of charge. PHP, like a lot of other open source programs, has been created as a collaborative effort, in which programmers continue to improve upon the code and share the changes with the open source community.

PHP can run on almost any platform. It is commonly said to be more stable and less resource-intensive than ASP.NET. ASP.NET is said by some developers to be slower and more cumbersome. ASP.NET, however, is easier to learn than PHP. While PHP isn't difficult, ASP.NET is very easy, especially if a developer has Visual Basic knowledge. Some developers also say PHP is more robust for adding advanced features like support for FTP servers, data parsing, and connectivity.

PHP Versus Java

Like JavaScript, PHP and Java are technically quite different, although the syntax of the languages is similar. Here is a brief review of how PHP and Java differ:

- PHP supports fewer data types than Java. In addition to Boolean, integer, float, string, array, and object, Java supports char, byte, short, and long data types.

- PHP requires that variables start with a dollar sign ($), while Java doesn't. Both PHP and Java use case-sensitive variables. In PHP, a variable is declared when it is created, and the type is implied by the assigned value. Within PHP, a variable type can be changed by assigning a new value. In Java, variables must be declared with a specific data type before use.

- PHP includes libraries and Java imports libraries.

- Within PHP, constants are defined through functions. In Java, constants are defined like other variables.

- PHP passes method parameters by value and by reference. Java passes by value only.

- Both PHP and Java support function calls, but function calls are easier with PHP.

- Java supports interfaces, multiple-thread processing, abstract classes and methods, and polymorphism. PHP does not.

- PHP supports public scope of class members and Java supports public, private, and protected.

- PHP allows errors to be ignored or raised. Within Java, error-handling is structured using try, catch, and finally, constructs.

- PHP is better suited to small, Web-based applications, since its features are geared toward script coding. Java is more general-purpose and suited for larger applications.

- PHP is an easier language to learn than Java.

- PHP is open source and Java is not.

- Java has been around a lot longer and has a larger user community. PHP has not been around very long, but has grown rapidly in popularity because of its short learning curve and ease of use.

PHP is currently considered the "in vogue" language to learn. Many site-serving companies support PHP. Java and JSP shine on large projects, where carefully developed objects can be reused and refined. Large projects imply in-house, dedicated servers to support the Web site, rather than having the site hosted.

Like Java, the PHP language is well-supported. PHP and Java technology may be used together in an application.

PHP's Advantages and Disadvantages

PHP is easily embedded in HTML and has the advantage of being executed on the server. One of the biggest advantages to PHP is that it is very easy for a programmer to learn and offers many advanced features to fulfill the development needs of a business application programmer. Table 10.2 reviews other advantages, as well as disadvantages, of using PHP. The review is relative to other Web development technologies.

Table 10.2: PHP's Advantages and Disadvantages	
Advantages	**Clarification**
Easy to learn	PHP has a very short learning curve. Programmers can learn the language and become productive quickly.
Easy to use	Scripting is easy to use. Many are of the opinion that PHP is easier to use than other technologies.
Inexpensive	PHP is free and open source for both commercial and non-commercial use and development.
Extensive server support	Support is provided for all common servers.
Extensive browser support	All popular browsers support PHP.
Extensive database access capability	PHP supports an extensive list of databases.
Widely used	Very popular, heavily used, and currently "in vogue," PHP has a very large base of developers and users. It is easy to find programmers who are fluent in PHP.
Extensive user support	Endless information, examples, and blogs exist to support the large community of PHP users and developers. Several sites are dedicated to providing information and support for PHP, including www.php.net and www.zend.com.
Many extensions	PHP has numerous extensions with a wide variety of features, such as XML manipulation and encryption. There is also extensive source code available that can be used to quickly to put together advanced applications.
Transparent compilation	PHP is compiled using a special byte-code format before it is executed. Compilation is transparent to programmers and users. Changes can be made to a PHP page and the results can be seen immediately in a browser without an additional compile step like JSP.
Quick performance	PHP has been noted for its execution speed. When used for heavy database interaction, PHP performs well compared to other programming languages.
Relatively slow computation	PHP is probably not the best choice for applications requiring heavy computation or intense, detailed business logic. Java technologies or .NET may be better in these cases.
Open source	Most organizations are receptive to open source technologies, but some are not.

Table 10.2: PHP's Advantages and Disadvantages (Continued)	
Disadvantages	**Clarification**
Viewable source code	PHP source code is frequently embedded in HTML, like other scripting languages, and can be easily viewed by users. For most applications, this is not an issue, but for applications that include sensitive information, it needs to be addressed.
Error-handling issues	PHP error-handling is currently not as robust as some of the other server-side Web development languages. The PHP community is very aware of this and efforts are in progress to improve error-handling.

PHP is a good fit for many application requirements. For an organization with little or no Web development skills, PHP is quick to learn. If the budget is limited, PHP may well be a good fit. If application requirements dictate accessing data from a variety of databases, PHP may also be the right choice. If the requirements include heavy computation and complicated business logic, however, other technologies may be a better fit.

Introduction to PHP

PHP is a server-side, cross-platform scripting language. Like JavaScript, PHP code can be embedded into HTML. Unlike JavaScript, PHP executes on the Web server, not the client browser. *Cross-platform* means that PHP scripts can run on many different operating systems and Web servers, and supports the most popular configurations. PHP is currently available for the following operating systems:

- i5/OS
- Linux
- Mac OS X
- Novell Netware
- OS/2
- RISC OS
- SGI IRIX 6.5.x
- Solaris (SPARC, INTEL)
- UNIX
- Windows

As mentioned earlier, PHP is free. The main implementation is provided through the PHP Group and released under the PHP license. PHP requires software to be downloaded, installed, and configured. The installation of PHP produces a configuration file named *php.ini* that contains configuration values, controls the behaviors of PHP, and provides the capability to configure PHP to work with most platforms comfortably.

Currently, two major versions of PHP are actively being developed: 5.x and 4.4x. On July 12, 2007, the PHP Group announced that active development on 4.4x would stop after December 31, 2007. Critical security updates will be provided for 4.4x through August 8, 2008. If you're new to PHP, therefore, download and use version 5.x.

PHP is simple to learn for someone with no Web programming experience, while offering advanced features for experienced programmers. The syntax is very similar to Perl and C. A PHP file may contain HTML tags, text, and scripts. PHP files have an extension of *.php*, *.php3*, or *.phtml*. This chapter uses *.php* for examples.

What Can PHP Do?

PHP, like most server-side scripting languages, is an excellent tool for creating dynamic Web sites incorporating database content. PHP uses external libraries and functions, making the language easy to use and providing extensive functionality. Functions make the language very robust and powerful. This chapter provides several examples of how functions can be used to incorporate PHP within business application Web sites.

Here are some specific examples of what PHP can be used for:

- Process an inquiry application requiring retrieval of data from a database, such as an inventory inquiry, an order inquiry, or an employee work-schedule inquiry.

- Read and process data.

- Connect to, read, and process database contents, as in an online-ordering or customer-feedback application.

- Based on a user's ID and password, or characteristics of a user's environment (such as browser, IP address, and time), serve different content. For example, based on a user's characteristics, display either a manager or an employee page.

- Provide a customer or employee feedback mechanism.

- Display images or text documents, such as a product catalog including detailed product pictures and product detail, or a contact list displaying employee pictures and contact information.

- Supply business-specific programming logic.

Preparing for PHP

To complete the examples in this chapter, a PHP-capable server needs to be installed and configured; PHP needs to be downloaded, installed, and tested; and a compatible database needs to be made available. Also, check to make sure your browser is PHP-compatible. (Most recent versions of popular browsers are.)

PHP can be downloaded from *http://www.php.net/downloads.php*. Instructions on how to download are provided on the site. The site also provides details on which servers and databases are supported for use with PHP. Server and database configuration is not covered in this chapter. The examples in this chapter use the Windows OS, PHP 5.2.3, MySQL for the database, and Microsoft's ISAPI IIS for the Web server.

PHP code is often indented to make it easier to read. While there is not an official standard for indenting, unofficial conventions for indentation are often used. Some of the examples in this chapter do not include indentation, however, for the sake of formatting the code to fit within a text page. Keep in mind that indentation is not necessary, but can make code easier to read and work with.

Basic PHP Syntax

When PHP parses a file, it looks for opening and closing tags, which tell it to interpret the code between them. Parsing allows PHP to be embedded in all sorts of different documents, as everything outside of the opening and closing tags is ignored by the PHP parser.

Tags

A PHP block usually starts with the **<?php** tag and ends with the **?>** tag. Everything in between is PHP program code rather than HTML. Alternatively, a **<script>** tag similar to that for JavaScript may be used. The tag **<script language= "php">** tells PHP that everything that follows is PHP program code rather than HTML until the closing **</script>** tag is encountered, as shown in Figure 10.1.

```
<html>
<body>
<script language="php">
 </script>
</body>
</html>
```

Figure 10.1: PHP script tags.

Figure 10.2 is a simple script that sends the text "Welcome to Bills Barbeque Barn!" to be displayed. Any application text can be displayed this way. Rather than "Welcome to Bills Barbeque Barn," for example, the text might be "XYZ Company Inventory Inquiry," "Mr. Widgets Purchase Order Inquiry Page," or whatever text is applicable to the business application being coded.

```
<html>
<body>
<?php
//  PHP1002.php
Echo "Welcome to Bills Barbeque Barn";
?>
</body>
</html>
```

Figure 10.2: A simple PHP script.

Statement Terminator

The semicolon is used to indicate the end of a PHP command. The semicolon is not required, but it is good practice to always include it to show that a command is complete.

Comments

Comments can be included anywhere within the PHP script to document your code or make it more readable. Comments used in PHP are no less important than comments used in any other programming language. They often make ongoing support easier because they enable other developers to understand your code. As with any other language in a business environment, documentation standards for PHP should be defined, including standards for comments.

Two types of comments can be used in PHP:

- Two slashes (//) indicate a single-line comment. Everything to the end of the current line is considered a comment and ignored.

- The combination "/*" and "*/" indicates a single- or multiple-line comment. Everything between the /* and */ characters is considered a comment and ignored.

Figure 10.3 shows both kinds of comment lines included in a PHP script.

```
</html>
<head>
</head>
<body>
<?php
/*  PHP1003.php
    This script displays welcome text
*/
echo "Welcome to Bills Barbeque Barn!"; // display welcome text
?>
</body>
</html>
```

Figure 10.3: PHP comments.

Echo

The **echo** command is used to send text to the browser for display. The command is quite simple, starting with the word *echo* followed by a variable, or the text you would like displayed in quotation marks, and ending with a semicolon. Figure 10.3 uses **echo** to display "Welcome to Bills Barbeque Barn!"

Variables

Variables are used for storing values, including text strings, numbers, or arrays. A variable in PHP must start with a dollar sign. Once a variable is set in PHP, it can be used over and over again within a script.

Unlike some other Web programming languages, PHP is a *loosely typed* language, meaning you can assign a value to a new variable whenever you would like, and start using the variable. Variables do not need to be declared before they are used. PHP will automatically convert variables to the correct data type depending on the values used to set the variables. In a *strongly typed* language, you need to declare or define the variable and the variable name and type before you are able to use it.

Here is a summary of the variable-naming rules for PHP:

- A variable must start with the dollar sign.
- A variable name must start with an underscore (_) or a letter.
- A variable cannot contain spaces. If a variable name contains more than one word, separate the words with underscores or use capitalization to distinguish them, as in *$variable_name* or *$variableName*.
- A variable name can only contain alphanumeric characters and underscores. Special characters cannot be used.

The syntax for setting a variable in PHP is as follows:

$variableName = value;

Figure 10.4 is an example of setting a variable value with a string and a variable with a number.

```
</html>
<head>
</head>
<body>
<?php
/* PHP1005 Defining Variables */
$text1 = "Welcome to Bills Barbeque Barn ";
$number1 = 1017;
echo $text1;
echo $number1;
?>
</body>
</html>
```

Figure 10.4: Setting a variable string and number value.

In this example, the text1 string is set to the value "Welcome to Bills Barbeque Barn" and the number1 number is set to the value 1017, so the message "Welcome to Bills Barbeque Barn 1017" would be displayed in the Web browser.

Expressions

The value of a variable assignment does not have to be a fixed value. It can be an expression. An expression is two or more values combined using an operator to produce a result, like this:

```
$sum = 16 + 30;
Echo $sum;
```

In this example, the variable **$sum** takes the value of the expression to the right of the equal sign. The value of 16 is added to 30, so the result would display the number 46 using the **echo** command.

Taking the example one step further, the same addition operation can be performed on two variables:

```
$qty1 = 16;
$qty2 = 30;
$totalqty = $qty1 + $qty2;
echo $totalqty;
```

The values of **$qty1** and **$qty2** are added together, and using **echo**, the number 46 would again be displayed.

Data types

Every variable that holds a value also has a data type that defines what kind of value it is holding. The basic data types in PHP are listed in Table 10.3.

Table 10.3: Data Types		
Data Type	**Description**	**Value**
Boolean	A truth value	Either true or false
Integer	A numeric value	Either a positive or negative whole number
Double or float	A floating-point numeric value	Any decimal number
String	An alphanumeric value	Any number of ASCII characters

The data type of a variable is set when a value is assigned. The data type is determined automatically based on the value assigned. The **gettype** function can be used to determine the PHP data type. Figure 10.5 is an example of using the **gettype** function. In this case, the result returned will be "double."

```
</html>
<head>
</head>
<body>
<?php
/* PHP1009 gettype Function Example */
$price = 9.999;
echo gettype($price);
?>
</body>
</html>
```

*Figure 10.5: The **gettype** function.*

Operators

The standard operators used by most other scripting languages are also used within PHP. Tables 10.4 through 10.7 list the operators supported.

Table 10.4: Arithmetic Operators			
Operator	Description	Example	Result
+	Addition	x=5, y=7 x+y	12
-	Subtraction	x=3, y=1 x-y	2
*	Multiplication	x=2, y=4 x*y	8
/	Division	x=4, y=2 x/y	2
%	Modulus(division remainder)	x=5, y=2 x%y	1 (remainder of 5/2)
++	Increment	x=2 x++	3
--	Decrement	x=2 x--	1

The basic assignment operator is the equals sign, =. It doesn't mean "equal to." It means that the left operand gets set to the value of the expression on the right. In addition to this basic assignment operator, there are "combined operators" for all of the binary arithmetic and string operators that allow you to use a value in an expression and then set its value to the result of that expression.

Table 10.5: Assignment Operators				
Operator	Description	Example	Result	Is the same as
=	Assignment	y=2 x=y	x=2	x=y
+=	Increment assignment	x=2, y=3 x+=y	x=5	x=x+y
-=	Decrement assignment	x=5, y=3 x-=y	x=2	x=x-y
*=	Multiplication assignment	x=5, y=3 x*=y	x=15	x=x*y
/=	Division assignment	x=6, y=2 x/=y	x=3	x=x/y
%=	Modulus assignment	x=6, y=5 x%=y	x=1	x=x%y

Comparison operators, as the name implies, allow you to compare two values.

Table 10.6: Comparison Operators			
Operator	Description	Example	Result
==	Is equal to	x=5, y=5, z=7 x==y x==z	True False
!=	Is not equal to	x=5, y=5, z=7 x!=y x!=z	False True
>	Is greater than	x=5, y=6, z=3 x>y x>z	False True
<	Is less than	x=5, y=6, z=3 x<y x<z	True False
>=	Is greater than or equal to	x=5, y=6, z=3 x>=y x>=z	False True
<=	Is less than or equal to	x=5, y=6, z=3 x<=y x<=z	True False

In addition to comparison operators, PHP also uses logical operators. Logical operators are typically used when you want to test more than one condition at a time.

Table 10.7: Logical Operators			
Operator	Description	Example	Result
&&	And	x=5 x==5 && x<3 x>3 && x==5	 False True
||	Or	x=5 x>3 || x>6 x==4 || x==3	 True False
!	Not	x=5 !(x==5) !(x==4)	 False True

Conditional Statements

Conditional statements are used to perform actions based on whether a condition is true or false. They provide the ability to perform different actions for different decisions. Conditional statements are case-sensitive and must be written in lowercase, as shown in Table 10.8.

Table 10.8: Conditional Statements	
Statement	Description
if	Code is executed only if a specified condition is true.
if else	One block of code is executed if the condition is true, and another block of code is executed if the condition is false.
elseif	One of multiple blocks of code is executed when the condition used in the block of code is true.
switch	This statement is similar to a series of if statements on the same expression. It is useful when you want to compare the same variable or expression with many different values, and execute a different block of code depending on which value it is equal to.

If Statements

The **if** statement is used when code is to be executed when a single condition is true.

> **If (*condition*)**
> *code to execute if condition is true*;

In the example in Figure 10.6, an initial welcome message is displayed, "Welcome to Bills Barbeque Barn Employee Page." Then, the password is set to "BBQEmployee." The **if** condition is now true, so another welcome greeting is displayed, "Welcome to the Employee Work Schedule Page." Note that the **
** tags result in the messages being on separate lines.

```
<html>
<body>
<?php
/* PHP1011 - Example if statement */
echo("Welcome to Bills Barbeque Barn Employee Page" . "<br>");
$password = "BBQEmployee";
if ($password=="BBQEmployee")
        echo ("Welcome to the Employee Work Schedule Page" .
  "<br>");
?>
</body>
</html>
```

*Figure 10.6: An example of the **if** statement.*

The **if else** statement is used when code is to be executed when a single condition is false.

> **if (condition)**
> **code to execute if condition is true;**
> **else**
> **code to execute if condition is false;**

The example in Figure 10.7 is very similar to Figure 10.6, but we have added additional code to include an **else**.

```
<html>
<body>
<?php
/* PHP1014 - Example if else statement */
echo("Welcome to Bills Barbeque Barn Employee Page" . "<br>");
$password = "BBQManager";
if ($password=="BBQEmployee")
        echo ("Welcome to the Employee Work Schedule Page" .
        "<br>");
else
        echo ("The Password is invalid." . "<br>");
?>
</body>
</html>
```

*Figure 10.7: An example of **if else**.*

Making this change, if the password value is anything other than "BBQEmployee," a message will be displayed informing the site user that the password is invalid, as shown in Figure 10.8.

> ***Password entered is not = "BBQEmployee"***
>
> Welcome to Bills Barbeque Barn Employee Page.
> The Password is Invalid

Figure 10.8: The results from Figure 10.7 for an invalid password.

The **if elseif else** statement is used when multiple conditions are tested. When the **if** condition is true, the block of code associated with that statement will be executed. When it is not true, the **elseif** condition will be tested, and if true, the associated block of code will be executed. The statement might contain multiple **elseif** statements. Finally, when the **if** and all of the **elseif** conditions are not true, the final **else** is used to associate a block of code to execute.

```
if (condition1)
    code to execute if condition is true;
elseif (condition2);
    code to execute if condition2 is true;
else
    code to execute if condition1 and 2 are false;
```

The **if elseif else** example will use forms and two documents, *PHP1017. html* and *PHP1017.php*, shown in Figure 10.9. Any form element in an HTML page will automatically be made available to your PHP scripts. The HTML page includes a form to prompt the user for a password. When the user enters a password and clicks Submit, the form data is sent to the PHP1017.php file. The password is then used for conditional logic.

```
HTML document PHP1017.html:

<html>
<body>
Welcome to Bills Barbeque Barn!
<form action="PHP1017.php" method="post">
Password: <input type="text" name="password"/>
<input type="submit" />
</form>
</body>
</html>

PHP document PHP1017.php:

<html>
<body>
<?php
```

*Figure 10.9: The **if elseif else** statement (part 1 of 2).*

```
/* PHP1017 - Example elseif statement */
if ($_POST["password"] == "BBQEmployee")
        echo ("Welcome to the Employee Work Schedule Page" .
        "<br>");
elseif ($_POST["password"] == "BBQManager")
        echo ("Welcome to the Manager Work Schedule Page" .
        "<br>");
else
        echo ("The Password Entered is Invalid" . "<br>");
?>
</body>
</html>
```

Figure 10.9: The *if elseif else* statement (part 2 of 2).

The conditional logic of the **if elseif else** statement controls the actions performed. As shown in Figure 10.10, if the user enters the password "BBQEmployee," the message "Welcome to the Employee Work Schedule" is displayed. If the user enters "BBQManager," the password "Welcome to the Manager Work Schedule Page" is displayed. Otherwise, the message "The Password Entered is Invalid" is displayed.

Password entered = "BBQEmployee"

Welcome to the Employee Work Schedule Page

Password entered = "BBQManager:

Welcome to the Manager Work Schedule Page

Any other Password entered:

The Password Entered is Invalid

Figure 10.10: The results from the code in Figure 10.9.

The Switch Statement

The **switch** statement is used to execute one of multiple blocks of code. It is often used in place of a long **if elseif else** statement to execute one of multiple blocks of code. The **case**, **default**, and **break** keywords are often used with **switch**. The **break** keyword will end execution of the **switch** when the **case** condition is true.

```
switch(expression)
case 1:
    execute code block 1;
    break;
case 2:
    execute code block 2;
    default:
    execute code block when case 1 and case 2 are false;
```

The example in Figure 10.11 is very similar to the one in Figure 10.9. In fact, the prompt screen is exactly the same. Again, the password is passed, but this time, the code uses switch, case, break, and default to handle the different conditions. The results will be the same as Figure 10.10.

```
HTML Document PHP1021.html:

<body>
Welcome to Bills Barbeque Barn!
<form action="PHP1021.php" method="post">
Password:
  <input type="text" name="password"/>
<input type="submit" />
</form>
</body>
</html>
```

```
PHP Document PHP1021.php:

<html>
<body>
<?php
/* PHP1021 - Example switch statement */

switch ($_POST["password"])
{
case "BBQEmployee":
        echo ("Welcome to the Employee Work Schedule Page" .
          "<br>");
        break;
case "BBQManager":
        echo ("Welcome to the Manager Work Schedule Page" .
          "<br>");
        break;
default:
        echo ("The Password Entered is Invalid" . "<br>");
}
?>
</body>
</html>
```

*Figure 10.11: The **switch** statement.*

Notice the syntax of **case** in Figure 10.11: curly braces enclose the statements, and **break** is used when a match is found so that the remaining case statements are not executed. The **default** statement provides the action when none of the criteria are true. The same example could be used for many other applications, including customer and vendor inquiries.

Loops

PHP has two kinds of loops, the **while** loop and the **for** loop. The **for** loop executes the same block of code a specified number of times. The **while** loop executes a block of code when a condition is true.

While loops

The syntax for a **while** loop is quite simple:

```
while(condition)
statement
```

The loop will repeat until the condition is no longer true. Figure 10.12 defines a loop that displays the line count when the condition variable **$count** is less than five. The variable **$count** is initialized to one before the loop begins and is incremented by one each time the loop is executed, resulting in the following:

BBQ Line 1
BBQ Line 2
BBQ Line 3
BBQ Line 4

```
<html>
<body>
<?php
/* PHP1023 - Example of while loop */
$count=1;
while($count<5)
  {
  echo "BBQ Line " . $count . "<br />";
  $count++;
  }
?>
</body>
</html>
```

Figure 10.12: The *while* loop.

The **do while** loop is a variation on the **while** loop. This loop always executes a block of code once, and then repeats the loop as long as the condition is true. The condition is tested after the loop statement(s) are executed.

```
do
{
statement;
statement;
}
while (condition);
```

Figure 10.13 defines a loop that will execute at least once and will execute while the condition variable **$count** is less than zero. The variable **$count** is incremented by one each time the loop is executed. The statement is true until **$count** is no longer less than zero. This loop always executes at least once, as shown in the results in Figure 10.14.

```
<html>
<body>
<?php
/* PHP1026 - Example of do while loop */
$count=0;
do
{
  echo "BBQ Line " . $count . "<br />";
  $count++;
}
while ($count<0);
?>
</body>
</html>
```

*Figure 10.13: The **do while** loop.*

BBQ Line 0

Same Example Change line of code while ($count<0) to while ($count<=5).

BBQ Line 0
BBQ Line 1
BBQ Line 2
BBQ Line 3
BBQ Line 4

Figure 10.14: The results from executing the code in Figure 10.13.

For loops

The **for** loop repeats the specified condition until the condition is false. A **for** loop begins with an expression to initialize counters. Next, the condition of the expression is evaluated and followed by an expression to increment the counter. If the condition is false, the loop terminates. If the condition is true, the loop's statements execute. Multiple statements can be included using curly braces and semicolons.

```
for (initialization; condition; increment)
{
statement;
statement;
}
```

The example in Figure 10.15 begins with variable **$count** being initialized to one. The loop will continue to run as long as **$count** is less than or equal to four, resulting in the following:

BBQ Line 1
BBQ Line 2
BBQ Line 3
BBQ Line 4

```
<html>
<body>
<?php
/* PHP1029 - Example for loop */
for ($count=1; $count<=4; $count++)
{
echo "BBQ Line " . $count . "<br />";
}
?>
</body>
</html>
```

*Figure 10.15: The **for** loop.*

The **foreach** loop is used to loop through arrays. For each loop, the value of the current array element is assigned to a variable. The array index is incremented by one, and the next cycle through the loop will look at the next element in the array.

```
foreach (array as value)
{
statement;
statement;
}
```

The example in Figure 10.16 executes the **echo** statement for each element in the BBQ sauce array, as shown in Figure 10.17.

```
<html>
<body>
<?php
/* PHP1032 - Example foreach loop */
$bbqsaucearray=array("Traditional.", "Sweet and Mild.", "Honey
  Mustard.", "Tangy Twist.", "Hot and Spicy.", "Flaming Hot");
foreach ($bbqsaucearray as $value)
{
echo $value . "<br />";
}
?>
</body>
</html>
```

*Figure 10.16: The **foreach** loop.*

Traditional.
Sweet and Mild.

Honey Mustard.

Tangy Twist.

Hot and Spicy.

Flaming Hot.

Figure 10.17: The results from the code in Figure 10.16.

Arrays

An array is a variable type that can store and index a set of values. Arrays are useful for data that has something in common or is logically grouped, like the array that contains BBQ sauces in Figure 10.16. An array can be visualized as a table, like a spreadsheet. Like most other programming languages, PHP is capable of using arrays, although its syntax might be a little different than you might be used to.

Arrays are stored with a unique key, usually referred to as an *index*. The index provides each element of data an ID so that it can be easily accessed. Array indexes are usually numeric, but can also be another assigned value.

Array indexing, if not specified, begins with the numeric index 0. In the example in Figure 10.18, the index is automatically assigned. In the example in Figure 10.19, the index is manually assigned.

```
$bbqsaucearray[ ] = "Traditional.";
$bbqsaucearray[ ] = "Sweet and Mild.";
$bbqsaucearray[ ] = "Honey Mustard..";
$bbqsaucearray[ ] = "Tangy Twist.";
$bbqsaucearray[ ] = "Hot and Spicy.";
$bbqsaucearray[ ] = "Flaming Hot.";
```

Figure 10.18: An array with an index automatically assigned.

```
$bbqsaucearray[0] = "Traditional.";
$bbqsaucearray[1] = "Sweet and Mild.";
$bbqsaucearray[2] = "Honey Mustard..";
$bbqsaucearray[3] = "Tangy Twist.";
$bbqsaucearray[4] = "Hot and Spicy.";
$bbqsaucearray[5] = "Flaming Hot.";
```

Figure 10.19: An array with an index manually assigned.

Once an array is defined and populated, it is ready to be used. An *associative array* uses a textual key for the index to make the index more descriptive. The examples in Figures 10.20 and 10.21 define arrays using associative indexes. The syntax is a little different for each. In Figure 10.20, the index is defined within single quotes and the element are within double quotes. In Figure 10.21, the index is in double quotes and the symbol "=>" is used to show the relationship between the index and the element value. Note that the array index must be unique.

```
$bbqprice['Traditional']   = "3.89";
$bbqprice['Sweet and Mild'] = "3.59";
$bbqprice['Honey Mustard']  = "3.69";
$bbqprice['Tangy Twist']    = "3.79";
$bbqprice['Hot and Spicy']  = "3.99";
$bbqprice['Flaming Hot']    = "3.49";
```

Figure 10.20: One way to define an array with an associative index.

```
$bbqprice = array("Traditional" => 3.89, "Sweet and Mild" =>
  3.59, "Honey Mustard" => 3.69, "Tangy Twist" => 3.79, "Hot and
  Spicy" => 3.99, "Flaming Hot" => 3.49);
```

Figure 10.21: An alternative way to define an array with an associative index.

Arrays can be very useful, and there are limitless possibilities for using them within business applications. In the example in Figure 10.22, the BBQ-sauce price array is used to sort and display the list of sauces ordered by price, as shown in Figure 10.23. (This code also uses **assort,** a predefined function that can be used with arrays. Functions are explained later in this chapter.)

```
<html>
<body>
<?php
/* PHP1039 - Example sorted associative array */
$bbqprice['Traditional']    = "3.89";
$bbqprice['Sweet and Mild'] = "3.59";
$bbqprice['Honey Mustard']  = "3.69";
$bbqprice['Tangy Twist']    = "3.79";
$bbqprice['Hot and Spicy']  = "3.99";
$bbqprice['Flaming Hot']    = "3.49";
asort($bbqprice);
foreach ($bbqprice as $sauce => $price)
{
echo "$sauce: $price <br />";
}
?>
</body>
</html>
```

Figure 10.22: An array with an associative index, sorted and displayed.

Flaming Hot: 3.49
Sweet and Mild: 3.59
Honey Mustard: 3.69
Tangy Twist: 3.79
Traditional: 3.89
Hot and Spicy: 3.99

Figure 10.23: The results from Figure 10.22.

Multidimensional Arrays

PHP can also use multidimensional arrays. A multidimensional array is an array that contains more arrays. Think of it like a spreadsheet that has multiple rows and multiple columns. The multidimensional array is very similar to a regular array in how it is defined and used. The example in Figure 10.24 uses a multidimensional sales array. Within the sales array are the arrays "Traditional," and "Hot," and "Spicy." The contents within the arrays represent the sales quantities by month; thus, there are 12 entries in each array.

```
<html>
<body>
<?php
/* PHP1041 Multidimensional array example sales by month for bbq
   sauces */
$sales = array
(
"Traditional"=>array
(
"5,000", "4,500", "4,750", "5,200", "5,000", "4,200",
"5,200", "4,960", "5,010", "4,325", "6,300", "7,200"
),
"Hot and Spicy"=>array
(
"3,000", "2,500", "3,750", "3,300", "3,000", "5,200",
"6,200", "3,020", "5,010", "3,325", "4,300", "5,300"
)
);
print_r ($sales);
echo "<br />";
echo "<br />";
echo "Sales for Traditional in January were ", $sales["Tradition
   al"][0], "<br />";
?>
</body>
</html>
```

Figure 10.24: A multidimensional array.

This code prints out the value of the array using the **print_r** statement, as show in Figure 10.25.

Array ([Traditional] => Array ([0] => 5,000 [1] => 4,500 [2] => 4,750 [3] => 5,200 [4] => 5,000 [5] => 4,200 [6] => 5,200 [7] => 4,960 [8] => 5,010 [9] => 4,325 [10] => 6,300 [11] => 7,200) [Hot and Spicy] => Array ([0] => 3,000 [1] => 2,500 [2] => 3,750 [3] => 3,300 [4] => 3,000 [5] => 5,200 [6] => 6,200 [7] => 3,020 [8] => 5,010 [9] => 3,325 [10] => 4,300 [11] => 5,300))

Sales for Traditional in January were 5,000

Figure 10.25: The results from Figure 10.24.

Functions

Functions make the PHP scripting language very powerful. A function is used to define a task that may consist of many lines of code. Once defined, the function can be called using a single instruction. PHP has hundreds of predefined functions that perform a wide range of tasks. Some of the functions are built into the PHP language, and others are available only after specific extensions are installed and activated within PHP.

In this chapter, we will review some of the predefined functions. Appendix C provides a more complete reference to these functions, but the list is still not all-inclusive. For a complete list, visit the official PHP Web site, *www.php.net*. This Web site provides extensive information on the PHP language and is a very useful reference.

Following is a list of some of the PHP built-in functions available. These functions are part of the PHP core language and require no special installation, except that the Linux platform requires a special update to the php.ini file for the calendar, FTP, and MySQL functions. Details on the configuration and update of php.ini can be found at *www.php.net*.

- *Array functions*—The array functions allow you to manipulate arrays. There are also specific functions for populating arrays from database queries.

- *Calendar functions*—The calendar functions are useful when working with different calendar formats.

- *Date/time functions*—The date/time functions allow you to extract and format the date and time on the server. These functions depend on the local settings on the server. Date/time functions require runtime configuration through settings in the php.ini file.

- *DB2 functions*—These functions enable access to IBM's DB2 Universal Database, IBM Cloudscape, and the Apache Derby databases using the DB2 Call Level Interface (DB2 CLI).

- *dBase functions*—These functions allow you to access records stored in dBase-format (.dbf) databases.

- *Directory functions*—The directory functions allow you to retrieve information about directories and their contents.

- *Error functions*—The error and logging functions allow errorhandling and logging. The error functions allow users to define error-handling rules and modify the way the errors can be logged. The logging functions allow users to log applications and send log messages to email, system logs, or other machines.

- *Filesystem functions*—The filesystem functions allow you to access and manipulate the file system.

- *Filter functions*—The filter functions validate and filter data coming from insecure sources, like user input.

- *FTP functions*—The FTP functions give client access to file servers through the File Transfer Protocol (FTP). The FTP functions are used to open, log in, and close connections, as well as upload, download, rename, delete, and get information on files from file servers. Not all of the FTP functions work with every server or return the same results. These functions are meant for detailed access to an FTP server. If you only want to read from or write to a file on an FTP server, consider using the *ftp://* wrapper with the filesystem functions.

- *HTTP functions*—The HTTP functions let you manipulate information sent to the browser by the Web server, before any other output has been sent.

- *Mail functions*—The mail functions allow you to send emails directly from a script. For the mail functions to be available, you must have an installed and working email system. The program to be used is defined by the configuration settings in the php.ini file.

- *Math functions*—The math functions can handle values within the range of integer and float types.

- *Miscellaneous functions*—Miscellaneous functions are those that do not fit within the other categories.

- *MySQL functions*—The MySQL functions allow you to access MySQL database servers.

- *SimpleXML functions*—The SimpleXML functions let you convert XML to an object. This object can be processed like any other object, with normal property selectors and array iterators. Some of these functions requires the newest PHP build.

- *String functions*—The string functions allow you to manipulate strings.

- *XML parser functions*—These functions let you parse, but not validate, XML documents.

As mentioned earlier, there are many more functions available through PHP, specific to particular databases, operating systems, FTP, Java, .NET, and many more. When coding business applications, you will use functions. These are the tools that make it easy to incorporate extended functionality within an application with very little coding.

Functions can be very useful, especially for code that is reused. Use a modular approach to coding by grouping tasks into functions to help keep code more manageable. In addition to predefined, built-in functions, PHP functions can be user-defined. Every function has a prototype that defines how many arguments it takes, the arguments' data types, and what value is returned by the function. Optional arguments are shown in square braces ([ ]). This applies to both predefined and user-defined functions.

A function begins with the word *function*, followed by a function name that should identify what it does, and parentheses that will hold any parameters. The name can start with a letter or an underscore, but not a number. The code executed when the function is called is contained within curly braces. Figure 10.26 is an example of creating a user-defined function that will display the welcome message "Welcome to Bills Barbeque Barn!"

```
<html>
<body>
<?php
/* PHP1043 User defined function to display welcome message */
function display_welcome()
 {
echo "Welcome to Bills Barbeque Barn!" . "<br />";
}
display_welcome();
?>
</body>
</html>
```

Figure 10.26: The **display_welcome()** user-defined function.

The example in Figure 10.27 uses another user-defined function to calculate sales tax. This example involves a parameter contained within the function's parentheses and used just like a variable.

```
<html>
<body>
<?php
/* PHP1045 User defined function to calculate sales tax */
function salestax($amount)
{
$total = $amount * .06;
return $total;
}
$price = 3.99;
$taxamount = salestax($price);
$total = $taxamount + $price;
echo "Unit Price : " . $price . "<br />";
echo "Tax Amount : " . salestax($price) . "<br />";
echo "Total : " . $total;
?>
</body>
</html>
```

Figure 10.27: A user-defined function with a parameter.

When the **salestax()** function is called in Figure 10.27, the block of code defined within the function will execute, using the argument stored in the variable **$amount**. In this example, **salestax()**is called once to calculate the value of the variable **$taxamount**. Next, the total is calculated by adding **$price** and **$taxamount**, and the value is returned from the function. The example then displays the unit price, tax amount, and total, as shown:

Unit Price : 3.99
Tax Amount : 0.2394
Total : 4.2294

The next example uses a function stored in a separate PHP file, shown in Figure 10.28. A separate file can contain common created functions for use on multiple site pages. The file is included within the current page using the **include** statement, as shown in Figure 10.29. The function in this example calculates an extended price using two parameters, the quantity and the price, passed to the function. After calling the function, the quantity, price, and extended price are displayed. Having a common function file enables you to make changes in one place to change the way a function works on many pages.

```
<html>
<body>
<?php
/* PHP1047 User defined functions */
function ext_price($price, $quantity)
{
$extprice = $price * $quantity;
return $extprice;
}
?>
</body>
</html>
```

Figure 10.28: A function included from a separate file.

```
<html>
<body>
<?php
/* PHP1048 Calculate extended price */
include ("PHP1047.php");
$quantity = 5;
$price = 3.99;
echo "quantity " . $quantity . "<br />";
echo "price " . $price . "<br />";
echo "extended price" . ext_price($quantity, $price);
?>
</body>
</html>
```

Figure 10.29: Calculating an extended price with a function from a separate file.

With these examples, you can see how easy it is to define and use functions in PHP. Predefined functions work the same way.

Getting Down to Business with PHP

Now the fun begins. We'll introduce, discuss, and work through examples that can be used to provide PHP functionality within business Web applications.

Cookies

A cookie is a small file that is stored on the visitor's computer. Each time the same computer requests a page with a browser, it will send the cookie, too. PHP provides the ability to create and retrieve cookie values. Most current versions of popular browsers are capable of supporting cookies. A form may also be used to retain and pass data. Use of cookies allows functionality that may be similar to what has been used for other business applications that display a name, ID, or other information specific to an application user. Is this critical to a business application? It might be, depending on the specifics of an application. It is common to provide user-specific information or to use environment details to control application logic or for informational purposes.

Cookies can be used for a variety of reasons. A cookie might be used to control the message displayed when the user visits a site, retain a password so a returning user won't be required to enter it, or store the date so the next time a visitor returns to the site, the date of the last visit is displayed. For example, a purchasing-department inquiry application might display the last date the user accessed the page, to make it easier for the user to identify new entries.

The predefined **setcookie()** function is used to create a cookie. This function must appear before the **<html>** tag. The instruction to create a cookie is sent as an HTTP header before a Web page is transmitted. A cookie has an expiration date. Some cookies only last as long as the Web browser is open and are kept in the client computer's memory. A cookie can also have a fixed expiration date and can be saved on the client hard drive. The cookie will be removed when the browser is closed if the **expires** attribute is not sent in the **setcookie()** function.

In the example in Figure 10.30, the visitor's name will be retained in the cookie **visitor_name**. The cookie is set to expire 60 days from the last visit, using the **time()** function (60 seconds x 60 hours x 24 hours x 60 days = 5,184,000 seconds). In this example, the cookie is retained on the log-out page. This is so we don't display the "welcome back" message the first time a user visits the page.

```php
<?php
// PHP1049 Logout page retain visitor name
// information will be retained for 60 days
setcookie(visitor_name, "Joe Walsh", time()+5184000);
?>
<html>
<head>
</head>
<body>
Thank you for visiting Bills Barbeque Barn!
</body>
</html></html>
```

Figure 10.30: Creating a cookie.

In Figure 10.31, there is a check to determine if the cookie exists. If it does, the name is used to format the "welcome back" message.

```
html>
<body>
<?php
/* PHP1050 check for cookie display welcome message */
if(isset($_COOKIE['visitor_name']))
{
$name = $_COOKIE['visitor_name'];
echo "Welcome back to Bills Barbeque Barn! " . $name;
}
else
{
echo "Welcome to Bills Barbeque Barn!";
}
?>
</body>
</html>
```

Figure 10.31: Checking for a cookie and retrieving its value.

This example will welcome back a site user who has visited within 60 days, as shown in Figure 10.32.

First time user visits site:

Welcome to Bills Barbeque Barn!

On users return visit within 60 days of last visit:

Welcome back to Bills Barbeque Barn! Joe Walsh

Figure 10.32: The results from the cookie created and used in Figures 10.30 and 10.31.

To delete a cookie, set the expiration date to a date in the past, as shown in Figure 10.33. The cookie will be removed.

```
<?php
// PHP1051 Delete Cookie
setcookie(visitor_name, " ", time()-5184600);
?>
<html>
<head>
</head>
<body>
</body>
</html>
```

Figure 10.33: Deleting a cookie.

The same cookie example may be used within many business applications, including a customer, vendor or employee inquiry page, or any other place where this user-specific information would be useful.

Date/Time

Dates are an important part of business applications and are often used in programming logic. PHP does not have a native date data type, but it does have the **date()** function, which formats a timestamp to a readable date and time. A *timestamp* is the number of seconds since midnight on January 1, 1970. This is also known as the *Unix timestamp*. The maximum value of a Unix timestamp depends on the system's architecture. Most systems use a 32-bit integer to store a timestamp, in which case the latest time that can be represented is 3:14 A.M. on January 19, 2038.

To find the current timestamp, use the **time()** function. To provide the date in a particular format, use the **date()** function with a format code included as a parameter. Figure 10.34 uses **time()**, followed by **date()** with various format codes for different types of date formatting.

```
<html>
<body>
<?php
/* PHP1053 Date and Time function example  */
echo "Time function: " . time() . "<br />";
echo "Date function Format Codes:" . "<br />";
echo "a---Lowercase am or pm-------------------------: " . date(a) . "<br />";
echo "A---Upper case AM or PM------------------------: " . date(A) . "<br />";
echo "d---Two digit day of month 01 - 31-------------: " . date(d) . "<br />";
echo "D---Three letter day name Mon - Sun------------: " . date(D) . "<br />";
```

*Figure 10.34: The **time()** and **date()** functions (part 1 of 2).*

```
echo "F---Full month name January - December---------: " . date(F) . "<br />";
echo "g---12 hour hour with no leading zero 0 - 23----: " . date(g) . "<br />";
echo "G---24 hour hour with no leading zero 0 - 23----: " . date(G) . "<br />";
echo "h---12 hour hour with leading zero 01 - 12------: " . date(h) . "<br />";
echo "H---24 hour hour with leading zero 00 - 23------: " . date(H) . "<br />";
echo "I---Minutes with leading zero 00 - 59----------: " . date(I) . "<br />";
echo "j---Day of month with no leading zero 1 - 31----: " . date(j) . "<br />";
echo "l---Full day name Monday - Sunday--------------: " . date(l) . "<br />";
echo "m---Month number with leading zeros 01 - 12-----: " . date(m) . "<br />";
echo "M---Three letter month name Jan - Dec----------: " . date(M) . "<br />";
echo "n---Month number with no leading zeros 1 - 12---: " . date(n) . "<br />";
echo "s---Seconds with leading zero 00 - 59----------: " . date(s) . "<br />";
echo "S---Ordinal suffix for day of mo st,nd,rd or th-: " . date(S) . "<br />";
echo "w---Number of day of week 0 - 6, 0 is Sunday----: " . date(w) . "<br />";
echo "W---Week number 0 - 53-------------------------: " . date(W) . "<br />";
echo "y---Two digit year number----------------------: " . date(y) . "<br />";
echo "Y---Four digit year number---------------------: " . date(Y) . "<br />";
echo "z---Day of year 0 - 365------------------------: " . date(z) . "<br />";
?>
</body>
</html>
```

*Figure 10.34: The **time()** and **date()** functions (part 2 of 2).*

Figure 10.35 shows the results from running the code in Figure 10.34 for Tuesday, August 21, 2007, at 10:01 P.M.

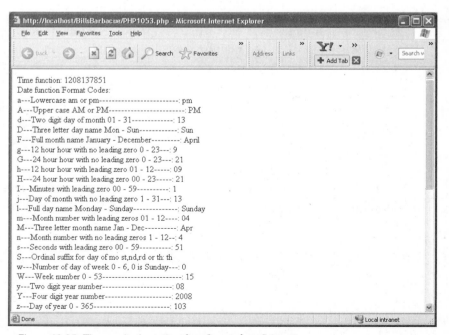

*Figure 10.35: The results from the **time()** and **date()** functions.*

Characters like dashes, slashes, and periods can be inserted in the **date()** parameter to provide additional formatting. For example, the code in Figure 10.36 would produce the results like this:

The current date is: Tuesday August 21,2007 23:1:58

The current date in YYYY/MM/DD format:2007/08/21

```
<html>
<body>
<?php
/* PHP1055 Formatted date function examples */
echo "The current date is: " . date("l F d,Y H:I:s") . "<br />";
echo "<br />";
echo "The current date in YYYY/MM/DD format:" . date("Y/m/d");
?>
</body>
</html>
```

*Figure 10.36: Adding additional formatting to **date()** examples.*

The **date()** function actually allows two parameters:

date(*format, timestamp*)

The previous examples used the **format** parameter. The **timestamp** parameter is optional. If it is not provided, the current time will be used.

The "make time" function, **mktime()**, can be used for date calculations. Its format is as follows:

mktime(*hour, minute, second, month, day, year, is_dst*)

The example in Figure 10.37 uses **mktime()** to calculate a date that is one year, one month, and one day in the future, to determine the account expiration date. If today's date was 08/21/2007, this example would display the following:

Your account will expire on: 09/22/2008

```
<html>
<body>
<?php
/* PHP1058 Make time function calculate date 1 year, 1 month and
   1 day from the current date example  */
$expire_date = mktime(0,0,0,date("m")+1, date("d")+1,date("Y")+1);
echo "Today's date is: " . date("m/d/Y") . "<br />";
echo "<br />";
echo "Your account will expire on: " . date("m/d/Y", $expire_
   date);
?>
</body>
</html>
```

*Figure 10.37: The **mktime()** function.*

This section has barely scratched the surface of date and time functionality, but the examples show how easy it is to work with dates in PHP and how powerful the predefined date functions are.

Email

Email is commonplace today. It is an accepted form of communication that can be incorporated into a business application for internal or external communication. For example, when an order is placed, an order-entry application might email the department responsible for processing orders with the message that activity to process the order should begin. An email could also be sent to the customer, with details about the order, including the expected delivery schedule.

While some traditional application-development languages do not provide functionality for easily sending email, email can be easily sent through PHP using the **mail()** function. All that is needed is an installed and working email system, and for the email server to be identified in the php. ini file. The authentication and authorization for your email server might need to be reviewed to determine the settings. In Figure 10.38, the default settings are used with the **sendmail_from** address changed.

```
[mail function]
; For Win32 only.
;SMTP = localhost
smtp_port = 25

; For Win32 only.
sendmail_from = myemail@sbcglobal.net
```

Figure 10.38: The php.ini email settings.

The format for the **mail()** function is as follows:

mail(*to,subject,message,headers,parameters*)

Sending a text message is the simplest way to send email using PHP. In Figure 10.39, a simple email message is sent to thank the customer for placing an order. In this example, the **ini_set()** function is used to set the value of the SMTP configuration.

```
<html>
<body>
<?php
/* PHP1062 Sending a text email example  */
ini_set('SMTP', 'mail.sbcglobal.net');
$to = "toemail@sbcglobal.net";
$subject = "Thank You";
$message = "Thank you for placing an order at Bills Barbeque
Barn!";
$from = "myemail@sbcglobal.net";
$headers = "From: $from";
mail($to,$subject,$message,$headers);
echo "Mail Sent.";
?>
</body>
</html>
```

Figure 10.39: A simple email example.

The message "mail sent" will be displayed on the site page. Figure 10.40 is the resulting email sent.

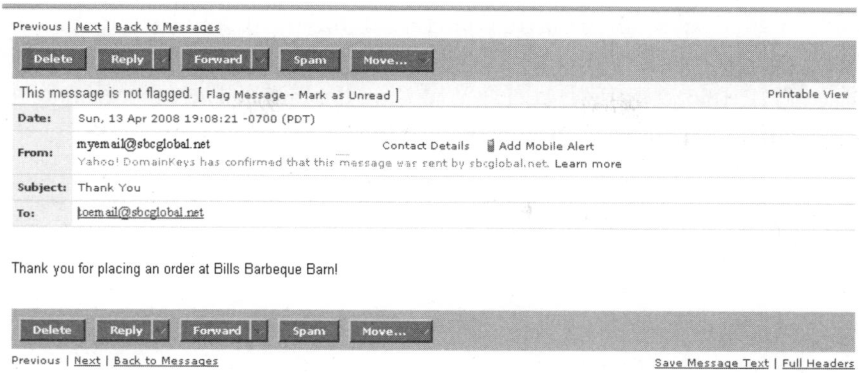

Previous | Next | Back to Messages

| Delete | Reply | Forward | Spam | Move... |

This message is not flagged. [Flag Message - Mark as Unread]   Printable View

Date:	Sun, 13 Apr 2008 19:08:21 -0700 (PDT)
From:	myemail@sbcglobal.net Contact Details Add Mobile Alert
	Yahoo! DomainKeys has confirmed that this message was sent by sbcglobal.net. Learn more
Subject:	Thank You
To:	toemail@sbcglobal.net

Thank you for placing an order at Bills Barbeque Barn!

| Delete | Reply | Forward | Spam | Move... |

Previous | Next | Back to Messages   Save Message Text | Full Headers

Figure 10.40: The email sent as a result of the code in Figure 10.39.

Email functions can also be used with forms. For example, you could use a feedback form to trigger an email. Figure 10.41 is such an HTML form, and Figure 10.42 is the PHP file used to send the email.

```html
<html>
<head>
<!** PHP1065 Customer service email form example **>
<br>
<form method="post" action="PHP1066.php">
  Email: <input name="email" type="text" /><br />
  Customer Service Message:<br />
  <textarea name="message" rows="15" cols="40">
  </textarea><br />
  <input type="submit" />
</form>
</head>
</html>
```

Figure 10.41: The HTML to create a customer-service feedback form.

```php
<head>
<?php
/* PHP1066 Email form example */
ini_set('SMTP', 'mail.sbcglobal.net');
  $to = "myemail@sbcglobal.net";
  $email = $_REQUEST['email'] ;
  $message = $_REQUEST['message'] ;
  mail( $to, "Customer Service Feedback",$message, $email );
  echo "Email sent";
?>
</head>
</html>
```

Figure 10.42: The PHP to send an email based on the form in Figure 10.41.

In this example, the form displayed in Figure 10.43 prompts for an email address and a customer-service message. When Submit is clicked, the PHP1066.php file is accessed to send the email. The **$to** variable is the email address that will receive the customer-service message.

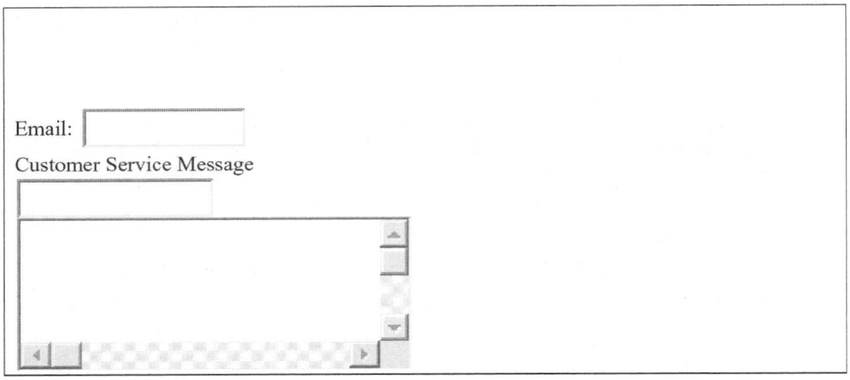

Figure 10.43: The form created from Figure 10.41.

The site user fills in the email address, enters a message, and clicks the Submit button. PHP1066.php is executed and displays the message "Email sent." The resulting email is shown in Figure 10.44.

Figure 10.44: A customer-service email.

Email Injection Attacks

The previous email examples have used hardcoded email addresses. PHP, like any language that uses the MIME and SMTP standards for sending email, has the potential problem of email injections. An *injection* is content inserted into the header level of an email. MIME and SMTP allow for multiple headers with the same name, enabling attackers to define additional recipients for a message or adding "bcc:" and "cc:." In addition, a message is open to attack. To prevent injections, input data should be validated or filtered when scripts are used for creating email.

The **preg_match()** function might be used to check for injections. This function performs a regular expression match, looking for a pattern, as shown in Figure 10.45. Alternatively, you might use the **strpos()** or **strstr()** function to check for the "at" sign (@) in an email address.

```
$email_address = '/^[^@\s]+@([-a-z0-9]+\.)+[a-z]{2,}$/i';
  if (!preg_match($email_address, $to_email))
  {
  echo "Email address entered is invalid.";
  }
```

*Figure 10.45: Checking for multiple email addresses using **preg_match()**.*

Another possibility for finding email injections is to use the **eregi()** function. The **eregi()** function is a case-insensitive regular expression match. Figure 10.46 shows an example of the use of this function.

```
<html>
<body>
<?php
/* PHP1071 email form example with email injection check */
function injectcheck($field)
  {
//eregi function used to perform case insensitive match on to:
  and cc:.
// using cc:  will also catch bcc:.

  if(eregi("to:",$field) || eregi("cc:",$field))
    {
    return TRUE;
    }
```

Figure 10.46: An email form with an email injection check (part 1 of 2).

```
   else
     {
     return FALSE;
     }
   }

//check to verify email field has been entered
echo $_REQUEST['email'];

if (isset($_REQUEST['email']))
   {
   //check email address for injection
   $emailcheck = injectcheck($_REQUEST['email']);
 echo $email;
   if ($emailcheck==TRUE)
     {
       echo "Email entered is invalid please correct and try
again.";
     }
   else
     {
     //send email
     $email = $_REQUEST['email'] ;
     $message = $_REQUEST['message'] ;
     mail("To: $email", "Subject: $subject",
     $message, "ubelhor@sbcglobal.net" );

         echo "Email sent to" . $email;
     }
   }
else
//if the email address hasn't been entered display the form
   {
   echo "<form method='post' action='PHP1072.php'>
   Email: <input name='email' type='text' /><br />
   Subject: <input name='subject' type='text' /><br />
   Customer Service Message:<br />
   <textarea name='message' rows='15' cols='40'>
   </textarea><br />
   <input type='submit' />
   </form>";
   }
?>
</body>
</html>
```

Figure 10.46: An email form with an email injection check (part 2 of 2).

Figure 10.47 is an email form that can be used as a template to send an email. The message, subject, and email address will need to be changed to valid values for the application.

```
<html>
<head>
<?php
/* PHP1072 Email form example */
ini_set('SMTP', 'mail.sbcglobal.net');
  $to = $_REQUEST['email'];
  $email = "email@sbcglobal.net";
  $message = $_REQUEST['message'] ;
  $subject = $_REQUEST['subject'] ;
  mail( $to, $subject,$message, $email );
  echo "Email sent";
?>
</head>
</html>
```

Figure 10.47: A template for an email form.

PHP Error Handling

PHP has a configurable error-reporting system that provides for a variety of error-reporting levels. The level can be changed through the error-reporting function with the error-reporting constants. Appendix C lists error-logging constants. To set the error-reporting level so that all warnings and notices are displayed, use the **error_reporting(E_ALL)**; setting.

The type of notices that are not displayed by default are not usually threatening and normally would not affect the execution of script. It might be helpful to use a different error level for development than for a production Web site. Displaying errors on the screen on a production Web site might pose a security risk, by exposing information that is not intended to be shared with site visitors, especially not potential intruders or competitors. The **log_errors** and **display_errors** configuration directives allow you to choose to have warnings displayed on the screen or written to a log file. The **display_errors** directive can be set to off in the php.ini file to prevent any errors from being displayed on screen.

Figure 10.48 is a snippet of the php.ini default settings. The semicolon indicates a comment line in the file. By default, **display_errors** is turned on. To turn it off, uncomment the line within the php.ini file designating **display_errors = Off** by removing the semicolon at the beginning of the line.

```
; - display_errors = Off          [Security]
;    With this directive set to off, errors that occur during the
execution of
;    scripts will no longer be displayed as a part of the script
output, and thus,
;    will no longer be exposed to remote users. With some errors,
the error message
;    content may expose information about your script, web server,
or database
;    server that may be exploitable for hacking. Production sites
should have this
;    directive set to off.
; - log_errors = On               [Security]
;    This directive complements the above one. Any errors that
occur during the
;    execution of your script will be logged (typically, to your
server's error log,
;    but can be configured in several ways). Along with setting
display_errors to off,
;    this setup gives you the ability to fully understand what may
have gone wrong,
;    without exposing any sensitive information to remote users.
```

Figure 10.48: The php.ini error settings.

Logging Errors

The **error_log()** function can be used to write an error message to the Web server log file or some other local file, or to send the error message by email. When **log_errors** is turned on in the php.ini file, errors will be logged. The default is to write the errors to the PHP log file on the Web server. Sending errors to the site administrator is also an option and can be coded to send only selected error messages. Figure 10.49 is an example of sending an email to the site administrator when a particular error occurs.

```
<html>
<head>
<?php
// PHP1074 - Send an email error message example
// Error handler function
function customError($errno, $errstr)
{
echo "<b>Error:</b> [$errno] $errstr<br />";
echo "Error has been sent to the Webmaster";
error_log("Error: [$errno] $errstr",1,
"toemail@sbcglobal.net","From: fromemail@sbcglobal.net");
}
```

Figure 10.49: Logging errors via email (part 1 of 2).

```
set_error_handler("customError",E_USER_WARNING);
//Check for and trigger error
$orderquantity=99;
if ($orderquantity>25)
  {
  trigger_error("Order  quantity  must  be  less  than  25",E_USER_
    WARNING);
  }
?>
</head>
</html>
```

Figure 10.49: Logging errors via email (part 2 of 2).

In this example, a custom error-handler function is created to send an email with the following error message to the Webmaster:

Error: [512] Order quantity must be less than 25

This error handler could be added to a common function file, to be used by all of the pages on a site. In this example, note that the **error_log** is passed parameters. The message type "1" is used to direct that the message is to be sent via email. Note also that the "to" and "from" addresses will need to be changed to valid email addresses.

Error-handling Components

Error handling is an important part of creating PHP scripts. Not handling errors can leave the site open to potential security risks, provide hackers or competitors the ability to access site information, or leave site visitors with the impression that the site is not friendly or professional. The previous examples cover some of the functionality of error handling. Now, let's look at the components more closely.

In Figure 10.50, the script tries to open a file that does not exist, so the following warning is displayed:

> **Warning: fopen(bbqbarn.txt) [function.fopen]: failed to open stream: No such file or directory in C:\Inetpub\wwwroot\BillsBarbeque\PHP1076.php on line 5**

This message provides a lot of information about the site that should not be shared.

```
<html>
<head>
<?php
// PHP1076 Example error handling open a file
$file = fopen("bbqbarn.txt", "r")
?>
</head>
Warning: fopen(bbqbarn.txt) [<A href="function.fopen">function.
fopen</A>]:
failed to open stream: No such file or directory in
C:\Inetpub\wwwroot\BillsBarbeque\PHP1076.php on line 5
</html>
```

Figure 10.50: A script to open a file, with inappropriate error handling.

To avoid this and handle the error, combine a check for the existence of the file with the **die()** function, as shown in Figure 10.51. This time, the results are much friendlier. If the file does not exist, the following message will be displayed:

File bbqbarn.txt not found

```
<html>
<head>
<?php
// PHP1078 Example error handling open a file
// with a check the file exists and using the die
// function to exit the script
if(!file_exists("bbqbarn.txt"))
{
die("File bbqbarn.txt not found");
}
else
{
$file = fopen("bbqbarn.txt", "r");
}
?>
</head>
</html>
```

*Figure 10.51: Error handling with **die()**.*

This example shows that when errors are handled properly, the results are much more secure and professional. Note that in this case, it works well to end the script and display a message, but ending the script might not always fit the application's needs.

A Custom Error-handler

The earlier example of sending an email to the Webmaster used a custom error-handler. Now, let's look at this component more closely. Creating an error handler is quite simple. Custom functions can be defined and saved in a common function file to be shared by site pages and Web applications, eliminating the need for the same code in multiple pages. Here is an example of a custom error function:

error_function(error_level, error_message, error_file, error_line, error_context)

The first two parameters, **error_level** and **error_message,** are required; the others are optional. The **error_level** parameter refers to the error report level. For example, a value of two corresponds to **E_WARNING**. (Refer to appendix C for error-value constants and more information on the parameters.)

The example from Figure 10.49 will be used for a custom error function. Figure 10.52 is the function definition. This custom function uses the **error_level** and **error_mesage** parameters. When the function is triggered, it receives the error level and an error message. It then sends an email.

```
// PHP1074 - Send an email error message example
// Error handler function
function customError($errno, $errstr)
  {
  echo "<b>Error:</b> [$errno] $errstr<br />";
  echo "Error has been sent to the Webmaster";
  error_log("Error: [$errno] $errstr",1,
  "toemail@sbcglobal.net","From: fromemail@sbcglobal.net");
  }
```

Figure 10.52: Creating a custom error function.

To trigger the **customError()** function, we first need to set the error handler to point to the function:

set_error_handler ("customError", E_USER_WARNING);

Next, we check for an error and trigger the error function. In Figure 10.53, an order quantity greater than 25 triggers the error. The actual value of the order in this example is 99, so the error function will be triggered.

```
//Check for and trigger error
$orderquantity=99;
if ($orderquantity>25)
  {
  trigger_error("Order  quantity  must  be  less  than  25",E_USER_
    WARNING);
  }
```

Figure 10.53: Triggering the error function.

When the error is triggered, the warning "Order quantity must be less than 25" is displayed. Then, the custom error function sends an email and causes the message "Error has been sent to the Webmaster" to be displayed.

More advanced error management can be done with exception handling, to change the normal flow of script execution when an error is encountered. This works through a check or validation, or when a specific condition is encountered. Combinations of **try**, **throw**, and **catch** can be used for more advanced error-handling.

Filters

Filters are used to make sure applications receive correct input. A number of predefined filter functions are provided with PHP to validate or sanitize input. (Appendix C lists some of them.) A custom filter can also be created.

Filters are used when a site requires external data input. Using external input on a Web site raises security considerations, but it also makes the site much more dynamic. Filtering can minimize the security risks and also improve and control data integrity. These are important factors for business applications.

Figure 10.54 uses the **filter_var()** filter function to validate that the integer value is a valid integer. The filter checks the variable input for the order quantity to determine if it is a valid integer. In this example, the results will be true, so the message "Order Quantity = 1" will be displayed. If you change the order quantity's value to *x*, which is not a valid integer, the message "Order Quantity is invalid" will be displayed.

```
<html>
<head>
<?php
// PHP1085 Filer validation example
$orderquantity = 1;
if(!filter_var($orderquantity, FILTER_VALIDATE_INT))
 {
 echo("Order Quantity is invalid");
 }
else
 {
 echo("Order Quantity = " . $orderquantity);
 }
?>
</head>
</html>
```

Figure 10.54: Filter validation.

Similar validate functions can be used for Boolean, float, regular expression, URL, email, and IP address entries.

Sanitize filter functions clean up data. The same example of order quantity will be used to demonstrate sanitization. In Figure 10.55, the input for the order quantity variable is "abcdefg12." The **filter_sanitize_number_int()** function cleans up the order quantity value by removing invalid characters. The result in this example is "12."

```
<html>
<head>
<?php
// PHP1088 Filter sanitization example
$orderquantity = "abcdefg12";
echo filter_var($orderquantity, FILTER_SANITIZE_NUMBER_INT);
?>
   </head>
</p>
</html>
```

Figure 10.55: Filter sanitization.

Similar prebuilt sanitization functions can be used for string, email, URL, and float entries.

In addition to predefined filter functions, custom functions can also be created. Figure 10.56 creates a custom function to replace all dashes in a phone number with spaces.

```
<html>
<head>
<?php
// PHP1090 Custom function with filter call back
function convert_phone_number($phone_number)
{
return str_replace("-", " ", $phone_number);
}
$phone_number = "248-701-9999";
echo filter_var($phone_number, FILTER_CALLBACK,
array("options"=>"convert_phone_number"));
?>
  </head>
</p>
</html>
```

Figure 10.56: A custom filter function.

This example uses the **filter_callback()** function and an array containing the custom function. The results will return the phone number "248-701-9999" as "248 701 9999."

Forms

Forms are often used for user input on Web sites. User input should always be validated. Input data might be validated using JavaScript on the client side. Client-side validation is faster and reduces the load on the server. A site with a lot of activity or a site that uses databases, however, poses concerns regarding site security. Server-side validation with PHP can be used when a form accesses a database.

Forms in HTML are quite simple and useful for submitting data, as shown in previous examples in this book. A good way to validate a form is to have the form and processing script in the same file, rather than within separate files, and have the form post to itself. By using this technique, any errors can be displayed on the same page as the form, and the previously entered data will be defaulted and automatically displayed on the form. Using this approach will make it easier to determine the error and the data entered resulting in the error.

All form elements are automatically available to PHP scripts. The **$_GET**, **$_POST**, and **$_REQUEST** variable submission methods are used in PHP to retrieve input from forms. The **$_GET** variable collects input values from a form that uses the HTML form method **get**. The data collected using **$_GET** is visible to everyone and will be displayed in the browser's address bar. The **$_GET** variable can only send a maximum of 100 characters. It should not be used for data that should not be seen when sending information, such as a password. Because the data can be seen in the URL, **$_GET** allows for bookmarking by saving the URL information. This may be helpful for repetitive tasks, like looking at an employee's work schedule.

Figure 10.57 is an example of using **$_GET** with a form. The example prompts the user for first and last name, validates the data input, and if a valid name is entered, displays an employee's work schedule.

```
HTML Document PHP1092.html:
<html>
<head>
<!-- PHP1092.html $_GET variable example -->
Welcome to Bills Barbeque Barn Employee Page!
<br>
Please enter your first and last name and press submit to view
    your schedule.
<form action="PHP1092.php" method="get">
First Name: <input type="text" name="first_name" />
Last Name: <input type="text" name="last_name" />
<br>
<input type="submit" />
</form>
</head>
</html>
```

```
PHP Document PHP1092.php:
<html>
<body>
<?php
/* PHP1092 - $_GET variable example */
if (! preg_match( "/^[A-Za-z]+$/", trim($_GET["first_name"]) ))
        echo ("Please enter your first name." . "<br>");
elseif (! preg_match( "/^[A-Za-z]+$/", trim($_GET["last_name"]) ))
        echo ("Please enter your last name." . "<br>");
else
        echo ("Employee Work Schedule Page." . "<br>");
        echo ("Welcome " . $_GET["first_name"] . " " . $_GET["last_
            name"] . "<br>");
?>
</body>
</html>
```

Figure 10.57: Using the $_GET variable.

The HTML in Figure 10.57 causes the page in Figure 10.58 to be displayed. In this example, the first and last name have been entered on the page's form.

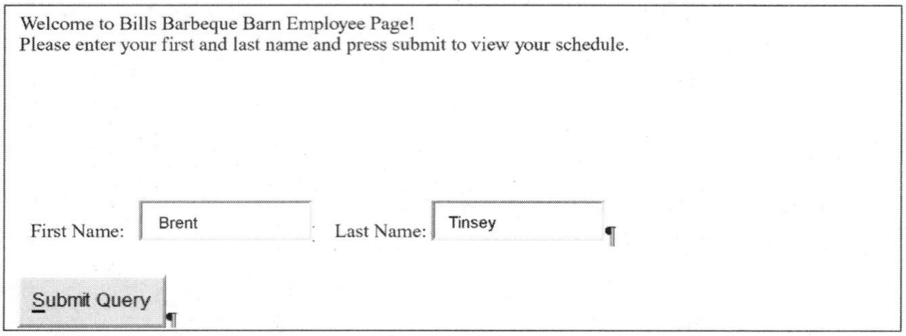

Figure 10.58: The Web page created from the HTML in Figure 10.57.

When the form is submitted, the file PHP1092.php is initiated. This document validates the data, checking that valid first and last names have been entered. If the first or last name is invalid, a message is displayed prompting for a valid entry. If the data is valid, the employee's work schedule is displayed. The work schedule page displays a welcome message and will also contain the values entered on the form for the first and last name in the browser's URL line, like this:

http://localhost/BillsBarbeque/PHP1092.php?first_name=Brent&last_name=Tinsey

Notice that the first and last name values are clearly visible, along with the Web site's path.

The PHP **$_REQUEST** variable contains the contents of **$_GET**, **$_POST**, and **$_COOKIE**. The **$_REQUEST** variable can be used to get the result from form data sent with either the **get** or **post** method. An application that uses both **get** and **post** for the same variable name may be a case where the **$_REQUEST** variable would be used. It might be argued that it is better to know where the data comes from and avoid using the **$_REQUEST** variable. It may also be argued that having two or more inputs to a script having the same name, for example one each from a **$_GET**, **$_POST**, and **$_COOKIE** variable, is a pretty confusing design. This may also open up some security issues. Regardless, the variable is available for use in PHP. Here is an example of using the **$_REQUEST** variable:

```
echo ("Welcome " . $_REQUEST["first_name"] . " " . $_
REQUEST["last_name"] . "<br>");
```

The **$_POST** variable is an array of variable names and values sent by the HTTP **post** method. The **$_POST** variable is used to collect values from a form with the HTML method **post**. Information collected and sent using this method is invisible to others and has no limit on the amount of information that is sent. When the **post** method is used in an HTML form, the **$_POST** variable can be used in a PHP script to catch the entered form data. **$_POST** has been used in previous examples in this chapter. Refer back, for example, to Figure 10.9.

The importance of form validation is obvious. The PHP language provides many options and flexibility for the application programmer. Care should be taken to make the application user-friendly and well-designed, just like applications in any other programming language. A good, well thought-out design will result in an improved application. When an error is identified through filtering or validation, the error should be clearly identified and information returned so the user can correct the error.

Sessions

When a user visits a dynamic Web site, an application is initiated, some activity occurs, and then the application is closed. This is very similar to a traditional computer session. The computer knows who the user is, when an application is started, and when it is ended. On the Internet, this information is not automatically retained on the Web server. A PHP session can be used to store the information on the server for later use. The information is only retained while the session is active and deleted when the session ends. If it must be kept, a permanent record of the data can be stored in a database.

Sessions work by creating a UID, a unique ID for each visitor. The UID is used to uniquely identify and store variables. The PHP session will be started, and then session information will be stored. Session information can also be deleted.

To start a session, use the **session_start()** function. As shown in Figure 10.59, this function must be placed before the **<html>** tag. Once started, a user's session is registered on the server, and user information can be saved using the assigned UID for the session.

```php
<?php
// PHP1097 PHP session example.
session_start();
if ($SESSION["last_visit"])
{
echo "Date of your last visit is: ";
echo date ("j F Y, H:i:s", $SESSION["last_visit"]);
echo "<br>";
echo "Total number of visits: "  . $_SESSION["number_visits"];
}
else
echo "This is your first visit";
$_SESSION["last_visit"] = time();
$_SESSION["number_visits"]++;
?>
<html>
<body>
Welcome to Bills BBQ Barn!
</body>
</html>
```

Figure 10.59: Starting a PHP session.

The PHP **$_SESSION** variable is used to store and retrieve session variables. In this example, we store the last visit information. The first time the user visits the site, the following message will be displayed:

This is your first visit Welcome to Bills BBQ Barn!

Each time the page is visited during the session, the values will be saved. If other Web site pages are visited and the user then returns to this page, the values will be remembered. If the browser is closed, the values will be reset. Each time the user returns to this page during a session, a message will be displayed with the date of the last visit and the number of times the page has been visited.

As mentioned earlier, a session may also be deleted. The **unset()** or **session_destroy()** function can be used for this purpose. The **unset()** function is used to reset a specific session variable.

```php
<?php
unset($SESSION[number_visits];
?>
```

The **session_destroy()** function will be used to destroy and reset the session. The stored session data will be deleted.

```
<?php
session_destroy();
?>
```

Working with Data

Web business applications often need to retrieve data from and store data in a database table or file on the server. PHP can be used for these tasks.

MySQL is the most popular open-source database server for use with Web applications, so it is used for the remaining examples in this chapter. In the examples that follow, you will learn how to connect to a MySQL database and input and output data. Some knowledge of SQL is helpful to better understand these examples, but it is not required. These examples could easily be used to access other databases by making slight changes. Examples can be found on the *www.php.net* Web site.

The code in Figure 10.60 connects to MySQL server and retrieves data from the master work schedule database, in a table named "workschedule." The retrieved data is displayed on a Web page.

```
<html>
<head>
<img src="images/bbqbarn.JPG">
<br>
Welcome to Bills Barbeque Barn Master Work Schedule Page!
<br>
Shift Date       Shift   Start Time  End Time
<body>
<?php
//  PHP10101 - Working with Data Example
// Connect to data source
mysql_connect("localhost", "userid", "password") or die(mysql_
  error());
// Select database
mysql_select_db("BillsBarbequeBarn") or die(mysql_error());
// Retrieve data
$data = mysql_query("SELECT * FROM workschedule")
or die(mysql_error());
// Display data in a table
Print "<table border cellpadding=3>";
while($info = mysql_fetch_array( $data ))
{
Print "<td>".$info['ShiftDate'] . "</td> ";
Print "<td>".$info['Shift'] . " </td>";
```

Figure 10.60: Retrieving data from a MySQL database (part 1 of 2).

```
Print "<td>".$info['StartTime'] . " </td>";
Print "<td>".$info['EndTime'] . " </td></tr>";\
}
Print "</table>";
?>
</body>
</head>
</html>
```

Figure 10.60: Retrieving data from a MySQL database (part 2 of 2).

There's not much code here, but it produces big results, as shown in Figure 10.61. It's really that simple.

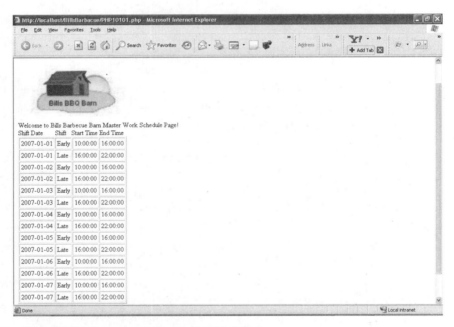

Figure 10.61: Data retrieved from a MySQL database.

In this example, we are connecting to a MySQL database, so the connection type is **mysql_connect**:

```
// Connect to data source
mysql_connect("localhost", "userid", "password") or die(mysql_
error());
```

The connection has three parameters: the connection, the user ID, and the password. The connection is the DSN where the data resides. In this example, *localhost* is the location, but it could be a DNS server name or an IP address. The user ID and password parameters are the IDs required to connect to the MySQL database. This statement also uses the **die()** function to end the script if a connection cannot be made.

The MySQL database name is "BillsBarbequeBarn":

```
// Select database
mysql_select_db("BillsBarbequeBarn") or die(mysql_error());
```

The **die()** function is used again, this time to end the script if the database is not found. Next, the data is retrieved:

```
// Retrieve data
$data = mysql_query("SELECT * FROM workschedule")
or die(mysql_error());
```

All fields and records are selected from the table "workschedule" and are stored in a variable named **$data**.

The data is accessed using the **mysql_fetch_array** statement. The data is put into the variable **$info**. The **while** statement continues to fetch data until no more exists. Finally, the contents are printed, listing the fields "ShiftDate," "Shift," "StartTime," and "EndTime" to be displayed in an HTML table:

```
// Display data in a table
Print "<table border cellpadding=3>";
while($info = mysql_fetch_array( $data ))
{
Print "<td>".$info['ShiftDate'] . "</td> ";
Print "<td>".$info['Shift'] . " </td>";
Print "<td>".$info['StartTime'] . " </td>";
Print "<td>".$info['EndTime'] . " </td></tr>";\
}
Print "</table>";
```

The example in Figure 10.62 adds a few more pieces to further show how data can be used within an application. This example begins with a form prompting the user to enter a first name and last name, as shown in Figure 10.63. When a valid name is entered and the Submit button is clicked, a work schedule for the employee is retrieved from a database and displayed. This application uses the same database and table as the previous one.

```
HTML Document PHP10107.html:

<html>
<head>
<!-- PHP10107.html Employee Schedule Inquiry example  -->
Welcome to Bills Barbeque Barn Employee Page!
<br>
Please enter your first and last name and press submit to view
your schedule.
<form action="PHP10107.php" method="get">
First Name: <input type="text" name="first_name" />
Last Name: <input type="text" name="last_name" />
<br>
<input type="submit" />
</form>
</head>
</html>
```

```
PHP Document PHP10107.php:

<html>
<head>
<img src="images/bbqbarn.JPG">
<br>
Bills Barbeque Barn Employee Work Schedule Page!
<br>
<body>
<?php
if (! preg_match( "/^[A-Za-z]+$/", trim($_GET["first_name"]) ))
{
        echo ("Please enter your first name." . "<br>");
    die;
}
elseif (! preg_match( "/^[A-Za-z]+$/", trim($_GET["last_name"])
))
{
        echo ("Please enter your last name." . "<br>");
    die;
}
else
echo ($_GET["first_name"] . " " . $_GET["last_name"] . "'s Work
  Schedule." . "<br>");

?>
<?php
// Connect to data source
$lname="'" . $_GET["last_name"] . "'";
$fname="'" . $_GET["first_name"] . "'";
mysql_connect("localhost", "userid", "password") or die(mysql_
  error());
```

Figure 10.62: Creating an application to retrieve an employee's work schedule from a
    database (part 1 of 2).

```
// Select database
mysql_select_db("BillsBarbequeBarn") or die(mysql_error());
// Retrieve data
$data = mysql_query("SELECT * FROM EmployeeSchedule WHERE
  LastName=$lname and FirstName=$fname order by ShiftDate")
or die(mysql_error());
// Display data in a table
Print "<table border cellpadding=3>";
while($info = mysql_fetch_array( $data ))
{
Print "<td>".$info['ShiftDate'] . "</td> ";
Print "<td>".$info['Shift'] . " </td>";
Print "<td>".$info['StartTime'] . " </td>";
Print "<td>".$info['EndTime'] . " </td>";
Print "<td>".$info['EmployeeNumber'] . " </td>";
Print "<td>".$info['FirstName'] . " </td>";
Print "<td>".$info['LastName'] . " </td></tr>";
}
Print "</table>";
?>
</body>
</head>
</html>
```

Figure 10.62: Creating an application to retrieve an employee's work schedule from a database (part 2 of 2).

Figure 10.63: The HTML form created by PHP10107.html.

The user is prompted for a first and last name using the form in file PHP10107.html. When the user clicks Submit, PHP10107.php is initiated. The code starts by validating the name entered. If the name is valid, the connection is made and data is retrieved using SQL. To format the SQL statement, the first and last name entered by the user are used for selection. The example first retrieves the fields using **$_GET**, and then formats the names within single quotes to follow correct syntax for the SQL statement:

```
$lname="'" . $_GET["last_name"] . "'";
$fname="'" . $_GET["first_name"] . "'";
```

With "Joe" entered for the first name and "Walsh" for the last name, the SQL statement would look like this:

```
SELECT * FROM EmployeeSchedule WHERE LastName='Walsh'
and FirstName='Joe' order by ShiftDate"
```

The SQL statement selects all records from the "EmployeeSchedule" table where the last name is "Walsh" and the first name is "Joe," and sorts the data in shift-date order:

```
// Retrieve data
$data=mysql_query("SELECT * FROM EmployeeSchedule WHERE
LastName=$lname and FirstName=$fname order by ShiftDate")
```

The **$lname** and **$fname** variables allow for passing the selection information using the user form displayed in PHP10107.html. These variables also format the selection criteria within single quotes to accommodate appropriate statement syntax.

Figure 10.64 shows the schedule displayed for Joe Walsh, with the date, shift, start and end times, employee number, first name, and last name. This technique works just as well with many other business inquiries.

Bills Barbeque Barn Employee Work Schedule Page!
Joe Walsh's Work Schedule.

2007-07-01	Early	10:00:00	16:00:00	2	Joe	Walsh
2007-07-02	Late	16:00:00	22:00:00	2	Joe	Walsh
2007-07-03	Early	10:00:00	16:00:00	2	Joe	Walsh

Figure 10.64: The results of the employee work schedule inquiry.

A dynamic application may require a database table to be updated. We will use a customer-service feedback application to show how this can be done. The code in Figure 10.65 prompts the user to enter feedback information in a form, validates the data, and updates the customer service database. The example is simple, but provides the techniques to complete the very important task of updating and storing data. The same method might be used to place online orders or update other data.

```
HTML file - PHP10113.html:

<html>
<head>
<!** PHP10113 Customer service feedback form example **>
Bills Barbeque Barn Customer Service Feedback Page
<br>
<form method="post" action="PHP10113.php">
  Email: <input name="email" type="text" /><br />
  First Name: <input name="firstname" type="text" /><br />
```

```
  Last Name: <input name="lastname" type="text" /><br />
  Phone Number: <input name="phonenumber" type="text" /><br />
  Follow Up (Yes or No): <input name="followup" type="text" /><br
/>
  Customer Service Message:<br />
  <textarea name="message" rows="5" cols="40">
  </textarea>
  <br />
  <input type="submit" />
</form>
</head>
</html>
```

```
PHP file - PHP10113.php:

<html>
<head>
<img src="images/bbqbarn.JPG">
<br>
Bills Barbeque Barn Customer Feedback Page!
<br>
<body>
<?php
$email_address = '/^[^@\s]+@([-a-z0-9]+\.)+[a-z]{2,}$/i';
$message=$_POST["message"];
$phonenumber=$_POST["phonenumber"];
$followup=$_POST["followup"]
if (!preg_match($email_address, trim($_POST["email"])))
 {
 echo "Email address entered is invalid.";
 die;
 }
elseif (! preg_match( "/^[A-Za-z]+$/", trim($_POST["firstname"])
))
{
        echo ("Please enter your first name." . "<br>");
   die;
}
elseif (! preg_match( "/^[A-Za-z]+$/", trim($_POST["lastname"])
))
{
        echo ("Please enter your last name." . "<br>");
   die;
}
elseif (strlen($phonenumber)<1)
{
        echo ("Please enter your phone number." . "<br>");
   die;
}
elseif (trim($_POST["phonenumber"] = " " ))
```

Figure 10.65: Updating a customer service database (part 1 of 2).

```
{
        echo ("Please enter your phone number." . "<br>");
    die;
}
elseif ($followup !== 'Yes' and $followup !== 'No')
{
        echo ("Please enter Yes or No for Follow Up." . "<br>");
    die;
}
elseif (strlen($message)<1)
//if (strlen($username)<1)
{
        echo ("Please enter your message." . "<br>");
    die;
}
?>
<?php
// Format Fields
$email="'" . $_POST["email"] . "'";
$lname="'" . $_POST["lastname"] . "'";
$fname="'" . $_POST["firstname"] . "'";
$phonenumber="'" . $_POST["phonenumber"] . "'";
$message="'" . $_POST["message"] . "'";
$followup="'" . $_POST["followup"] . "'";
// Connect to data source
mysql_connect("localhost", "userid", "password") or die(mysql_
error());
// Select database
mysql_select_db("BillsBarbequeBarn") or die(mysql_error());
// Add data
$data = mysql_query("INSERT INTO CustomerService (DateReceived,
  TimeReceived, EmailAddress, FirstName, LastName, PhoneNumber,
  Message, FollowUp, Status) VALUES(CURDATE(), CURTIME(), $email,
  $fname, $lname, $phonenumber, $message, $followup, 'Open')")
or die(mysql_error());
echo "<br>";
echo "Your Customer Service Message has been sent!"
?>
</body>
</head>
</html>
```

Figure 10.65: Updating a customer service database (part 2 of 2).

The code in PHP10113.html displays the customer service form in Figure 10.66. Once data is entered in the form and the Submit button is clicked, the PHP10113.php document is initiated. The data is retrieved using **$_POST**, and then validated. If the data is valid, the MySQL connection is made and the database table is updated, using the **INSERT INTO** MySQL syntax. The fields to be updated are listed, and the values are populated using the data retrieved from the form.

Bills Barbeque Barn Customer Service Feedback Page

Email:

First Name:

Last Name:

Phone Number:

Follow Up (Yes or No):
Customer Service Message:

Submit Query

Bottom of Form

Figure 10.66: The customer service feedback form.

Note in Figure 10.65 that the status is defaulted to the value 'Open', the date received is defaulted to the current date, and the time received is defaulted to the current time. Once the update is complete, the message in Figure 10.67 is displayed, letting the user know the data has been sent.

Bills Barbeque Barn Customer Feedback Page!

Your Customer Service Message has been sent!

Figure 10.67: Letting the user know the result of the data update.

PHP may also be used to work with a text file. The file must first be opened using the **fopen()** function. The function uses two parameters. The first is for the file name, and the second is for the mode. The example in Figure 10.68 opens the file in read-only mode. Table 10.9 lists valid modes that can be used with **fopen()**.

```
$file=fopen("PHP10119.txt","r");
```

Figure 10.68: The file open function.

Table 10.9: Valid Modes for the File Open Function	
Mode	Description
r	Read-only; starts at the beginning of the file.
r+	Read/write; starts at the beginning of the file.
w	Write-only; opens and clears the contents of the file or creates a new file if the file referenced does not exist.
w+	Read/write; opens and clears the contents of the file or creates a new file if the file referenced does not exist.
a	Append; opens and writes to the end of the file or creates a new file if the file referenced does not exist.
a+	Read/append; preserves file's contents and writes to the end of the file.
x	Write-only; creates a new file and returns false and an error if the file already exists.
x+	Read/write; creates a new file and returns false and an error if the file already exists.

The example in Figure 10.69 reads the text file PHP10119.txt to display the offers from Bills Barbeque Barn for the month of July. The text file is read and displayed using the **fopen()** and **fclose()** functions. To access a file, it must be opened. It is also important to close the file.

The **while** loop uses the end-of-file function, **feof(),** to read through the file line-by-line and display the contents using **echo**. The loop will complete when the end of the file is reached, and the contents of the text file will be displayed to the screen, as shown in Figure 10.70.

```
Text File - PHP10119.txt:

Bills Barbeque Barn July Special Offers!
*******************************************************
10% off all merchandise ordered online
reference offer bbqonline0707
*******************************************************
20% your entire food bill on your next visit to
Bills Barbeque Barn
reference offer bbqonsite0707
*******************************************************
Offers valid July 1, 2007 through July 31, 2007
```

```
PHP File - PHP10119.php:

<html>
<head>
<img src="images/bbqbarn.JPG">
<br>
Bills Barbeque Barn Special Offers Page!
<br>
<body>
<?php
// PHP10119 - Read and display text file example
$file = fopen("PHP10119.txt", "r") or exit("Unable to open
  file!");
// Display the file line until the end of the file is reached
while(!feof($file))
  {
  echo fgets($file). "<br />";
  }
fclose($file);
?>
</body>
</head>
</html>
```

Figure 10.69: The code to read and display a text file.

The list of monthly specials for Bills Barbeque Barn is a good example of
this kind of application. The promotions can be easily changed by replacing
the contents of the text document, without having to make changes to the
Web site application. This same technique could be used for product-specific
information, employee procedures, or order comments.

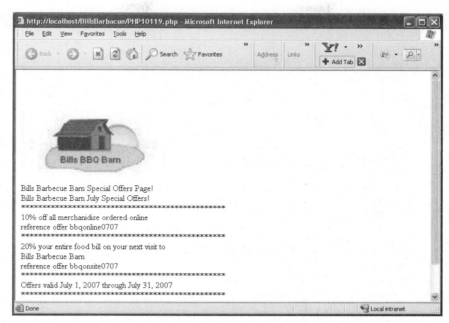

Figure 10.70: Displaying a text file on a Web page.

Although the examples in this chapter use MySQL, connections to other databases can also be used. Figures 10.71 through 10.73 show examples of a few other database connections.

```php
<?php

$db_host      = "server.mynetwork";
$db_user      = "dbuser";
$db_pass      = "dbpass";

odbc_connect($db_host, $db_user, $db_pass, "SQL_CUR_USE_ODBC");

@odbc_setoption($this->db_connectid, 1, SQL_ATTR_COMMIT, SQL_
  TXN_NO_COMMIT)
   or die('Failed setoption: ' . odbc_error() . ":" . odbc_
   errormsg());

@odbc_setoption($this->db_connectid, 1, SQL_ATTR_DBC_DEFAULT_
  LIB, $this->dbname)
    or die('Failed select: ' . odbc_error() . ":" . odbc_
    errormsg());

?>
```

Figure 10.71: Making an ODBC connection.

```php
<?php

$database     = 'SAMPLE';
$user         = 'db2inst1';
$password     = 'ibmdb2';

db2_connect($database, $user, $password);

?>
```

Figure 10.72: Making a DB2 connection

```
INSERT INTO table VALUES(val1, val2, ... valn);
//MySQL Insert Statement

INSERT INTO table VALUES(val1, val2, ... valn);
INSERT INTO schema.table VALUES(val1, val2, ... valn);
//DB2 Insert Statements
```

Figure 10.73: Using a DB2 table reference.

Summary

This chapter has covered a lot of ground, but has barely scratched the surface of the capability and functionality of PHP. PHP can be used for advanced validation, XML processing, FTP, file uploads, and much more.

It is obvious that PHP can bring dynamic capability to a business Web application. If your goal is to get to the Web fast, PHP should be considered. Its user base continues to grow, and the language continues to evolve, thanks to the efforts of the PHP community.

CHAPTER 11

Web Development with ASP

I n this chapter, you'll explore Microsoft's Active Server Pages, also know as *ASP*. The latest version of ASP is included within Microsoft's .NET Framework, and is referred to as *ASP.NET*. This chapter goes into detail on what ASP.NET is, what tools you need to work with it, how it integrates with HTML, and how it integrates with your database.

ASP Compared to Other Tools

As you might guess from the word "Server" in "Active Server Pages," the processing for ASP.NET takes place primarily on the server itself. Be aware, however, that there are differences between ASP.NET and the older version of ASP. ASP.NET is compiled, where its predecessor was not. This gives ASP.NET a distinct performance advantage. There are also numerous additional controls available for ASP.NET.

Because ASP.NET is built on Microsoft's .NET Framework, it interacts with the Common Language Runtime. Therefore, developers can code in any of the .NET languages. Most commonly, this would be either VB.NET or C#. This book uses VB.NET because it provides a distinct alternative to some of the other languages discussed in this book. VB.NET is also a very popular programming language, so examples in that language will be valuable to a large number of readers.

ASP Versus PHP

As you learned in the previous chapter, PHP is open source and quite portable, as it can be run on almost any platform. PHP is commonly said to be more stable and less intensive on resource requirements than ASP. For some programmers who are already familiar with Visual Basic, however, ASP might be easier to learn than PHP.

Some people say that PHP is more robust for advanced features like working with FTP servers, parsing data, and connectivity. Others, however, contend that the available controls within ASP make many programming jobs dramatically easier.

ASP Versus Java

ASP and Java are different in many ways. For one thing, the syntax of the languages is different. For another, Java is open source, while ASP is provided and supported by Microsoft. Microsoft provides many ASP objects to assist in developing Web applications. To find similar objects for Java, you might need to include additional open-source material from a third party, or develop the tools yourself.

ASP Versus CGI

CGI is at its best when you have extensive amounts of useful code already written that perform the tasks needed by your Web application. With CGI, you can easily interact with these existing applications without needing to learn a lot of new programming languages.

When creating truly sophisticated Web pages that perform important tasks such as validating input data, however, CGI can become labor-intensive, depending on exactly what platform you are working with, what languages you use, and the available toolset. ASP may be better suited than CGI for businesses that are developing new applications where there is little legacy code to reuse, or if the legacy code can be accessed via stored procedures. Where the exact nature of the server side of a CGI application changes from server to server, the ASP server-side coding is always consistent.

ASP's Advantages and Disadvantages

Like any other tool, ASP has advantages and disadvantages. The following are a few of its advantages:

- Object-oriented

- Less code required

- Powerful prebuilt controls available

- Can be used with any .NET programming language

- Server-compiled pages for faster performance on subsequent calls

- Better security; code never sent to remote browser

Here are its main disadvantages:

- Microsoft-specific

- Windows-based

- Fairly complex

- Difficult to control much of the HTML code

ASP Processing

While it is possible to incorporate client-side ASP.NET processing through scripting languages such as VB Script or JavaScript, the focus of ASP. NET coding remains on the server. ASP.NET source files end with a suffix of *.aspx* rather than *.htm* or *.html* as would normally be the case for Web pages. This suffix signals the server that the document contains HTML code as well as special ASP.NET code that must be processed before the contents of the document are sent to the remote user. Figure 11.1 illustrates this process, and shows how the ASP.NET server-side code is replaced at run time with dynamic HTML content. (For the sake of simplicity, throughout the rest of this chapter, we'll refer to ASP.NET as just *ASP*.)

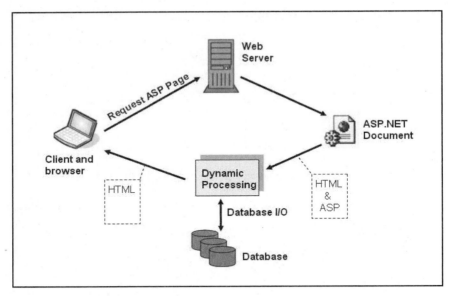

Figure 11.1: Processing an ASP document.

Figure 11.2 shows ASP code inserted inside HTML. This code creates the Web page shown in Figure 11.3.

```
<html>
<head>
<link rel="stylesheet" type="text/css"  href="TESTcss.css">
</head>
<body>
<%Response.Write("<p>Paragraph One")%>
<%Response.Write("<p>Paragraph Two")%>
<%Response.Write("<p>Paragraph Three")%>
</body>
</html>
```

Figure 11.2: The ASP code to create three paragraphs.

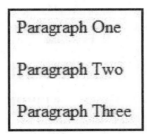

Figure 11.3: An ASP.NET
page with three paragraphs.

The code contains very familiar-looking HTML, but there are three lines containing a new type of code in the middle of the document. Anywhere in an HTML page that you need to execute server-side logic, insert ASP code delimited by "<%" and "%>".

This example uses the **response.write** method, which simply inserts the given string into the HTML page. The string can contain HTML tags, plain text, or a combination of the two, as in Figure 11.2.

```
Tags

        response.write("..")
```

Processing the ASP document and properly handling the code within it requires a special server, such as Microsoft's IIS (Internet Information Server). This server is an optional component of Windows that can be installed using the Add or Remove Program wizard in the Windows Control Panel. You might need the Install CD to complete the installation.

What Tools to Use

To develop pages using ASP.NET, you may want to install a tool that will assist in creating the Web pages. Microsoft provides a free tool, the Microsoft Visual Web Developer 2008 Express Edition. (At the time of this writing, however, we were using the 2005 edition, not 2008.) You can download the tool and get more information from Microsoft's Web site, *http://www.microsoft.com/express/vwd*.

Once installed, this tool will assist in editing and managing pages that incorporate ASP.NET. To get started, create a new Web site using the wizard in the File pull-down menu, shown in Figure 11.4. This wizard creates the shell of a Web page, as shown in Figure 11.5. Simply insert HTML and ASP code into this document as needed.

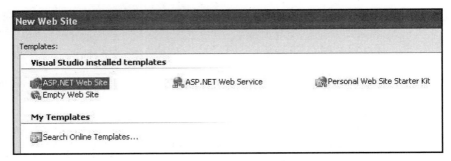

Figure 11.4: The ASP.NET wizard.

```
 1   <%@ Page Language="VB" AutoEventWireup="false" CodeFile="Default.aspx.vb"
 2       Inherits="_Default" %>
 3
 4   <!DOCTYPE html PUBLIC "-//W3C//DTD XHTML 1.0 Transitional//EN"
 5       "http://www.w3.org/TR/xhtml1/DTD/xhtml1-transitional.dtd">
 6
 7   <html xmlns="http://www.w3.org/1999/xhtml" >
 8   <head runat="server">
 9       <title>Untitled Page</title>
10   </head>
11   <body>
12       <form id="form1" runat="server">
13       <div>
14
15       </div>
16       </form>
17   </body>
18   </html>
19
```

Figure 11.5: Default HTML/ASP code generated by the wizard.

In the code created by the wizard, you'll see lines that are not absolutely required. The examples in this chapter may omit some or all of this default code, allowing us to better focus on the samples being discussed. Until you are sure you understand the implications of changing the default code, however, it's best to leave it as–is in your own development efforts. Initially, focus on adding new code within the **<div>** and **</div>** tags (between lines 13 and 15).

To view the rendered output from this or any other ASP.NET page, simply right-click on the page and select the option "View in Browser." If the current page has unsaved changes, you will be prompted to save them before the page is rendered. However, if this page links to other pages that have changes, those changes will be ignored, and the last saved version of those pages will be used.

When viewing pages this way, the Visual Web Developer tool will activate temporary server processes on specific ports to handle the request. Information on these server processes can be found in the system tray.

Server Information

If you want to use IIS to present and test your Web page, first make sure that you've installed the IIS Windows component as discussed earlier in the chapter. Once that is installed, direct your browser to the URL "http://localhost." This presents the default page shown in Figure 11.6.

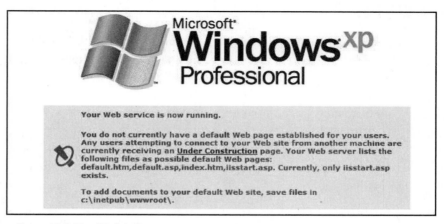

Figure 11.6: The IIS default page.

As this page explains, you do not yet have a default Web site configured for users attempting to connect to your server. Anyone who does attempt to connect will receive a notice that your page is under construction. To define a default page for the IIS server, load the files for your Web site into the folder "c:\inetpub\wwwroot\," as indicated in Figure 11.6. Set the initial page to "default.aspx" or "default.htm." Also, make sure that you have the latest version of the .NET Framework installed, which you can verify though the administrative tools in the Windows Control Panel.

The default.aspx page can be accessed by simply using the URL "http://locahost." To access other documents in the c:\inetpub\wwwroot\ folder, simply reference them in the localhost directory, such as "http://locahost/your-file.aspx."

The IIS server is fine for hosting a single Web site or FTP site. For more sophisticated implementations that involve multiple sites, however, consider upgrading to Windows Server.

Writing VB Script in Your Web Pages

ASP developers who need to include client-side logic within their Web pages often choose VB Script rather than JavaScript, since VB Script bears a strong resemblance to ASP code. VB Script can be included in either the **<head>** or **<body>** sections of a Web page. The **<script>** and **</script>** tags act as delimiters for the code.

More advanced ASP controls provide much of the capability that developers have often had to code manually through client-side scripts using such tools as VB Script or JavaScript. While you certainly can continue to perform such functions with client-side scripts, you might find that using some of the newer ASP controls will improve your capability and productivity. As with all things, there will likely be some learning curve involved as you begin working with these new controls. In the long run, however, an investment in developing those skills should more than pay for itself.

Learning to use client-side VB Script is also good preparation for getting started with ASP programming. You'll be familiarizing yourself with the VB language syntax and also learning to do manually what ASP will later automate. The scripts can include procedures, functions, and a variety of logical operations, allowing you to create Web pages with dynamic client-side processing. Client-side processing often provides far better performance and responsiveness than server-based logic.

What kinds of tasks lend themselves to client-side processing? One of the most popular uses for client-side scripting is to edit the information being typed on a Web page. If the input fields on a Web page are edited with VB Script, the code executes as soon as possible, without needing to connect to the remote Web server first.

The **document.write** method is perhaps the most important tool in VB Script. It allows you to write text into the HTML document. This text can include HTML tags, or be just plain text. This is similar in

function to the response.write ASP method mentioned earlier. The sample code in Figure 11.7 shows how to use the document.write method to print text on a Web page, shown in Figure 11.8.

```
<html>
<head>
<link rel="stylesheet" type="text/css" href="TESTcss.css">
</head>
<body>
<script>
<!--
document.write("<CENTER><H1>VB SCRIPT HEADING</H1></CENTER>")
-->
</script>
<%Response.Write("<p>Paragraph One")%>
<%Response.Write("<p>Paragraph Two")%>
<%Response.Write("<p>Paragraph Three")%>
</body>
</html>
```

Figure 11.7: ASP.NET code with client-side VB Script.

VB SCRIPT HEADING

Paragraph One

Paragraph Two

Paragraph Three

*Figure 11.8: A heading created with **document.write**.*

Tags

```
<script type="text/vbscript">
<!--
    ...
-->
</script>
```

Notice in Figure 11.7 that the VB Script code inside the **<script>** tag is enclosed within an HTML comment tag. This technique is popularly used to deal with browsers that do not support VB Script. Without the comment, any browser that does not support VB Script might simply print the code with the tags as if it were text content. To prevent the VB Script code from being displayed this way, it is contained in an HTML comment. Any browser that supports VB Script will ignore the comment tags and execute the code. A browser that does not support VB Script will see the HTML comment and ignore all the code within it. For this reason, some VB Script developers enclose all their VB Script code in HTML comment tags.

Tags

```
MsgBox(text,options,title)
```

Another popular tool in VB Script is the message box, which displays the specified text to the user. There are a large number of message-box options relating to what buttons are available and what icon is displayed for the message box. The third parameter is the title for the message box. There are additional parameters beyond the ones discussed here. These additional parameters deal with option help-text documents, which are beyond the scope of this topic.

The code in Figure 11.9 creates the sample message box shown in Figure 11.10.

```
<html>
<head>
<link rel="stylesheet" type="text/css" href="TESTcss.css">
</head>
<body>
<script type="text/vbscript">
document.write("<CENTER><H1>VB SCRIPT HEADING</H1></CENTER>")
dim rsp
rsp=MsgBox("This is a test message",16,"Sample Message Box")
</script>
<%Response.Write("<p>Paragraph One")%>
<%Response.Write("<p>Paragraph Two")%>
<%Response.Write("<p>Paragraph Three")%>
</body>
</html>
```

Figure 11.9: Using the **MsgBox** function.

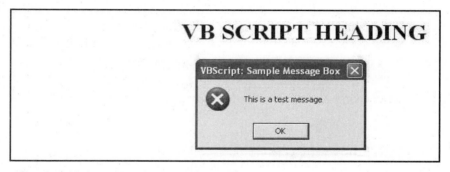

Figure 11.10: A sample message box from VB Script.

The value returned by the **MsgBox** function indicates what option the user took. The list of possible values is as follows:

- 1 = OK button clicked

- 2 = Cancel button clicked

- 3 = Abort button clicked

- 4 = Retry button clicked

- 5 = Ignore button clicked

- 6 = Yes button clicked

- 7 = No button clicked

As you can see in Figure 11.10, not all of the possible buttons are displayed in every message box. The available buttons are controlled by the numeric value in the second parameter of the function. Four different options are controlled by this number; simply add up the numeric value of one option in each set to determine what value to place in the second parameter.

The first option controls the buttons displayed:

- 0 = OK button
- 1 = OK and Cancel buttons
- 2 = Abort, Retry, and Ignore buttons
- 3 = Yes, No, and Cancel buttons
- 4 = Yes and No buttons
- 5 = Retry and Cancel buttons

For example, if you want to show the Retry and Cancel buttons on a message box, you would use 5 as your numeric value in the second parameter. This could change as other options are selected.

The second option controls the icon:

- 0 = No icon
- 16 = Critical icon ("X")
- 32 = Query icon ("?")
- 48 = Message icon ("!")
- 64 = Information icon ("i")

To add an exclamation icon to a message box, you would add 48 to the previous value of 5, for a total of 53.

The third option indicates which button is the default in case the user presses the Enter key rather than clicking on a button:

- 0 = First button
- 256 = Second button
- 512 = Third button
- 768 = Fourth button

To define the Cancel button as the default, you would add 256 to the numeric value of 53, for a total of 309.

The fourth option indicates the modal nature of the message box. This controls whether or not the user can switch from the message box to some other application:

- 0 = Application modal
- 4096 = System modal

A value of zero makes the message box modal for the application. This essentially means the Web page is locked until the user clicks a button in the message box. A value of 4096 defines the message box as modal for the entire system, meaning the user cannot perform any work on the computer until the message box is responded to. To define the message box as modal just for the application, you would add zero to the numeric value, so it would remain 309. If possible, avoid system-modal message boxes, as they can be very frustrating for users.

You can do far more with VB Script than we've discussed here. Throughout the remainder of this chapter, we'll continue to explore the capabilities of VB Script, but understand that there is no way to fully explore them in a single chapter of a book.

Defining Variables

In the example in Figure 11.9, you can see how the variable **rsp** is defined using the **dim** statement. It's not mandatory that variables be defined before using them, but it is a good idea and is generally considered to be good programming practice. To require that all variables in your VB Script be defined before they are used, add the **option explicit** statement to the beginning of a section of VB Script.

Figure 11.11 shows an example of this statement.

```
script type="text/vbscript">
<!--
option explicit
document.write("<CENTER><H1>VB SCRIPT HEADING</H1></CENTER>")
dim rsp
rsp=MsgBox("This is a test message",309,"Sample Message Box")
-->
</script>
```

*Figure 11.11: VB Script with **option explicit**.*

Variables in VB Script are not given explicit data types; they can hold either text or numeric data. To display the content of a variable in the Web page, use the **document.write** method. This method was mentioned earlier. An example of it for displaying a variable is shown in Figure 11.12.

```
<script type="text/vbscript">
<!--
option explicit
document.write("<CENTER><H1>VB SCRIPT HEADING</H1></CENTER>")
dim rsp
rsp=MsgBox("This is a test message",309,"Sample Message Box")
document.write("rsp = " & rsp)
-->
</script>
```

Figure 11.12: Displaying a variable.

Using Arrays

Arrays are defined using the **dim** statement, by simply following the variable name with parentheses containing a numeric value. Arrays are zero-based, so the number of elements in an array is one more than the number in parentheses. For example, in Figure 11.13, the **dim rsp(4)** statement defines an array with five elements. The first element is loaded with "Number One."

```
<script type="text/vbscript">
<!--
option explicit
document.write("<CENTER><H1>VB SCRIPT HEADING</H1></CENTER>")
dim rsp(4)
rsp(0)="Number One"
document.write("rsp = " & rsp(0))
-->
</script>
```

Figure 11.13: Using an array.

Arrays are useful when you have a number of similar values that you need to work with. We continue to discuss arrays throughout the remainder of this chapter.

Defining Subprocedures

Subprocedures are sections of VB Script that are identified by a name and can be executed as needed from anywhere within the HTML document.

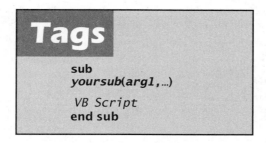

```
sub
yoursub(arg1,...)

VB Script
end sub
```

```
call yoursub(arg1,...)
```

Subprocedures are particularly useful when you have a task that must be repeated in more than one place. In such situations, subprocedures provide a single point of control, making the code easier to write and maintain. You can pass one or more arguments (parameters) into the subprocedure, if needed. These parameters are listed in the parentheses after the subprocedure name, separated by commas. To run the code in a subprocedure, use the **call** statement, including any arguments needed. The code in Figure 11.14 shows an example of a subprocedure and how it might be called. The resulting Web page is shown in Figure 11.15.

```
<html>
<head>
<link rel="stylesheet" type="text/css" href="TESTcss.css">
</head>
<body>
<script type="text/vbscript">
<!--
document.write("<CENTER><H1>VB SCRIPT HEADING</H1></CENTER>")
dim showimg
call askimages(showimg)
sub askimages(ans)
ans=MsgBox("Show Images?",36,"Image Question")
end sub
-->
</script>
<%Response.Write("<p>Paragraph One")%>
<%Response.Write("<p>Paragraph Two")%>
<%Response.Write("<p>Paragraph Three")%>
</body>
</html>
```

Figure 11.14: Coding and calling a subprocedure.

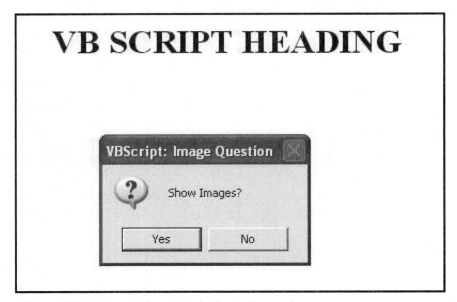

Figure 11.15: A message box created using a subprocedure.

In the code in Figure 11.14, the variable **showimg** is defined and then passed to the **askimages** subprocedure. At this point, it has not been assigned a value. We are primarily passing it to the subprocedure so that we can receive the updated value after the subprocedure executes. Within the subprocedure, we have defined the argument as **ans**. The **ans** variable is local to the subprocedure, meaning it cannot be used anywhere except inside **askimages**. The subprocedure displays a message box, and then loads the **ans** variable with the return information, which indicates which button was pressed. This value is then returned into the **showimg** variable as the subprocedure ends.

Obviously, this code is somewhat simplistic. We are not yet doing very much with the information received from the user. As you become more familiar with VB Script throughout the chapter, we'll make the sample code more and more useful.

Defining Functions

Functions are similar to subprocedures, but are more specialized. They are procedures that must return one and only one value.

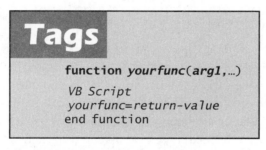

```
function yourfunc(arg1,…)

VB Script
yourfunc=return-value
end function
```

```
… yourfunc(arg1,…)…
```

Functions may have parameters passed to them, just as subprocedures do. Any changes made to the arguments in the function are passed back to the variables used to call the function. In addition, a single value must be loaded into a variable with the same name as the function. This value is the return value of the function.

Functions are called differently than subprocedures. To call a function, place it and its arguments, if any, in your VB Script, just as you would a variable. The code in Figure 11.16 shows how a function is used to provide a value for a variable.

```
<html>
<head>
<link rel="stylesheet" type="text/css" href="TESTcss.css">
</head>
<body>
<script type="text/vbscript">
<!--
document.write("<CENTER><H1>VB SCRIPT HEADING</H1></CENTER>")
dim showimg
showimg = askimages()
function askimages()
askimages=MsgBox("Show Images?",36,"Image Question")
end function
-->
</script>
<%Response.Write("<p>Paragraph One")%>
<%Response.Write("<p>Paragraph Two")%>
<%Response.Write("<p>Paragraph Three")%>
</body>
</html>
```

Figure 11.16: Coding and calling a function.

Anywhere that you might use a constant value in your VB Script code, you can probably substitute a function call that returns a value, as in Figure 11.16 when the variable **showimg** is loaded with the statement **"showimg = askimages()."** As this statement is processed, the **askimages** function is called with no arguments. (Note the empty parentheses.) As the function executes, the **askimages** variable in the function is loaded with the result of the message box. That value is returned to the calling statement and is used in place of the function. Therefore, the statement might be thought of as performing as **"showimg = askimages."** This means that the **showimg** variable is essentially set equal to the value of the **askimages** variable in the function.

Built-in Functions

Writing your own functions, as shown in the previous example, is a powerful way to extend the capabilities of the language you are coding in. Most languages include some built-in functions. These functions typically perform common tasks, such as data and time manipulation, data type conversions, string manipulation, and basic arithmetic. VB Script has a large number of built-in functions. Some of these, such as **MsgBox**, we've already discussed. Reviewing each of these functions is beyond the scope of this book, but to help you get started with VB Script, lists of built-in functions are given in Tables 11.1 through 11.6.

Table 11.1 shows the VB Script functions for working with dates and times. Use the Date function to return the current system date. The Time function returns the current system time. To return both the current date and time, use the Now function.

Table 11.1: Date and Time Functions	
Function	**Description**
Date	Returns the current system date
DateAdd	Returns a date after adding a specified time interval
DateDiff	Returns the difference between two dates
DatePart	Returns the specified part of a date
DateSerial	Returns the date for a specified year, month, and day
DateValue	Returns a date
Day	Returns the day of the month (between one and 31)
FormatDateTime	Returns a formatted date or time
Hour	Returns the hour of the day (between zero and 23)
IsDate	Returns a Boolean value that indicates if a specified value can be converted to a date
Minute	Returns the minute of the hour (between zero and 59)
Month	Returns the month of the year (between one and 12)
MonthName	Returns the name of a month
Now	Returns the current system date and time
Second	Returns the second of the minute (between zero and 59)
Time	Returns the current system time
Timer	Returns the number of seconds since 12:00 A.M.
TimeSerial	Returns the time for a specific hour, minute, and second
TimeValue	Returns a time
Weekday	Returns the day of the week (between one and seven)
WeekdayName	Returns the name of a specified day of the week
Year	Returns the year

Table 11.2 lists functions for conversion and formatting. To convert a value into a currency amount, use the FormatCurrency function. Use the FormatPercent function to convert a value into a percent.

Table 11:2: Conversion and Formatting Functions	
Function	Description
Asc	Converts the first letter in a string to ANSI code
CBool	Converts an expression to a variant of subtype Boolean
CByte	Converts an expression to a variant of subtype Byte
CCur	Converts an expression to a variant of subtype Currency
CDate	Converts a valid date and time expression to the variant of subtype Date
CDbl	Converts an expression to a variant of subtype Double
Chr	Converts the specified ANSI code to a character
CInt	Converts an expression to a variant of subtype Integer
CLng	Converts an expression to a variant of subtype Long
CSng	Converts an expression to a variant of subtype Single
CStr	Converts an expression to a variant of subtype String
FormatCurrency	Returns an expression formatted as currency
FormatDateTime	Returns an expression formatted as a date or time
FormatNumber	Returns an expression formatted as a number
FormatPercent	Returns an expression formatted as a percentage
Hex	Returns the hexadecimal value of a specified number
Oct number	Returns the octal value of a specified number

Table 11.3 lists common math functions in VB Script. Use the Int function to return the integer portion of a number. The Fix function does the same thing as Int, but behaves differently if used with negative numbers. For a negative value, Int returns the next lowest integer and Fix returns the next greater integer.

Table 11.3: Math Functions	
Function	**Description**
Abs	Returns the absolute value of a specified number
Atn	Returns the arctangent of a specified number
Cos	Returns the cosine of a specified number (angle)
Exp	Returns e raised to a power
Hex	Returns the hexadecimal value of a specified number
Int	Returns the integer part of a specified number
Fix	Returns the integer part of a specified number
Log	Returns the natural logarithm of a specified number
Oct	Returns the octal value of a specified number
Rnd	Returns a random number less than one but greater or equal to zero
Sgn	Returns an integer that indicates the sign of a specified number
Sin	Returns the sine of a specified number (angle)
Sqr	Returns the square root of a specified number
Tan	Returns the tangent of a specified number (angle)

Table 11.4 contains a list of functions for manipulating arrays. Use the UBound function to return the highest used subscript for an array. The LBound function returns the lowest subscript used for an array.

Table 11.4: Array Functions	
Function	**Description**
Array	Returns a variant containing an array
Filter	Returns a zero-based array that contains a subset of a string array based on a filter criteria
IsArray	Returns a Boolean value that indicates whether a specified variable is an array
Join	Returns a string that consists of a number of substrings in an array
LBound	Returns the smallest subscript for the indicated dimension of an array
Split	Returns a zero-based, one-dimensional array that contains a specified number of substrings
UBound	Returns the largest subscript for the indicated dimension of an array

Table 11.5 lists VB Script's string-manipulation functions. The UCase function converts a string into uppercase, while LCase converts it into lowercase. Use the Mid function to extract a portion of a string.

Table 11.5: String Functions	
Function	**Description**
InStr	Starting at the first character of the string, returns the position of the first occurrence of one string within another
InStrRev	Starting at the last character of the string, returns the position of the first occurrence of one string within another
LCase	Converts a specified string to lowercase
Left	Returns a specified number of characters from the left side of a string
Len	Returns the number of characters in a string
LTrim	Removes spaces on the left side of a string
RTrim	Removes spaces on the right side of a string
Trim	Removes spaces on both the left and right sides of a string
Mid	Returns a specified number of characters from a string
Replace	Replaces a specified part of a string with another string a specified number of times
Right	Returns a specified number of characters from the right side of a string
Space	Returns a string that consists of a specified number of spaces
StrComp	Compares two strings and returns a value that represents the result of the comparison
String	Returns a string that contains a repeating character of a specified length
StrReverse	Reverses a string
UCase	Converts a specified string to uppercase

Table 11.6 contains other miscellaneous VB Script functions. Use the MsgBox function to display a pop-up message box. The InputBox function is similar to the message box, but it also allows for the input of a value.

Table 11.6: Miscellaneous Functions	
Function	Description
CreateObject	Creates an object of a specified type
Eval	Evaluates an expression and returns the result
GetLocale	Returns the current locale ID
GetObject	Returns a reference to an automation object from a file
GetRef	Allows you to connect a VB Script procedure to a DHTML event on your pages
InputBox	Displays a dialog box where the user can write some input and/or click a button, and returns the contents
IsEmpty	Returns a Boolean value that indicates whether a specified variable has been initialized or not
IsNull	Returns a Boolean value that indicates whether a specified expression contains no valid data (null)
IsNumeric	Returns a Boolean value that indicates whether a specified expression can be evaluated as a number
IsObject	Returns a Boolean value that indicates whether the specified expression is an automation object
LoadPicture	Returns a picture object; available only on 32-bit platforms
MsgBox	Displays a message box, waits for the user to click a button, and returns a value that indicates which button the user clicked
RGB	Returns a number that represents an RGB color value
Round	Rounds a number
ScriptEngine	Returns the scripting language in use
ScriptEngineBuildVersion	Returns the build version number of the scripting engine in use
ScriptEngineMajorVersion	Returns the major version number of the scripting engine in use
ScriptEngineMinorVersion	Returns the minor version number of the scripting engine in use
SetLocale	Sets the locale ID and returns the previous locale ID
TypeName	Returns the subtype of a specified variable
VarType	Returns a value that indicates the subtype of a specified variable

Where to Place VB Script

In the examples so far in this chapter, the VB Script was coded within the body of the HTML document. This causes the VB Script to execute as the page contents are loaded. Typically, this is done if the VB Script is controlling the content included on the page.

VB Script can also be included within the heading section of the HTML document. This code is loaded before the page is displayed and is very popular for coding functions and procedures that are called from elsewhere on the page. The code in Figure 11.17 illustrates how VB Script can be written in both the body and heading sections of an HTML document.

```
<html>
<head>
<link rel="stylesheet" type="text/css" href="TESTcss.css">
<script type="text/vbscript">
<!--
sub writeheadings()
document.write("<CENTER><H1>VB SCRIPT HEADING</H1></CENTER>")
end sub
function askimages()
askimages=MsgBox("Show Images?",36,"Image Question")
end function
-->
</script>
</head>
<body>
<script type="text/vbscript">
<!--
option explicit
dim showimg
call writeheadings()
showimg = askimages()
-->
</script>
<%Response.Write("<p>Paragraph One")%>
<%Response.Write("<p>Paragraph Two")%>
<%Response.Write("<p>Paragraph Three")%>
</body>
</html>
```

Figure 11.17: Placing code in the header and body HTML sections.

In this example, the **writeheadings** procedure and the **askimages** function are placed in the header section of the HTML document. This allows the code to load as the Web page is displayed, enabling it to execute more quickly, when needed. Creating standardized subprocedures to produce common sections of your Web page can be a valuable tool in designing easily maintained Web pages.

If Statements

The **if** statement is an important feature of VB Script. This statement allows us to make decisions and dynamically control the behavior of the Web page as it's processed. There are several different formats for the **if** statement. It can be a single line of code where some condition causes a single statement to execute.

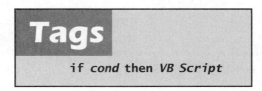

```
Tags

if cond then VB Script
```

It can also be coded with an **end if** that marks the end of an entire block of code that executes when the condition is true.

```
Tags

if cond then
    VB Script
end if
```

You can add an **else** statement to define a block of code that executes if the given condition is false.

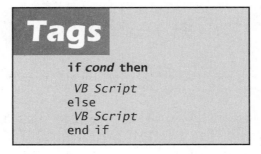

```
Tags

if cond then
    VB Script
else
    VB Script
end if
```

The condition is a logical operation that compares two or more values, for example, **showimg** = **6**. In earlier examples in this chapter, **showimg** holds the return value from a message box. A value of 6 from a message box indicates that its Yes button has been clicked. We could add an **if** statement that adds an image to the Web page when the user clicks the Yes button. That code is shown in Figure 11.18.

```
<script type="text/vbscript">
<!--
option explicit
dim showimg
call writeheadings()
showimg = askimages()
if showimg = 6 then
    document.write("<img src=" & chr(34) & "Grandma_Spicy.jpg" &
    chr(34) & ">")
end if
-->
</script>
```

Figure 11.18: Using an **if** *statement.*

If the **showimg** variable is equal to six, then the image of Grandma's spicy
BBQ sauce is displayed. This is not the most efficient way to code this **if**
statement, however. We can eliminate the **showimg** variable and call the
askimages function directly from the **if**. Note, though, that this is only
more efficient if the user's response to the question is needed just once.
If it is needed in more than one place in the code, it's probably better to
define a variable to hold the value rather than executing the code twice.
The alternative code is shown in Figure 11.19.

```
<script type="text/vbscript">
<!--
option explicit
call writeheadings()
if askimages() = 6 then
    document.write("<img src=" & chr(34) & "Grandma_Spicy.jpg" &
    chr(34) & ">")
end if
-->
</script>
```

Figure 11.19: Using a function in an **If** *statement.*

In both the **if** examples, you can see how the **chr(34)** function is used to
insert double quotes into the HTML tag. The **src** attribute of the **<img>**
tag is typically enclosed in double quotes. Coding those within the
document.write method, however, would conflict with the double quotes
being used to delimit the text written into the Web page. To avoid that
conflict, we use the **chr(34)** function, which inserts the double quotes into
the HTML document without conflicting with the double quotes used in
the VB Script.

To create a list of mutually exclusive conditions, we can add **elseif** to the **if** statement.

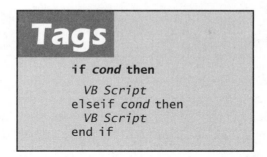

```
if cond then
    VB Script
elseif cond then
    VB Script
end if
```

For example, to test a variable for a series of different values, we could use **elseif** as shown in Figure 11.20. This example shows the **showimg** variable being tested for a 6, meaning that the Yes button was clicked, or a 7, indicating that the No button was clicked, or anything else, which would have to be the Cancel button. Because the same value is being tested more than once, we use the **showimg** variable to hold the return value from the **askimages** function.

```
<script type="text/vbscript">
<!--
option explicit
dim showimg
showimg = askimages()
call writeheadings()
if showimg = 6 then
    document.write("<img src=" & chr(34) & "Grandma_Spicy.jpg" &
    chr(34) & ">")
elseif showimg = 7 then
    document.write("They said No Images")
else
    document.write("They Canceled")
end if
-->
</script>
```

Figure 11.20: Using **elseif**.

And/Or Conditions

We can make the conditions in our statements increasingly complex using "and/or" logic. This allows us to define multiple conditions that must be true before a section of code is executed, and to define optional conditions that can cause the code to execute.

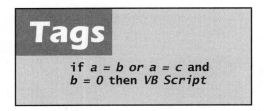

If **and** is used, the conditions on both sides of the **and** must be true for the code to execute. When an **or** is used, if the condition on either side of it is true, the code executes. Each **or** represents a completely new condition. An **and** listed on one side of the **or** has no impact on the tests being performed on the other side.

Select Statements

Another way to handle mutually exclusive sets of tests is with the **select** statement.

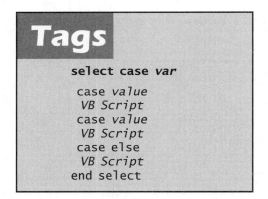

This statement defines a single value that is tested, and then defines what it is tested for and what code runs when one of those tests is true. In this statement, all of the tests are mutually exclusive. As soon as one is found to be true and its associated code is executed, processing continues after the **end select**. The code in Figure 11.21 shows how we could rewrite the previous **if/elseif** example using **select** instead.

```
<script type="text/vbscript">
<!--
option explicit
call writeheadings()
select case askimages()
    case 6
      document.write("<img src=" & chr(34) & "Grandma_Spicy.jpg" &
      chr(34) & ">")
    case 7
      document.write("They said No Images")
    case else
      document.write("They Canceled")
end select
-->
</script>
```

*Figure 11.21: Using **case** and **select**.*

For Next/Each Loops

Sometimes, we need to loop through a section of code a certain number of times. In these cases, the **for next** loop is extremely useful.

This loop defines an index variable that is loaded with the starting numeric value before the VB Script code within the loop is executed. After it executes the code the first time, the index is increased by one, and the code repeats. This continues until the limit value is reached. To increment the index by a value other than one, use the optional **step** parameter. To exit the loop before the limit is reached, use the **exit for** statement. This loop can be very useful in handling arrays.

Figure 11.22 shows how the **for next** loop can be used to display images on a page. This example shows additional code in the **writeheading** procedure that loads the URLs of a series of images into the **img** array. The script in the body of the page uses a **for next** loop to cycle through the array, asking the user if each image should be displayed on the page. Obviously, you would not typically ask the user that question, but it illustrates how the technique works using a simple example.

```
<html>
<head>
<link rel="stylesheet" type="text/css" href="TESTcss.css">
<script type="text/vbscript">
<!--
sub writeheadings()
document.write("<CENTER><H1>VB SCRIPT HEADING</H1></CENTER>")
img(0) = "Granma_Spicy.jpg"
img(1) = "Granma_Sweet.jpg"
img(2) = "Granma_Secret.jpg"
img(3) = "Granma_Home.jpg"
img(4) = "Granma_Fire_n_Spice.jpg"
end sub
sub askimages(x)
if MsgBox("Show Image " & x,36,"Show Image " & x) = 6 then
    document.write("<img src=" & chr(34) & img(x) & chr(34) & ">")
end if
end sub
-->
</script>
</head>
<body>
<script type="text/vbscript">
<!--
option explicit
dim img(4)
Dim n
call writeheadings()
for n = 0 to 4
   call askimages(n)
next
-->
</script>
<%Response.Write("<p>Paragraph One")%>
<%Response.Write("<p>Paragraph Two")%>
<%Response.Write("<p>Paragraph Three")%>
</body>
</html>
```

Figure 11.22: A **for next** loop.

A variation on the **for next** loop is the **for each** loop.

This loop is designed to work with arrays. It loops through each element in an array, incrementing the index by one. You can break out of the loop with the **exit** statement. We could rewrite the **for next** loop in Figure 11.22 as a **for each** loop, as shown in Figure 11.23.

```
for each n in imgs
   call askimages(n)
next
```

*Figure 11.23: A **for each** loop.*

Do While/Until Loops

Another form of loop is the **do while**, which loops as long as the given condition is true. There are two different formats for coding the **do while**, one that tests the condition before executing the code in the loop, and another that tests the condition after the loop has processed at least once.

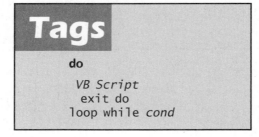

To exit the loop before the condition is not true, you can use the **exit do** statement, which is very similar to the **exit for** statement. The same loop coded with **for** in the previous examples could be coded with **do while** loops, as shown in Figures 11.24 and 11.25.

```
n = 0
do while n < 5
    call askimages(n)

n = n + 1
```

Figure 11.24: A **do while** loop.

```
n = 0
do
    call askimages(n)
    n = n + 1
loop while n < 5
```

Figure 11.25: An alternative **do while** loop.

Another form of loop is the **do until**.

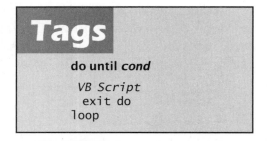

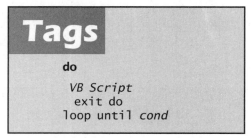

This statement is very similar to the **do while**, but it stops looping when the given condition is true. It can also be coded in two forms, one that tests the condition before the code executes, and the other that tests after it has executed at least once.

The **do until** loops could also be used in the previous examples. Figures 11.26 and 11.27 show how each version of the **do until** loop would work.

```
n = 0
do until n = 5
   call askimages(n)
   n = n + 1
loop
```

*Figure 11.26: A **do until** loop.*

```
n = 0
do
   call askimages(n)
   n = n + 1
loop until n = 5
```

*Figure 11.27: An alternative **do until** loop.*

ASP Code to Create a Simple Table

Now that you have learned the basics of VB Script, it's time to take a closer look at the server-side code for ASP.NET. Since this chapter is just a brief introduction to the topic, we'll avoid a lengthy discussion of all the possible things you could do with ASP.NET. That could fill multiple books. Instead, we'll focus on a few practical examples that show typical uses for ASP. NET in business applications.

Tables 11.7 through 11.11 contain lists of common ASP.NET controls for manipulating web pages. Table 11.7 focuses on HTML controls, which are ASP. NET tools used to replicate the function of common HTML tags. For example, to create a table in the Web page, you would use the HtmlTable control.

Table 11.7: HTML Controls in ASP.NET	
HTML Server Control	**Description**
HtmlAnchor	Controls the <a> tag
HtmlButton	Controls the <button> tag
HtmlForm	Controls the <form> tag
HtmlGeneric	Controls a generic HTML element, such as <body>, <div>, <span>, <p>, or <font>
HtmlImage	Controls the <image> tag

Table 11.7: HTML Controls in ASP.NET (Continued)	
HTML Server Control	**Description**
HtmlInputButton	Controls the \<input type="button">, \<input type="submit">, or \<input type="reset"> buttons
HtmlInputCheckBox	Controls the \<input type="checkbox"> tag
HtmlInputFile	Controls the \<input type="file"> tag
HtmlInputHidden	Controls the \<input type="hidden"> tag
HtmlInputImage	Controls the \<input type="image"> tag
HtmlInputRadioButton	Controls the \<input type="radio"> button
HtmlInputText	Controls the \<input type="text"> or \<input type="password"> tags
HtmlSelect	Controls the \<select> tag
HtmlTable	Controls the \<table> tag
HtmlTableCell	Controls the \<td> and \<th> tags
HtmlTableRow	Controls the \<tr> tag
HtmlTextArea	Controls the \<textarea> tag

Table 11.8 lists standard controls in ASP.NET. These controls provide the ability to create specialized objects such as buttons, datagrids, and calendars. This set of controls also includes tools for connecting to databases, such as the AccessDataSource.

Table 11.8: Standard Controls in ASP.NET	
Control	**Description**
AccessDataSource	Defines a connection to a Microsoft Access database
AdRotator	Displays a sequence of images
Button	Displays a push button
Calendar	Displays a calendar
CalendarDay	Controls a day in a calendar control
CheckBox	Displays a check box
CheckBoxList	Creates a multi-selection check box group
DataGrid	Displays the fields of a data source in a grid
DataList	Displays items from a data source by using templates

Table 11.8: Standard Controls in ASP.NET (Continued)	
Control	**Description**
DetailsView	Presents a single row from a data source with navigation buttons
DropDownList	Creates a drop-down list
FormView	Presents a single row from a data source
GridView	Controls an enhanced data grid
HyperLink	Creates a hyperlink
Image	Displays an image
ImageButton	Displays a clickable image
Label	Displays static content which is programmable (can apply styles to its content)
LinkButton	Creates a hyperlink button
ListBox	Creates a single- or multi-selection drop-down list
ListItem	Creates an item in a list
Literal	Displays static content which is programmable (cannot apply styles to its content)
ObjectDataSource	Defines a database connection
Panel	Provides a container for other controls
PlaceHolder	Reserves space for controls added by code
RadioButton	Creates a radio button
RadioButtonList	Creates a group of radio buttons
BulletedList	Creates a list in bullet format
Repeater	Displays a repeated list of items bound to the control
SqlDataSource	Defines an ADO.NET SQL connection
Style	Sets the style of controls
Table	Creates a table
TableCell	Creates a table cell
TableRow	Creates a table row
TextBox	Creates a text box
Xml	Displays an XML file or the results of an XSL transform
XmlDataSource	Defines an XML data source

Table 11.9 lists ASP.NET validation controls. These unique controls provide client-side editing of user input on the Web page. For example, RangeValidator provides the ability to assign a specific range to another control. Entries that are outside that range will be caught before the page is transmitted to the server.

Table 11.9: Validation Controls in ASP.NET	
Validation Server Control	**Description**
CompareValidator	Compares the value of one control to another control or value
CustomValidator	A custom method to validate input
RangeValidator	Verifies that a value is within a range
RegularExpressionValidator	Verifies that input matches a specified pattern
RequiredFieldValidator	Makes an input control a required field
ValidationSummary	Displays a report of all validation errors in a Web page

Table 11.10 lists controls used to navigate between pages. These specialized controls allow the user to navigate between pages in the Web site. Use the Menu control to create pop-up menus.

Table 11.10: Navigation Controls in ASP.NET	
Control	**Description**
Menu	Displays static and popup navigation options
SiteMapPath Web	Displays a hierarchical path back to the main page
TreeView	Displays static, dynamic or data bound trees

Table 11.11 contains ASP.NET controls for managing user login. The Login control allows users to log in. The LoginName control displays the name of the currently logged-in user.

Table 11.11: Log-in Controls in ASP.NET	
Control	**Description**
Login	Controls user log-in interface
PasswordRecovery	Retrieves or resets passwords
LoginName	Displays user's name
ChangePassword	Controls updating passwords
LoginView	Displays templates based on log-in status
LoginStatus	Detects status and displays log-in options
CreateUserWizard	Creates a new user

The first example is a simple Web page that lists all of the employees in an employee master table stored in an Access database. The ASP. NET code is shown in Figure 11.28. It produces the example shown in Figure 11.29.

```
<%@ Import Namespace="System.Data.OleDb" %>

<script runat="server">
sub Page_Load
dim dbconn,sql,dbcomm,dbread
        dbconn = New OleDbConnection("Provider=Microsoft.Jet.
  OLEDB.4.0;data source=" & Server.MapPath("App_Data\BBQData.
  mdb"))
dbconn.Open()
        sql = "SELECT * FROM EmpMast"
dbcomm=New OleDbCommand(sql,dbconn)
dbread=dbcomm.ExecuteReader()
        emps.DataSource = dbread
        emps.DataBind()
dbread.Close()
dbconn.Close()
end sub
</script>

<html>
<head>
<link href="asp.css" rel="stylesheet" type="text/css">
</head>
<body>

<form id="Form1" runat="server">
<asp:DataList
id="emps"
runat="server">

<HeaderTemplate>
```

Figure 11.28: ASP.NET code to list employees (part 1 of 2).

```
<asp:Table ID="Table1" runat=server>
<asp:TableHeaderRow>
<asp:TableHeaderCell   Width="40"   BackColor=#CCCCCC>Emp</asp:
   TableHeaderCell>
<asp:TableHeaderCell  Width="100"  BackColor=#CCCCCC>Name</asp:
   TableHeaderCell>
<asp:TableHeaderCell Width="100" BackColor=#CCCCCC>Title</asp:
   TableHeaderCell>
</asp:TableHeaderRow>
</asp:Table>
</HeaderTemplate>

<ItemTemplate>
<asp:Table ID="Table2" runat=server>
<asp:tablerow ID="Tablerow1" runat=server>
<asp:tablecell ID="Number" runat=server CssClass=Number>
<%#Container.DataItem("EmpNbr")%>
</asp:tablecell>
<asp:tablecell ID="Name" runat=server cssclass=Name>
<%#Container.DataItem("EmpName")%>
</asp:tablecell>
<asp:tablecell ID="Title" runat=server cssclass=Title>
<%#Container.DataItem("EmpTitle")%>
</asp:tablecell>
</asp:tablerow>
</asp:Table>
</ItemTemplate>
<FooterTemplate>
Source: BBQData Database
</FooterTemplate>

</asp:DataList>
</form>

</body>
</html>
```

Figure 11.28: ASP.NET code to list employees (part 2 of 2).

Emp	Name	Title
1	BBQ Bill	Big Boss
2	Grandma	Real Boss
3	Jane Smith	Manager
4	Joe Miller	Manager
5	Karl Dunns	Cook
6	Tim Tyler	Cook
7	Kathy Randal	Cook
8	Sandy Brown	Cook
9	Tom Clark	Server
10	Steve Hanes	Server
11	Adam Greene	Server
12	Alice Landon	Server
13	Rebecca Walters	Server
14	Tammy Yates	Server

Source: BBQData Database

Figure 11.29: A simple table created from the ASP.NET in Figure 11.28.

You can use this example as a simple template to display data from any table in your database. Similar code could be used in your business applications to list such things as current production orders, a shipping schedule, a contact list, or a daily sales activity log. While there are certainly many other ways to list data, this one is reasonably easy.

In the pages that follow, the code in Figure 11.28 is broken into smaller sections and discussed piece-by-piece.

Section 1 of 3

The section of code in Figure 11.30 defines the OLEDB connection to the Access database.

```
<%@ Import Namespace="System.Data.OleDb" %>

<script runat="server">
sub Page_Load
dim dbconn,sql,dbcomm,dbread
        dbconn = New OleDbConnection("Provider=Microsoft.Jet.
  OLEDB.4.0;data source=" & Server.MapPath("App_Data\BBQData.
  mdb"))
dbconn.Open()
        sql = "SELECT * FROM EmpMast"
dbcomm=New OleDbCommand(sql,dbconn)
dbread=dbcomm.ExecuteReader()
        emps.DataSource = dbread
        emps.DataBind()
dbread.Close()
dbconn.Close()
end sub
</script>
```

Figure 11.30: Section 1 of the ASP.NET code for Figure 11.29.

This example uses Access rather than SQL Server because it is easier for you to recreate an Access database for testing purposes. The script is defined as a server-side script by the statement **<script runat="server">**. The **Page_Load** subprocedure is automatically executed as the page loads. The **dim** statement defines a number of loosely typed variables. The **dbconn** statement defines the connection to the Access database **BBQData.mdb**, located in the **APP_Data** folder. The **Server.MapPath** function returns the name and path of the Access database. Its path is relative to the ASP file. In this case, both the ASP file and the database reside in the same folder.

The **sql** variable contains the **SELECT** statement, which selects all of the columns from the table **EmpMast**. In the sample database, this table includes the employee number, name, and title. Just because we selected all of the data doesn't mean we need to use it, but it is available if needed. The **emps** datalist contains the result of the **SELECT** statement and is loaded by binding the datalist to the data reader. Once the datalist is loaded, the reader and database connection are closed.

Section 2 of 3

The section of the ASP.NET file shown in Figure 11.31 begins the HTML code.

```
<html>
<head>
<link href="asp.css" rel="stylesheet" type="text/css">
</head>
<body>

<form id="Form1" runat="server">
<asp:DataList
id="emps"
runat="server">

<HeaderTemplate>
<asp:Table ID="Table1" runat=server>
<asp:TableHeaderRow>
<asp:TableHeaderCell   Width="40"    BackColor=#CCCCCC>Emp</asp:
   TableHeaderCell>
<asp:TableHeaderCell  Width="100"  BackColor=#CCCCCC>Name</asp:
   TableHeaderCell>
<asp:TableHeaderCell Width="100" BackColor=#CCCCCC>Title</asp:
   TableHeaderCell>
</asp:TableHeaderRow>
</asp:Table>
</HeaderTemplate>
```

Figure 11.31: Section 2 of the ASP.NET code for Figure 11.29.

The header section contains a link to a cascading style sheet, also stored in the same folder as the ASP file. The body section contains a simple form named **Form1**. (Forms were discussed in chapter 9.) It also defines the **emps** datalist. The ASP page will automatically produce a table that holds the information from the datalist. This table is built using properties set by three specialized controls: **HeaderTemplate**, **ItemTemplate**, and **FooterTemplate**. In this section, **HeaderTemplate** defines a table and a table header row containing header cells for each column in the table. The width and background color of these cells is set here. In the next section, you'll see that the cell properties are set through the style sheet.

Section 3 of 3

The **ItemTemplate** control defines the formatting of each record read from the datalist, as shown in Figure 11.32.

```
<ItemTemplate>
<asp:Table ID="Table2" runat=server>
<asp:tablerow ID="Tablerow1" runat=server>
<asp:tablecell ID="Number" runat=server CssClass=Number>
<%#Container.DataItem("EmpNbr")%>
</asp:tablecell>
<asp:tablecell ID="Name" runat=server cssclass=Name>
<%#Container.DataItem("EmpName")%>
</asp:tablecell>
<asp:tablecell ID="Title" runat=server cssclass=Title>
<%#Container.DataItem("EmpTitle")%>
</asp:tablecell>
</asp:tablerow>
</asp:Table>
</ItemTemplate>
<FooterTemplate>
Source: BBQData Database
</FooterTemplate>

</asp:DataList>
</form>

</body>
</html>
```

Figure 11.32: Section 3 of the ASP.NET code for Figure 11.29.

In this case, each record is defined as being a table with one row and three cells. The width, color, and other properties are defined in the style sheet linked to in the header section. The cells are each defined with their own class name using the **cssclass** property. Each cell is associated with a data item from the datalist using the **Container.DataItem** function, which identifies the desired column from the datalist. The names of the data items correspond to the column names from the table read in the **SELECT** statement. A **FooterTemplate** defines the text displayed at the bottom of the table, and then the datalist, form, and Web page are all closed.

The code for the cascading style sheet associated with this ASP.NET example is shown in Figure 11.33. The table and table row elements have their width set to 300 pixels. The background color of the table is set to gray. The style sheet contains several subclasses for the table data element. Each of the columns has its own class with a specific width and color. Some of the classes shown here are used in later examples.

```
.data {width:20%; position:absolute; top:10; left:20;
}
.TblTitle {background-color:#CCCCCC;
}
table {width:300; background-color:gray;
}
tr {width:300;
}
td.number {width:40; background-color:white;
}
td.name {width:100; background-color:white;
}
td.title {width:100; background-color:white;
}
td.date {width:90; background-color:white;
}
td.start {width:90; background-color:white;
}
td.stop {width:90; background-color:white;
}
```

Figure 11.33: The code for a cascading style sheet.

Creating a More Advanced Table

The previous example showed how to use ASP.NET to create a simple list. That is fine for many business functions; it's possible that all you need to do is present a list of current orders, inventory, scheduling information, or similar information. However, this is not always sufficient. You might have layers of pages where, for example, the first page presents a list of employees whose names are hypertext links. Clicking an employee's name displays a second page with the schedule information for that employee. Figure 11.34 shows the code for building the initial list of employees, shown in Figure 11.35.

```
<%@ Page Language="VB" Debug="true" %>
<%@ Import Namespace="System.Data.OleDb" %>

<script runat="server">
sub Page_Load
      Dim dbconn, sql, dbcomm, dbread
      dbconn = New OleDbConnection("Provider=Microsoft.Jet.
  OLEDB.4.0;data source=" & Server.MapPath("App_Data\BBQData.
  mdb"))
dbconn.Open()
      sql = "SELECT * FROM EmpMast"
dbcomm=New OleDbCommand(sql,dbconn)
dbread=dbcomm.ExecuteReader()
      emps.DataSource = dbread
      emps.DataBind()
```

Figure 11.34: The ASP.NET code that creates the page in Figure 11.35 (part 1 of 2).

```
dbread.Close()
dbconn.Close()
    End Sub

</script>

<html>
<head>
<link href="asp.css" rel="stylesheet" type="text/css">
</head>
<body>
<div class="data">
<form id="Form1" runat="server">
<asp:DataList
id="emps"
runat="server">

<HeaderTemplate>
<asp:Table ID="Table1" runat=server>
<asp:TableHeaderRow>
<asp:TableHeaderCell Width="40" BackColor=#CCCCCC>Emp</asp:
  TableHeaderCell>
<asp:TableHeaderCell Width="100" BackColor=#CCCCCC>Name</asp:
  TableHeaderCell>
<asp:TableHeaderCell Width="100" BackColor=#CCCCCC>Title</asp:
  TableHeaderCell>
</asp:TableHeaderRow>
</asp:Table>
</HeaderTemplate>

<ItemTemplate>
<asp:Table runat=server>
<asp:tablerow runat=server>
<asp:tablecell ID="Number" runat=server CssClass=Number>
<%#Container.DataItem("EmpNbr")%>
</asp:tablecell>
<asp:tablecell ID="Name" runat=server CssClass=Name>
<ahref="test6.aspx?Emp=<%#Container.DataItem("EmpNbr")%>
  &Nam=<%#Container.DataItem("EmpName")%>"><%#Container.
  DataItem("EmpName")%></a>
</asp:tablecell>
<asp:tablecell ID="Title" runat=server CssClass=Title>
<%#Container.DataItem("EmpTitle")%>
</asp:tablecell>
</asp:tablerow>
</asp:Table>
</ItemTemplate>
<FooterTemplate>
Source: BBQData Database
</FooterTemplate>

</asp:DataList>
</form>
</div>
</body>
</html>
```

Figure 11.34: The ASP.NET code that creates the page in Figure 11.35 (part 2 of 2).

Emp	Name	Title
1	BBQ Bill	Big Boss
2	Grandma	Real Boss
3	Jane Smith	Manager
4	Joe Miller	Manager
5	Karl Dunns	Cook
6	Tim Tyler	Cook
7	Kathy Randal	Cook
8	Sandy Brown	Cook
9	Tom Clark	Server
10	Steve Hanes	Server
11	Adam Greene	Server
12	Alice Landon	Server
13	Rebecca Walters	Server
14	Tammy Yates	Server
Source: BBQData Database		

Figure 11.35: A table with linked items

The lines in Figure 11.34 that create the hypertext link are shown again in Figure 11.36.

```
<asp:tablecell ID="Name" runat=server CssClass=Name>
<ahref="test6.aspx?Emp=<%#Container.DataItem("EmpNbr")%>
  &Nam=<%#Container.DataItem("EmpName")%>"><%#Container.
  DataItem("EmpName")%></a>
</asp:tablecell>
```

Figure 11.36: The code to create a hypertext link.

In this case, we use a simple anchor tag and assemble the **href** property. It begins with the name of the next ASP page to open. Then, additional information is added to the URL to pass the employee number and name as parameters to the next page. The list of parameters starts with a question mark. Each parameter begins with the parameter name followed by an equal sign, and then the value for the parameter. Ampersands separate the parameters. The data passed in this manner is referred to as the *query string*. For example, the query string for Grandma in the second row of the table would look like this:

test6.aspx?Emp=2&Nam=Grandma

Notice how the data items are rendered into the page without needing any kind concatenation.

The code for the schedule data page is shown in Figure 11.37, and the results for the employee Grandma are shown in Figure 11.38.

```
<%@ Page Language="VB" Debug="true" %>
<%@ Import Namespace="System.Data.OleDb" %>

<script runat="server">
sub Page_Load

      Dim dbconn, sql, dbcomm, dbread, empnbr
      empnbr = Request.QueryString("Emp")

      dbconn = New OleDbConnection("Provider=Microsoft.Jet.
  OLEDB.4.0;data source=" & Server.MapPath("App_Data\BBQData.
  mdb"))
      dbconn.Open()
      sql = "SELECT Format(SchDate, 'Short Date') as
  SDate,Format(SchStart, 'Medium Time') as SStart,Format(SchEnd,
  'Medium Time') as SEnd,SchJob FROM SchMast Where SchEmp = " &
  empnbr
      dbcomm = New OleDbCommand(sql, dbconn)
      dbread = dbcomm.ExecuteReader()
      emps.DataSource = dbread
      emps.DataBind()
      dbread.Close()
      dbconn.Close()
    End Sub

</script>

<html>
<head>
<link href="asp.css" rel="stylesheet" type="text/css">
</head>
<body>

<form id="Form1" runat="server">
<asp:DataList
id="emps"
runat="server">

<HeaderTemplate>
<asp:Table ID="Table1" runat=server>
<asp:TableHeaderRow>
<asp:TableHeaderCell colspan="3" BackColor=#CCCCCC><% Response.
  Write(Request.QueryString("Nam"))%></asp:TableHeaderCell>
</asp:TableHeaderRow>
<asp:TableHeaderRow>
```

Figure 11.37: The ASP code to create the page in Figure 11.38 (part 1 of 2).

```
<asp:TableHeaderCell Width="100" BackColor=#CCCCCC>Date
</asp:TableHeaderCell>
<asp:TableHeaderCell Width="100" BackColor=#CCCCCC>Clock In
</asp:TableHeaderCell>
<asp:TableHeaderCell Width="100" BackColor=#CCCCCC>Clock Out
</asp:TableHeaderCell>
</asp:TableHeaderRow>
</asp:Table>
</HeaderTemplate>

<ItemTemplate>
<asp:Table runat=server >
<asp:tablerow runat=server>
<asp:tablecell ID="Date" runat=server CssClass=Date>
<%#Container.DataItem("SDate")%>
</asp:tablecell>
<asp:tablecell ID="Start" runat=server cssclass=Start>
  <%#Container.DataItem("SStart")%>
</asp:tablecell>
<asp:tablecell ID="Stop" runat=server cssclass=Stop>
<%#Container.DataItem("SEnd")%>
</asp:tablecell>
</asp:tablerow>
</asp:Table>
</ItemTemplate>
<FooterTemplate>
Source: BBQData Database
</FooterTemplate>

</asp:DataList>
</form>

</body>
</html>
```

Figure 11.37: The ASP code to create the page in Figure 11.38 (part 2 of 2).

Grandma		
Date	**Clock In**	**Clock Out**
12/8/2007	12:00 PM	10:00 PM
12/9/2007	12:00 PM	10:00 PM
Source: BBQData Database		

Figure 11.38: Selected schedule data.

This code is very similar to that shown in Figure 11.34, except that it has input parameters to read from the query string. The employee number is read with the following statement:

empnbr = Request.QueryString("Emp")

This statement loads the value of the **Emp** parameter into the **empnbr** variable. This variable is then used in assembling the **SELECT** statement. For this page to work correctly, the **SELECT** statement needs to limit the data displayed to only the schedule entries for one employee—"Grandma," in this case. The code sample in Figure 11.39 shows how the **SELECT** statement was assembled. At the end of this statement, you can see how the **empnbr** variable is concatenated into the **Where** clause.

```
            sql = "SELECT Format(SchDate, 'Short Date') as
SDate,Format(SchStart, 'Medium Time') as SStart,Format(SchEnd,
'Medium Time') as SEnd,SchJob FROM SchMast Where SchEmp = " &
empnbr
```

*Figure 11.39: The code to build a precise **SELECT** statement.*

The **Format** function modifies each of the date and time variables from the Access database to display the appropriate information. The employee name from the query string is displayed in the table headings using this simple statement:

<%Response.write(Request.QueryString("Nam"))%>

The **response.write** method was discussed earlier in this chapter.

Updating Data in a Database

Suppose we want to create a page to update the schedule data in the Access database discussed in the previous examples. There are a number of ways we can accomplish that. One of the standard data controls included in ASP is **FormView**. This control is designed to manage a connection to a database, allowing an application user to navigate through all the rows in a table. As the user moves through the database, he or she can edit, delete, or insert records. Of course, those are configurable options, so if you don't want to allow them, you can disable them.

The code in Figure 11.40 creates the **FormView** control shown in Figure 11.41.

```
<%@ Page Language="VB" Debug="true" %>
<%@ Import Namespace="System.Data.OleDb" %>
<%@ Import Namespace="System.Web.UI.WebControls" %>


<html>
<body>

<form id="Form1" runat="server">
<asp:FormView
        datasourceid="SchedSource"
        allowpaging="True"
        datakeynames="SchEmp,SchDate"
        id="sched"
        runat="server"
        BackColor=lightgray
        BorderWidth=3
        borderstyle=Inset>
<edititemtemplate>
    SchEmp:
    <asp:Label ID="SchEmpLabel1" runat="server" Text='<%#
Eval("SchEmp") %>'></asp:Label><br />
    SchDate:
    <asp:Label ID="SchDateLabel1" runat="server" Text='<%#
Eval("SchDate") %>'></asp:Label><br />
    SchStart:
    <asp:TextBox ID="SchStartTextBox" runat="server" Text='<%#
Eval("SchStart") %>'></asp:TextBox><br />
    SchEnd:
    <asp:TextBox ID="SchEndTextBox" runat="server" Text='<%#
Bind("SchEnd") %>'>
    </asp:TextBox><br />
    SchJob:
    <asp:TextBox ID="SchJobTextBox" runat="server" Text='<%#
Bind("SchJob") %>'>
    </asp:TextBox><br />
    <asp:LinkButton ID="UpdateButton" runat="server"
CausesValidation="True" CommandName="Update"
        Text="Update">
    </asp:LinkButton>
    <asp:LinkButton ID="UpdateCancelButton" runat="server"
CausesValidation="False" CommandName="Cancel"
        Text="Cancel">
    </asp:LinkButton>
</edititemtemplate>
    <InsertItemTemplate>
    SchEmp:
    <asp:TextBox  ID="SchEmpTextBox"  runat="server"  Text='<%#
Bind("SchEmp") %>'>
        </asp:TextBox><br />
    SchDate:
```

Figure 11.40: The code to update a database (part 1 of 3).

```
        <asp:TextBox ID="SchDateTextBox" runat="server" Text='<%#
Bind("SchDate") %>'>
      </asp:TextBox><br />
      SchStart:
      <asp:TextBox ID="SchStartTextBox" runat="server" Text='<%#
Bind("SchStart") %>'>
      </asp:TextBox><br />
      SchEnd:
       <asp:TextBox ID="SchEndTextBox" runat="server" Text='<%#
Bind("SchEnd") %>'>
      </asp:TextBox><br />
      SchJob:
       <asp:TextBox ID="SchJobTextBox" runat="server" Text='<%#
Bind("SchJob") %>'>
      </asp:TextBox><br />
      <asp:LinkButton      ID="InsertButton"       runat="server"
CausesValidation="True" CommandName="Insert"
         Text="Insert">
      </asp:LinkButton>
       <asp:LinkButton ID="InsertCancelButton" runat="server"
CausesValidation="False" CommandName="Cancel"
         Text="Cancel">
      </asp:LinkButton>
  </InsertItemTemplate>
  <ItemTemplate>
      SchEmp:
      <asp:Label  ID="SchEmpLabel"   runat="server"   Text='<%#
Eval("SchEmp") %>'></asp:Label><br />
      SchDate:
      <asp:Label  ID="SchDateLabel"  runat="server"   Text='<%#
Eval("SchDate") %>'></asp:Label><br />
      SchStart:
      <asp:Label  ID="SchStartLabel" runat="server"   Text='<%#
Eval("SchStart") %>'></asp:Label><br />
      SchEnd:
      <asp:Label  ID="SchEndLabel"   runat="server"   Text='<%#
Bind("SchEnd") %>'></asp:Label><br />
      SchJob:
      <asp:Label  ID="SchJobLabel"   runat="server"   Text='<%#
Bind("SchJob") %>'></asp:Label><br />
      <asp:LinkButton      ID="EditButton"       runat="server"
CausesValidation="False" CommandName="Edit"
         Text="Edit">
      </asp:LinkButton>
      <asp:LinkButton      ID="DeleteButton"       runat="server"
CausesValidation="False" CommandName="Delete"
         Text="Delete">
      </asp:LinkButton>
      <asp:LinkButton ID="NewButton" runat="server"
CausesValidation="False" CommandName="New"
         Text="New">
```

Figure 11.40: The code to update a database (part 2 of 3).

```
        </asp:LinkButton>
    </ItemTemplate>
</asp:FormView>

        <asp:AccessDataSource  ID="schedsource"  runat="server"
DataFile="~/App_Data/BBQData.mdb"
            selectcommand="SELECT        Format(SchDate,      'Short
Date')   as   SchDate,Format(SchStart,  'Medium  Time')   as
SchStart,Format(SchEnd, 'Medium Time') as SchEnd,SchEmp,SchJob
FROM [SchMast] ORDER BY [SchEmp], [SchDate], [SchStart]"
DeleteCommand="DELETE FROM [SchMast] WHERE [SchEmp] = ? AND
[SchDate] = ? AND [SchStart] = ?" InsertCommand="INSERT INTO
[SchMast] ([SchEmp], [SchDate], [SchStart], [SchEnd], [SchJob])
VALUES (?, ?, ?, ?, ?)" UpdateCommand="UPDATE [SchMast] SET
[SchEnd] = ?, [SchJob] = ? WHERE [SchEmp] = ? AND [SchDate] = ?
AND [SchStart] = ?">
        <DeleteParameters>
            <asp:Parameter Name="SchEmp" Type="Int32" />
            <asp:Parameter Name="SchDate" Type="DateTime" />
        </DeleteParameters>
        <UpdateParameters>
            <asp:Parameter Name="SchEnd" Type="DateTime" />
            <asp:Parameter Name="SchJob" Type="String" />
            <asp:Parameter Name="SchEmp" Type="Int32" />
            <asp:Parameter Name="SchDate" Type="DateTime" />
            <asp:Parameter Name="SchStart" Type="DateTime" />
        </UpdateParameters>
        <InsertParameters>
            <asp:Parameter Name="SchEmp" Type="Int32" />
            <asp:Parameter Name="SchDate" Type="DateTime" />
            <asp:Parameter Name="SchStart" Type="DateTime" />
            <asp:Parameter Name="SchEnd" Type="DateTime" />
            <asp:Parameter Name="SchJob" Type="String" />
        </InsertParameters>

    </asp:AccessDataSource>
</form>
</body>
</html>
```

Figure 11.40: The code to update a database (part 3 of 3).

```
SchEmp: 1
SchDate: 12/3/2007
SchStart: 08:00 AM
SchEnd: 05:00 PM
SchJob: Manager
Edit Delete New
    1 2 3 4 5 6 7 8 9 10 ...
```

*Figure 11.41: A form for updating
data in a database.*

This simple form lists each of the columns in the table, and presents a navigation tool at the bottom so that the user can move through all the records. It also provides options to edit or delete the current record, or even insert a new record.

All of this is done with very little coding on your part if you use the tools in the Visual Web Developer. Simply open a new file within your Web site, and select the **Web Form** option. When the new file is opened in edit mode, select the **Design** option in the lower left corner of the page. This switches you from views of the code to looking at the palette. Using the toolbox typically located on the left side of the screen, drag a **FormView** from the data controls onto the page. Then drag an **AccessDataSource** onto the page. Figure 11.42 shows the page with these two controls added.

FormView - FormView1

Right-click or choose the Edit Templates task to edit template content. The ItemTemplate is required.

AccessDataSource - AccessDataSource1

Figure 11.42: A new page in design mode.

Once these are located on the screen, you can right-click the **AccessDataSource** and select the **Configure Data Source** option. This walks you through a series of prompts asking you where the database is that you want to connect to, what table in the database you want to connect to, and what columns within the table you want to use. You also have the option to have this wizard generate the appropriate **SELECT, INSERT, UPDATE,** and **DELETE** commands for you.

Right-click the **FormView** and select the **AutoFormat** option, and you can select from one of several preconfigured layout options. For this example, select **Black & Blue 2**. Then, select the properties of the **FormView** and update the data source to point at the **AccessDataSource** you've already placed on the page. They are not automatically associated since, in more sophisticated applications, you might have multiple data sources in use on the same page. If you used the data in the EmpMast table, your control would look like the example in Figure 11.43.

*Figure 11.43: The new page
after configuring the options.*

That is essentially all it takes to create an editable interface to your
Access database. To see it in action, simply right-click the page and
select **View in Browser**. This launches the page and allows you to
update your database.

With the control completed, let's go back to reviewing some of the code
from Figure 11.40. The snippet shown in Figure 11.44 shows the definition
of the **FormView**. In this case, we define the keys to the table as the
employee number and schedule data. The background color, style, and
width are also set here.

```
<form id="Form1" runat="server">
<asp:FormView
        datasourceid="SchedSource"
        allowpaging="True"
        datakeynames="SchEmp,SchDate"
        id="sched"
        runat="server"
        BackColor=lightgray
        BorderWidth=3
        borderstyle=Inset>
```

*Figure 11.44: The **FormView** definition from the application in Figure 11.40.*

The code snippet in Figure 11.45 shows only **EditTemplate**. This controls
the look and behavior of the form while in edit mode. As you can see,
the two key fields, **SchEmp** and **SchDate,** are displayed in **Label** controls.
These are read-only, so no updating of these columns is allowed. The other
fields are all shown in textboxes, which allow for easy updating. This
section is completed by the Update and Cancel buttons.

```
<edititemtemplate>
   SchEmp:
   <asp:Label   ID="SchEmpLabel1"   runat="server"   Text='<%#
Eval("SchEmp") %>'></asp:Label><br />
   SchDate:
   <asp:Label   ID="SchDateLabel1"   runat="server"   Text='<%#
Eval("SchDate") %>'></asp:Label><br />
   SchStart:
   <asp:TextBox ID="SchStartTextBox" runat="server" Text='<%#
Eval("SchStart") %>'></asp:TextBox><br />
   SchEnd:
   <asp:TextBox   ID="SchEndTextBox"   runat="server"   Text='<%#
Bind("SchEnd") %>'>
   </asp:TextBox><br />
   SchJob:
   <asp:TextBox   ID="SchJobTextBox"   runat="server"   Text='<%#
Bind("SchJob") %>'>
   </asp:TextBox><br />
   <asp:LinkButton      ID="UpdateButton"      runat="server"
CausesValidation="True" CommandName="Update"
      Text="Update">
   </asp:LinkButton>
   <asp:LinkButton    ID="UpdateCancelButton"    runat="server"
CausesValidation="False" CommandName="Cancel"
      Text="Cancel">
   </asp:LinkButton>
</edititemtemplate>
```

*Figure 11.45: The **EditTemplate** code.*

The code snippet in Figure 11.46 shows **InsertTemplate**. In this case, all of the columns are editable, since even the key fields need to be provided here.

```
<InsertItemTemplate>
   SchEmp:
   <asp:TextBox ID="SchEmpTextBox" runat="server" Text='<%#
Bind("SchEmp") %>'>
   </asp:TextBox><br />
   SchDate:
   <asp:TextBox ID="SchDateTextBox" runat="server" Text='<%#
Bind("SchDate") %>'>
   </asp:TextBox><br />
   SchStart:
   <asp:TextBox      ID="SchStartTextBox"      runat="server"
Text='<%# Bind("SchStart") %>'>
   </asp:TextBox><br />
   SchEnd:
   <asp:TextBox ID="SchEndTextBox" runat="server" Text='<%#
Bind("SchEnd") %>'>
   </asp:TextBox><br />
   SchJob:
```

*Figure 11.46: The **InsertTemplate** code (part 1 of 2).*

```
        <asp:TextBox ID="SchJobTextBox" runat="server" Text='<%#
Bind("SchJob") %>'>
        </asp:TextBox><br />
            <asp:LinkButton ID="InsertButton" runat="server"
CausesValidation="True" CommandName="Insert"
        Text="Insert">
        </asp:LinkButton>
            <asp:LinkButton ID="InsertCancelButton" runat="server"
CausesValidation="False" CommandName="Cancel"
        Text="Cancel">
        </asp:LinkButton>
    </InsertItemTemplate>
```

Figure 11.46: The **InsertTemplate** code (part 2 of 2).

The code snippet in Figure 11.47 shows **ItemTemplate**, which defines the look and behavior of the form while the user is simply browsing data, not editing or inserting. As you can see in this example, all of the columns are displayed as read-only **Label** controls. Buttons for switching to edit or delete mode complete the template.

```
    <ItemTemplate>
        SchEmp:
            <asp:Label ID="SchEmpLabel" runat="server" Text='<%#
Eval("SchEmp") %>'></asp:Label><br />
        SchDate:
            <asp:Label ID="SchDateLabel" runat="server" Text='<%#
Eval("SchDate") %>'></asp:Label><br />
        SchStart:
            <asp:Label ID="SchStartLabel" runat="server" Text='<%#
Eval("SchStart") %>'></asp:Label><br />
        SchEnd:
            <asp:Label ID="SchEndLabel" runat="server" Text='<%#
Bind("SchEnd") %>'></asp:Label><br />
        SchJob:
            <asp:Label ID="SchJobLabel" runat="server" Text='<%#
Bind("SchJob") %>'></asp:Label><br />
            <asp:LinkButton ID="EditButton" runat="server"
CausesValidation="False" CommandName="Edit"
        Text="Edit">
        </asp:LinkButton>
            <asp:LinkButton ID="DeleteButton" runat="server"
CausesValidation="False" CommandName="Delete"
        Text="Delete">
        </asp:LinkButton>
            <asp:LinkButton ID="NewButton" runat="server"
CausesValidation="False" CommandName="New"
        Text="New">
        </asp:LinkButton>
    </ItemTemplate>
```

Figure 11.47: The **ItemTemplate** code.

The last code snippet, in Figure 11.48, shows **AccessDataSource**. You'll see that we added the same **Format()** function to the **SELECT** statement that we used in an earlier example. Again, this formats the data and time fields from the Access database correctly for our needs. After the **SELECT** statement, the **DELETE**, **INSERT**, and **UPDATE** commands are all listed. Whenever a field from the **FormView** is referenced, parameter markers are used in the code (the question marks). Then, the parameters are defined below.

```
</asp:FormView>
        <asp:AccessDataSource ID="schedsource" runat="server"
DataFile="~/App_Data/BBQData.mdb"
        selectcommand="SELECT Format(SchDate, 'Short Date') as SchD
ate,Format(SchStart, 'Medium Time') as SchStart,Format(SchEnd,
'Medium Time') as SchEnd,SchEmp,SchJob FROM [SchMast] ORDER
BY [SchEmp], [SchDate], [SchStart]" DeleteCommand="DELETE  FR
OM [SchMast] WHERE [SchEmp] = ? AND [SchDate] = ?" InsertCom
mand="INSERT INTO [SchMast] ([SchEmp], [SchDate], [SchStart],
[SchEnd], [SchJob]) VALUES (?, ?, ?, ?, ?)" UpdateCommand="UPDATE
[SchMast] SET [SchEnd] = ?, [SchJob] = ? WHERE [SchEmp] = ? AND
[SchDate] = ?">
            <DeleteParameters>
                <asp:Parameter Name="SchEmp" Type="Int32" />
                <asp:Parameter Name="SchDate" Type="DateTime" />
            </DeleteParameters>
            <UpdateParameters>
                <asp:Parameter Name="SchEnd" Type="DateTime" />
                <asp:Parameter Name="SchJob" Type="String" />
                <asp:Parameter Name="SchEmp" Type="Int32" />
                <asp:Parameter Name="SchDate" Type="DateTime" />
                <asp:Parameter Name="SchStart" Type="DateTime" />
            </UpdateParameters>
            <InsertParameters>
                <asp:Parameter Name="SchEmp" Type="Int32" />
                <asp:Parameter Name="SchDate" Type="DateTime" />
                <asp:Parameter Name="SchStart" Type="DateTime" />
                <asp:Parameter Name="SchEnd" Type="DateTime" />
                <asp:Parameter Name="SchJob" Type="String" />
            </InsertParameters>

        </asp:AccessDataSource>
</form>
</body>
</html>
```

*Figure 11.48: The **AccessDataSource** code.*

Connecting to SQL Server

All of the examples in this chapter have involved an Access database. One of the reasons for this is because it is somewhat simpler to distribute an Access database than a SQL Server database, so we can make the database available to our readers through MC Press's Web site, *www.mcpressonline.com*. Go to the Forums and then MC Product Reviews and Downloads. You will find the files under the book title in the Download forum.

If you want to use an SQL Server database instead, however, it is an easy change to make. Simply go to the **Data Controls** in the toolbox, drag the **SQLDataSource** onto the page, and configure it in much the same fashion as the **AccessDataSource** discussed earlier. Once it is configured, simply attach the appropriate data controls to the data source by changing their **Datasource** property, and you're connected.

Summary

The large number of specialized controls combined with a robust programming language makes ASP.NET an extremely diverse development environment. We've only touched the basics of programming with it in this chapter. To truly master ASP.NET takes considerable effort, but we hope the examples here have helped you see that you can create productive and effective Web pages fairly easily, once you get the basics figured out.

12

Java Server Pages

First Java, then JavaScript, and now Java Server Pages. They have similar names, but are different programming tools. Yes, it is confusing! Chapter 8 introduced JavaScript, the client-side scripting language that can be embedded in HTML to make Web pages more dynamic. This chapter introduces Java Server Pages (JSP). Like JavaScript, JSP makes Web pages more dynamic. Like PHP and ASP.NET, JSP is a server-side programming tool.

JSP Overview

JSP technology provides a simple, fast way to create dynamic Web-page content. The JSP specifications are developed through an industry-wide initiative led by Sun Microsystems. The specifications define the interaction between the server and JSP, and describe the format and syntax of JSP. JSP can be viewed as a high-level abstraction of servlets and is implemented as an extension of the Servlet API.

JSP is a Java technology that allows programmers to dynamically generate HTML in response to a Web client's request. The technology allows Java code and certain predefined actions to be embedded in static Web content. In this chapter, you will be introduced to the JSP used in HTML, learn the basics of JSP syntax, and learn by example how to use JSP within Web applications. Learning JSP does not require Java knowledge or experience, but if you are already familiar with Java, JSP programming will be easy.

The JSP syntax adds additional tags, called JSP *actions*, to be used to invoke built-in functionality. These tags allow for the creation of JSP *tag libraries* that act as extensions to the standard HTML and XML tags. Tag libraries provide a platform-independent way of extending the capabilities of a Web server. JSP pages are platform- and Web-server independent.

JSP pages use XML tags and scriptlets written in the Java programming language to encapsulate the logic that generates the content for a Web page. A JSP page usually has the extension *.jsp*, or it may use the extension *.jspx* for XML deployment. This chapter works with the *.jsp* extension. Any formatting tags (HTML or XML) are passed directly back to the response page. In this way, JSP separates the page logic from the design and display.

JSP pages are compiled into Java *servlets* by a JSP compiler. A servlet is a program written in the Java programming language that runs on the server. A JSP compiler may generate a servlet in Java code that is then compiled by the Java compiler, or it may generate byte code for the servlet directly. A servlet may call *JavaBeans* to perform processing on the server. JavaBeans are classes written in Java. They are used to encapsulate many objects into a single "bean" object. The bean can be passed around and shared, rather than having many individual objects.

In the real world, you'll often find many individual objects all of the same kind. Similarly, there are many cars of the same make and model. Each one was built from the same set of blueprints, and therefore contains the same components. In object-oriented terms, an individual car is an *instance* of the class of objects known as "cars." A *class* is the blueprint from which individual objects are created. A *superclass* is a class that is inherited. *Inheritance* is the process by which one object acquires the properties of another object.

JSP technology is designed to simplify the process of creating pages by separating Web presentation from Web content. In a dynamic Web site, there will proably be a combination of static data and dynamically generated data. The data will be sent in response to a client request, through the browser. A JSP engine interprets tags and generates the content required by, for example, calling a bean, accessing a database with the JDBC API, or including a file. It then sends the results back to the browser in the form of an HTML or XML page. The logic that generates the content is encapsulated in tags and beans processed on the server.

It is much easier to work with JSP pages than to do everything with servlets. Servlets are the counterpart to non-Java dynamic Web-content technologies such as PHP, CGI, and ASP.NET. Servlets are programs that run on a Web server and build Web pages on the fly. JSP technology is a key component in a highly scalable architecture for Web-based applications.

What JSP Is Used for

JSP can be used for many applications. Here are just a few examples:

- Web pages that use data from business databases, for example, an application that displays inventory stock or current product prices for an online order system.

- Web pages based on data submitted by a user, for example, an online customer-service application or an online ordering application. Other examples are an online work schedule for employees or a search engine.

- Web pages with data that changes often, for example, a special events page that is updated frequently. The events may change, requiring a new page, or a previously built page might be returned if the information is still up-to-date.

Why use JSP instead of other tools? There are many reasons. Here are a few:

- JSP servlets are efficient, easy to use, portable, platform-independent, and inexpensive.

- JSP makes it easy and convenient to add dynamic content to an otherwise static HTML page.

- Comparing JSP to JavaScript, JavaScript is limited to the client environment. It can generate HTML dynamically on the client, which is a useful capability, but with the exception of cookies, HTTP and form-submission data is not available to JavaScript. JavaScript can't access server-side resources like databases. Often, JSP will be used with JavaScript.

- Comparing JSP to pure servlets, JSP is more convenient to write and modify, and provides the same functionality. JSP separates the look from the content. This might be an important consideration, especially for a large organization that has some staff members who work on page design and others who work on the dynamic content of the site.

- Comparing JSP to traditional CGI, JSP's servlets allow you to do several things that are difficult or impossible with CGI. For example, servlets can talk directly to the Web server. A CGI program cannot.

Also, with traditional CGI, a new process is started for each HTTP request. With JSP servlets, the Java Virtual Machine (JVM) stays up, and each request is handled by a lightweight Java thread, not a heavyweight operating system process. Traditional CGI loads the request in memory for each CGI program request. Servlets have multiple threads, but only a single copy of the servlet class.

- JSP is a similar technology to .NET, discussed in chapter 11. However, the dynamic part of JSP is written in Java, not Visual Basic or some other Microsoft-specific language, so JSP is portable and can be used with non-Microsoft operating systems and servers, unlike .NET. In an environment that uses non-Microsoft technology or requires multiple platforms, JSP would be the likely choice. JSP can also be used on a Microsoft server.

- PHP is portable like JSP, and arguably easier to learn. However, PHP is fairly new compared to JSP. Currently, much more information is available on Java technologies like JSP than on PHP technology, although this might change in the future. JSP is sponsored by Sun, and PHP is sponsored by Zend. Sun has been around a lot longer and is a much larger organization. Does this matter? Big names are sometimes important when choosing technology. For example, company policy might consider it important, when considering the possible support that will be received. Also, PHP is open source. Some organizations are comfortable with using open source technologies, while others are not.

JSP has been around quite awhile and has been incorporated for dynamic Web development in many environments, large and small. However, all of the alternatives to JSP have positive qualities. It might be a difficult choice, and many factors should be considered. Keep in mind your resources' expertise and your organization's goals, including longer-term goals. Of course, don't lose site of the purpose of your Web application! The decision on tools may likely be to use a combination, including JSP.

JSP's Advantages and Disadvantages

Like all other Web development tools, JSP has advantages and disadvantages. Here are some of its advantages:

- Portability. JSP is available on any JVM machine.

- Java is a very popular language, with extensive support and resource knowledge.

- Java is a robust and very functional language.

- You can easily incorporate extensive functionality through JSP without completely mastering Java.

- JSP provides full security functionality.

- Performance is strong.

- JSP separates content from presentation, and thus the designer role from the developer role.

- JSP allows for multi-threading and multi-tasking to accommodate resources.

- JSP is easily incorporated for use with other languages and tools.

- Strong error-identification and error-handling are included.

Here are JSP's perceived disadvantages:

- It's a little harder to learn than some other server-side languages.

- It is a compiled language. The extra step of compiling is required prior to executing code.

- It can be difficult to debug.

What Is Needed to Use Java Server Pages

Here's what you need to get started with JSP:

- JSP pages are usually compiled into Java servlet classes. Therefore, to use JSP, you need a JVM that supports the Java platform servlet specifications. Most platforms support JVM.

- Obtain and install the JSP Servlet and Development kits. Both can be downloaded free from the Sun Web site at *http://java.sun.com*. Directions on how to download, install, and configure the tools are provided on the site.

- Install a JSP-capable Web server. You will find a list of these servers on the Sun Web site. The server will need to be downloaded, installed, and configured.

- Decide on an editor. JSP can be coded using a simple text editor like Notepad, or a more full-featured editor that provides functions like syntax-checking. Dreamweaver, Eclipse, and WDSc are a few full-featured editors that support JSP.

A Simple JSP Script

Pages built using JSP technology are typically implemented using a one-time translation phase that is performed the first time the page is called. The page is compiled into a Java servlet class and remains in server memory, providing quick response time for subsequent calls.

JSP simply puts Java inside HTML pages. To turn any existing HTML page into JSP, you can just change its extension from *.htm* or *.html* to *.jsp*. For example, consider the simple HTML page in Figure 12.1.

```
<html>
<body>
<!-- JSP1201 - Simple JSP Example -->
Welcome to Bill's Barbeque Barn
</body>
</html>
```

Figure 12.1: A simple JSP script.

Just give that file the extension *.jsp* and load it in your browser. The same message will be displayed in the browser as if this were an HTML file:

Welcome to Bill's Barbeque Barn

The first time the page loads, it will take a little longer. The JSP file will be turned into a Java file in the form of a compiled and loaded Java servlet class. The compile only takes place once and will load quickly the next time it's run. If the JSP file is changed, it will be compiled again the first time the changed file is loaded.

JSP Syntax Summary

A JSP page is a text document that contains two basic elements: static data, which can be expressed in any text-based format like HTML, and JSP code, which constructs dynamic content.

Tags are used within JSP code. All JSP tags are case-sensitive. In JSP, a pair of single quotes ('..') is equivalent to a pair of double quotes (".."). Either single or double quotes can be used. Also, spaces are not allowed between an equal sign and an attribute value. The basic JSP elements are listed in Table 12.1.

Table 12.1: JSP Syntax		
Element	Syntax	Description
jsp:forward action	<%jsp:forward page= "relative URL"/>	Forwards a client request to an HTML file, a JSP file, or a servlet for processing.
jsp:getProperty action	<%jsp:getProperty name="propertyName" value="val"/>	Gets the value of a bean property so that you can display it in a JSP page.
jsp:include action	<jsp:include page="relative URL" flush="true"/>	Sends a request to an object and includes the result in a dynamic JSP file.

jsp:plugin action	<jsp:plugin type="type" atrribute="value"*> .... </jsp:plugin> Type values:
	  bean
	  applet
	  Attribute values:
	  codebase="classFileDirectory Name"
	  name="instanceName"
	  archive="URIToArchive,..."
	  align="value" (valid values bottom, top, middle, left or right)
	  height=displayPixels"
	  width="displayPixels"
	  hspace="leftRightPixels"
	  vspace="topBottomPixels"
	  jreversion="value" (valid values JREVersionNumber or 1.1"
	  nspluginurl=URLToPlugin"
	  iepluginurl="URLToPlugin"
		Downloads a Java plugin to the client Web browser to execute a Java applet or bean.

jsp:setProperty action	<jsp:setProperty att=val*/>	Sets a property value or values in a bean.
jsp.useBean action	<jsp:useBean att=val*/> or jsp: useBean att=val*> .... </jsp:useBean>	Finds or builds a Java bean.
Hidden comment	<%-- comment --%>	Used to document the JSP file. Hidden comments are not sent to the client.
HTML comment	<!-- comment -->	Creates a comment. HTML comments are sent to the client in the viewable page source.
HTML comment with an expression	<!-- comment [<%= expression %>] -->	Comment with expression. The expression is dynamic and is evaluated when the page is loaded in the Web browser.

Table 12.1: JSP Syntax (Continued)		
Element	Syntax	Description
Declaration	<%! declaration %>	Declares a variable or method valid in the page scripting language. The declaration can be referenced by other declarations, scriptlets, or expressions within the page.
Expression	<%= expression %>	Defines a Java expression that is evaluated at page request time, converted to a string, and sent inline to the output stream of the JSP response.
Include directive	<%@ include file="URL" %>	Includes a static file, parsing the file's JSP elements.
Page directive	<%@ page attribute="value" %> Legal attributes with default values in **bold**: autoflush="**true**|false" buffer="sizekb|none" contentType="MIME-Type" errorPage="url" extends="package.class" import="package.class" info="text" isErrorPage="true|**false**" isThreadSafe="**true**|false" language="java" session="**true**|false"	Gives directions to the servlet engine about general setup. This defines attributes that apply to an entire JSP page.
Taglib directive	<%@ taglib uri="URIToTagLibrary" prefix="tagPrefix" %>	Defines a tag library and prefix for the custom tags used in the JSP page.
Scriptlet	<% code %>	Contains a code fragment valid in the page scripting language. This tag embeds a Java source code scriptlet in HTML page. The Java code is executed, and the output is inserted in sequence with the rest of the HTML page.

Four main types of JSP constructs can be embedded in a Web page. These constructs are listed in Table 12.2.

Table 12.2: JSP Constructs	
Construct	**Description**
Template text	Regular HTML.
Scripting elements, objects, and variables	Used to specify Java code that will become part of a servlet. There are many predefined variables that can be accessed and used.
Directives	Used to control the structure of a servlet.
Actions	Used to specify existing components to be used and to control the behavior of the JSP engine.

Template Text

Most of a JSP page usually consists of static HTML known as template text. The HTML looks just like normal HTML. It follows the same syntax rules as and is passed through to the client. Figure 12.1 is an example of using all template text for a JSP page.

Scripting Elements

JSP scripting elements are used to insert Java code into the servlet that will be generated from the JSP page. There are three basic kinds of scripting elements: the declaration tag, the expression tag, and the scriptlet tag.

Declaration Tag

A declaration tag is used to declare one or more variables or method. The variable or method is placed inside the body of the **Java** servlet class and outside of existing methods. Declarations do not create output and are usually used with expressions and scriptlets.

A variable or method must be declared before it can be used in the JSP file. To declare more than one variable or method within a declaration element, separate them with semicolons. Variables and methods declared in an imported package may also be used. A *package* is a namespace that organizes a set of related classes and interfaces. Conceptually, packages are similar to folders on your computer. You might keep images in one folder, HTML in another, and scripts in another. Because software written in the Java programming language can be composed of hundreds of individual classes, it makes sense to keep things organized by placing related classes and interfaces in packages. Figure 12.2 gives some examples of declaration tag syntax.

```
<%! Declaration; Declaration;  %>

<%! int price = 0; %>
<%!
int price = 0; quantity = 0;
string greeting= "Welcome";
%>
```

Figure 12.2: Declaration tag syntax.

To simplify code in JSP expressions and scriptlets, use the predefined variables listed in Table 12.3. Predefined variables are also referred to as *implicit objects*.

Table 12.3: Predefined Variables			
Predefined Variable/ Implicit Object	Scope	Description	Some Useful Methods
Application	Application	HttpServletRequest associated with the request. Allows access to content of request parameters through getParameter, the request type, and incoming HTTP headers.	getMimeType, getRealPath
Config	Page	ServletConfig object for the page.	getInitParameter, getInit ParameterNames
Exception	Page	Exceptions not caught by application code.	getMessage, getLocalizedMessage, printStackTrace,toString
Out	Page	The PrintWriter used to send output to the client. To make the response object useful, there is a buffered version of PrintWriter called JspWriter. The buffer size can be adjusted or turned off through the buffer attribute of the page directive. JSP expressions are placed in the output stream and usually do not need to refer to out. It is usually used in scriptlets.	clear, clearBuffer, flush, getBufferSize, getRemaining
Page	Page	The servlet itself.	Not typically used by JSP page authors

Table 12.3: Predefined Variables (Continued)			
Predefined Variable/ Implicit Object	Scope	Description	Some Useful Methods
pageContext	Page	An instance that contains data associated with the whole page. A given HTML page may be passed among multiple JSPs.	findAttribute, getAttribute, getAttributesScope, getAtributeNamesInScope
Response	Page	HttpServletResponse associated with the response to the client. Since the output stream is buffered, it is legal to set HTTP status codes and response headers. It is not legal to set HTTP status codes and response headers in regular servlets once output has been sent to the client.	Not typically used by JSP page authors
Request	Request	HttpServletRequest associated with a request. Allows access to content, including parameters through getParmeter, request type, and incoming HTTP headers.	getAttribute, getParameter, getParameterNames, getParameterValues
Session	Session	HttpSession object associated with the request. Session are created automatically. If the session attribute is turned off through the session attribute of a page directive, an error will occur when trying to use session when the JSP page is compiled into a servlet.	getId, getValue, getValueNames, putValue

Expression Tag

An expression tag is used to define an expression. The expression is evaluated, converted to a string, and inserted where the expression appears in the JSP file. The conversion to a string allows the use of an expression within a line of text with or without an HTML tag in the JSP file. The expression is used to insert Java values directly into the page output. A semicolon cannot be used to end an expression, unlike a scriptlet, which requires a semicolon. Expressions can be simple or complex and can be composed of multiple expressions. An expression is evaluated from left to right.

Any valid Java expression can be used within the expression tag. There are also predefined variables that can be used within the expression tag. These variables are referred to as *expression objects* and can be used for a request, a response, session information, and output. The expression objects are also referred to as implicit objects.

Figure 12.3 gives some examples of expression tag syntax. In this figure, an expression is used to get the remote host name, and the import directive is used to display the current date. The example is being served on the localhost. The result of the code is shown in Figure 12.4.

```
<%= expression %>

<HTML>
<HEAD>
<!-- JSP1204 - Expression Tag Example -->
<TITLE>Bills Barbeque Barn</TITLE>
</HEAD>
<BODY BGCOLOR="#CCCCFF" TEXT="#000000">
<TABLE BORDER=5 BGCOLOR="#6699CC">
   <TR><TH CLASS="TITLE">
       Expression Tag Example JSP1204</TABLE>
<P>
Example of Expression and Directives:
<UL>
   <LI><B>Expression.</B><BR>
    Bills Barbeque Barn Host Name: <%= request.getRemoteHost()
       %>.
  <LI><B>Directive and Expression.</B><BR>
  <%@ page import = "java.util.*" %>
  Current Date: <%= new Date() %>
</UL>
</BODY>
</HTML>
```

Figure 12.3: Expression tag syntax.

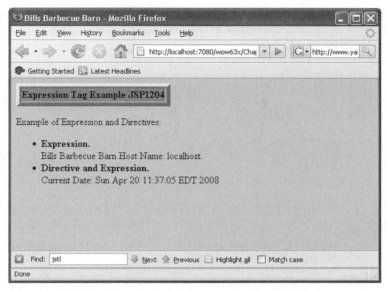

Figure 12.4: The page displayed from the code in Figure 12.3.

Scriptlet Tag

A scriptlet tag is used to insert code into the servlet method that will be built to generate the JSP page. The tag places the code statements inside the service method **JSPService()** of the **Java** servlet class. Scriptlets are often used to perform more complex tasks than those performed by expressions. Scriptlets have the same access to the predefined variables as expressions. Scriptlets are executed when the client request is processed. When output is generated from the scriptlet, it is stored in the **out** object. Text, HTML tags, and JSP elements must be outside of the scriptlet.

A scriptlet can contain variable or method declarations, language statements, and/or expressions that are valid in the page scripting language. A scriptlet can be used for many tasks, including writing valid scripting language statements, writing expressions, declaring variables or methods, and using objects declared with the **jsp:useBean** element. The beginning scriptlet tag is **<%** and the ending tag is **%>**. A semicolon is required to end a scriptlet statement.

In Figure 12.5, two scriptlets are used. Notice the scriptlets start with **<%** and end with **%>**. The first one declares and initializes the date value. The second one generates the date output using the **out** variable. The scriptlet does not generate HTML. The HTML output is created by using the **out** variable. This variable does not need to be declared because it is already predefined for a scriptlet to use.

```
<HTML>
<HEAD>
<TITLE>Bills Barbeque Barn</TITLE>
</HEAD>
<%
        // JSP1206 - Scriptlet Example
     // This scriptlet declares and initializes the date
     java.util.Date date = new java.util.Date();
%>
Welcome To Bills Barbeque Barn!  <BR>
Today is:
<%
    // This scriptlet generates HTML date output
    out.println( String.valueOf( date ));
%>
</BODY>
</HTML>
```

Figure 12.5: Scriptlet syntax.

JSP Directives

JSP directives, listed in Table 12.4, control how the JSP compiler generates the servlet. A directive affects the overall structure of a servlet class. There are two types of directives: **include** and **page**. The **include** directive inserts a file into the servlet class at the time the JSP is compiled into a servlet. The **page** directive provides such capabilities as importing classes, allowing multiple pages to execute at the same time, and allowing the JSP page to participate in a session.

Table 12.4: JSP Directives	
Directive	Description
<%@include file="path" %>	Includes a file path on the local system to be included when the JSP page is compiled into a servlet.
<%@ page autoFlush="true" %>	Indicates whether JSP should automatically flush the page buffer when it is full. The default is true. When the buffer is set to none, the autoFlush directive cannot be set to false. When autoFlush is set to false, an exception will be encountered when the buffer is full and overflows.

Table 12.4: JSP Directives (Continued)	
Directive	**Description**
<%@ page buffer=sizkb %>	Gives the size of the page buffer in kb, or none for no buffer. The default is 8kb. If a size is designated, the output is buffered with the size specified. For pages with a lot of output activity, it might be desirable to control the buffer size.
<%@ page contentType="descr iption" %>	Sets the MIME content type and character encoding of the page used by the JSP file for the response it sends to the client. Any MIME type or character set that is valid for the JSP container can be used. The default value is MIME type text/html, and the default character set is ISO-8859-1.
<%@ page errorPage="path" %>	Defines a page to display if an unhandled error occurs while running the JSP page. When a slash (/) is used to start the path, the path will be relative to the JSP file's root directory.
<%@ page extends="Java class" %>	Changes the generated servlet's class. The extends attribute should be used with caution, as it might affect quality and performance. It will also result in errors when a superclass is already being used by the server.
<%@ page import="package" %>	Provides a means to extend page functionality by importing packages or classes beyond the default list of imported classes and packages for JSP pages. The classes and packages can include java.lang.*, javax.servlet.*, javax.servlet.jsp.*, and javax.servlet. http.*. You can list multiple classes by separating them with commas. This page directive must be designated before the element that calls the imported class. It is the only attribute that can appear multiple times on the same page.
<%@ page info="description" %>	Gives a brief description of the JSP page in the form of a string that can be retrieved using the Servlet. getServletInfo() method.
<%@ page isErrorPage="true" %>	Indicates whether to give an error page access to the exception implicit variable. When set to true, the page can be used for the exception object in a JSP file. The default is false.
<%@ page isThreadSafe="true" %>	Control whether or not the JSP page is thread safe, meaning it will function correctly during simultaneous execution of multiple threads (program parts). Thread safe also means the application will satisfy the need for multiple threads to access the same shared data and the need for a shared piece of data to be accessed by only one thread at a given time. The default value is true. When true the JSP container, can send multiple concurrent client requests to the JSP page. In that case, code should be included to synchronize access to instance variables and the multiple client threads.

Table 12.4: JSP Directives (Continued)	
Directive	**Description**
<%@ page language="language" %>	Designates the language used for writing the script, declarations, expressions, and any files included within the JSP page. Currently, java is the default and only legal language choice.
<%@ page session="true" %>	Tells JSP whether the page participates in a session. The default is true, making session data available to the page. When the value is false, the session object cannot be used.
<%@ page taglib prefix="x" uri="libraryname" %>	Configures tags with the prefix x to use the tag library. Tag libraries are discussed later in this chapter.

The start tag for a directive is **<%@** and the end tag is **%>**. The statement consists of the directive, attribute, and value in the form **<%@** *directive, attribute="value"* **%>**. Multiple attribute settings can be used within a single directive, as shown in Figure 12.6.

```
Syntax:

<%@ directive attribute="value"
             attribute="value"
               attribute="value"
               attribute="value" %>

Code example:

%@page language="java"
import="java.sql.*,java.util.*"
session="true"
errorPage="ErrorPage.jsp" %

.
```

Figure 12.6: The syntax for a directive with multiple attribute settings.

Include Directive

The **include** directive is used to bring a file's content into the current file. The file is included at the time the JSP page is compiled into a servlet. The contents of the file are included as a part of the servlet object. In the example in Figure 12.7, the JSP file *JSP1209date.jsp*, containing code to retrieve the current date, will be included within the file *JSP1208.jsp*. The code for file *JSP1209date.jsp* is shown in Figure 12.8.

```
<html>
<body>
<!-- JSP1208 - JSP Include Directive Example -->
Welcome To Bills Barbeque Barn!  <BR>
                The current date and time is:
<%@ include file="JSP1209date.jsp" %>
</body>
</head>
</html>
```

*Figure 12.7: An example of the JSP **include** directive.*

```
<!-- JSP1209date - JSP include directive example current date -->

<%= (new java.util.Date() ).toLocaleString() %>
```

*Figure 12.8: The JSP file included with the **include** directive.*

The message displayed when this file is run is as follows:

> **Welcome To Bills Barbeque Barn!**
> **The current date and time is: Sep 7, 2007 9:07:39 PM**

This simple example shows how easily additional code can be incorporated into a JSP file. If the included JSP file is changed, the JSP files that include this file must be recompiled.

Page Directive

The **page** directive applies to the current JSP file and any static files included within the JSP page. This directive can be used more than once on a JSP page, but can only use each attribute once within the page, with the exception of the **import** attribute. Usually, **page** directives are placed together at the top of the JSP file. Consistently grouping directives together at the top is a standard that makes it easier for the developer, but they can be placed anywhere.

Figure 12.9 uses some of the **page** directive's attributes. In this example, the **errorPage** attribute references a page named *JSP1213errorpage.jsp*. The code for that page is shown in Figure 12.10.

```
<html>
<body>
<!-- JSP1211 - JSP Page Directives Example -->
Welcome to Bill's Barbeque Barn <BR>
<%@ page autoFlush="true" %>
<%@ page buffer="8kb" %>
<%@ page contentType="text/html" %>
<%@ page errorPage="JSP1213errorpage.jsp" %>
<%@ page import = "java.util.*" %>
<%@ page info="JSP Page Directives Example" %>
<%@ page isErrorPage="false" %>
<%@ page isThreadSafe="true" %>
<%@ page language="java" %>
<%@ page session="true" %>
            Current Date: <%= new Date() %>
</body>
</html>
```

Figure 12.9: Using the JSP *page* directive.

```
<html>
<body>
<!-- JSP1213errorpage - JSP Page Directives Example Error Page -->
<%@ page isErrorPage="true" %>
Welcome to Bill's Barbeque Barn <BR>
An Error Has Been Encountered!!
</body>
</html>
```

Figure 12.10: An *errorPage* file.

This page will only be called when an unhandled error is encountered on the page. In that case, the following message will be displayed:

**Welcome to Bill's Barbeque Barn
An Error Has Been Encountered!!**

The page may contain text to be displayed or additional application code.

JSP Actions

JSP actions are executed at runtime and provide built-in Web server functionality. JSP actions are used to modify, use, or create objects that are represented by JavaBeans. Actions use XML syntax. Several standard actions are provided for use with JSP, listed in Table 12.5. Custom actions can be developed using the Java language.

Table 12.5: JSP Actions		
Action	Use	Description
jsp:fallback	Show content.	Content to show if a browser supports applets.
jsp:forward	Forward requester to a new page.	Used to hand off a request and response to a JSP or servlet. Once handed off, the control will not return the current page.
jsp:getProperty	Insert the property of a JavaBean into output.	Used to get a property from a designated JavaBean.
jsp:include	Include a file when a page is requested.	Comparable to a subroutine. The servlet will temporarily hand the request and response off to a specified JSP. Control will return to the current JSP once the other has completed. This action allows code to be shared by multiple other JSPs.
jsp:param	Designate an additional parameter.	May be used inside a jsp:forward, jsp:include, or jsp:params action. This action designates a parameter to be included in addition to the request's current parameters.
jsp:plugin	Generate browser code that makes an <object> or <embed> tag for a Java plugin.	Generates a browser-specific tag to include an applet.
jsp:setProperty	Set the property of a JavaBean.	Sets a property in a designated JavaBean.
jsp:useBean	Find or instantiate a JavaBean.	Creates or allows reuse of a JavaBean available to the current JSP page.

jsp:fallback

The **<jsp:fallback>** tag enables you to substitute HTML for browsers that are not supported by the **<jsp:plugin>** action, or when the plugin fails. The HMTL found between the **<fallback>** and **<jsp:fallback>** tags is the content that will be shown if the browser doesn't support applets. Most current browsers, however, support the **<jsp:plugin>** action.

For example, if the plugin in Figure 12.11 fails, the following content will be displayed:

Welcome to Bill's Barbeque Barn
The java applet cannot be run!!

```
<html>
<body>
<!-- JSP1215 - jsp:fallback Action Example -->
Welcome to Bill's Barbeque Barn <BR>
<jsp:plugin type="applet" code="BillsBarbeque"
  codebase="/bills/" height="800" width="500">
<jsp:params>
<jsp:param name="author" value="Laura"/>
</jsp:params>
<jsp:fallback>
<font color=#FF0000 > The java applet cannot be run!!</font>
</jsp:fallback>
</jsp:plugin>
</body>
</html>
```

Figure 12.11: Using the ***<jsp:fallback>*** *action.*

In this case, the plugin will fail because it does not exist.

jsp:forward

The **<jsp:forward>** tag is used to hand off the request and response to another JSP or servlet. The control will not return to the current JSP. In the example in Figure 12.12, *JSP1217.jsp* uses the **<jsp:forward>** action tag to direct the page to *JSP1218.jsp*, shown in Figure 12.13. The control remains with *JSP1218.jsp* and does not return. The parameter **forwardedFrom** is set in the request before the hand off. The result will be the following:

Welcome to Bill's Barbeque Barn
We have been forwarded from JSP1217.jsp!

```
<html>
<body>
<!-- JSP1217 - JSP Actions jsp:forward Example -->
<jsp:forward page="JSP1218.jsp" >
<jsp:param name="forwardedFrom" value="JSP1217.jsp" />
</jsp:forward>
</body>
</html>
```

Figure 12.12: The JSP file forward from using ***<jsp:forward>***.

```
<html>
<body>
<!-- JSP1218 - JSP Actions jsp:forward Example -->
Welcome to Bill's Barbeque Barn <BR>
We have been forwarded from JSP1217.jsp!
</body>
</html>
```

Figure 12.13: JSP Action jsp:forward example.

jsp:getProperty

The **<jsp:getProperty>** tag gets the property from the specified JavaBean. In the example in Figure 12.14, the month, day, year, hours, and minutes are retrieved from the JavaBean named "clock." The bean is referenced with the parameter name in the **<jsp:getProperty>** statements, and the property identifies the property being retrieved.

In the results shown in Figure 12.15, the month is actually September. This is because the **java.util.Date** class uses the numbers for months from zero to 11: zero is January, one is February, and 11 is December. The year is the current year minus 1900.

```
<%@ page language="java" contentType="text/html" %>
<html>
<body>
<!-- JSP1220 - JSP Actions jsp:getProperty Example -->
Welcome to Bill's Barbeque Barn <BR>
<jsp:useBean id="clock" class="java.util.Date" />
The current date and time is:
<ul>
<li>Month: <jsp:getProperty name="clock" property="month" />
<li>Day: <jsp:getProperty name="clock" property="date" />
<li>Year: <jsp:getProperty name="clock" property="year" />
<li>Hours: <jsp:getProperty name="clock" property="hours" />
<li>Minutes: <jsp:getProperty name="clock" property="minutes" />
</ul>
</body>
</html>
```

*Figure 12.14: Using the **<jsp:getProperty>** action.*

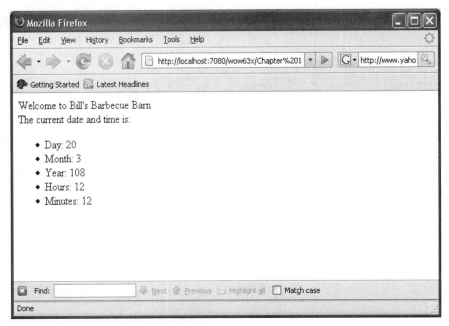

Figure 12.15: The results from Figure 12.14.

There are other ways to display a date, but for the purposes of this example, this is a simple way to show how **jsp:getProperty** works.

jsp:include

The **<jsp:include>** action tag is similar to the concept of a subroutine, which is used in many application development languages, including RPG on the System i. The Java servlet temporarily hands the request and response off to the specified JSP. Control will then return to the current JSP, once the other JSP finishes. The **<jsp:include>** tag allows JSP code to be shared among multiple JSPs rather than duplicated.

The example in Figure 12.16 includes the page *JSP1223.jsp*, shown in Figure 12.17. The include allows for reuse of code. Notice the **flush** parameter. Usually, this will be set to true. However, there might be instances when it should be set to false, such as when multiple actions, directives, or parameter values need to be retained.

```
<html>

<body>
<!-- JSP1222 - JSP Actions jsp:include Example -->
<p>Welcome to Bill's Barbeque Barn</p>
<jsp:include page="JSP1223.jsp" flush="true"/>
</body>
</html>
```

*Figure 12.16: Using the <**jsp:include**> action.*

```
<!-- JSP1223 - JSP Actions jsp:include Example -->
<%@ page import = "java.util.*" %>
<%
Date todaysdate = new Date();
out.print("<p>Current Date:" + todaysdate + ".</p>");
%>
```

Figure 12.17: The JSP page included in Figure 12.16.

In this example, the first JSP displays "Welcome to Bill's Barbeque Barn," and the second JSP displays the current date. There are two include mechanisms here: the include directive and the include action. The include directive includes the content of the file during the translation phase. The include action includes the content of the file during the execution of the request-processing phase. For the include directive, the JSP engine adds the content of the inserted page during the translation phase so it does not have an impact on performance. For the include action, the JSP engine adds the content of the inserted page at run time, which adds extra overhead to the application.

Take care when including large pages in instances when performance can noticeably be impacted. Generally, though, the include action has a small negative impact on performance but a great improvement in flexibility.

jsp:param

The **<jsp:param>** tag can be used inside of a **<jsp:forward>**, **<jsp:include>**, or **<jsp:plugin>** block. The tag specifies a parameter that will be available for use by the forward, include, or plugin code.

The example in Figure 12.18 uses **<jsp:param>** in coordination with **<jsp:forward>**. This example is very similar to the forward example in Figure

12.12 and Figure 12.13. In this case, the parameter is passed to the forward page, JSP1226.jsp, which retrieves the parameter using the **getParameter** request. The **forwardedFrom** parameter is then printed. The result would be the following message:

Welcome to Bill's Barbeque Barn
Forwarded From: JSP1225.jsp.

```
<html>
<body>
<!-- JSP1225 - JSP Actions jsp:param Example -->
<jsp:forward page="JSP1226.jsp" >
<jsp:param name="forwardedFrom" value="JSP1225.jsp" />
</jsp:forward>
</body>
</html>
```

Figure 12.18: Using the <jsp:param> action.

```
<html>
<body>
<!-- JSP1226 - JSP Actions jsp:param Example -->
Welcome to Bill's Barbeque Barn <BR>
<%
String forwardedFrom = request.getParameter("forwardedFrom");
out.print("<p>Forwarded From: " + forwardedFrom + ".</p>");
%>
</body>
</html>
```

Figure 12.19: JSP Action jsp:param example.

Not only does the application forward the user to a new page, but it also passes a parameter to be used within the page. Although this example is simple, it should give you an idea of how powerful and useful the **<jsp: param>** action is.

jsp:plugin

The **<jsp:plugin>** action is used to include the Java plugin applets on a Web page. The Java plugin allows you to use a Java Runtime Environment (JRE) supplied by Sun Micorsystems, instead of using the JVM implemented through the client Web browser. Java plugin technology is part of the JRE standard edition and establishes a connection between popular browsers and the Java platform. The connection enables Web site applets to be run within a browser on a user's desktop.

A plugin can be used to avoid problems between applets and specific types of Web browsers. The syntax used for Internet Explorer and Netscape, for example, is different. The servlet code generated when using **<jsp:plugin>** dynamically senses the type of browser and sends **<object>** and **<embed>** elements for that browser. The plugin serves as a bridge between the browser and JRE.

A plugin is executable code that is stored in a library file. A developer "tells" the browser to use this external JRE by placing special HTML tags on a Web page. Once this is done, a browser can run Java applets or JavaBean components that have access to the features of this external JRE.

To use a plugin, it must be downloaded and might also need to be configured. Sun provides detailed information on plugins that can be downloaded for a variety of uses at *http://java.sun.com/products/plugin/index.jsp*. There are many sources on the Web to download plugins. Some sources provide plugins for a fee, while many provide plugins for free. In addition, a developer can create a new plugin.

In the example in Figure 12.20, the applet code referenced is *com.example. MyApplet*. This example shows a uniform way of embedding applets in a Web page. The **<object>** tag provides a common way of embedding applets. Currently, **<jsp:plugin>** does not allow for dynamically called applets. Parameters can be passed as constants, but not as variable values.

```
<jsp:plugin type=applet height="100%" width="100%"
archive="myjarfile.jar,myotherjar.jar"
codebase="/jspapplets"
code="com.example.MyApplet" >
<jsp:params>
<jsp:param name="enableDebug" value="true" />
</jsp:params>
<jsp:fallback>
Your browser does not support applets.
</jsp:fallback>
</jsp:plugin>
```

Figure 12.20: Using the **<jsp:plugin>** *action.*

jsp:setProperty

The **<jsp:setProperty>** action sets the property in the specified JavaBean. Four possible attributes can be used for the **jsp:setProperty** action, listed in Table 12.6.

Table 12.6: Attributes for <jsp:setProperty>	
Attribute	**Description**
Name	This attribute is required and designates the bean the property will be set for. The <jsp:useBean> action must appear before the <jsp:setProperty> action.
property	This attribute is required and designates the property to be set. When a value of "*" is used, all request parameters with names that match the bean property names will be passed to the setter methods.
value	This attribute is optional and designates the value for the property. You cannot use both the value and param attributes for a single <jsp: setProperty> action. One or the other may be used, although neither is required. String values are automatically converted to numbers, Boolean, byte, and character through the standard valueOf method in the target wrapper class. For example, a value of "17" of an integer property will be converted through the Integer.valueOf method.
param	This attribute is optional and designates the request parameter used to retrieve the property. If the request does not have a parameter, nothing will be done. In other words, a null value will not be passed to the setter method of the property.

The bean can supply default values. The param attribute can be used to override the property values. The bean itself can be used to supply default values, or the request parameters can be used to provide values.

The following code is used to set the numberOfFields property to the value provided from the value of the numFields request parameter:

<jsp:setProperty name="promptBean" property="numberOfFields" param="numFields" />

If the numFields request parameter does not exist, nothing will be done.

When both the value and param attributes are not used it is the same as using a param name that matches the property name. When both the value and param attributes are not used, "*" can be used to iterate through available properties and request parameters matching those with identical names:

<jsp:setProperty name="promptBean" property="*" /> |

jsp:useBean

The **<jsp:useBean>** action is used to instantiate Java objects that comply with the JavaBean specification and refer to the beans from JSP pages. In other words, it creates or reuses a JavaBean available to the JSP page. Several attributes can be used with **<jsp:useBean>**, listed in Table 12.7.

Table 12.7: Attributes for <jsp:UseBean>	
Attribute	**Description**
BeanName	The name of the bean provided to instantiate the method of Beans. The type and beanName can be provided and the class> attribute omitted.
Class	The full package name of the bean.
Id	The name of the variable that will reference the bean. If the id and scope is the same as a previously used bean object, it will be used instead of instantiating a new bean.
Scope	The context in which the bean should be made available to the application. There are four possible values: application, page, request, and session. A <jsp:useBean> entry will only result in a new object being instantiated if there is no previous object with the same id and scope.
Type	The type of the variable that will refer to the object. The name of the variable is designated through the id attribute. The type must match the classname or be a superclass or an interface that the class implements.

The example in Figure 12.21 shows the use of the **<jsp:useBean>** and **<jsp:setProperty>** actions and also the use of a user-created JavaBean. The user is prompted to enter his or her name. Once the name is entered and submitted, a "hello" message is displayed. The example uses the Bean Manager to instantiate an instance of the class **JavaSource.NameBean** and store the class in the attribute **promptBean**. The attribute will be available for use throughout the current run time of the request because the scope attribute value is **request**. The attribute can be shared within all JSPs included or forwarded from the main JSP that first received the request. The **scope** attribute can be one of four values, listed in Table 12.8.

```
<%@ page import="JavaSource.*" %>
<jsp:useBean id="promptBean" class="JavaSource.NameBean"
   scope="request"></jsp:useBean>
<jsp:setProperty name="promptBean" property="*" />
<HTML>
<!-- JSP1230 - JSP Actions jsp:useBean and jsp:setProperty Example -->
<H3>Welcome to Bill's Barbeque Barn Inquiry Page!</H3>
<% if (promptBean.getNewName().equals("")) { %>
User Unknown.
<% } else { %>
Welcome
<%= promptBean.getNewName() %>
!
<% } %>
<P>Please Enter Your Name?
<FORM METHOD=get><INPUT TYPE=TEXT name=newName size=20> <INPUT
        TYPE=SUBMIT VALUE="Submit Your Name"></FORM>
</BODY>
</HTML>
```

*Figure 12.21: Using the **<jsp:useBean>** and **<jsp:setProperty>** actions.*

Table 12.8: Values for the Scope Attribute	
Value	Description
application	This is the same as using a global variable. The attribute is available to every instance and is never de-referenced.
Page	The attribute is available to the current JSP page only.
Request	The attribute is available for the lifetime of the request. Once the request has been processed by all of the JSPs, the attribute will be de-referenced.
Session	The attribute is available for the lifetime of the user's current session.

Figure 12.21 references the user-defined bean "NameBean." Although the focus of this chapter is JSP, the Java source code for this user-defined JavaBean is given in Figure 12.22. You will often see JSP and Java used together within applications. This example helps you understand how this is done. This does not mean that to use JSP, you must know how to code Java. There are many existing JavaBeans that can easily be included in an application, found on the Sun Web site (*www.Sun.com*) and many other sites on the Web.

```
/*JSP1231 Java NameBean Example */
package JavaSource;

public class NameBean {

  String newName="";

  public void NameBean() {  }

  public String getNewName() {
       return newName;
  }
  public void setNewName(String newName) {
       this.newName = newName;
  }
}
```

Figure 12.22: The Java code for a user-defined bean.

The components in this example include the JSP file *JSP1230.jsp* and the user-defined bean in *NameBean.java*. Figure 12.23 is the screen that will be displayed when the application is run.

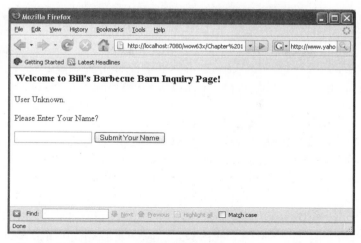

Figure 12.23: The screen displayed from the code in Figure 12.21.

The first time the page is displayed upon initiation of the application, the user is prompted to enter his or her name. Also, the text "User Unknown" is displayed. This is because the following code checks for the value of **promptBean.getNewName**:

<% if (promptBean.getNewName().equals("")) { %>

Once the user enters a name and clicks **Submit**, the page will be redisplayed with the entered name and a new message, as shown in Figure 12.24.

Figure 12.24: The screen after entering a name.

This example is not a complete application, but it should give you an idea of the possibilities for **<jsp:useBean>** and **<jsp:setProperty>** in business applications. The bean incorporates use of an HTML form to prompt for the **name** value, use the entered value within the JSP code, and then display the value. These are activities very familiar to a business developer.

The **<jsp:useBean>** action lets you load a JavaBean to a JSP page. This is a very useful capability, allowing the reusability of Java classes without sacrificing the convenience that JSP adds over servlets alone. The beans should be stored in a directory included in the site's class path.

JSP Implicit Objects

Implicit objects in JSP are objects that are automatically available within JSP. They are Java objects that the JSP container provides to a developer to access in expressions and scriptlets. They are called "implicit" because they are automatically instantiated. The implicit object is created by the JSP environment, so you do not need to initialize it. The JSP implicit objects in Table 12.9 are exposed by the JSP container and can be referenced by the application developer. The implicit objects act as wrappers around underlying Java classes or interfaces that are typically defined with the servlet API.

Implicit objects are provided as a convenience for programmers and are commonly used by developers. They are introduced in this section and included in code examples throughout this chapter. Implicit objects are only visible within the system-generated **_jspService()** method. They are not visible within user-defined methods created in declarations.

Table 12.9: JSP Implicit Objects	
Implicit Object	**Description**
Application	Represents the ServletContext obtained from the servlet configuration object. It is used to find information about the servlet engine and environment. The information is shared by all JSPs and servlets in the application.
Config	Represents ServletConfig for the JSP. It provides access to the servlet instance initialization parameters. In other words, it is the servlet configuration data.
Exception	Provides the uncaught throwable object that results in an error page being invoked. It is used for exceptions not caught by application code.

Table 12.9: JSP Implicit Objects (Continued)	
Implicit Object	**Description**
Out	This JSPWriter object is used to write the data to the response output stream.
Page	Represents the servlet instance generated from the JSP page as an HTTPJSPPage. It is the same as using the Java keyword this in scriptlet code.
PageContext	Represents a PageContext instance that contains data associated with the whole page. An HTML page may be passed to multiple JSPs. It is a convenient API for accessing scoped namespaces and servlet-related objects. The pageContext object provides wrapper methods for common servlet-related functionality.
Request	This HttpServletRequest object provides HTTP request information, including methods for getting cookie, header, and session data. It represents the client request.
Response	The HTTPServlet response object provides HTTP response information, including cookies and other header information. It represents the page response.
Session	This HTTPSession object can be used to track information about a user from one request to another. The session directive is set to true by default, so the session is valid by default.

A request-and-response cycle consists of a request where the client asks for data from the server, and a response where the server sends the data to the client. This cycle is represented by the request and response implicit objects, as shown in Figure 12.25. The request object handles the information sent from the client, and the response object handles the information sent to the client. Table 12.10 lists request and methods, and Table 12.11 lists response methods.

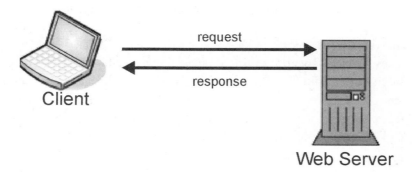

Figure 12.25: The request and response cycle.

Table 12.10: Request Methods		
Return Type	Method	Description
HttpSession	getSession()	Returns the session associated with the request
String	getHeader(String headerName)	Returns the value associated with the header name of the request
Enumeration	getHeaderNames()	Returns all of the header names associated with a request
Cookie[]	getCookies()	Returns the cookies associated with a request
Object	getAttribute(String attributeName)	Returns the object that is paired with an attribute's name
void	setAttribute(String nameOfTheAttribute, Object valueOfThe Attribute)	Sets an attribute named nameOfTheAttribute to the value of valueOfTheAttribute

Table 12.11: Response Methods		
Return Type	Method	Description
Void	addCookie(Cookie cookie)	Adds the specified cookie to the response
Void	addHeader(String headerName, String value)	Adds the header to the response
Void	sendError(int statusCode) throws IOException	Sends a predefined error message back to the client
Void	sendRedirect(String newURL) throws IOException	Redirects the client browser to a different URL

Web application information can be stored in the application, session, and page scope, as shown in Figure 12.26. The *page scope* refers to the information that pertains to a specific instance of a given page. The server keeps the page-specific information as long as the page exists. The *session scope* contains information pertaining to a session instance. The server keeps session-specific information until the session has been ended. The *application scope* contains information that is available to all sessions in an application, as long as the application is running.

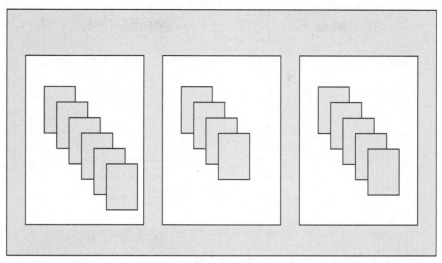

Figure 12.26: Web application, session, and page scopes.

You can access information stored in the application, page, and session scope using the application, pageContext, and session implicit objects. The methods for these objects are listed in Tables 12.12, 12.13, and 12.14, respectively.

Table 12.12: Application Methods		
Return Type	**Method**	**Description**
Object	getAttribute(String attributeName)	Returns the object that is paired with an attribute's name
Void	setAttribute(String name OfTheAttribute, Object valueOfTheAttribute)	Sets an attribute named nameOfTheAttribute to the value of valueOfTheAttribute
Enumeration	getAttributeNames()	Returns an array of the names of the attributes for a given application

Table 12.13: pageContext Methods		
Return Type	**Method**	**Description**
Object	findAttribute(String attributeName)	Searches the page, session, application, and request scopes for an attribute named attributeName and returns the attribute or null if the attribute does not exist

Table 12.13: pageContext Methods (Continued)		
Return Type	Method	Description
Object	getAttribute(String attributeName)	Returns the object that is paired with an attribute's name
Void	setAttribute(String nameOfTheAttribute, Object valueOfTheAttribute)	Sets an attribute named nameOfTheAttribute to the value of valueOfTheAttribute
HttpServlet Request	getRequest()	Returns the request object associated with the page
HttpServlet Response	getResponse()	Returns the response object associated with the page

Table 12.14: Session Methods		
Return Type	Method	Description
Object	getAttribute(String attributeName)	Returns the object that is paired with an attribute named attributeName
Void	setAttribute(String nameOfTheAttribute, Object valueOfTheAttribute)	Sets an attribute named nameOfTheAttribute to the value of valueOfTheAttribute
String	getAttributeNames()	Gets the name of all attributes.

JSP Standard Tag Libraries

In addition to using the predefined JSP actions, you can create custom actions using the JSP Tag Extension API. Custom actions are created by writing a Java class that implements one of the tag interfaces and providing a tag-library XML description file that specifies the tags and the Java classes that implement the tags. JSP tag libraries define declarative, modular functionality that can be reused by any JSP page. The tag libraries reduce the requirement to embed large amounts of Java code in JSP pages by moving the functionality of the tags into tag implementation classes.

JSP standard tag libraries are also referred to as *JSTL*. JSTL encapsulates, as simple tags, the core functionality common to many Web applications. JSTL has support for common structural tasks such as iteration, conditions, control flow, and text inclusion; tags for manipulating XML documents; internationalization tags; and SQL tags. For example, with JSTL, <forEach> can be used to standardize iteration. This standardization lets you learn a single tag and use it on multiple JSP containers.

The expression language that JSTL defines is an integral part of the JSP 2.0 specification. You might also be interested in JSTL's current extensibility mechanisms. JSTL provides a framework for integrating custom tags with JSTL tags. All of the information needed to dive into JSTL can be found on the Sun Web site at *http://java.sun.com/products/jsp/jstl/*. The page includes downloads, API specifications, documentation, and forums specific to JSTL. Table 12.15 lists available JSTL libraries and the links you can use to find out more about them.

Table 12.15: JSP Standard Tag Libraries		
Library	**URL**	**Prefix**
JSTL core	*http://java.sun.com/jsp/jstl/core*	c
JSTL fmt	*http://java.sun.com/jsp/jstl/xml*	fmt
JSTL sql	*http://java.sun.com/jsp/jstl/fmt*	sql
JSTL xml	*http://java.sun.com/jsp/jstl/sql*	xml
JSTL functions	*http://java.sun.com/jsp/jstl/functions*	fn

The standard tag libraries provide many standard tags and functions. Table 12.16 lists many of these tags, and Table 12.17 lists many of these functions.

Table 12.16: JSTL Standard Tags		
Library	**Tag**	**Description**
core	catch	Catches any throwable error that occurs in its body and optionally exposes it
	choose	A simple conditional tag that establishes a context for mutually exclusive conditional operations, marked by <when> and <otherwise>
	if	A simple conditional tag that evaluates its body if the supplied condition is true and optionally exposes a Boolean scripting variable representing the evaluation of this condition
	import	Retrieves an absolute or relative URL and exposes its contents to either the page, a string in "var", or a Reader in 'varReader'
	forEach	The basic iteration tag, accepting many different collection types and supporting subsetting and other functionality
	forTokens	Iterates over tokens, separated by the supplied delimiters
	out	Like <%= ... >, but for expressions
	otherwise	A subtag of <choose> that follows <when> tags and runs only if all of the prior conditions evaluated to false
	param	Adds a parameter to a containing <import> tag's URL
	redirect	Redirects to a new URL

Library	Tag	Description
		Table 12.16: JSTL Standard Tags (Continued)
	remove	Removes a scoped variable (from a particular scope, if specified)
	set	Sets the result of an expression evaluation in a scope
	url	Creates a URL with optional query parameters
	when	A subtag of <choose> that includes its body if its condition evaluates to true
fmt	request Encoding	Sets the request character encoding
	setLocale	Stores the given locale in the locale configuration variable
	timeZone	Specifies the time zone for any time formatting or parsing actions nested in its body
	setTimeZone	Stores the given time zone in the time zone configuration variable
	bundle	Loads a resource bundle to be used by its tag body
	setBundle	Loads a resource bundle and stores it in the named scoped variable or the bundle configuration variable
	message	Maps key to localized message and performs parametric replacement
	param	Supplies an argument for parametric replacement to a containing <message> tag
	format Number	Formats a numeric value as number, currency, or percentage
	parse Number	Parses the string representation of a number, currency value, or percentage
	formatDate	Formats a date and/or time using the supplied styles and pattern
	parseDate	Parses the string representation of a date and/or time
sql	transaction	Provides nested database action elements with a shared connection, set up to execute all statements as one transaction
	query	Executes the SQL query defined in its body or through the sql attribute.
	update	Executes the SQL update defined in its body or through the sql attribute
	param	Sets a parameter in an SQL statement to the specified value
	dateParam	Sets a parameter in an SQL statement to the specified java.util. Date value
	setData-Source	Creates a simple DataSource suitable only for prototyping
xml	choose	A simple conditional tag that establishes a context for mutually exclusive conditional operations, marked by <when> and <otherwise>
	out	Like <%= ... >, but for XPath expressions

Table 12.16: JSTL Standard Tags (Continued)

Library	Tag	Description
	if	An XML conditional tag, which evaluates its body if the supplied XPath expression evaluates to true
	forEach	The XML iteration tag
	otherwise	A subtag of <choose> that follows <when> tags and runs only if all of the prior conditions evaluated to false
	param	Adds a parameter to a containing <transform> tag's Transformer
	parse	Parses XML content from a "source" attribute or 'body'
	set	Saves the result of an XPath expression evaluation in a "scope"
	transform	Conducts a transformation given a source XML document and an XSLT stylesheet
	when	A subtag of <choose> that includes its body if its expression evaluates to true

Table 12.17: JSTL Standard Functions

Type	Function Tag	Description
Boolean	contains(java.lang. String, java.lang.String	Tests whether an input string contains the specified substring
Boolean	containsIgnoreCase (java.lang.String, java. lang.String)	Tests whether an input string contains the specified substring in a case-insensitive way
Boolean	endsWith (java.lang. String, java.lang. String)	Tests whether an input string ends with the specified suffix
Boolean	startsWith (java.lang. String, java.lang.String	Tests if an input string starts with the specified prefix
Int	indexOf (java.lang. String, java.lang. String)	Returns the index within a string of the first occurrence of a specified substring
Int	Length (java.lang. Object)	Returns the number of items in a collection, or the number of characters in a string
java.lang. String	escapeXml (java.lang. String)	Escapes characters that could be interpreted as XML markup
java.lang. String	join (java.lang.String[], java.langString	Joins all elements of an array into a string
java.lang. String	replace (java.lang. String, java.lang. String, java.lang. String)	Returns a string resulting from replacing an input string in all occurrences of a "before" and "after" substring
java.lang. String	split (java.lang.String, java.lang.String)	Splits a string into an array of substrings

Table 12.17: JSTL Standard Functions (Continued)		
Type	**Function Tag**	**Description**
java.lang. String	substring (java.lang. Stirng, int, int)	Returns a subset of a string
java.lang. String	substringAfter (java. lang.String, java.lang. String)	Returns a subset of a string following a specific substring
java.lang. String	substringBefore (java. lang.String, java.lang. String)	Returns a subset of a string before a specific substring
java.lang. String	toLowerCase (java. lang.String)	Converts all of the characters of a string to lowercase
java.lang. String	toUpperCase (java. lang.String)	Converts all of the characters of a string to uppercase
java.lang. String	trim (java.lang.String)	Removes whitespace from both ends of a string

Sessions

On a typical visit to a Web site, a user will probably view several pages. The session object allows an application developer to associate data specific to an individual site visitor. Data can be stored in and retrieved from a session. The three Web pages in Figures 12.27, 12.28, and 12.29 show an application using sessions to store and retrieve the user name. Figure 12.27 is an HTML file that prompts for the site user's name. Figure 12.28 is a JSP page that stores the name and provides a link to another site page. Figure 12.29 is the page referenced in the link provided.

```
<HTML>
<BODY>
<!-- JSP1237.html Session Example -->
Welcome To Bills Barbeque Barn Home Page!   <BR>
<FORM METHOD=POST ACTION="JSP1238.jsp">
Please Enter Your Name and Press the Submit Button. <INPUT TYPE=TEXT
   NAME=siteusername SIZE=30>
<P><INPUT TYPE=Submit>
</FORM>
</BODY>
</HTML>
```

Figure 12.27: The HTML page of the sessions example.

```
<%--JSP1238.jsp Session Example --%>
<%
   String name = request.getParameter( "siteusername" );
   session.setAttribute( "theUserName", name );
%>
<HTML>
<BODY>
<A HREF="JSP1239.jsp">Link to Bill's Barbeque Barn Inventory
   Inquiry Page.</A>
</BODY>
</HTML>
```

Figure 12.28: The first JSP page of the sessions example.

```
<%--JSP1239.jsp Session Example --%>
<HTML>
<BODY>
Bill's Barbeque Barn Product Inventory Inquiry Page! <BR> <BR>
Welcome <%= session.getAttribute( "theUserName" ) %> !
</BODY>
</HTML>
```

Figure 12.29: The second JSP page of the sessions example.

The page JSP1237.html is displayed first, as shown in Figure 12.30. It prompts for and retains the user's name in the session. The name retained using the **session.setAttribute** is "theUserName."

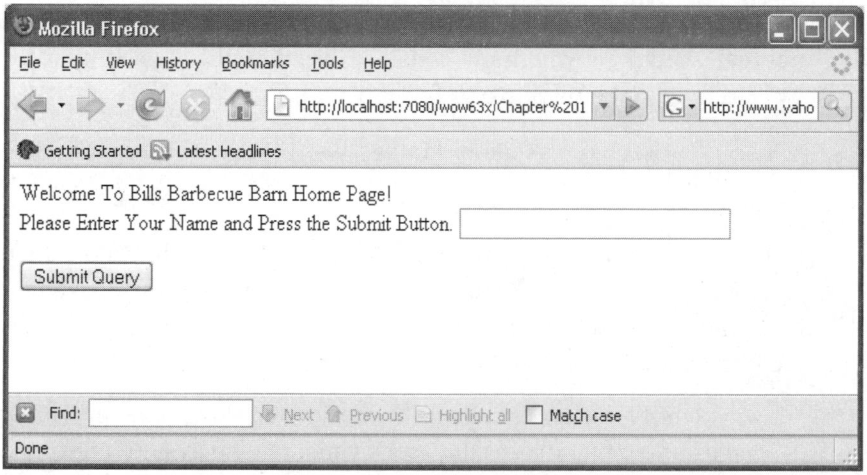

Figure 12.30: The page displayed from the HTML in Figure 12.27.

Once the user has entered a name and clicked **Submit**, the user is directed to the *JSP1238.jsp* page through this message:

Link to Bill's Barbeque Barn Inventory Inquiry Page.

This page uses the request **getParameter** to retrieve the name entered and the session **setAttribute** to retain the name entered. When the site user clicks the link provided, he or she will be routed to the JSP1239.jsp page, displaying a message like this:

Bill's Barbeque Barn Product Inventory Inquiry Page!

Welcome Brent Tinsey !

The session value is retrieved using the session **getAttribute** and is used to display a "Welcome" message.

This example shows how useful sessions can be within JSP. Additional data can be retained by adding another attribute. Sessions provide many practical uses for business application developers.

Sessions are enabled by default. The session object is stored on the server side, so each session object will use a little bit of the system resources. Using sessions also increases the server traffic, as the session ID is sent from the server to the client. The client will send the session ID along with each request made. If a site has heavy traffic and the stored session data is not really required, you might consider disabling the session in a JSP page by setting he **page** directive to false, like this:

<%@ page session="false" %>

Cookies

Cookies are small bits of information sent to and saved by a browser. Cookies can be retrieved and reused when a visitor returns to a site, providing the visitor with conveniences that enhance the user experience. Here are a few ways a cookie may be used:

- Identify a user during a Web site session, like in the previous example that retains the user's name to display a greeting.

- Enable the user to bypass entering a user name and password on a return visit to a site.

- Customize a site by incorporating cookie information into site application logic. For example, a page with instructions on how to use the site would not be displayed on a return visit.

The **javax.servlet.http.Cookie** class is used to create a JSP cookie. The information contained within a cookie can uniquely identify a client. A cookie consists of a cookie name, a cookie value, and optional attributes. The request method **getCookies()** is used to retrieve cookie information and return the values in an array of cookie objects. The cookie is added to the Set-Cookie response header by using the **addCookie** method of **HttpServletResponse**. Figure 12.31 shows the code to add a cookie.

```
..Cookie userCookie = new Cookie("username", "siteusername");
..response.addCookie(userCookie);
```

Figure 12.31: Adding a cookie.

Cookie objects have the methods listed in Table 12.18.

Table 12.18: Methods for Getting and Setting Cookie Attributes	
Cookie Object Method	**Description**
getComment() setComment()	Gets or sets the comment describing the purpose of the cookie, or returns null if a comment has not been defined.
getDomain() setDomain()	Gets or sets the domain to which the cookie applies. Cookies normally are returned to the exact hostname that sent them. This method can be used to instruct the browser to return the user to other hosts within the same domain.
getMaxAge() setMaxAge()	Gets or sets the maximum allowed age of the cookie. The value is stored in seconds that will elapse before a cookie expires. When the maximum age is not set, the cookie will only be retained for the current session and will not be stored on the client.
getName() setName()	Gets or sets the name of the cookie.
getPath() setPath()	Gets or sets the path to which the cookie applies.
getSecure() setSecure()	Gets or sets the Boolean value indicating whether a cookie should only be sent over an encrypted connection like SSL.
getValue() setValue()	Gets or returns the value of a cookie.

A cookie may be used to prompt for a value and can store and retain that value for a designated period of time to use when a site visitor returns to the site. The cookie is dependent upon the specific client connecting. Figure 12.32 is an example of JSP to request a cookie.

```jsp
<%--JSP1245.jsp Cookie Example --%>
<%@ page language="java" %>
<%
String cookieName = "siteusername";
Cookie cookies [] = request.getCookies ();
Cookie myCookie = null;
if (cookies != null)
{
for (int i = 0; i < cookies.length; i++)
{
if (cookies [i].getName().equals (cookieName))
{
myCookie = cookies[i];
break;
}
}
}
%>
<html>
<body>
<%
if (myCookie == null) {
%>
No Cookie found with the name <%=cookieName%> <BR>
Welcome to Bill's Barbeque Barn! <BR>
<form method="post" action="JSP1246.jsp">
<p><b>Please Enter Your Name: </b><input type="text"name="siteu
    sername"><BR>
<input type="submit" value="Submit">
</form>
<%
} else {
%>
<p>
Welcome <%=myCookie.getValue()%> To Bill's Barbeque Barn!
<%
}
%>
</body>
```

Figure 12.32: Requesting a cookie.

In this example, **request.getCookies()** is used to determine if the **siteusername** cookie exists. If it doesn't exist, the user is prompted to "Please Enter Your Name" using an HTML form. When the user clicks **Submit**, the browser is directed to the *JSP1246.jsp* page, shown in Figure 12.33.

```
<%--JSP1246.jsp Cookie Example Set Cookie Provide Link --%>
<%@ page language="java" import="java.util.*"%>
<%
String siteusername=request.getParameter("siteusername");
if(siteusername==null) siteusername="";
Date now = new Date();
String timestamp = now.toString();
Cookie cookie = new Cookie ("siteusername",siteusername);
cookie.setMaxAge(90 * 24 * 60 * 60);
response.addCookie(cookie);
%>
<html>
<head>
<title>Cookie Saved</title>
</head>
<body>
<p><a href="JSP1245.jsp">Next Page to view the cookie value</a><p>
</body>
```

Figure 12.33: Creating a cookie.

This page creates the cookie, retains the value for **siteusername**, and provides a link to return back to the "Welcome" page. If the cookie value exists for **siteusername**, its value is retrieved using **getValue()** and displayed on the "Welcome" page. The "Welcome" page will be displayed when the client returns to the site or after the cookie has been created and the user clicks the link to return to the "Welcome" page. In this example, note that the cookie will not expire for 90 days, because **cookie. setMaxAge(90 * 24 * 60 * 60)** multiplies 90 days, 24 hours, 60 minutes, and 60 seconds.

The "Welcome" page displayed if no cookie is found is shown in Figure 12.34. After the user's name is entered and retained in **siteusername,** a message containing a link to return back to the home page will be displayed, like this:

Next Page to view the cookie value

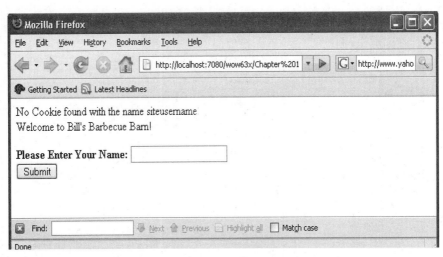

Figure 12.34: The "Welcome" page prompting for a user name.

This example should inspire some thought as to how cookies can be used in business applications. On sites requiring an ID and password, a cookie can even be compared to a database value to determine if the user is still valid.

Accessing a Database

As a business application developer, you must be able to access stored data. JSP can be used to connect and retrieve data from most databases, including SQL Server, MySQL, DB2, and Oracle. The examples in this chapter use MySQL on a local system. The examples can be used with other databases with minor changes, including the appropriate connection type.

Displaying Database Records

In the first example, an employee table will be displayed containing an automatically assigned employee ID, last name, first name, and position. To prepare for this example, MySQL needs to be loaded and configured on your PC as a local source. This chapter isn't intended to teach MySQL, but we will briefly walk through the creation of a MySQL database to be used with the examples. Here is the MySQL statement to create the BillsBarbequeBarn database:

CREATE DATABASE BillsBarbequeBarn;

Here is the MySQL statement to create an employee table:

```
CREATE TABLE employee (id INT( 7 ) NOT NULL AUTO_INCREMENT ,
LastName VARCHAR( 30 ) , FirstName VARCHAR( 30 ) , Position
VARCHAR(30),
PRIMARY KEY (id)) TYPE = MYISAM ;
```

Next, you need to add a few records to the table, to have something to display from it, like this:

```
INSERT INTO employee (LastName, FirstName, Position)
VALUES('Ubelhor', 'Laura', 'Waitress');
```

The id field is defined as an auto-increment field, so its numeric value will automatically be assigned when a record is added. Add a few more records in the table, changing the values of the last name, first name, and position.

This example uses a single JSP file, shown in Figure 12.35, to provide a display screen listing employees in order by last name and then first name.

```
<%--JSP1253.jsp Accessing and Displaying Data  Example--%>
<%@ page language="java" import="java.sql.*" %>
  <%
        String driver = "org.gjt.mm.mysql.Driver";
        Class.forName(driver).newInstance();
        Connection con=null;
        ResultSet rst=null;
        Statement stmt=null;
    try{
            String url="jdbc:mysql://localhost/Billsbarbequ
                eBarn?user=youruserid&password=yourpassword";
            con=DriverManager.getConnection(url);
            stmt=con.createStatement();
        }catch(Exception e){
                    System.out.println(e.getMessage());
                }
                rst=stmt.executeQuery("select * from employee
                    order by LastName, FirstName");
    %>
<html>
  <body>
  <center><h2>Employee List</h2>
  <table border="1" cellspacing="0" cellpadding="0">
        <tr><td><b>Employee No</b></td><td><b>Last Name
            </b><td><b>FirstName</b></td><td><b>Position
            </b></td></tr>
```

Figure 12.35: Accessing data with JSP (part 1 of 2).

```
        <%
            while(rst.next()){
    %>
        <tr><td><%=rst.getInt("Id")%></td>
        <td><%=rst.getString("LastName")%></td>
        <td><%=rst.getString("FirstName")%></td>
        <td><%=rst.getString("Position")%></td>
        </tr>
        <%
                    }
                    rst.close();
            stmt.close();
            con.close();
        %>
        <tr>
    </table>
    </center>
    <body>
<html>
```

Figure 12.35: Accessing data with JSP (part 2 of 2).

The example begins with the following directive:

<%@ page language="java" import="java.sql.*" %>

Java, of course, is identified as the language for the JSP file. The directive is important because the java.sql* classes are imported and can be used throughout the JSP code. The **import** statement provides access to the java. sql classes required to access the data and run MySQL statements. Other classes can be imported to access a variety of databases.

A connection is needed when accessing a database. As discussed earlier in this chapter, a variable or method must be declared before it can be used in the JSP file. We declare variables and make a connection to the database using the code in Figure 12.36.

```
    String driver = "org.gjt.mm.mysql.Driver";
    Class.forName(driver).newInstance();
    Connection con=null;
    ResultSet rst=null;
    Statement stmt=null;
```

Figure 12.36: The code to declare variables and load the database driver.

In this example, the variable **con** is the connection type, **rst** is the object that will hold the result set from the database query, and **stmt** is the object that will be used to execute the query.

To connect to the database, we need to load the database driver. In this case, a MySQL driver is loaded. Calling **Class.forName(driver)** results in the driver class being loaded. JSP can access many databases, as mentioned earlier. Here are some additional drivers that can be used:

> **String driver = "com.mysql.jdbc.Driver";**
> **String driverName = "com.ibm.as400.access.AS400JDBCDriver";**
> **String Driver = "oracle.jdbc.driver.OracleDriver";**

After the driver is loaded, the next step is to make the connection. The code to do this is shown in Figure 12.37.

```
url="jdbc:mysql://localhost/BillsbarbequeBarn?user=userid&pass
    word=password";
con=DriverManager.getConnection(url);
```

Figure 12.37: Making the connection.

The URL path is first defined, so it can be used by the connection. The JDBC URL for MySQL consists of *jdbc:mysql://* followed by the name of the MySQL server, in this example *localhost*, followed by the database, *BillsbarbequeBarn*, followed by the user ID and password. The ID and password need to be valid, with authority to access the database. When the URL is passed to the **getConnection()** method of the **DriverManager** class, the connection object is returned, which completes the connection to the database.

The connection could be defined a little differently, passing the URL, user ID, and password as separate parameters, like this:

> **con = DriverManager.getConnection (url, userName, password);**

You might opt to do this for security purposes. The ID and password will be provided through a prompted parameter.

With the connection made, we are ready to run the query using the database specified in the connection and a designated table. A statement object is created by calling the **createStatement()** method. After creating the statement object we are ready to execute the query. The statement variable name is **stmt**, and the recordset variable is **rst**. The query is executed on the statement object, as shown in Figure 12.38. The **executeQuery()** method runs the SQL statement and returns a single result object in **rst**. The method also returns the number of records from the table included in the query, based on the selection criteria.

```
rst=stmt.executeQuery("select * from employee order by LastName,
    FirstName");
```

Figure 12.38: Query execution.

In summary, the statement is created, the **executeQuery()** method is called on the **stmt** object, and the SQL query string is passed in method **executeQuery()** to the **rst** result set. Using an asterisk in the statement means all of the fields within the table are included in the result. All records in the table will be retrieved in order by last name and first name.

The example also includes code to address any errors encountered, shown in Figure 12.39. In this example, **try** and **catch** are used. These are one construct, and must be included in the same block of code. If an exception is encountered, a message will be displayed. Errors will be discussed in more detail later in this chapter.

```
try{
    }catch(Exception e){
                    System.out.println(e.getMessage());
        }
                }
```

Figure 12.39: Catching errors.

After executing the query and having a result set returned, the results are available for use in the application. The result set represents a table including the fields designated in the query statement. The table cursor initially is positioned before the first row selected. To access the first row in a result set, the **next()** method is used, as shown in Figure 12.40. This method moves the cursor to the next record. It returns a value of true if the next row is valid, or false if there are no more records within the result set.

```
    while(rst.next()){
%>
    <tr><td><%=rst.getInt("Id")%></td>
    <td><%=rst.getString("LastName")%></td>
    <td><%=rst.getString("FirstName")%></td>
    <td><%=rst.getString("Position")%></td>
    </tr>
    <%
    }
```

Figure 12.40: Reading rows from the result set.

The **getString()** method retrieves a string value from the current row. In this example, the ID, last name, first name, and position values are retrieved. The **getInt()** or **getDate()** methods would be used to retrieve integer or date values. (Refer to Appendix D for a list of JDBC types, for other data type methods that may be used.)

The values are retrieved and displayed. We loop through the record set until we have reached them. We finish by closing the table and connection, as shown in Figure 12.41.

```
            rst.close();
    stmt.close();
    con.close();
```

Figure 12.41: Closing the connection.

The result that will be displayed to the user is shown in Figure 12.42. Notice that the employee ID, last name, first name, and position are displayed in order by last name, followed by first name.

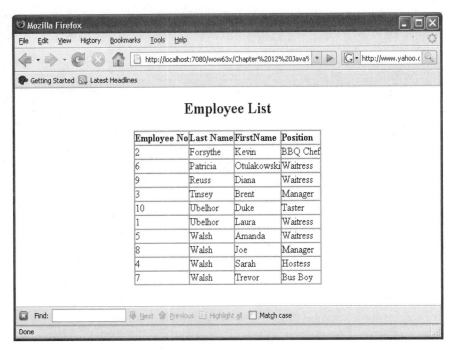

Figure 12.42: The results from accessing a database with JSP.

Adding Data to a Database

In the next example, a record will be added to a table and the table will be displayed after the record is added. The **executeUpdate()** method is used to insert a record in the table. As in the previous example, we will work with the employee table. Figure 12.43 shows the single JSP file that provides an entry form, adds records to the employee table, and displays the contents of the employee table.

```
<%--JSP1266.jsp Accessing a Database - Add and Display Example--%>
<%@ page language="java" import="java.sql.*" %>
..<%
        String driver = "org.gjt.mm.mysql.Driver";
        Class.forName(driver).newInstance();
        Connection con=null;
        ResultSet rst=null;
        Statement stmt=null;
    try{
                Stringurl="jdbc:mysql://localhost/Billsbarbeque
                Barn?user=youruserid&password=yourpassword";
```

Figure 12.43: Adding and displaying data (part 1 of 4).

```
                    con=DriverManager.getConnection(url);
                    stmt=con.createStatement();
          }catch(Exception e){
                        System.out.println(e.getMessage());
                    }
      if(request.getParameter("action") != null){
          String lastname=request.getParameter("lastname");
         String firstname=request.getParameter("firstname");
         String position=request.getParameter("position");
stmt.executeUpdate("insert  into  employee(LastName,FirstName,
   Position)
values('"+lastname+"','"+firstname+"','"+position+"')");
          rst=stmt.executeQuery("select * from employee order by
   position");
      %>
<html>
  <body>
  <center><h2>Employee List</h2>
  <table border="1" cellspacing="0" cellpadding="0">
        <tr><td><b>Number</b></td><td><b>Employee Number</b>
          </td><td><b>Last Name</b><td><b>FirstName</b>
          </td><td><b>Position</b></td></tr>
        <%
        int no=1;
                    while(rst.next()){
   %>
        <tr><td><%=no%></td>
        <td><%=rst.getInt("Id")%></td>
        <td><%=rst.getString("LastName")%></td>
        <td><%=rst.getString("FirstName")%></td>
        <td><%=rst.getString("Position")%></td>
        </tr>
        <%
              no++;
                  }

        rst.close();
                  stmt.close();
                  con.close();
            %>
            <tr>
  </table>
Total Number of Employees: < %=no - 1%>  <br>
        <A HREF="JSP1252.jsp">Add Another Employee.</A>

  </center>
  <body>
<html>
<%}else{%>

<html>
```

Figure 12.43: Adding and displaying data (part 2 of 4).

```
            <head>
            <title>Employee Entry FormDocument</title>
<script language="javascript">
            function validate(objForm){
                    if(objForm.lastname.
                      value.length==0){
                            alert("Please enter
                              Last  Name!");
                            objForm.lastname.
                              focus();
                            return false;
                }
                if(objForm.firstname.value.
                   length==0){
                            alert("Please enter First
                              Name!");
                            objForm.firstname.
                              focus();
                            return false;
                }
                if(objForm.position.value.
                   length==0){
                            alert("Please enterPosi
                              tion!");
                            objForm.position.focus();
                            return false;
                }
                return true;
            }
</script>
        </head>
        <body><center>
        <form action="JSP1266.jsp" method="post"
          name="entry"
          onSubmit="return validate(this)">
        <input type="hidden" value="list" name="action">
        <table border="1" cellpadding="0" cellspacing="0">
                <tr>
                        <td>
                            <table>
        <tr><td colspan="2" align="center"><h2>Employee
          Entry
          Form</h2></td></tr>
        <tr><td colspan="2"> </td></tr>
        <tr><td>LastName:</td><td><inputname="lastname"
          type="text"
          size="30"></td></tr>
        <tr><td>FirstName:</td><td><inputname="firstname"
          type="text"
          size="30"></td></tr>
        <tr><td>Position:</td><td><input name="position"
type="text"
```

Figure 12.43: Adding and displaying data (part 3 of 4).

```
                    size="30"></td></tr>
                    <tr><td colspan="2" align="center">
                        <input type="submit"
                    value="Submit"></td></tr>
                                            </table>
                                </td>
                        </tr>
                </table>
                </form>
                </center>
                </body>
        </html>
<%}%>
```

Figure 12.43: Adding and displaying data (part 4 of 4).

When the JSP file is run, the entry screen in Figure 12.44 will be displayed. The screen prompts for the employee information to be entered.

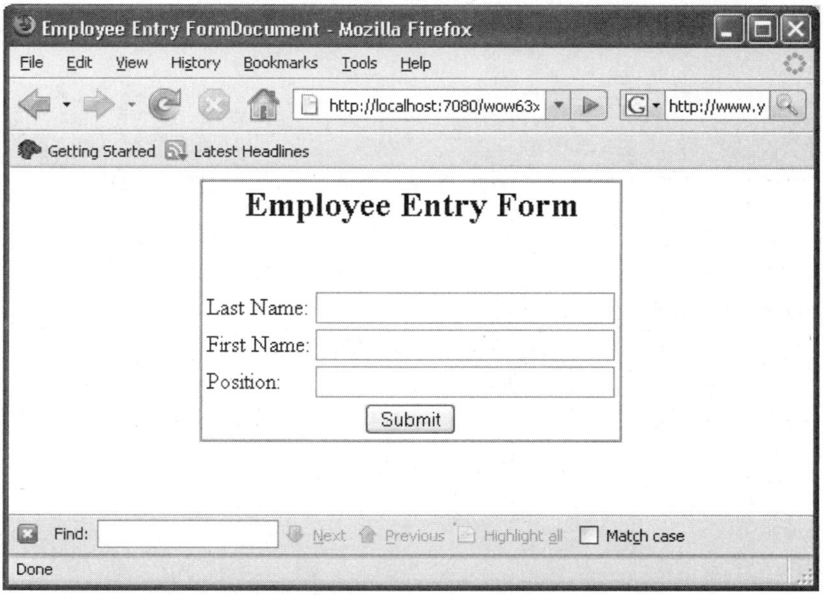

Figure 12.44: The employee entry form.

The code includes JavaScript edit checks requiring the last name, first name, and position to be entered, shown in Figure 12.45. JavaScript, introduced in chapter 8, is often used with JSP for such things as client-side validation.

```
script language="javascript">
                function validate(objForm){
                        if(objForm.lastname.value.
                         length==0){
                                alert("Please  enter  Last
                                 Name!");
                                 objForm.lastname.focus();
                                 return false;
                        }
                        if(objForm.firstname.value.
                         length==0){
                                alert("Please enter First
                                 Name!");
                                 objForm.firstname.
                                  focus();
                                 return false;
                        }
                        if(objForm.position.value.
                         length==0){
                                alert("Please enter
                                 Position!");
                                 objForm.position.focus();
                                 return false;
                        }
                        return true;
                }
        </script>
```

Figure 12.45: JavaScript data validation.

If the last name, first name, or position is missing when the user clicks **Submit**, a message like the one in Figure 12.46 will be displayed.

*Figure 12.46: A JavaScript
validation message.*

When all required data is entered and the user clicks **Submit**, we loop back again through the code. This time the "action" is not null, so the code in Figure 12.47 is executed. This code constructs MySQL statements to insert the new data into the employee table and display all of the records in the table, in order of position.

```
if(request.getParameter("action") != null){
      String lastname=request.getParameter("lastname");
    String firstname=request.getParameter("firstname");
    String position=request.getParameter("position");
        stmt.executeUpdate("insert into employee(LastName,Firs
          tName,Position)
         values('"+lastname+"','"+firstname+"','"+position
          +"')");

        rst=stmt.executeQuery("select * from employee order by
          position"));
```

Figure 12.47: Code to execute MySQL ***insert*** *and* ***select*** *statements.*

In our example, the database already contained ten employees. We added employee 12, Jessie Weaver, Manager. The resulting display is shown in Figure 12.48.

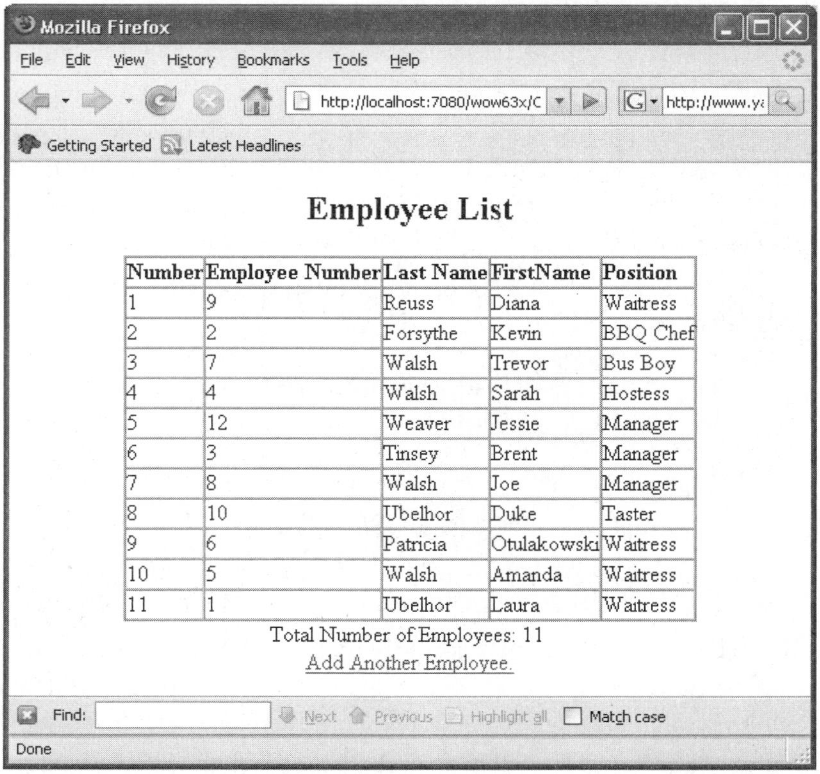

Number	Employee Number	Last Name	FirstName	Position
1	9	Reuss	Diana	Waitress
2	2	Forsythe	Kevin	BBQ Chef
3	7	Walsh	Trevor	Bus Boy
4	4	Walsh	Sarah	Hostess
5	12	Weaver	Jessie	Manager
6	3	Tinsey	Brent	Manager
7	8	Walsh	Joe	Manager
8	10	Ubelhor	Duke	Taster
9	6	Patricia	Otulakowski	Waitress
10	5	Walsh	Amanda	Waitress
11	1	Ubelhor	Laura	Waitress

Figure 12.48: The results of adding a new employee.

Notice the "Add Another Employee" link. When that link is clicked, the application runs again, and the employee entry form will be re-displayed.

In this example, the employee ID is automatically assigned without entry because that field is defined to auto-increment in the MySQL table definition. The integer **no**, used to increment the record count and assign a number to the entries, is not the same as the employee ID. This example adds a line of code to display the total employee count, using the accumulated value of **no**. Because this integer is incremented each time the loop is executed, and the loop is executed until a value of false is returned for the result set, the integer count is one more than the record count. The code in Figure 12.49 deals with this.

```
Total Number of Employees: <%=no - 1%> <br>
```

Figure 12.49: Displaying the total number of employees.

Updating a Database

The next example takes access to a database further, providing capabilities to add, update, and delete rows in a table. Again, the employee table of the BillsBarbequeBarn database will be used. The table includes the fields employee number, last name, first name, and position.

This application consists of four JSP files:

- The employee list page (the main application page), JSP1275EEDisplay.jsp

- The employee add page, JSP1275Add.jsp

- The employee update page, JSP1275Update.jsp

- The employee delete page, JSP1275Delete.jsp

The main application page, shown in Figure 12.50, displays a list of the employee table entries and provides options to add, update, or delete an employee. The rows of the employee table are displayed in order by last name, followed by first name. The employee list page also provides a total number of employees.

```
<%--JSP1275EEDisplay.jsp Employee Modification Example--%>
<%@ page language="java" import="java.sql.*" %>
 <%
        String driver = "org.gjt.mm.mysql.Driver";
        Class.forName(driver).newInstance();
        Connection con=null;
        ResultSet rst=null;
        Statement stmt=null;
   try{
            String
url="jdbc:mysql://localhost/Billsbarbequ eBarn?user=youruserid
  &password=yourpassword";
            con=DriverManager.getConnection(url);
            stmt=con.createStatement();
      }catch(Exception e){
                    System.out.println(e.getMessage());
            }
            rst=stmt.executeQuery("select * from employee
order by LastName, FirstName");
    %>
<html>
  <body>
  <center><h2>Employee List</h2>
  <table border="1" cellspacing="0" cellpadding="0">
        <tr><td><b>Employee No</b></td>
        <td><b>Last Name</b></td>
        <td><b>FirstName</b></td>
        <td><b>Position</b></td>
        <td><b>Update</b></td>
        <td><b>Delete</b></td>
        </tr>
        <%
        int no=1;
            while(rst.next()){
   %>
        <tr><td><%=rst.getInt("Id")%></td>
        <td><%=rst.getString("LastName")%></td>
        <td><%=rst.getString("FirstName")%></td>
        <td><%=rst.getString("Position")%></td>
                <td><a
 href="JSP1275EEUpdate.jsp?id=<%=rst.
                getInt("Id")%>">Update</a></b>
                <td><a
 href="JSP1275EEDelete.jsp?id=<%=rst.
                getInt("Id")%>">Delete</a></b>
        </tr>
        <%
                no++;
                    }

        rst.close();
                stmt.close();
                con.close();
        %>
```

Figure 12.50: The main JSP page for updating employee data (part 1 of 2).

```
                   <tr>
     </table>
       Total Number of Employees: <%=no - 1%>  <br>
            <A HREF="JSP1275EEAdd.jsp">Add An Employee.</A>
     </center>
     <body>
 <html>
```

Figure 12.50: The main JSP page for updating employee data (part 2 of 2).

The file in Figure 12.50 creates and makes the connection, displays all of the entries in the employee table, and displays the accumulated count, as shown in Figure 12.51.

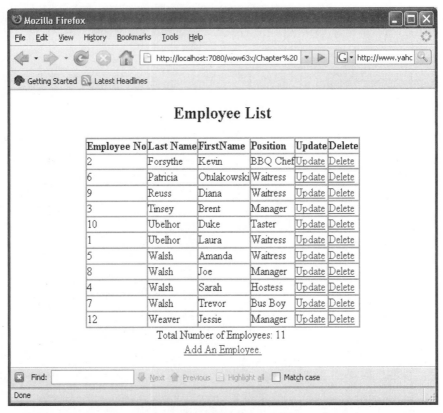

Figure 12.51: The initial screen for the application to update employee data.

Notice there are additional columns for updating and deleting records. A link to add an employee is also displayed. When the user clicks a link, the application is directed to the add, change, or delete page to complete the appropriate action, as shown in Figure 12.52. The employee number is the key to accessing the employee record.

```
<td><a    href="JSP1275EEUpdate.jsp?id=<%=rst.getInt("Id")%>">Update
   </a></b>
<td><a    href="JSP1275EEDelete.jsp?id=<%=rst.getInt("Id")%>">Delete
   </a></b>


<A HREF="JSP1275EEAdd.jsp">Add An Employee.</A>
```

Figure 12.52: Links for updating, deleting, or add employee records.

For the update and delete functions, the parameter **Id** will be passed by using the record set type variable to retrieve the **Id** value. Notice the <%= %> tags used, to allow use of the **getint()** method.

The add function is very similar to the earlier example of adding records to a table. However, in this example, the add page is accessed through an HTML link. When the user clicks the link on the main page, the JSP file in Figure 12.53 will be executed and the screen in Figure 12.54 will be displayed.

```
<%--JSP1275EEAdd.jsp Add an Employee Example--%>
<%@ page language="java" import="java.sql.*" %>
  <%
          String driver = "org.gjt.mm.mysql.Driver";
          Class.forName(driver).newInstance();
          Connection con=null;
          ResultSet rst=null;
          Statement stmt=null;
    try{
              String
url="jdbc:mysql://localhost/BillsbarbequeBarn?user=youruserid
  &password=yourpassword";
              con=DriverManager.getConnection(url);
              stmt=con.createStatement();
        }catch(Exception e){
                      System.out.println(e.getMessage());
                }
    if(request.getParameter("action") != null){
        String lastname=request.getParameter("lastname");
    String firstname=request.getParameter("firstname");
    String position=request.getParameter("position");
    stmt.executeUpdate("insert  into  employee(LastName,FirstNa
```

Figure 12.53: Adding an employee (part 1 of 3).

```
             me,Position)     values('"+lastname+"','"+firstname+"','"
        +position+"')");
    %>
  <html>
 Employee Record Successfully Added! <br> <br>
 <A HREF="JSP1275EEDisplay.jsp">Return to Employee Display.</A>
 </hmtl>
 <%}else{%>
 <html>

                <head>
                <title>Employee Entry FormDocument</title>
        <script language="javascript">
                    function validate(objForm){
                            if(objForm.lastname.value.
                              length==0){
                                    alert("Please enter Last
                                      Name!");
                                    objForm.lastname.focus();
                                    return false;
                            }
                            if(objForm.firstname.value.
                              length==0){
                                    alert("Please enter First
                                      Name!");
                                    objForm.firstname.focus();
                                    return false;
                            }
                            if(objForm.position.value.
                              length==0){
                                    alert("Please enter
                                      Position!");
                                    objForm.position.focus();
                                    return false;
                            }
                            return true;
                    }
         </script>
         </head>
         <body><center>
         <form action="JSP1275EEAdd.jsp" method="post" name="entry
           "onSubmit="return validate(this)">
         <input type="hidden" value="list" name="action">
         <table border="1" cellpadding="0" cellspacing="0">
 <tr>
 <td>
 <table>
 <tr><td  colspan="2"  align="center"><h2>Employee   Entry   Form
   </h2></td></tr>
 <tr><td colspan="2"> </td></tr>
 <tr><td>Last Name:</td><td><input name="lastname" type="text"
   size="30"></td></tr>
 <tr><td>First Name:</td><td><input name="firstname" type="text"
   size="30"></td></tr>
```

Figure 12.53: Adding an employee (part 2 of 3).

```
<tr><td>Position:</td><td><input name="position" type="text"
   size="30"></td></tr>
<tr><td colspan="2" align="center"><input type="submit"
   value="Add Employee"></td></tr>
                                      </table>
                            </td>
                  </tr>
            </table>
<A HREF="JSP1275EEDisplay.jsp">Return to Employee Display Page
   Without Adding an Employee.</A>
                  </form>
                  </center>
                  </body>
   </html>
<%}%>
```

Figure 12.53: Adding an employee (part 3 of 3).

JavaScript code is used for field validation on the client side. Like the example earlier in this chapter, the validation checks to make sure a last name, first name, and position are entered. When the user clicks the Add Employee button and there are no field validation errors, the action parameter value is set to "Add Employee." The value is not null, so the SQL statement is executed to insert a record. The user also has the option to return to the main application page without adding an employee through the use of an HTML link.

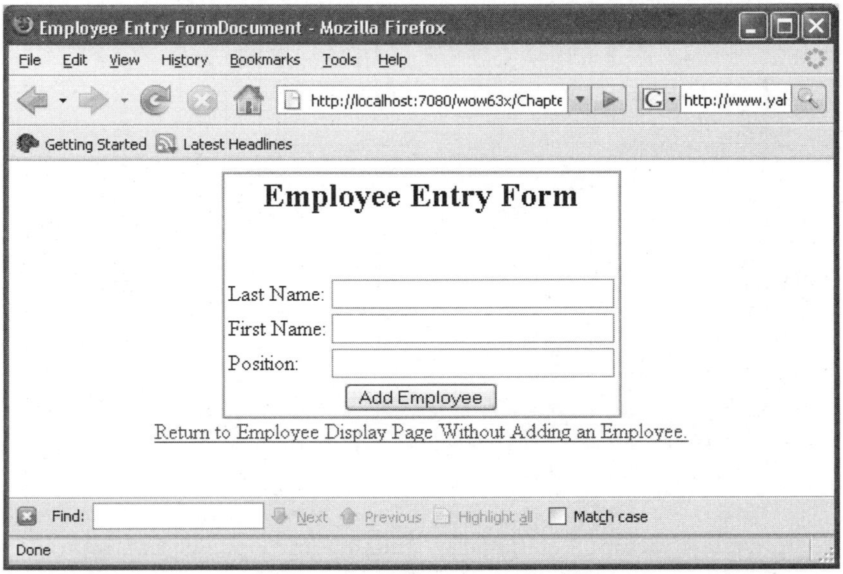

Figure 12.54: The screen to add an employee.

When the action parameter is set to "Add Employee," the following message is displayed:

Employee Record Successfully Added!

Return to Employee Display.

The user clicks the "Return to Employee Display" link to return to the main application page. In this example, employee 13 has been added, as shown in Figure 12.55. Notice the employee count has been incremented. The new entry is displayed at the top of the page because the records are displayed by last name and first name.

Figure 12.55: The main application page after employee 13 is added.

The update feature is initiated by clicking an "Update" link reference. It will execute the JSP in Figure 12.56, passing the **id** parameter with the value of the employee number.

```
<%--JSP1275EEUpdate.jsp Update an Employee Example--%>
<%@ page language="java" import="java.sql.*" %>
 <%
        String driver = "org.gjt.mm.mysql.Driver";
        Class.forName(driver).newInstance();
        Connection con=null;
        ResultSet rst=null;
        Statement stmt=null;
   try{
             String
url="jdbc:mysql://localhost/Billsbarbequ
eBarn?user=youruserid&password=yourpassword";
             con=DriverManager.getConnection(url);
             stmt=con.createStatement();
       }catch(Exception e){
                     System.out.println(e.getMessage());
             }
   if(request.getParameter("action") != null){
   int selectionId = Integer.parseInt(request.
     getParameter("id"));
   String lastname=request.getParameter("lastname");
   String firstname=request.getParameter("firstname");
   String position=request.getParameter("position");
       stmt.executeUpdate("UPDATE employee SET LastName='
         "+ lastname +"', FirstName=' "+ firstname +"',
         Position=' "+ position +"' where Id =12");

   %>
 <html>
Employee Id <%= request.getParameter ("id") %> Successfully
   Updated! <br> <br>
<A HREF="JSP1275EEDisplay.jsp">Return to Employee Display.</A>
</html>
<%}else{%>
<%
int selectionId = Integer.parseInt(request.getParameter("id"));
String lastname=null;
String firstname=null;
String position=null;
rst=stmt.executeQuery("select * from employee where Id =
   " + selectionId + "");
       if (rst.next())
       {
       lastname = rst.getString("LastName");
       firstname = rst.getString("FirstName");
       position = rst.getString("Position");

       }
       else
       {
             lastname = "Unknown.";
             firstname = "Unknown.";
             position = "Unknown.";
```

Figure 12.56: Updating an employee (part 1 of 3).

```
        }
%>
<html>
                <head>
                    <script language="javascript">
                    function validate(objForm){
                            if(objForm.lastname.value.
                                length==0){
                                    alert("Please enter Last
                                        Name!");
                                    objForm.lastname.focus();
                                    return false;
                            }
                            if(objForm.firstname.value.
                                length==0){
                                    alert("Please enter First
                                        Name!");
                                    objForm.firstname.
                                        focus();
                                    return false;
                            }
                            if(objForm.position.value.
                                length==0){
                                    alert("Please enter
                                        Position!");
                                    objForm.position.focus();
                                    return false;
                            }
                            return true;
                    }
            </script>
        </head>
        <body><center>
        <form action="JSP1275EEUpdate.jsp" method="post" name="update"
          onSubmit="return validate(this)">
        <input type="hidden" value="list" name="action">
        <input type="hidden" value=<%= request.getParameter ("id")%>
          name="id"">
        <table border="1" cellspacing="0" cellpadding="0">
                    <tr><td colspan="4" align="center"><h2>Employee
                        Update Form</h2></td></tr>
                    <tr><td><b>Employee No</b></td>
                    <td><b>Last Name</b></td>
                    <td><b>FirstName</b></td>
                    <td><b>Position</b></td>
                    </tr>
                    <tr><td><%=selectionId%></td>
                    <td><input name="lastname" type="text" size="30"
                        value="<%=lastname%>"></td>
                    <td><input name="firstname" type="text" size="30"
                        value="<%=firstname%>"></td>
```

Figure 12.56: Updating an employee (part 2 of 3).

```
                  <td><input name="position" type="text" size="30"
                     value="<%=position%>"></td>
</tr>
<tr><td    colspan="4"    align="center"><input    type="submit"
   value="Update Employee <%= request.getParameter ("id") %>">
   </td></tr>
                  </table>
<A HREF="JSP1275EEDisplay.jsp">Return to Employee Display Page
   Without Updating Employee.</A>
                  </form>

                  </center>
                  </body>
   </html>
<%}%>
```

Figure 12.56: Updating an employee (part 3 of 3).

When the update page is initially displayed, the action value is null. Using the **id** parameter passed, a query is executed as shown in Figure 12.57, retrieving the matching employee record.

```
rst=stmt.executeQuery("select * from employee where Id = " +
   selectionId + "");
```

Figure 12.57: The query to select an employee record by ID.

Prior to executing the query, the **selectionId** integer is defined and the value is set to the passed **id** parameter using the **getParameter()** method. The update form is displayed using the retrieved table row values from the query for the matching selection. The row values are displayed within the form table by inserting JSP code to set the value of the display field, as shown in Figure 12.58.

```
<td><input name="lastname" type="text" size="30"
   value="<%=lastname%>"></td>
```

Figure 12.58: Setting HTML form field values.

The update also has a validation check to ensure the fields are not blank. If the last name, first name, or position are blank, a message will be displayed prompting the user to enter the missing value.

Figure 12.59 shows the update function if the "Update" link for employee 9 is clicked on the main application page. After making corrections to swap the first and last names, the user clicks the "Update Employee 9" button. Alternatively, the user can click the "Return to Employee Display Page Without Updating Employee" link. This HTML link will return the user to the main application page without completing the update.

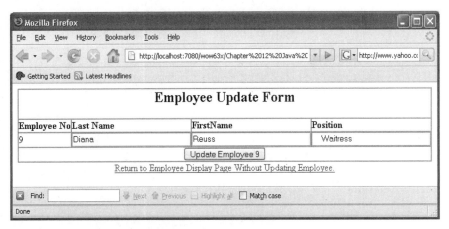

Figure 12.59: An employee update form.

The "Update Employee 9" button shown in Figure 12.59 displays the employee number using JSP code embedded within the JSP tags, as shown in Figure 12.60.

```
<%= request.getParameter ("id") %>
```

Figure 12.60: Displaying the employee number on a button.

When the "Update Employee 9" button is clicked, hidden field values will be available for use on the **post** action, as shown in Figure 12.61. The **id** field will be used for the MySQL **update** statement's selection criteria. On submit, the action value is set to "Update Employee," and the value will no longer be null, triggering **executeUpdate** to be run.

```
<input type="hidden" value="list" name="action">
<input type="hidden" value=<%= request.getParameter ("id")%>
   name="id"">
```

Figure 12.61: Hidden form values.

The form field values for last name, first name, and position will be used to update the table row with an employee ID matching the **id** field value. After the update is complete, an HTML page with the following message is displayed:

Employee Id 9 Successfully Updated!

Return to Employee Display.

By pressing the "Return to Employee Display" link, the main application page will again display the employee list, as shown in Figure 12.62.

Figure 12.62: The updated employee list.

Notice employee 9's position in the list has changed to reflect her correct last name, *Reuss*.

The final function in this application is deleting a record. When the "Delete" link is clicked, the JSP file in Figure 12.63 will be loaded. Again, the **id** value for the selected row is passed as a parameter using JSP code embedded in the HTML link reference and the **getint()** method.

```
<%--JSP1275EEDelete.jsp Delete an Employee Example--%>
<%@ page language="java" import="java.sql.*" %>
  <%
        String driver = "org.gjt.mm.mysql.Driver";
        Class.forName(driver).newInstance();
        Connection con=null;
        ResultSet rst=null;
        Statement stmt=null;
    try{
                String url="jdbc:mysql://localhost/Billsbarbequ
                    eBarn?user=youruserid&password=yourpassword";
                con=DriverManager.getConnection(url);
                stmt=con.createStatement();
        }catch(Exception e){
                    System.out.println(e.getMessage());
                }
    if(request.getParameter("action") != null){
            int    selectionId   =   Integer.parseInt(request.
                getParameter("id"));
        stmt.executeUpdate("delete  from  employee  where  Id  ="
            + selectionId );

            %>
 <html>
Employee  Id  <%=  request.getParameter  ("id")  %>  Successfully
Deleted!  <br>  <br>
<A HREF="JSP1275EEDisplay.jsp">Return to Employee Display.</A>
</html>
<%}else{%>
<%
int selectionId = Integer.parseInt(request.getParameter("id"));
String lastname=null;
String firstname=null;
String position=null;
rst=stmt.executeQuery("select  *  from  employee  where  Id  =  "  +
    selectionId + "");
        if (rst.next())
        {
        lastname = rst.getString("LastName");
        firstname = rst.getString("FirstName");
        position = rst.getString("Position");

        }
        else
        {
                lastname = "Unknown.";
                firstname = "Unknown.";
                position = "Unknown.";
```

Figure 12.63: Deleting an employee (part 1 of 2).

```
            }
%>
<html>
                <head>
                </head>
                <body><center>
                <form action="JSP1275EEDelete.jsp" method="post"
                    name="delete"">
                                <input type="hidden" value="list"
name="action">
                                <input  type="hidden"  value=<%=
request.getParameter ("id")%> name="id"">
                                <table border="1" cellspacing="0"
cellpadding="0">
                <tr><td colspan="4" align="center"><h2>Employee
                    Delete Form</h2></td></tr>
                <tr><td><b>Employee No</b></td>
                <td><b>Last Name</b></td>
                <td><b>FirstName</b></td>
                <td><b>Position</b></td>
                </tr>
                <tr><td><%=selectionId%></td>
                <td><%=lastname%></td>
                <td><%=firstname%></td>
                <td><%=position%></td></tr>
                <tr><td colspan="4"align="center"><input
                    type="submit"
value="Delete Employee <%= request. getParameter ("id") %>">
</td> </tr>
                </table>
            <A  HREF="JSP1275EEDisplay.jsp">Return to Employee
            Display Page Without Deleting Employee.</A>
                </form>

                </center>
                </body>
    </html>
<%}%>
```

Figure 12.63: Deleting an employee (part 2 of 2).

The delete JSP file is very similar to the update JSP file. The biggest difference is that the page retrieves the employee row and displays the fields within an HTML form as display values, instead of form input fields. Also, the **executeQuery** statement uses a **delete** SQL statement. No field edit checks are required because the application will not be changing the values of the fields. The application again provides the capability to return to the main employee page without deleting the employee through an HTML link.

The HTML page in Figure 12.64 is displayed after clicking the "Delete" link next to employee 10.

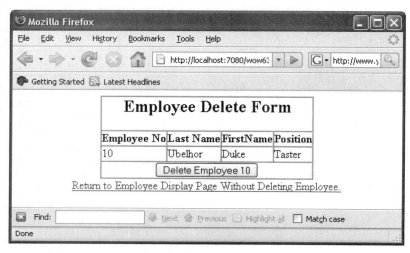

Figure 12.64: An employee delete page.

When the user clicks the "Delete Employee 10" button the action value will be set to "Delete Employee," initiating **executeUpdate** and using the passed **id** value to select the row to be deleted from the employee table, as shown in Figure 12.65.

```
Execute Update:

if(request.getParameter("action") != null){
int selectionId = Integer.parseInt(request.getParameter("id"));
   stmt.executeUpdate("delete from employee where Id ="
          + selectionId );


Retrieve Id:

<html>
Employee Id <%= request.getParameter ("id") %> Successfully
   Deleted! <br> <br>
<A HREF="JSP1275EEDisplay.jsp">Return to Employee Display.</A>
</html>
```

Figure 12.65: Initiating executeUpdate for deletion.

When the deletion is complete, the page shown in Figure 12.66 will be displayed. The HTML code includes embedded JSP code to use the **getParameter()** function to retrieve the employee ID to display.

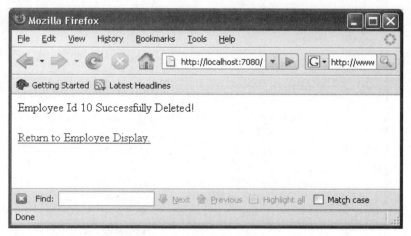

Figure 12.66: The deletion confirmation screen.

When the "Return to Employee Display" link is clicked, the application again returns to the main application page, shown in Figure 12.67. Notice that employee 10, Duke Ubelhor, is no longer included on the list, so the total number of employees has changed from 12 to 11.

Figure 12.67: The employee list after a deletion.

The ability to retrieve, display and update data is critical for business application developers. The examples in this section have shown some of the options for coding this functionality with JSP. As you have seen, Javascript is often embedded within HTML and used with JSP to shift tasks like editing fields to the client side, rather than using shared server-side resources.

Although these examples used MySQL, they will work with slight changes to access a System i DB2 database, SQL Server database, Oracle database, or other database sources. Similarly, although these examples used an employee update application, they could easily be changed to update other business databases, such as those for inventories, orders, or general ledgers.

Exception Handling

Exception handling is an important part of application development, as mentioned earlier in this chapter. An exception is an uncaught throwable object that results in an error. An exception might occur while connecting to a database when a server is down, when a buffer is full and overflows, or when a request method fails.

Exceptions can be caught by coding to throw an exception to a **try** and **catch** block. In the example in Figure 12.68, if an exception occurs while making the connection to a database, it is caught, and a message is displayed.

```
    try{
                String
url="jdbc:mysql://localhost/Billsbarbequ eBarn?user=youruserid
  &password=yourpassword";
                con=DriverManager.getConnection(url);
                stmt=con.createStatement();
        }catch(Exception e){
                    System.out.println(e.getMessage());
                }
```

*Figure 12.68: A **try catch** exception.*

In the code, **Exception** is an implicit object that acts as a wrapper around underlying Java classes or interfaces typically defined with the servlet API. It is used for exceptions not caught by application code.

An exception may also be caught by designating an error page in the page directive. If an exception is thrown, the control will be transferred to the designated error page. Using this form of exception, you can provide a more meaningful error message for the user and also provide details for system administration about the exception encountered. Think carefully about whether or not to provide these system details. For exceptions that have a critical impact on the application, they may be more significant.

The example in the following pages illustrates the runtime error-handling features of JSP pages. The example includes three pages:

- The product list page (the main application page), JSP1296.html.
- The form handler page, JSP1297.jsp
- The exception-handler error page, JSP1298.jsp

The HTML page in Figure 12.69 displays a form requesting the user to make a product selection. The page would also probably include code to list products, but this example has been kept simple to illustrate exception error-handling. The input field will be used in the form-handler page shown in Figure 12.70.

```
<%--JSP1296.html Exception Handling Example--%>
<html>
<head>
Bill's Barbeque Barn Product List Page.
</head>
<body>
<form action="JSP1297.jsp" method="post">
Please Enter The Product Number:
<input type="text" name="product" />
<input type="submit" value="Submit" />
</form>
</body>
</html>
```

Figure 12.69: A product list HTML page.

```
<%--JSP1297.jsp Exception Handling Form Handler Example--%>
<%@ page errorPage="JSP1298.jsp" %>
<html>
<head>
Bill's Barbeque Barn Product Selection Page.
</head>
<body>
<%
int product;
product = Integer.parseInt(request.getParameter("product"));
%>
<p>Thank You For Selecting Product Number <%= product %>.</p>
<p><a href="JSP1296.html">Return To Bill's Barbeque Barn Product
    List Page.</a>.</p>
</body>
</html>
```

Figure 12.70: A JSP form-handler page.JSP1297.jsp Product Selection Page Form Handler Exception Handling example.

The JSP file in Figure 12.71 is the exception-handling page initiated when the user clicks the form's **Submit** button.

```
<%--JSP1298.jsp Exception Handling Exception Handler Error Page
   Example--%>
<%@ page isErrorPage="true" import="java.io.*" %>
<html>
<body>
An error has occurred the Product Selection is invalid! <br>
<%= exception.toString() %><br>
<%
out.println("<!--");
StringWriter sw = new StringWriter();
PrintWriter pw = new PrintWriter(sw);
exception.printStackTrace(pw);
out.print(sw);
sw.close();
pw.close();
out.println("-->");
%>
</body>
</html>
```

Figure 12.71: A JSP exception-handler page.

When the application is initiated, the screen in Figure 12.72 will be displayed.

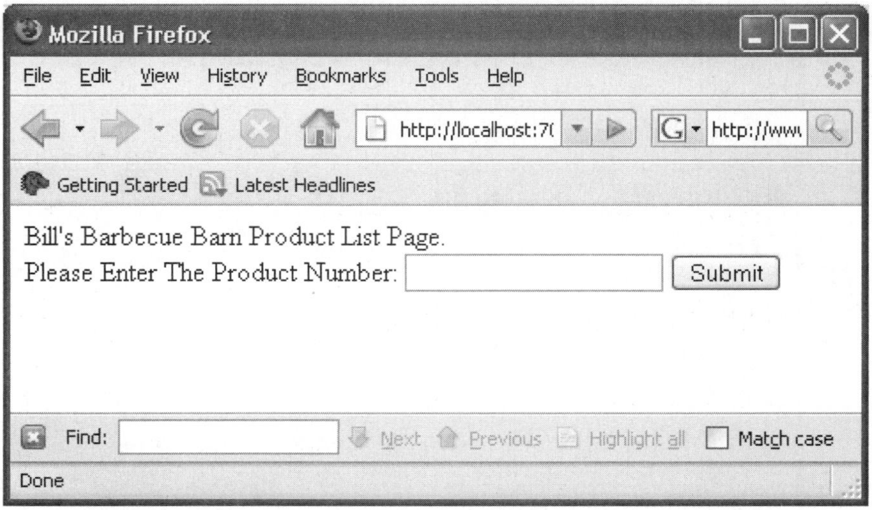

Figure 12.72: The main screen.

The page prompts the user to enter a product number and click **Submit**. The input from the field is then received and used in the form-handler page. The first line of code on the page, shown in Figure 12.73, includes a directive to specify an **errorPage**.

```
<%@ page errorPage="JSP1298.jsp" %>
```

Figure 12.73: Specifying an error page.

The page then declares the product as an integer variable. The entered value is parsed using the method **Integer.parseInt()** and the value is retrieved using the method **request.getParameter()**, as shown in Figure 12.74. The argument for the method is the name of the form field product.

```
<%
int product;
product = Integer.parseInt(request.getParameter("product"));
%>
```

Figure 12.74: Form-handler code get parameter request.

Suppose the user enters *1* for the product number. This is a valid integer, so an exception will not occur. The page shown in Figure 12.75 will be displayed. The product number entered is displayed, and the user is provided a link to return to the main product list.

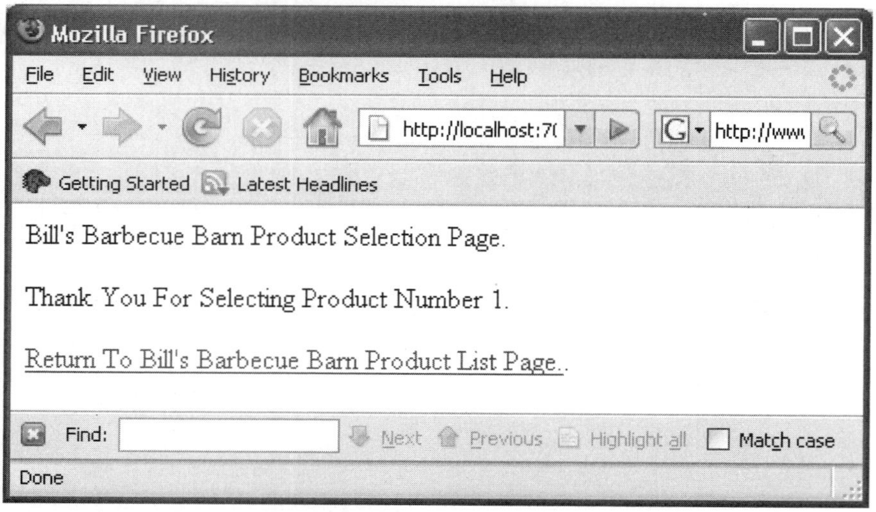

Figure 12.75: The result when no exception is thrown.

Suppose, however, the user enters an invalid value. To make the JSP exception-handler error page, the **isErrorPage** attribute is specified, as shown in Figure 12.76.

```
<%@ page isErrorPage="true" import="java.io.*" %>
```

*Figure 12.76: The **isErrorPage** attribute.*

In the declarative, the **java.io** class is also designated to provide functionality for the **PrintWriter** and **StringWriter** classes. Because **errorPage** has been declared, it has been made the name of the exception object of the type **java.lang.Throwable** available.

In addition to the exception, a programmer-defined message has been provided for the user when an exception is encountered.

If the users enters *A*, an exception will be created, and the following messages will be displayed:

An error has occurred the Product Selection is invalid!
java.lang.NumberFormatException: For input string: "A"

The user is informed that an error has occurred. In addition, the stack trace information has been included inside HTML comment tags, so the user will only see the message and not the stack trace information. This information could be used by system administrators or developers to provide details about the exception error that occurred. Figure 12.77 is the code that creates the stack trace information.

```
<%
out.println("<!--");
StringWriter sw = new StringWriter();
PrintWriter pw = new PrintWriter(sw);
exception.printStackTrace(pw);
out.print(sw);
sw.close();
pw.close();
out.println("-->");
%>
```

Figure 12.77: Capturing stack trace exception details.

To capture stack trace details, the **PrintWriter** and **StringWriter** classes are used. They are available because in the declarative, the import **java.io***** package was included. To view the stack trace, display the page source.

Exception handling is important. As you have seen, you can use JSP to control the messages displayed to a user, and also can control how an application reacts when an error is encountered.

Summary

JSP is a widely used, proven technology for Web development. The language is very robust and can be used on a wide array of platforms and with a multitude of databases. JSP can be used alone or, more frequently, with other tools, including JavaScript and Java.

In this chapter, you have covered the basics of JSP. You have also seen how it can be used for dynamic tasks, including data retrieval and update. Other code examples can easily be found on the Web, and now that you have a basic understanding of JSP, you'll be able to understand and use these examples.

Fueled with the understanding of JSP provided through this chapter, you can determine how JSP can be used for your specific business application needs. You are now ready to take the next step, incorporating JSP into your Web application projects.

13

Differences in Common Browsers

An important part of your Web application project is how the site will appear to end-users. It is unlikely that all of the visitors to your site will be using the same browser, hardware, operating system, and browser configuration settings. In one browser, your site might display perfectly, while in another browser, it might look quite different or not work properly at all.

There is a long list of Internet browsers available. It would be impossible to code your site to work exactly the same with all of them. However, by understanding browser differences, you can take them into consideration when designing and developing your site to maximize consistency for end users. You should attempt to accommodate as many of your site's users as possible, within the limitations of time, money, and resources.

W3C Standards and Guidelines

The Web and HTML have been around a long time. The language you use for writing a Web page is standardized by the World Wide Web Consortium, or W3C, which was created in October 1994 by Tim Berners-Lee,the original architect of the Web. The W3C is an international consortium made up of about 500 member organizations, a full-time staff, and the public, who work together to develop Web standards. W3C's mission is to lead the Web to its full potential by developing protocols and guidelines that ensure its long-term growth.

W3C primarily pursues its mission through the creation of Web standards and guidelines. Since 1994, W3C has published more than 90 standards called "W3C Recommendations." W3C also engages in education and outreach, develops software, and serves as an open forum for discussion about the Web. In order for the Web to reach its full potential, the most fundamental Web technologies must be compatible with one another and allow any hardware and software used to access the Web to work together. W3C refers to this goal as *Web interoperability*. By publishing open (non-proprietary) standards for Web languages and protocols, W3C seeks to avoid market and Web fragmentation. W3C's purpose is to develop open standards so the Web evolves with interoperability. W3C is the reason the Web works, no matter what business or organization builds tools to support it.

Creators and vendors of browsers are not required to follow the guidelines and standards provided by W3C. Fortunately, W3C compliance has had an impact on the popularity of browsers and has had a significant impact on the interoperability of current browsers. Therefore, most current browsers comply to varying degrees with the standards set by W3C. Most browsers are available for download from the Internet for no charge, so the option to choose a browser is left in the hands of individuals and organizations.

A sophisticated Web site developer takes into consideration the differences in common browsers and designs Web applications to minimize the impact of those differences. Creating several different versions of the same Web site can accommodate some of the various browser requirements, but it can put a great strain on budget and resources, and it still leaves you open to variations and omissions. A text-only version of a site can be created, which will be less affected by browser differences. Even when a text-only site is well-maintained, however, it often lacks the appeal of a dynamic, graphical site.

Addressing Differences in Common Browsers

The first step to addressing browser differences is to list which browsers should be considered for your project. Set a goal. If you feel you can expend the time, money, and resources, set your goal high. A good design should be able to work with about 90-95% of your audience. Your Web site should be tested using the list of browsers identified. Understand that it is next to impossible to build a Web site that displays perfectly on every version of every browser running on every computer. If you tried this, you would probably have to leave out many features that you really wanted to include on your Web site.

A page written in pure HTML, without any style sheets or scripts, can look the same in almost any browser. However, upon closer examination, even text-only pages may look different when viewed in different browsers. Some differences might be so minor that you don't readily notice them. Others might be obvious. The more complex the pages on your site, the more likely there will be browser differences.

Browser Issues to Consider

Within the constraints of time, money, and resources, it is usually impossible to design a Web application for all users. Therefore, identify the software used by most of your audience, and design to maximize the effectiveness of your Web site for them. Constraints imposed on users by their hardware, settings, and connection speed must also be considered.

Part of the process of designing and testing a Web application is listing its browser-support issues, as shown in Figure 13.1. Once this list is created, you will probably be able to use it for all of your Web applications. The list should be revisited periodically to accommodate changes in application purposes and common browsers. The rest of this chapter discusses the topics in this list.

Bill's BBQ Barn Web Site Application Supported Browser Checklist	
1	Web Site Audience
2	Language
3	Common Browsers
4	Browser Features and Settings
5	Hardware
6	Monitor Settings
7	Operating System Support
8	Internet Connection Speed
9	Image Format Support
10	Minimizing the Impact of Browser Differences
11	Text Format Support
12	Browser Testing Checklist

Figure 13.1: An application's supported browser checklist.

Web Site Audience

Your audience consists of the people who visit and use your Web site and applications. Always keep in mind that your site is for people, who are the key to its success.

The purpose of your site should be carefully defined. This purpose determines who the site's users will be. For example, will employees visit your site to determine their work schedules or to order supplies? Will customers be viewing your site to purchase items or to log customer-service requests? Determining how the site will be used will determine who your audience is.

Let's use the example of Bill's BBQ Barn to create a list of site users. Its Web site consists of pages providing information about Bill's BBQ Barn, a customer product-ordering form, a customer-service application, an application to update employee information, and an employee work-schedule inquiry. The audience for Bill's BBQ Barn includes the following groups:

- Local restaurant customers inquiring to find restaurant information
- Customers looking to order products
- Customers accessing the customer-service application to log and view requests
- Employees accessing online work schedules
- Internal staff updating employee data

Next, you will need to consider how your site's users will be accessing the Internet and what types of browsers will be used. In the case of Bill's BBQ Barn, we know most of the site visitors will be local people accessing the Web site from home. We also know the majority of our customers and all of our employees are from the local area. However, we want to include potential customers outside of our local area.

Now that we know who our audience is, we are equipped to do some research. A staff developer is assigned to determine what kinds of browsers the majority of our visitors will be using. The developer does some research and comes back with the following:

- The local community has been aggressively promoting new technology and has provided free training on how to use the Web. Therefore, those accessing our site locally will probably be using newer browsers and high-speed Internet connections.

- Customers outside the local area who purchase our types of products have a higher than average income, and are likely to be tech-savvy users with relatively new browsers.

Based on this research, we can determine a list of supported browsers to reach our goal of 90-95% of our target audience.

If your users were only internal staff accessing the site through a local area network, it would be easy for you to learn what kinds of browsers to support. With more complex patterns of users, it might be more difficult to determine the types of browsers being used. If you already have a Web site up and running, your log files will help you learn who your audience is. Most Web servers save access information in a log file—typically derived from the W3C draft *ELF*, or *Extended Log File*, format. This log file includes significant information regarding your visitors, including the user agent for the software used to access your site. This agent can help you identify the types of browsers being used to view your site.

The log file can be analyzed using any number of log analysis tools, or a counting service can be used to complete analysis and provide statistics. If external visitors are critical to the success of your site, the log file can help find the balance between not excluding a significant percentage of your users and wasting time on browsers that seldom access your site. Some browsers, such as Opera, can spoof other user agents, so you might not get a completely accurate representation of all browser types from the log. You will, however, be able to determine most of the browsers accessing your site.

To whom do you want to target your site? The easy answer to this is "most users." You'll have to decide, however, what your cut-off point is. Do you want to support the bleeding edge? Are you willing to risk that the 15% you exclude aren't a critical part of your audience? There are a number of things to consider. How much time you should spend on this task is likely determined by how dependent your site is on external users whose browsers you can't easily find out.

Language

Most browsers are available in more than one language. Does your site need to support more than one? This consideration will help you create the list of supported browsers. If you require multiple-language support, you will need to change the settings for your browser. This can be done through your Internet Options settings, shown in Figure 13.2 for the Windows operating system. In Windows, this is found through the **Control Panel**.

Select the **Languages** tab, and a screen similar to Figure 13.3 will be displayed, listing the languages supported by your browser.

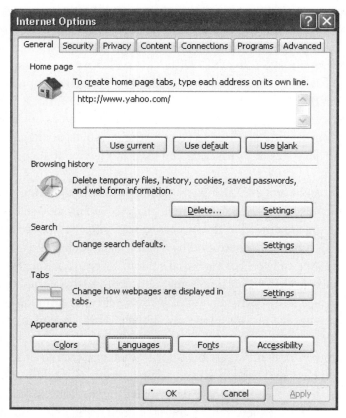

Figure 13.2: The Internet Options dialog box in Windows.

Figure 13.3: Language preferences.

If you require additional languages, click the **Add** button. A list of languages will be displayed, as shown in Figure 13.4.

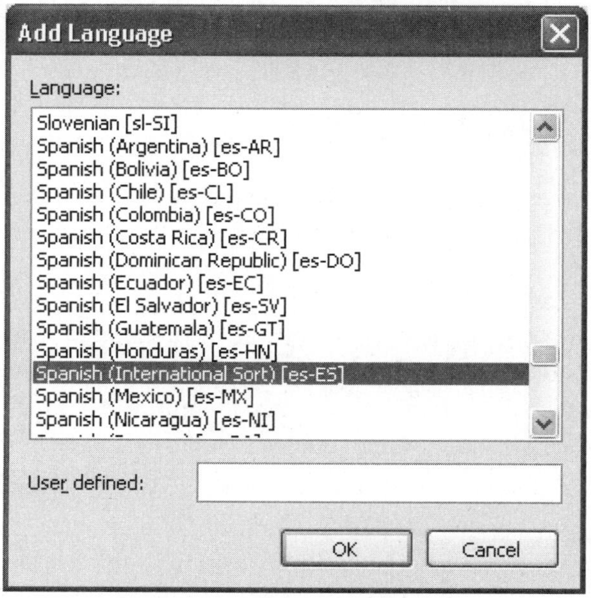

Figure 13.4: The Internet Options language list.

Select the language you would like to include, and click **OK**. The language will be added to the list of languages supported by your browser, as shown in Figure 13.5. Repeat the process until your browser includes all of the languages you would like to support. Keep in mind that this process will need to be repeated for all of the browsers on your supported list.

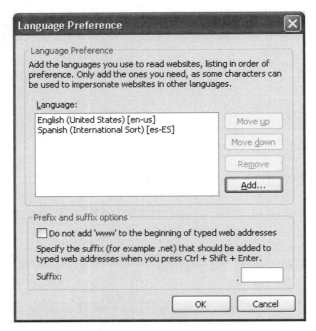

Figure 13.5: Spanish added to the languages supported.

Common Browsers

Many browsers are available to Internet users. Some of these are listed in Table 13.1. This list has changed and grown over the years, and is sure to continue to change.

As of June 2007, IE version 6.0 was the most commonly used browser, but IE version 7.0 is gaining in popularity. IE has been the leader in browser usage for several years. When compiling your list of commonly used browsers, check several sources for statistics and consider browser versions, as shown in Table 13.2.

Table 13.1: Commonly Used Browsers		
Logo	Abbreviation	Description
	IE	Internet Explorer
	FX	Firefox, identified as Mozilla before 2005
	MOZ	Mozilla
	SA	Safari developed by Apple to support the Mac OS; support for Windows XP added January 2007 (and Konqueror, both identified as Mozilla before 2007)
	O	Opera
	N	Netscape, identified as Mozilla after 2006
	AOL	AOL Explorer, based on Internet Explorer; previously known as AOL Browser

Table 13.2: Browser Popularity, June 2007	
Browser	Estimated Popularity, by Percentage of Users
IE6	37.3%
FX	34%
IE7	19.7%
IE5	1.5%
Moz	1.4%
SA	1.3%
O	1.8%

Although Internet Explorer is currently the most popular browser, it is not correct to assume that what it supports is valid. IE has many nonstandard features that are not supported by other browsers. The true industry standards are those published by standards organizations such as ECMA, ISO, and THW W3C.

Consideration should be given to whether you include support for old browsers. If you do not, you may exclude some of your key market demographics. If you do, you will have increased maintenance costs, as you will need to duplicate some functionality. Similarly, consideration should be given to whether you support the newest browsers. Consider your site's audience, and how fast these users are to adopt new technology. New browsers provide new features and can also present new considerations for development. If you decide not to test with new browsers, you will not be prepared to accommodate functionality and features that might one day be required for your key audience.

Browsers support many different features that you should take into consideration before deploying your site to an audience. Do not assume that all of your site's users will have the same browser features and settings. This can be a complicated task if your site is complex and uses advanced features like cookies, JavaScript, Flash, pop-ups, PHP, ASP.NET, or JSP. Keep it simple. If there are advanced features that add important value to your site's audience, you might need to include additional code to make sure a visit to your site is as pleasant as possible.

Hardware

Is your Web site intended to be run on devices other than a personal computer, such as a handheld device? This certainly will affect many decisions made regarding compatibility. PCs running Windows are the dominant device used to access the Internet. It would be easy if testing your site with a PC running Windows meant that it would work with Mac operating systems and other platforms, but it doesn't. Testing will increase significantly if you need to support multiple platforms. You might need to test several browsers on more than one machine.

Excluding non-Windows operating systems might be a costly mistake. Consider, do you have staff on the shop floor using handheld devices? Sales staff on the road using Blackberries or cell phones to access applications? Research and statistics are the key. Consider your audience and make a list of devices you will support. That list will need to be included within your site's test plan.

Monitor Settings

Not everyone accessing the Web has the same monitor you are using. If you design your Web site to be displayed on a monitor with 1024x768 resolution, visitors who have lower resolutions, like 800x600, might have problems reading your pages. Some users may have still lower resolution settings, like 640x480, but the trend is toward 800x600 as the low-resolution standard.

Test your site's display on different-sized monitors with different resolution settings. Site pages will look quite different using different screen sizes and resolutions, as shown in Figures 13.6, 13.7, and 13.8. Since you can't control what resolution your visitors will be using, the safest thing is to ensure that your pages will display well to the broadest audience. Currently, more than 90% of users have their monitors set to 1280x1024, 1024x768, or 800x600 resolution, but common monitor settings will change as technology changes. With this knowledge, plan to revisit your test plan to make updates as monitor technology changes.

Figure 13.6: A Web page displayed at 800x600 resolution.

Figure 13.7: The Web page from Figure 13.6 displayed at 1024x768.

Figure 13.8: The Web page from Figure 13.6 displayed at 1152x864.

When designing and developing Web applications, remember that monitor settings can have an impact. Don't try to cram too much data on a page. Test the application using different resolution settings to make sure what application users see is readable and not unexpected.

Operating System Support

The visitors to your Web site will be using a variety of operating systems on their computers or other devices. You cannot assume that they will be using the same operating system as your developers. You need to understand which operating systems your audience is most likely to use. Again, research is the key. Fortunately, the hard work has already been done for you. You can easily find statistics through many sources, such as magazines articles, books, surveys, and of course, Web sites. The Web is probably the easiest source to use. You can simply retrieve the information and draw your own conclusions.

As of this writing, a single operating system, Microsoft's XP, dominates the personal computer market, with over 80% of the market share. The second is Windows 2000 (8% share), followed by Windows 98 (5%), and the Macintosh (3%). With that information, the list of operating systems that might be considered include the following:

- Windows XP
- Windows 2000
- Windows 98
- Vista
- Windows 2003
- Linux
- Mac OS

Design your site to work well with the most popular operating systems. Your goal is to accommodate as close to 100% of your audience as possible within the limitation of resources and time. The following list includes steps to supporting users with various operating systems:

- Find out which operating systems are commonly available.
- Collect and review statistics.
- Draw conclusions from the statistics, based on your audience.
- Create a list of operating systems your site will support.
- Make sure to have equipment available to test on.
- Include operating system testing within your test plan.

Internet Connection Speed

Technology has changed greatly over the years, providing Internet users options for much quicker connections than in the past. Many Internet users have high-speed connections, including ISN, satellite, DSL, E1, cable, T2, Ethernet, E3, T3, OC3, and T4. However, there are still users who have dial-up connections. A dial-up connection is usually very low-priced, and in some rural areas, it might still be the only option available for Internet connectivity. Most dial-up connections can support a speed of 56 Kbps, although there are still a few out there that only support 28.8 or 14.4 Kbps.

If your target audience includes users who will be accessing the Internet from home, you will probably have some who use dial-up connections. For example, if your organization sells furniture over the Internet, most of your site's users are probably accessing the site from home. Don't assume because your site loads quickly on your desktop, your audience will have the same results. Consider the lowest speed you will support, and be sure to include this as a part of your test process.

Image Format Support

Images can be created in many formats, as identified in chapter 3. GIF and JPEG are the most common image formats in HTML, but browsers do not all support the same image formats. For applications and sites where images are critical, image format is very important.

The larger the image, the more resources it will require. Usually, the better the image quality, the larger the image file. Vector files can minimize this impact, but are not commonly compatible with all browsers. Also, the sizes of graphics can vary greatly when viewed on different computers, according to the resolution of the monitor.

Minimizing the Impact of Different Browsers

It is easy to see that it is important to recognize browser differences. These differences have a great impact on how your site will be displayed, and the impression the audience will be left with. The goal is to design your application to look as expected to as many of the site visitors as possible, within reason. We will next consider things we can do to minimize the effects of browser differences.

Keep It Simple

Keep it simple! Browser differences will create problems if the code or the page is needlessly complex. Simplicity will result in a site that is appealing and easier to use. This does not mean your site has to be plain. If it is too simplistic, you might not accomplish what you intended for your audience. A good site will leave your audience with a positive image.

Keeping things simple can be accomplished through using the available technology wisely. The best choice is usually to use HTML or XHTML to specify structure, and to use CSS to specify appearance, with carefully chosen CSS classes for page elements that reoccur throughout the site. If you choose not to use CSS, the likely result will be larger, harder to maintain sites, with inconsistent pages.

You must have a balance in your site design. Design and content should be separated. Large organizations, with large Web sites and Web applications, often have staff organized so one group takes care of appearance and site support, and a separate group focuses on coding applications. Even if developers don't support the site design and are not entirely responsible for site appearance, they should understand conceptually the design of the site, so applications are designed and coded with the site's design in mind.

Keeping it simple means focusing on effectiveness. This will result in a better site, less code, and easier testing. Before incorporating a feature, consider its impact on the end user's experience. Consider whether complicated code to provide an extra "wow" factor will return value for the site's purpose. Keeping your site pages consistent will add value and will also reduce the complexity of your site. You don't want your visitors wondering whether they are still on the same site or have traveled to another.

Common elements should be reused. If you have code that will be useful on other pages within your site, reuse it. By using common elements, you reduce the need to recode and retest. Sometimes, you can spend just a little more time making a component a bit more general, but it will pay off in allowing you to reuse and simplify code throughout your site. (We touched on this in the JavaScript and JSP chapters.)

Use Dynamic Components Carefully

Business applications include programming languages like Java, JavaScript, PHP, and .NET. When using programming languages with your site, use standard, proven components and techniques.

Using dynamic components for your site adds an additional level of complexity and increases the risk of having an unfavorable impact due to browser differences. Creating a dynamic page also increases development costs because it takes more time to code, test, and support your site.

Avoid Over-precise Control

You should avoid over-precise control of your Web page layouts. If you take an over-precise approach, you might create fragile pages that break when browsers don't display them the way you expect. You will waste time fighting with the ways different browsers do layout and how user preferences affect layout.

Trying to control layout precisely can result in problems including blocks overlapping, vertical gaps appearing between rows, content being cropped because it is too large to fit within a block, and crowded pages. Layout problems can also affect applications. For example, an application that displays data might be fine for a simple display with a few columns, but might not be able to accommodate all of the information required for the application because the page layout does not allow flexibility for fitting the required content.

Code to Detect Different Browsers

If it is critical that your site display in a variety of browsers, you might want to accommodate different browsers through coding techniques. The following are some coding techniques that can be used to detect and react to the browser being used.

Let's look first at detecting the browser and using a different CSS for a page, by including code in the **<head>** section of an HTML page. In Figure 13.9, the file *versionie5.css* will be used when the browser is IE version 5. The file *versionie6.css* will be used when the browser is IE version 6.

```
<!--[if IE 5]>
<link rel="stylesheet" type="text/css" href="versionie5.css" />
<![endif]-->
<!--[if IE 6]>
<link rel="stylesheet" type="text/css" href="versionie6.css" />
<![endif]-->
```

Figure 13.9: A check for IE versions.

The comparison operators listed in Table 13.3 may also be used. For example, in Figure 13.10, the file *lessthanversion5.css* will be used when the browser is less than or equal to version IE 5.

Table 13.3: Comparison Operators	
Operator	Description
!	Not
Lt	Less than
Lte	Less than or equal to
Gt	Greater than
Gte	Greater than or equal to

```
<!--[if lte IE 5]>
<link rel="stylesheet" type="text/css" href="lessthanequalvers
  ion5.css" />
<![endif]-->
```

Figure 13.10: A check for a version of IE less than or equal to 5.

Summary

Browser differences will always be an important factor that needs to be considered for Web site development projects. When dealing with browser differences, try capturing your Web site's statistics to see what types of browsers and operating systems are being used by visitors to your site.

The list of browsers supported by your site should be reviewed periodically. Changes in the list should be reflected in your test plan. Operating systems, screen resolutions, the most popular browsers, and other factors will change over time. The recommendations in this chapter will help improve your site's quality and reduce the impact of these differences.

CHAPTER 14

Best Practices

There are a number of things to keep in mind to help make your Web site more effective and productive. Some of these best practices include keeping the site's overall purpose in mind, using a clear and easily maintained folder structure, and avoiding cutting-edge techniques. These and other important suggestions are discussed in this chapter.

Focus on the Site's Objective

When designing your site and Web applications, keep the focus on your objective. Don't add components and content needlessly. A good site should provide the following:

- Offer site visitors what they want and need.

- Be up-to-date.

- Load quickly.

- Be easy to use.

- Be simple.

If your site has too much content, slow-loading pages, is hard to use, does not provide current information, or does not provide what visitors are looking for, not only will visitors have an unfavorable impression, but you will also increase the potential for unfavorable results due to browser differences.

Structure Your Site

Keep your site's file structure simple. Don't haphazardly structure your site files or use no structure at all. This is especially critical for larger sites, but it is also important for small ones. It is easy to have a Web application's structure get out of hand and become disorganized. Create a simple structure to easily organize the components of your site. Use simple, meaningful file names. For example, if you have a logo image, you might name the file *Logo.jpg*. Similarly, your "about us" Web page might be named *AboutUs.html*. Let's consider a site with the following components: HTML, CSS, JavaScript, images, and document files.

The example in Figures 14.1 and 14.2 is simplistic, but the message is clear: organizing your files in a simple structure makes it easier to locate them. If you put all of your image files in an "images" folder, then you know any code referencing an image file will use the format *images/imagefilename.xxx*.

```
C:\BillsBBQBarnSite
Abc.html
Abc.js
Abc.jpg
BBQ.html
CC.html
CC.jpg
CC.doc
DD.doc
```

Figure 14.1: Unstructured site files.

```
ABC.html
BBQ.html
CCC.html
\JSFiles
Abc.js
CC.js
\Images
ABC.jpg
CC.jpg
\Docs
CC.doc
DD.doc
```

Figure 14.2: Structured site files.

When defining pathnaming and filenaming conventions, remember that Windows is not case-sensitive, but other operating systems are. For example, Windows would deem *Images* and *images* to refer to the same folder, but some other operating systems would not.

The design of your site and applications is critical. The more complex your site and applications, the more critical it is to have a great design. The time and effort spent up-front on design will result in a good end product and will also save you support time in the long run. Incorporate the file-structure definition and filenaming conventions as a part of your development standards.

Avoid the Cutting Edge

It can be very tempting to use cutting-edge coding techniques. However, "cutting edge" can also mean "bleeding edge." Be careful to choose your coding techniques wisely. Choose tools that fit your business needs.

Browser consideration is a critical part of the decision of which tools to use. Don't reinvent the wheel. Research tools before jumping in. Choose tools with a track record and proven capability for Web development. There are many popular, proven tools for Web development, including JavaScript, PHP, JSP, .NET, HTML, and CSS. It is likely you'll use a combination of these.

Do not lose site of your goal. Code to fit your application requirements, not to use technology for the sake of trying something new. If your company objective is to only use cutting-edge technology, be prepared to spend more time, money, and other resources on Web application development.

Use CSS

Use only CSS for layout consistency, and put the CSS in files that all pages share. Browsers have many properties whose default values are not defined in the specifications, and these properties can vary from browser to browser. You should, therefore, specify CSS properties fully to prevent differences in browser defaults. For example, default margins and padding are not defined in the specifications and may differ for different browsers; to ensure consistent results, your CSS should set both. Make sure designers and application developers work together in developing the CSS, and take into consideration the business application requirements.

You might need to use different CSS code for different browsers and possibly for different versions of browsers. This can be done by detecting the version of the browser and coding to point to the CSS file designed for it.

Deal with Coding Issues

Coding errors are one of the leading causes of browser display problems. Making sure your code is error-free can have the biggest impact on preventing problems because of browser differences. Poor code can affect a page's look, performance, and errors encountered. Poorly coded sites will result in browser issues.

Use well-formed HTML. Tags should be nested properly. No end tags should be omitted. Some browsers will not display your site as desired if the HTML is not well-formed. The same applies to script and program code. You might want to use a code checker to identify and make corrections. Code checkers warn about deviant code.

Don't assume there are no coding errors in a page that looks right. Some errors might not be obvious when you test your work. A browser that does not conform to the standards may wrongly produce results. Some browsers, most notably IE, try hard to recover from errors gracefully by guessing what the designer intended, which covers up errors. Often, the first sign that there is a problem with your code is that your page looks bad with a different browser or an updated browser. This also applies to application programming. Tools like WDSC, Eclipse, and DreamWeaver can be used for PHP, HTML, JSP, JavaScript, and .NET. Coding errors are rarely justified.

Coding to Specifications and Standards

As mentioned earlier, specifications are issued by the W3C. You can find the specifications at *www.w3.org*. Design to the standards. Use a *DOCTYPE* declaration (DTD) within your HTML and XHTML. This declaration makes modern browsers honor standards more strictly, so that browsers act more alike. Figure 14.3 shows the DOCTYPE reference for strict HTML 4.01 code.

A DOCTYPE declaration should appear at the beginning of an HTML or XHTML file to specify the standard applicable to the file. The declaration must be exact in both spelling and case, to be effective. You can find a list of valid DOCTYPEs on the W3C Web site.

```
<!DOCTYPE html PUBLIC "-//W3C//DTD HTML
"http://www.w3.org/TR/html4/strict.dtd">
```

Figure 14.3: A DOCTYPE example.

Pay close attention to details for efficient, effective design. It can be so easy to slap together page elements and overlook details. This applies to both site design and application design. Being able to focus on the details is a skill that must be practiced over time. A good way to learn is from your mistakes. When you find an error, ask yourself where you went wrong. Every failure is an opportunity to learn.

Some people continue to use older, less capable browsers even when much better versions are available. Therefore, avoid using poorly supported elements of standards for several years, until so few people use the old browsers that you can reasonably exclude older browsers from your consideration. If you must use something that might not be supported, include a proven work-around that works with all browsers.

Code Checkers and Validators

Different browsers handle errors differently. Syntax errors can be found during testing, or you might decide to use a code validator or code checker. *Validators* check your files to determine if the CSS, HTML, XHTML, JavaScript, PHP, JSP, and ASP.NET syntax is correct and written in accordance with coding specifications. Using a validator is a fast and simple way to identify the most blatant errors. Before manual testing, fix all syntax errors and critical warnings found by the validator. Reviewing a validator's error messages will also help you learn more about HTML, CSS, PHP, JavaScript, JSP, and .NET, to improve the quality of your work.

Code checkers are sometimes also called *syntax checkers* or *lint programs*. They check for problems in HTML or CSS. Some of the checks are similar to what validators do. Others are beyond what validators do, checking for browser incompatibility, broken links, missing files, missing tags, and other problems. For example, if an **<img>** tag's **src** attribute names an image file that does not exist, a validator will not report an error, because it does not violate HTML syntax to refer to a missing image file. A code checker, however, should report an error, or at least a warning, because it is very likely that the code specifies either the wrong file or one that has not yet been created.

It is easy to find code validators and checkers on the Web. Validators are often available for free. Code checkers are sometimes free, but are usually sold for a fee. The W3C Web site provides a free code validator and a free code checker for CSS and HTML. Code checkers and validators depend on the DOCTYPE line to determine the designated standards being used.

Coding Standards and Techniques

There are many techniques for coding. Ask 10 programmers to code an application, and they will probably all code it differently. Some programmers, for example, have a tendency to use complex code or to show off their "wow-factor" skills. You don't want to end up with code that can only be maintained by the developer who created it. Coding should be done with the mindset that someone else might have to maintain the application. Having standards will ensure that inconsistencies are minimized and will affect ongoing support. This applies whether your organization is new to Web development or is experienced. The time spent on standards upfront will minimize development and support requirements later.

When creating new pages or changing existing pages, do your work one step at a time, with verifiable results at each step. This approach makes it easier to develop and test your work. If a new problem appears, you know that it is caused by what you have just done. Therefore, you only have to review the little bit of work since your previous step. This process is called *incremental development*. Making massive changes before testing any of them can make testing and debugging a time-consuming and frustrating task.

Documentation

Documentation is a key factor when developing and updating applications. A well-documented program is much easier to support and maintain. Documentation should not be an afterthought. It should be prepared so another developer can use it to easily understand the code. This can be critical when incorporating new code or when debugging or correcting a programming error. Software design is an art in which great attention to detail is essential. Poorly documented software means that some details will be unclear, likely will be misunderstood, and often will cause errors.

Documentation embedded within an application should be used wisely because it will increase page load times in HTML, CSS, and JavaScript files. You might decide to have documentation stored in a separate file.

Documentation must be up-to-date. Incorrect or out-of-date documentation can be worse than useless, leading developers down the wrong path at a cost of time and effort.

JavaScript Support Coding

JavaScript will probably be one of the tools you will use for Web development. Most modern browsers support the use of JavaScript. Older browsers, however, might not support JavaScript, or a user might have disabled it. Coding techniques can be used to accommodate browsers that are not JavaScript-enabled.

One possible method is to embed **<script>** tags within the HTML comment block. Browsers that don't support JavaScript will consider the code to be a comment and ignore it, while browsers that do support JavaScript will execute the code.

In Figure 14.4, when the browser being used supports JavaScript, an alert box like the one in Figure 14.5 will be displayed. When the browser doesn't support JavaScript, the code will be treated like an HTML comment and ignored.

```
<html>
<head>
<script language="javascript">
<!-- CS1320 - JavaScript Support Example -->
<!-- Just a comment to JavaScript Non Supported Browsers
alert ("JavaScript Is Supported By The Browser Being Used!");
-->
</script>
</head>
<body>
</body>
</html>
```

Figure 14.4: JavaScript support in an HTML comment.

Figure 14.5: The alert displayed by a JavaScript-enabled browser.

You might want to design an application to react one way when a user's browser is able to support JavaScript, and another way when it does not support JavaScript. This can be accomplished by using the **<noscript>** tag embedded within the HTML. JavaScript-enabled browsers recognize **<noscript>** and ignore everything from the beginning **<noscript>** tag to the ending **</noscript>** tag. When a browser doesn't support JavaScript, **<noscript>** is unknown to the browser and is ignored, but not the contents within the **<noscript>** and **</noscript>** tags.

Figure 14.6 is another way to display the alert box in Figure 14.5 when JavaScript is supported. When JavaScript is not supported, the following message will be displayed:

The browser being used doesn't support JavaScript!

```
<html>
<head>
<script language="javascript">
<!-- CS1322 - JavaScript Support <noscript> Example -->
<!-- Just a comment to JavaScript Non Supported Browsers
alert ("JavaScript Is Supported By The Browser Being Used!");
-->
</script>
<noscript>
The browser being used doesn't support JavaScript!
</noscript>
</head>
<body>
</body>
</html>
```

Figure 14.6: An example of **<noscript>***.*

These techniques can easily be used to incorporate code specific to your application. If the browser you are using is JavaScript-enabled, temporarily turn off JavaScript support, and run the examples.

Pages could get quite complicated and large if you incorporated JavaScript code to accommodate JavaScript-enabled browsers, and other code for browsers that don't support JavaScript. Another possibility is to create separate pages for JavaScript-enabled browsers and for those not supporting JavaScript. For example, in Figure 14.7, when JavaScript is enabled, the page *CS1326.html* shown in Figure 14.8 will be loaded.

```
<html>
<head>
<!-- CS1325 - JavaScript Support Example -->
<script language="javascript">
<!--
window.location.href="CS1326.html";
//-->
</script>
</head>
<body>
<noscript>
The browser being used doesn't support JavaScript!
</noscript>
</body>
</html>
```

Figure 14.7: Loading a separate page for JavaScript-enabled browsers.

```
<html>
<body>
<script language="javascript">
<!-- CS1326 - JavaScript Support Example -->
alert ("JavaScript Is Supported By The Browser Being Used!");
-->
</script>
JavaScript Enabled Page!
</body>
</html>
```

Figure 14.8: The CS1326.html file.

This example can be applied to most applications. Note that the code has been embedded within the HTML in a combination of **<head>** and **<body>** tags.

Fonts

There are a handful of browser-safe fonts that can be used to minimize differences in common browsers. Usually, using the native fonts provided as standard to the operating system is pretty safe. Basic PC fonts include the following:

- Arial
- **Arial Black**
- Comic Sans
- Courier New
- Georgia
- Lucida Console
- Tahoma
- Times New Roman

These fonts are commonly seen on Web pages. Font appearance can also be affected by size and color. Black is a pretty safe bet for consistent display, but other colors are often required to emphasize text. Using browser-safe fonts will make it more likely that text will be displayed consistently in different browsers. Test different browsers with the font types, sizes, and colors that have been chosen.

Text

You can put your text in tables, which most browsers recognize. Then, you can control the width of the text on the page. This way, it won't matter what the visitor's browser is set at. It will look the same for everyone.

Test

Testing is a critical part of your Web project, just as it would be in any other application development project. This step should not be skimped. The goal of testing is to find any fundamental flaws in the design, to identify coding errors, and to ensure that your site displays as expected for your audience. The test plan should include testing of all pages in your Web site. If you have a large, complex site, we recommend that initial testing be completed after only a few pages have been coded. Initial testing will identify design flaws early on and minimize the time required to address them.

Testing needs to be comprehensive, and testers should try hard to make the design fail. A well-designed test plan will uncover flaws well before your audience views your site and Web applications. Test first with the most common browser used by your audience. After you are satisfied with your test results, move on to test the rest of the browsers your site will support. You might want to incorporate the use of automated tools to validate and test your site. As discussed earlier, a variety of automated tools are available, including code validators and checkers. The expense of such tools may well be justified by minimizing coding errors and saving time testing a large, complex site. Testing should not be considered complete until the problems identified have been corrected and retested.

Consider your tolerance for defects. It would be easy to say that you have zero tolerance for errors, but this is not practical, taking into consideration browser differences. If your Web site caters to a small or informal audience, your bug tolerance will be much higher than if your Web site is your corporate statement. The purpose and audience of your site will likely provide the key to determining your tolerance for errors and defects. You will have to consider how large an audience you will support and how much expense you are willing to expend to support it.

Make a formal test plan. Use your list of browsers, settings, hardware, and operating systems as a test checklist, as shown in Table 14.1. Incorporate the test plan as part of your standard development procedures. The test plan should be designed so it can be used for new development and for site changes. The test plan should include a detailed identification of the problems encountered, with planned actions to be taken to correct the errors.

Table 14.1: Test Plan Support Example				
Browsers Supported	Operating Systems Supported	Monitor Resolution Supported	Monitor Size Supported	Connection Speed Supported
IE 6	Windows XP	800 x 600	17"	Dial-up, 56kbps
IE7	Windows 2000	1024 x 768	19"	DSL
Firefox		1280 x 1024		
Mozilla				
Opera				

Figure 14.9 is an example test plan that includes support of the English language. This plan is based on the criteria in Table 14.1. Of course, the plan that fits your organization's needs might be more complex and include additional information.

Site: Bill's BBQ Barn Web Site
Site Page: Home Page
Language Supported: English (United States) [en-us]
Special Features and Notes:
Date: July 16, 2007
Name of Tester: Rickelle Walsh
Test Completion Date: July 18, 2007
Test Passed: No
Language Supported: English (United States) [en-us]
Instructions: If the test is valid, enter OK in the corresponding box. If the test fails, enter an X in the corresponding box and make a note identifying the description of the failure.

Operating System	Monitor Resolution	Monitor Size	Connection Speed	IE 6	IE 7	Firefox	Mozilla	Opera
Win XP	800x600	17"	Dial-up	Ok	Ok	X Text is hard to read	Ok	Ok
Win XP	1024x768	17"	Dial-up	Ok	Ok	Ok	Ok	Ok
Win XP	1280x1024	17"	Dial-up	Ok	Ok	Ok	Ok	Ok
Win XP	800x600	17"	DSL	Ok	Ok	X Text is hard to read	Ok	Ok
Win XP	1024x768	17"	DSL	Ok	Ok	Ok	Ok	Ok
Win XP	1280x1024	17"	DSL	Ok	Ok	Ok	Ok	Ok
Win XP	800x600	19"	Dial-up	Ok	Ok	X Text is hard to read	Ok	Ok
Win XP	1024x768	19"	Dial-up	Ok	Ok	Ok	Ok	Ok
Win XP	1280x1024	19"	Dial-up	Ok	Ok	Ok	Ok	Ok
Win XP	800x600	19"	DSL	Ok	Ok	X Text is hard to read	Ok	Ok
Win XP	1024x768	19"	DSL	Ok	Ok	Ok	Ok	Ok
Win XP	1280x1024	19"	DSL	Ok	Ok	Ok	Ok	Ok
Win 2000	800x600	17"	Dial-up	Ok	Ok	X Text is hard to read	Ok	Ok
Win 2000	1024x768	17"	Dial-up	Ok	Ok	Ok	Ok	Ok
Win 2000	1280x1024	17"	Dial-up	Ok	Ok	Ok	Ok	Ok

Figure 14.9: An example of a test plan (part 1 of 2).

Win 2000	800x600	17"	DSL	Ok	Ok	X Text is hard to read	Ok	Ok
Win 2000	1024x768	17"	DSL	Ok	Ok	Ok	Ok	Ok
Win 2000	1280x1024	17"	DSL	Ok	Ok	Ok	Ok	Ok
Win 2000	800x600	19"	Dial-up	Ok	Ok	X Text is hard to read	Ok	Ok
Win 2000	1024x768	19"	Dial-up	Ok	Ok	Ok	Ok	Ok
Win 2000	1280x1024	19"	Dial-up	Ok	Ok	Ok	Ok	Ok
Win 2000	800x600	19"	DSL	Ok	Ok	X Text is hard to read	Ok	Ok
Win 2000	1024x768	19"	DSL	Ok	Ok	Ok	Ok	Ok
Win 2000	1280x1024	19"	DSL	Ok	Ok	Ok	Ok	Ok

Figure 14.9: An example of a test plan (part 2 of 2).

Summary

Web design projects have some similarity to traditional application design projects. There is no substitute for good planning, design, documentation, and testing. Developing and following coding standards improves your ability to create functional and easily maintained Web sites. Be sure to test your Web pages with the most common browsers. Also test them with the most common screen resolutions. The use of both Cascading Style Sheets and JavaScript are highly recommended to extend the capabilities of your Web site and to make it easy to maintain.

HTML Tags

Tag	Description
<!--...-->	Defines a comment
<!DOCTYPE>	Defines the document type
<a>	Defines an anchor
<abbr>	Defines an abbreviation
<acronym>	Defines an acronym
<address>	Defines an address element
<applet>	Defines an applet
<area>	Defines an area inside an image map
<b>	Defines bold text
<base>	Defines a base URL for all the links in a page
<basefont>	Defines a base font
<bdo>	Defines the direction of text display
<big>	Defines big text
<blockquote>	Defines a long quotation
<body>	Defines the body element
 	Inserts a single line break
<button>	Defines a push button
<caption>	Defines a table caption
<center>	Defines centered text
<cite>	Defines a citation
<code>	Defines computer code text
<col>	Defines attributes for table columns
<colgroup>	Defines groups of table columns
<dd>	Defines a definition description

Continued	
Tag	**Description**
<del>	Defines deleted text
<dir>	Defines a directory list
<div>	Defines a section in a document
<dfn>	Defines a definition term
<dl>	Defines a definition list
<dt>	Defines a definition term
<em>	Defines emphasized text
<fieldset>	Defines a fieldset
<font>	Defines text font, size, and color
<form>	Defines a form
<frame>	Defines a sub window (a frame)
<frameset>	Defines a set of frames
<h1> to <h6>	Defines header 1 to header 6
<head>	Defines information about the document
<hr>	Defines a horizontal rule
<html>	Defines an html document
<i>	Defines italic text
<iframe>	Defines an inline sub window (frame)
<img>	Defines an image
<input>	Defines an input field
<ins>	Defines inserted text
<isindex>	Defines a single-line input field
<kbd>	Defines keyboard text
<label>	Defines a label for a form control
<legend>	Defines a title in a fieldset
<li>	Defines a list item
<link>	Defines a resource reference
<map>	Defines an image map
<menu>	Defines a menu list
<meta>	Defines meta information
<noframes>	Defines a noframe section
<noscript>	Defines a noscript section
<object>	Defines an embedded object
<ol>	Defines an ordered list
<optgroup>	Defines an option group

Continued	
Tag	**Description**
<option>	Defines an option in a drop-down list
<p>	Defines a paragraph
<param>	Defines a parameter for an object
<pre>	Defines preformatted text
<q>	Defines a short quotation
<s>	Defines strikethrough text
<samp>	Defines sample computer code
<script>	Defines a script
<select>	Defines a selectable list
<small>	Defines small text
<span>	Defines a section in a document
<strike>	Defines strikethrough text
<strong>	Defines strong text
<style>	Defines a style definition
<sub>	Defines subscripted text
<sup>	Defines superscripted text
<table>	Defines a table
<tbody>	Defines a table body
<td>	Defines a table cell
<textarea>	Defines a text area
<tfoot>	Defines a table footer
<th>	Defines a table header
<thead>	Defines a table header
<title>	Defines the document title
<tr>	Defines a table row
<tt>	Defines teletype text
<u>	Defines underlined text
<ul>	Defines an unordered list
<var>	Defines a variable

B

Special Characters

Character	Code	Name
"	&#34;	&quot;
&	&#38;	&amp;
<	&#60;	&lt;
>	&#62;	&gt;
Non-breaking space		
¡	&#161;	&iexcl;
¢	&#162;	&cent;
£	&#163;	&pound;
¤	&#164;	&curren;
¥	&#165;	&yen;
¦	&#166;	&brvbar;
§	&#167;	&sect;
¨	&#168;	&uml;
©	&#169;	&copy;
ª	&#170;	&ordf;
«	&#171;	&laquo;
¬	&#172;	&not;
®	&#173;	&reg;
¯	&#174;	&macr;
°	&#175;	&deg;
°	&#176;	&deg;
±	&#177;	&plusmn

Continued		
Character	**Code**	**Name**
²	&#178;	&sup2;
³	&#179;	&sup3;
´	&#180;	&acute;
µ	&#181;	&micro;
¶	&#182;	&para;
·	&#183;	&middot;
¸	&#184;	&cedil;
¹	&#185;	&sup1;
º	&#186;	&ordm;
»	&#187;	&raquo;
¼	&#188;	&frac14;
½	&#189;	&frac12;
¾	&#190;	&frac34;
¿	&#191;	&iquest;
À	&#192;	&Agrave;
Á	&#193;	&Aacute;
Â	&#194;	&Acirc;
Ã	&#195;	&Atilde;
Ä	&#196;	&Auml;
Å	&#197;	&Aring;
Æ	&#198;	&AElig;
Ç	&#199;	&Ccedil;
È	&#200;	&Egrave;
É	&#201;	&Eacute;
Ê	&#202;	&Ecirc;
Ë	&#203;	&Euml;
Ì	&#204;	&Igrave;
Í	&#205;	&Iacute;
Î	&#206;	&Icirc;
Ï	&#207;	&Iuml;
Ð	&#208;	&ETH;
Ñ	&#209;	&Ntilde;
Ò	&#210;	&Ograve;
Ó	&#211;	&Oacute;
Ô	&#212;	&Ocirc;
Õ	&#213;	&Otilde;

Continued		
Character	**Code**	**Name**
Ö	&#214;	&Ouml;
×	&#215;	&times;
Ø	&#216;	&Oslash;
Ù	&#217;	&Ugrave;
Ú	&#218;	&Uacute;
Û	&#219;	&Ucirc;
Ü	&#220;	&Uuml;
Ý	&#221	&Yacute;
Þ	&#222;	&THORN;
ß	&#223;	&szlig;
à	&#224;	&agrave;
á	&#225;	&aacute;
â	&#226;	&acirc;
ã	&#227;	&atilde;
ä	&#228;	&auml;
å	&#229;	&aring;
æ	&#230;	&aelig;
ç	&#231;	&ccedil;
è	&#232;	&egrave;
é	&#233;	&eacute;
ê	&#234;	&ecirc;
ë	&#235;	&euml;
ì	&#236;	&igrave;
í	&#237;	&iacute;
î	&#238;	&icirc;
ï	&#239;	&iuml;
ð	&#240;	&eth;
ñ	&#241;	&ntilde;
ò	&#242;	&ograve;
ó	&#243;	&oacute;
ô	&#244;	&ocirc;
õ	&#245;	&otilde;
ö	&#246;	&ouml;
÷	&#247;	&divide;
ø	&#248;	&oslash;
ù	&#249;	&ugrave;

Continued		
Character	**Code**	**Name**
ú	&#250;	&uacute;
û	&#251;	&ucirc;
ü	&#252;	&uuml;
ý	&#253;	&yacute;
þ	&#254;	&thorn;
ÿ	&#255;	&yuml;

PHP Functions, Constants, Filters, & Parameters

Array Functions

Function	Description
array()	Creates an array
array_change_key_case()	Returns an array with all keys in lowercase or uppercase
array_chunk()	Splits an array into chunks of arrays
array_combine()	Creates an array by using one array for keys and another for values
array_count_values()	Returns an array with the number of occurrences for each value
array_diff()	Compares array values, and returns the differences
array_diff_assoc()	Compares array keys and values, and returns the differences
array_diff_key()	Compares array keys, and returns the differences
array_diff_uassoc()	Compares array keys and values, with an additional user-made function check, and returns the differences
array_diff_ukey()	Compares array keys, with an additional user-made function check, and returns the differences
array_fill()	Fills an array with values
array_filter()	Filters elements of an array using a user-made function
array_flip()	Exchanges all keys with their associated values in an array
array_intersect()	Compares array values, and returns the matches
array_intersect_assoc()	Compares array keys and values, and returns the matches

Continued	
Function	**Description**
array_intersect_key()	Compares array keys, and returns the matches
array_intersect_uassoc()	Compares array keys and values, with an additional user-made function check, and returns the matches
array_intersect_ukey()	Compares array keys, with an additional user-made function check, and returns the matches
array_key_exists()	Checks if the specified key exists in the array
array_keys()	Returns all the keys of an array
array_map()	Sends each value of an array to a user-made function, which returns new values
array_merge()	Merges one or more arrays into one array
array_merge_recursive()	Merges one or more arrays into one array
array_multisort()	Sorts multiple or multi-dimensional arrays
array_pad( )	Inserts a specified number of items, with a specified value, to an array
array_pop()	Deletes the last element of an array
array_product()	Calculates the product of the values in an array
array_push()	Inserts one or more elements to the end of an array
array_rand()	Returns one or more random keys from an array
array_reduce()	Returns an array as a string, using a user-defined function
array_reverse()	Returns an array in the reverse order
array_search( )	Searches an array for a given value and returns the key
array_shift()	Removes the first element from an array, and returns the value of the removed element
array_slice()	Returns selected parts of an array
array_splice()	Removes and replaces specified elements of an array
array_sum( )	Returns the sum of the values in an array
array_udiff()	Compares array values in a user-made function and returns an array
array_udiff_assoc()	Compares array keys, and compares array values in a user-made function, and returns an array
array_udiff_uassoc()	Compares array keys and array values in user-made functions, and returns an array
array_uintersect()	Compares array values in a user-made function and returns an array
array_uintersect_assoc()	Compares array keys, and compares array values in a user-made function, and returns an array
array_uintersect_uassoc()	Compares array keys and array values in user-made functions, and returns an array

Continued	
Function	**Description**
array_unique( )	Removes duplicate values from an array
array_unshift( )	Adds one or more elements to the beginning of an array
array_values( )	Returns all the values of an array
array_walk( )	Applies a user function to every member of an array
array_walk_recursive( )	Applies a user function recursively to every member of an array
arsort( )	Sorts an array in reverse order and maintains index association
asort( )	Sorts an array and maintains index association
compact( )	Creates an array containing variables and their values
count( )	Counts elements in an array, or properties in an object
current( )	Returns the current element in an array
each( )	Returns the current key-and-value pair from an array
end( )	Sets the internal pointer of an array to its last element
extract( )	Imports variables into the current symbol table from an array
in_array( )	Checks if a specified value exists in an array
key( )	Fetches a key from an array
krsort( )	Sorts an array by key in reverse order
ksort( )	Sorts an array by key
list( )	Assigns variables as if they were an array
natcasesort( )	Sorts an array using a case-insensitive "natural order" algorithm
natsort( )	Sorts an array using a "natural order" algorithm
next( )	Advance the internal array pointer of an array
pos( )	Alias of current( )
prev( )	Rewinds the internal array pointer
range( )	Creates an array containing a range of elements
reset( )	Sets the internal pointer of an array to its first element
rsort( )	Sorts an array in reverse order
shuffle( )	Shuffles an array
sizeof( )	Alias of count( )
sort( )	Sorts an array
uasort( )	Sorts an array with a user-defined function and maintains index association
uksort( )	Sorts an array by keys using a user-defined function
usort( )	Sorts an array by values using a user-defined function

Array Constants

Constant	Description
CASE_LOWER	Used with array_change_key_case() to convert array keys to lowercase
CASE_UPPER	Used with array_change_key_case() to convert array keys to uppercase
SORT_ASC	Used with array_multisort() to sort in ascending order
SORT_DESC	Used with array_multisort() to sort in descending order
SORT_REGULAR	Used to compare items normally
SORT_NUMERIC	Used to compare items numerically
SORT_STRING	Used to compare items as strings
SORT_LOCALE_STRING	Used to compare items as strings, based on the current locale
COUNT_NORMAL	Used to return the number of elements in an array
COUNT_RECURSIVE	Used to return the number of recursive elements in an array
Extract Type and Prefix Parameters	**Description**
EXTR_OVERWRITE	If there is a collision, overwrite the existing variable.
EXTR_SKIP	If there is a collision, don't overwrite the existing variable.
EXTR_PREFIX_SAME	If there is a collision, prefix the variable name with *prefix*
EXTR_PREFIX_ALL	Prefix all variable names with *prefix*.
EXTR_PREFIX_INVALID	Only prefix invalid/numeric variable names with *prefix*.
EXTR_PREFIX_IF_EXISTS	Only create prefixed variable names if the non-prefixed version of the same variable exists in the current symbol table.
EXTR_IF_EXISTS	Only overwrite the variable if it already exists in the current symbol table, otherwise do nothing.
EXTR_REFS	Extracts variables as references.

Calendar Functions

Function	Description
cal_days_in_month()	Returns the number of days in a month for a specified year and calendar
cal_from_jd()	Converts a Julian day count into a date of a specified calendar
cal_info()	Returns information about a given calendar
cal_to_jd()	Converts a date to a Julian day count
easter_date()	Returns the Unix timestamp for midnight on Easter of a specified year
easter_days()	Returns the number of days after March 21, on which Easter falls for a specified year
FrenchToJD()	Converts a French Republican date to a Julian day count
GregorianToJD()	Converts a Gregorian date to a Julian day count
JDDayOfWeek()	Returns the day of a week
JDMonthName()	Returns a month name
JDToFrench()	Converts a Julian day count to a French Republican date
JDToGregorian()	Converts a Julian day count to a Gregorian date
jdtojewish()	Converts a Julian day count to a Jewish date
JDToJulian()	Converts a Julian day count to a Julian date
jdtounix()	Converts a Julian day count to a Unix timestamp
JewishToJD()	Converts a Jewish date to a Julian day count
JulianToJD()	Converts a Julian date to a Julian day count
unixtojd()	Converts a Unix timestamp to a Julian day count

Date/Time Functions

Function	Description
checkdate()	Validates a Gregorian date
date_default_timezone_get()	Returns the default time zone
date_default_timezone_set()	Sets the default time zone
date_sunrise()	Returns the time of sunrise for a given day and location
date_sunset()	Returns the time of sunset for a given day and location
date()	Formats a local time/date
getdate()	Returns an array that contains date and time information for a Unix timestamp
gettimeofday()	Returns an array that contains current time information

Continued	
Function	**Description**
gmdate()	Formats a GMT/UTC date/time
gmmktime()	Returns the Unix timestamp for a GMT date
gmstrftime()	Formats a GMT/UTC time/date according to local settings
idate()	Formats a local time/date as integer
localtime()	Returns an array that contains the time components of a Unix timestamp
microtime()	Returns the microseconds for the current time
mktime()	Returns the Unix timestamp for a date
strftime()	Formats a local time/date according to local settings
strptime()	Parses a time/date generated with strftime()
strtotime()	Parses an English textual date or time into a Unix timestamp
time()	Returns the current time as a Unix timestamp

Date Constants

Constant	**Description**
DATE_ATOM	Atom (example: 2005-08-15T16:13:03+0000)
DATE_COOKIE	HTTP cookies (example: Sun, 14 Aug 2005 16:13:03 UTC)
DATE_ISO8601	ISO-8601 (example: 2005-08-14T16:13:03+0000)
DATE_RFC822	RFC 822 (example: Sun, 14 Aug 2005 16:13:03 UTC)
DATE_RFC850	RFC 850 (example: Sunday, 14-Aug-05 16:13:03 UTC)
DATE_RFC1036	RFC 1036 (example: Sunday, 14-Aug-05 16:13:03 UTC)
DATE_RFC1123	RFC 1123 (example: Sun, 14 Aug 2005 16:13:03 UTC)
DATE_RFC2822	RFC 2822 (Sun, 14 Aug 2005 16:13:03 +0000)
DATE_RSS	RSS (Sun, 14 Aug 2005 16:13:03 UTC)
DATE_W3C	World Wide Web Consortium (example: 2005-08-14T16:13:03+0000)

Directory Functions

Function	Description
chdir()	Changes the current directory
chroot()	Changes the root directory of the current process
dir()	Opens a directory handle and returns an object
closedir()	Closes a directory handle
getcwd()	Returns the current directory
opendir()	Opens a directory handle
readdir()	Returns an entry from a directory handle
rewinddir()	Resets a directory handle
scandir()	Lists files and directories inside a specified path

Error and Logging Functions

Function	Description
debug_backtrace()	Generates a backtrace
debug_print_backtrace()	Prints a backtrace
error_get_last()	Gets the last error that occurred
error_log()	Sends an error to the server error log, to a file, or to a remote destination
error_reporting()	Specifies which errors are reported
restore_error_handler()	Restores the previous error handler
restore_exception_handler()	Restores the previous exception handler
set_error_handler()	Sets a user-defined function to handle errors
set_exception_handler()	Sets a user-defined function to handle exceptions
trigger_error()	Creates a user-defined error message
user_error()	Alias of trigger_error()

Error Function Parameters

Parameter	Description
error_level	Required; specifies the error report level for the user-defined error; corresponds to logging constant numbers
error_message	Required; specifies the error message for the user-defined function
error_file	Optional; specifies the filename in which the error occurred
error_line	Optional; specifies the line number in which the error occurred
error_context	Optional; specifies an array containing all variables and their values in use when the error occurred

Error and Logging Constants

Error Value Constant		Description
1	E_ERROR	Fatal run-time errors; errors that cannot be recovered from; execution of the script halted
2	E_WARNING	Non-fatal run-time errors; execution of the script not halted
4	E_PARSE	Compile-time parse errors; should only be generated by the parser
8	E_NOTICE	Run-time notices; found something that might be an error, but could also happen when running normally
16	E_CORE_ERROR	Fatal errors at PHP startup; like an E_ERROR in the PHP core
32	E_CORE_WARNING	Non-fatal errors at PHP startup; like an E_WARNING in the PHP core
64	E_COMPILE_ERROR	Fatal compile-time errors; like an E_ERROR generated by the Zend Scripting Engine
128	E_COMPILE_WARNING	Non-fatal compile-time errors; like an E_WARNING generated by the Zend Scripting Engine
256	E_USER_ERROR	Fatal user-generated error; like an E_ERROR set by the programmer using the PHP function trigger_error()
512	E_USER_WARNING	Non-fatal user-generated warning; like an E_WARNING set by the programmer using the PHP function trigger_error()
1024	E_USER_NOTICE	User-generated notice; like an E_NOTICE set by the programmer using the PHP function trigger_error()
2048	E_STRICT	Run-time notices; PHP-suggested changes to your code to help interoperability and compatibility of the code
4096	E_RECOVERABLE_ERROR	Catchable fatal error; like an E_ERROR but can be caught by a user-defined handle; see also set_error_handler()
8191	E_ALL	All errors and warnings, except of level E_STRICT

File System Functions

Function	Description
basename()	Returns the filename component of a path
chgrp()	Changes the file group
chmod()	Changes the file mode

Continued	
Function	**Description**
chown()	Changes the file owner
clearstatcache()	Clears the file status cache
copy()	Copies a file
delete()	See unlink() or unset()
dirname()	Returns the directory name component of a path
disk_free_space()	Returns the free space of a directory
disk_total_space()	Returns the total size of a directory
diskfreespace()	Alias of disk_free_space()
fclose()	Closes an open file
feof()	Tests for end-of-file on an open file
fflush()	Flushes buffered output to an open file
fgetc()	Returns a character from an open file
fgetcsv()	Parses a line from an open file, checking for CSV fields
fgets()	Returns a line from an open file
fgetss()	Returns a line, with HTML and PHP tags removed, from an open file
file()	Reads a file into an array
file_exists()	Checks whether or not a file or directory exists
file_get_contents()	Reads a file into a string
file_put_contents()	Writes a string to a file
fileatime()	Returns the last access time of a file
filectime()	Returns the last change time of a file
filegroup()	Returns the group ID of a file
fileinode()	Returns the inode number of a file
filemtime()	Returns the last modification time of a file
fileowner()	Returns the user ID (owner) of a file
fileperms()	Returns the permissions of a file
filesize()	Returns the file size
filetype()	Returns the file type
flock()	Locks or releases a file
fnmatch()	Matches a filename or string against a specified pattern
fopen()	Opens a file or URL

Continued	
Function	**Description**
fpassthru()	Reads from an open file until EOF, and writes the result to the output buffer
fputcsv()	Formats a line as CSV and writes it to an open file
fputs()	Alias of fwrite()
fread()	Reads from an open file
fscanf()	Parses input from an open file according to a specified format
fseek()	Seeks in an open file
fstat()	Returns information about an open file
ftell()	Returns the current position in an open file
ftruncate()	Truncates an open file to a specified length
fwrite()	Writes to an open file
glob()	Returns an array of filenames/directories matching a specified pattern
is_dir()	Checks whether a file is a directory
is_executable()	Checks whether a file is executable
is_file()	Checks whether a file is a regular file
is_link()	Checks whether a file is a link
is_readable()	Checks whether a file is readable
is_uploaded_file()	Checks whether a file was uploaded via HTTP POST
is_writable()	Checks whether a file is writeable
is_writeable()	Alias of is_writable()
link()	Creates a hard link
linkinfo()	Returns information about a hard link
lstat()	Returns information about a file or symbolic link
mkdir()	Creates a directory
move_uploaded_file()	Moves an uploaded file to a new location
parse_ini_file()	Parses a configuration file
pathinfo()	Returns information about a file path
pclose()	Closes a pipe opened by popen()
popen()	Opens a pipe
readfile()	Reads a file and writes it to the output buffer

Continued	
Function	**Description**
readlink()	Returns the target of a symbolic link
realpath()	Returns the absolute pathname
rename()	Renames a file or directory
rewind()	Rewinds a file pointer
rmdir()	Removes an empty directory
set_file_buffer()	Sets the buffer size of an open file
stat()	Returns information about a file
symlink()	Creates a symbolic link
tempnam()	Creates a unique temporary file
tmpfile()	Creates a unique temporary file
touch()	Sets access and modification time of a file
umask()	Changes file permissions for files
unlink()	Deletes a file

File System Constants

Constant	Description
GLOB_BRACE	Expands {a,b,c} to match 'a', 'b', or 'c'
GLOB_ONLYDIR	Return only directory entries which match the pattern
GLOB_MARK	Adds a slash to each item returned
GLOB_NOSORT	Return files as they appear in the directory (no sorting)
GLOB_NOCHECK	Return the search pattern if no files matching it were found
GLOB_NOESCAPE	Backslashes do not quote metacharacters
PATHINFO_DIRNAME	The path being checked returns directory name
PATHINFO_BASENAME	The path being checked returns basename
PATHINFO_EXTENSION	The path being checked returns extionsion
FILE_USE_INCLUDE_PATH	Search for the file in the include path
FILE_APPEND	Append file
FILE_IGNORE_NEW_LINES	Do not add newline at the end of each array element
FILE_SKIP_EMPTY_LINES	Skip empty lines

Filter Functions

Function	Description
filter_has_var()	Checks if a variable of a specified input type exist
filter_id()	Returns the ID number of a specified filter
filter_input()	Gets input from outside the script and filters it
filter_input_array()	Gets multiple inputs from outside the script and filters them
filter_list()	Returns an array of all supported filters
filter_var_array()	Gets multiple variables and filters them
filter_var()	Gets a variable and filters it

Filters

Filter	Description
FILTER_CALLBACK	Calls a user-defined function to filter data
FILTER_SANITIZE_STRING	Strips tags, optionally strips or encodes special characters
FILTER_SANITIZE_STRIPPED	Alias of "string" filter
FILTER_SANITIZE_ENCODED	URL-encodes string, optionally strips or encodes special characters
FILTER_SANITIZE_SPECIAL_CHARS	HTML-escapes '"<>& and characters with ASCII values less than 32
FILTER_SANITIZE_EMAIL	Removes all characters, except letters, digits, and the following special characters: !#$%&'*+-/=?^_`{|}~@.[]
FILTER_SANITIZE_URL	Removes all characters except letters, digits, and the following special characters: $-_.+!*'(),{} |\\^~[]`<>#%";/?:@&=
FILTER_SANITIZE_NUMBER_INT	Removes all characters except digits and +-
FILTER_SANITIZE_NUMBER_FLOAT	Removes all characters except digits, +-, and optionally eE
FILTER_SANITIZE_MAGIC_QUOTES	Applies addslashes()
FILTER_UNSAFE_RAW	Does nothing, optionally strips or encodes special characters
FILTER_VALIDATE_INT	Validates a value as an integer, optionally from the specified range
FILTER_VALIDATE_BOOLEAN	Returns TRUE for "1," "true," "on," or "yes"; FALSE for "0," "false," "off," "no," or ""; NULL otherwise
FILTER_VALIDATE_FLOAT	Validates a value as float

Continued	
Filter	**Description**
FILTER_VALIDATE_REGEXP	Validates a value against regexp, a Perl-compatible regular expression
FILTER_VALIDATE_URL	Validates a value as a URL, optionally with required components
FILTER_VALIDATE_EMAIL	Validates a value as email
FILTER_VALIDATE_IP	Validates a value as an IP address, optionally only IPv4 or IPv6 or not from private or reserved ranges

FTP Functions

Function	**Description**
ftp_alloc()	Allocates space for a file to be uploaded to the FTP server
ftp_cdup()	Changes the current directory to the parent directory on the FTP server
ftp_chdir()	Changes the current directory on the FTP server
ftp_chmod()	Sets permissions on a file via FTP
ftp_close()	Closes an FTP connection
ftp_connect()	Opens an FTP connection
ftp_delete()	Deletes a file on the FTP server
ftp_exec()	Executes a program/command on the FTP server
ftp_fget()	Downloads a file from the FTP server and saves it to an open file
ftp_fput()	Uploads from an open file and saves it to a file on the FTP server
ftp_get_option()	Returns runtime behaviors of the FTP connection
ftp_get()	Downloads a file from the FTP server
ftp_login()	Logs on to an FTP connection
ftp_mdtm()	Returns the last modified time of a specified file
ftp_mkdir()	Creates a new directory on the FTP server
ftp_nb_continue()	Continues retrieving/sending a file (non-blocking)
ftp_nb_fget()	Downloads a file from the FTP server and saves it to an open file (non-blocking)
ftp_nb_fput()	Uploads from an open file and saves it to a file on the FTP server (non-blocking)

Continued	
Function	**Description**
ftp_nb_get()	Downloads a file from the FTP server (non-blocking)
ftp_nb_put()	Uploads a file to the FTP server (non-blocking)
ftp_nlist()	Lists the files in a specified directory on the FTP server
ftp_pasv()	Turns passive mode on or off
ftp_put()	Uploads a file to the FTP server
ftp_pwd()	Returns the current directory name
ftp_quit()	Alias of ftp_close()
ftp_raw()	Sends a raw command to the FTP server
ftp_rawlist()	Returns a detailed list of files in the specified directory
ftp_rename()	Renames a file or directory on the FTP server
ftp_rmdir()	Removes a directory on the FTP server
ftp_set_option()	Sets runtime options for the FTP connection
ftp_site()	Sends a SITE command to the server
ftp_size()	Returns the size of the specified file
ftp_ssl_connect()	Opens a secure SSL-FTP connection
ftp_systype()	Returns the system type identifier of the FTP server

FTP Constants

Constant	Description
FTP_ASCII	FTP transfer mode ASCII
FTP_TEXT	FTP transfer mode Text
FTP_BINARY	FTP transfer mode binary
FTP_IMAGE	FTP transfer mode image
FTP_TIMEOUT_SEC	Set FTP timeout
FTP_AUTORESUME	Determines resume position and start position for get and put requests automatically
FTP_FAILED	Indicates asynchronous transfer has failed
FTP_FINISHED	Indicates asynchronous transfer has finished
FTP_MOREDATA	Indicates asynchronous transfer is still active

HTTP Functions

Function	Description
header()	Sends a raw HTTP header to a client
headers_list()	Returns a list of response headers sent (or ready to send)
headers_sent()	Checks if/where the HTTP headers have been sent
setcookie()	Sends an HTTP cookie to a client
setrawcookie()	Sends an HTTP cookie without URL-encoding the cookie value

Mail Functions

Function	Description
ezmlm_hash()	Calculates the hash value needed by the EZMLM mailing list system
mail()	Allows you to send emails directly from a script

Mail Parameters

Parameter	Description
To	Required; specifies the receiver(s) of the email
Subject	Required; specifies the subject of the email; cannot contain any newline characters
Message	Required; defines the message to be sent; each line should be separated with a LF (\n); lines should not exceed 70 characters
Headers	Optional; specifies additional headers, like From, Cc, and Bcc; additional headers should be separated with a CRLF (\r\n)
Parameters	Optional; specifies an additional parameter to the sendmail program

Math Functions

Function	Description
abs()	Returns the absolute value of a number
acos()	Returns the arccosine of a number
acosh()	Returns the inverse hyperbolic cosine of a number
asin()	Returns the arcsine of a number
asinh()	Returns the inverse hyperbolic sine of a number

Continued

Function	Description
atan()	Returns the arctangent of a number as a numeric value between -PI/2 and PI/2 radians
atan2()	Returns the angle theta of an (x,y) point as a numeric value between -PI and PI radians
atanh()	Returns the inverse hyperbolic tangent of a number
base_convert()	Converts a number from one base to another
bindec()	Converts a binary number to a decimal number
ceil()	Returns the value of a number rounded upwards to the nearest integer
cos()	Returns the cosine of a number
cosh()	Returns the hyperbolic cosine of a number
decbin()	Converts a decimal number to a binary number
dechex()	Converts a decimal number to a hexadecimal number
decoct()	Converts a decimal number to an octal number
deg2rad()	Converts a degree to a radian number
exp()	Returns the value of Ex
expm1()	Returns the value of Ex – 1
floor()	Returns the value of a number rounded downwards to the nearest integer
fmod()	Returns the remainder (modulo) of the division of the arguments
getrandmax()	Returns the maximum random number that can be returned by a call to the rand() function
hexdec()	Converts a hexadecimal number to a decimal number
hypot()	Returns the length of the hypotenuse of a right-angle triangle
is_finite()	Returns true if a value is a finite number
is_infinite()	Returns true if a value is an infinite number
is_nan()	Returns true if a value is not a number
lcg_value()	Returns a pseudo-random number in the range of (0,1)
log()	Returns the natural logarithm (base-E) of a number
log10()	Returns the base-10 logarithm of a number
log1p()	Returns log (1+number)
max()	Returns the number with the highest value of two specified numbers
min()	Returns the number with the lowest value of two specified numbers
mt_getrandmax()	Returns the largest possible value that can be returned by mt_rand()

Continued	
Function	**Description**
mt_rand()	Returns a random integer using Mersenne Twister algorithm
mt_srand()	Seeds the Mersenne Twister random number generator
octdec()	Converts an octal number to a decimal number
pi()	Returns the value of PI
pow()	Returns the value of x to the power of y
rad2deg()	Converts a radian number to a degree
rand()	Returns a random integer
round()	Rounds a number to the nearest integer
sin()	Returns the sine of a number
sinh()	Returns the hyperbolic sine of a number
sqrt()	Returns the square root of a number
srand()	Seeds the random number generator
tan()	Returns the tangent of an angle
tanh()	Returns the hyperbolic tangent of an angle

Math Constants

Constant	Description
M_E	Returns e (approx. 2.718)
M_EULER	Returns Euler's constant (approx. 0.577)
M_LNPI	Returns the natural logarithm of PI (approx. 1.144)
M_LN2	Returns the natural logarithm of 2 (approx. 0.693)
M_LN10	Returns the natural logarithm of 10 (approx. 2.302)
M_LOG2E	Returns the base-2 logarithm of E (approx. 1.442)
M_LOG10E	Returns the base-10 logarithm of E (approx. 0.434)
M_PI	Returns PI (approx. 3.14159)
M_PI_2	Returns PI/2 (approx. 1.570)
M_PI_4	Returns PI/4 (approx. 0.785)
M_1_PI	Returns 1/PI (approx. 0.318)
M_2_PI	Returns 2/PI (approx. 0.636)
M_SQRTPI	Returns the square root of PI (approx. 1.772)
M_2_SQRTPI	Returns 2/square root of PI (approx. 1.128)
M_SQRT1_2	Returns the square root of 1/2 (approx. 0.707)
M_SQRT2	Returns the square root of 2 (approx. 1.414)
M_SQRT3	Returns the square root of 3 (approx. 1.732)

Miscellaneous Functions

Function	Description
connection_status()	Returns the current connection status
connection_timeout()	Deprecated in PHP 4.0.5
constant()	Returns the value of a constant
define()	Defines a constant
defined()	Checks whether a constant exists
die()	Prints a message and exits the current script
eval()	Evaluates a string as PHP code
exit()	Prints a message and exits the current script
get_browser()	Returns the capabilities of the user's browser
highlight_file()	Outputs a file with the PHP syntax highlighted
highlight_string()	Outputs a string with the PHP syntax highlighted
ignore_user_abort()	Sets whether a remote client can abort the running of a script
pack()	Packs data into a binary string
php_check_syntax()	Deprecated in PHP 5.0.5
php_strip_whitespace()	Returns the source code of a file with PHP comments and whitespace removed
show_source()	Alias of highlight_file()
sleep()	Delays code execution for a number of seconds
time_nanosleep()	Delays code execution for a number of seconds and nanoseconds
time_sleep_until()	Delays code execution until a specified time
uniqid()	Generates a unique ID
unpack()	Unpacks data from a binary string
usleep()	Delays code execution for a number of microseconds

MySQL Functions

Function	Description
mysql_change_user()	Deprecated; changes the user of the current MySQL connection
mysql_client_encoding()	Returns the name of the character set for the current connection
mysql_close()	Closes a non-persistent MySQL connection
mysql_connect()	Opens a non-persistent MySQL connection
mysql_create_db()	Deprecated; creates a new MySQL database; use mysql_query() instead

Continued	
Function	**Description**
mysql_data_seek()	Moves the record pointer
mysql_db_name()	Returns a database name from a call to mysql_list_dbs()
mysql_db_query()	Deprecated; sends a MySQL query; use mysql_select_db() and mysql_query() instead
mysql_drop_db()	Deprecated; deletes a MySQL database; use mysql_query() instead
mysql_errno()	Returns the error number of the last MySQL operation
mysql_error()	Returns the error description of the last MySQL operation
mysql_escape_string()	Deprecated; escapes a string for use in a mysql_query; use mysql_real_escape_string() instead
mysql_fetch_array()	Returns a row from a recordset as an associative array and/or a numeric array
mysql_fetch_assoc()	Returns a row from a recordset as an associative array
mysql_fetch_field()	Returns column information from a recordset as an object
mysql_fetch_lengths()	Returns the length of the contents of each field in a result row
mysql_fetch_object()	Returns a row from a recordset as an object
mysql_fetch_row()	Returns a row from a recordset as a numeric array
mysql_field_flags()	Returns the flags associated with a field in a recordset
mysql_field_len()	Returns the maximum length of a field in a recordset
mysql_field_name()	Returns the name of a field in a recordset
mysql_field_seek()	Moves the result pointer to a specified field
mysql_field_table()	Returns the name of the table the specified field is in
mysql_field_type()	Returns the type of a field in a recordset
mysql_free_result()	Frees result memory
mysql_get_client_info()	Returns MySQL client info
mysql_get_host_info()	Returns MySQL host info
mysql_get_proto_info()	Returns MySQL protocol info
mysql_get_server_info()	Returns MySQL server info
mysql_info()	Returns information about the last query
mysql_insert_id()	Returns the AUTO_INCREMENT ID generated from the previous INSERT operation
mysql_list_dbs()	Lists available databases on a MySQL server

Continued	
Function	**Description**
mysql_list_fields()	Deprecated; lists MySQL table fields; use mysql_query() instead
mysql_list_processes()	Lists MySQL processes
mysql_list_tables()	Deprecated. Lists tables in a MySQL database. Use mysql_query() instead
mysql_num_fields()	Returns the number of fields in a recordset
mysql_num_rows()	Returns the number of rows in a recordset
mysql_pconnect()	Opens a persistent MySQL connection
mysql_ping()	Pings a server connection or reconnects if there is no connection
mysql_query()	Executes a query on a MySQL database
mysql_real_escape_string()	Escapes a string for use in SQL statements
mysql_result()	Returns the value of a field in a recordset
mysql_select_db()	Sets the active MySQL database
mysql_stat()	Returns the current system status of the MySQL server
mysql_tablename()	Deprecated; returns the table name of a field; use mysql_query() instead
mysql_thread_id()	Returns the current thread ID
mysql_unbuffered_query()	Executes a query on a MySQL database (without fetching/buffering the result)

MySQL Constants

Constant	**Description**
MYSQL_CLIENT_COMPRESS	Uses compression protocol
MYSQL_CLIENT_IGNORE_SPACE	Allows space after function names
MYSQL_CLIENT_INTERACTIVE	Allows interactive timeout seconds of inactivity before closing the connection
MYSQL_CLIENT_SSL	Uses SSL encryption (only available with version 4+ of the MySQL client library)
MYSQL_ASSOC	Returns columns into the array with the fieldname as the array index
MYSQL_BOTH	Returns columns into the array having both a numerical index and the fieldname as the array index
MYSQL_NUM	Returns columns into the array having a numerical index (starting at zero)

SimpleXML Functions

Function	Description
_construct()	Creates a new SimpleXMLElement object
addAttribute()	Adds an attribute to the SimpleXML element
addChild()	Adds a child element the SimpleXML element
asXML()	Gets an XML string from a SimpleXML element
attributes()	Gets a SimpleXML element's attributes
children()	Gets the children of a specified node
getDocNamespaces()	Gets the namespaces of an XML document
getName()	Gets the name of a SimpleXML element
getNamespaces()	Gets the namespaces from XML data
registerXPath-Namespace()	Creates a namespace context for the next XPath query
simplexml_import_dom()	Gets a SimpleXMLElement object from a DOM node
simplexml_load_file()	Gets a SimpleXMLElement object from an XML document
simplexml_load_string()	Gets a SimpleXMLElement object from an XML string
xpath()	Runs an XPath query on XML data

String Functions

Function	Description
addcslashes()	Returns a string with backslashes in front of the specified characters
addslashes()	Returns a string with backslashes in front of predefined characters
bin2hex()	Converts a string of ASCII characters to hexadecimal values
chop()	Alias of rtrim()
chr()	Returns a character from a specified ASCII value
chunk_split()	Splits a string into a series of smaller parts
convert_cyr_string()	Converts a string from one Cyrillic character-set to another
convert_uudecode()	Decodes a uuencoded string
convert_uuencode()	Encodes a string using the uuencode algorithm
count_chars()	Returns how many times an ASCII character occurs within a string and returns the information
crc32()	Calculates a 32-bit CRC for a string
crypt()	One-way string encryption (hashing)

Continued	
Function	**Description**
echo()	Outputs strings
explode()	Breaks a string into an array
fprintf()	Writes a formatted string to a specified output stream
get_html_translation_table()	Returns the translation table used by htmlspecialchars() and htmlentities()
hebrev()	Converts Hebrew text to visual text
hebrevc()	Converts Hebrew text to visual text and new lines (\n) into tags
html_entity_decode()	Converts HTML entities to characters
htmlentities()	Converts characters to HTML entities
htmlspecialchars_decode()	Converts some predefined HTML entities to characters
htmlspecialchars()	Converts some predefined characters to HTML entities
implode()	Returns a string from the elements of an array
join()	Alias of implode()
levenshtein()	Returns the Levenshtein distance between two strings
localeconv()	Returns local numeric and monetary formatting information
ltrim()	Strips whitespace from the left side of a string
md5()	Calculates the MD5 hash of a string
md5_file()	Calculates the MD5 hash of a file
metaphone()	Calculates the metaphone key of a string
money_format()	Returns a string formatted as a currency string
nl_langinfo()	Returns specific local information
nl2br()	Inserts HTML line breaks in front of each newline in a string
number_format()	Formats a number with grouped thousands
ord()	Returns the ASCII value of the first character of a string
parse_str()	Parses a query string into variables
print()	Outputs a string
printf()	Outputs a formatted string
quoted_printable_decode()	Decodes a quoted-printable string
quotemeta()	Quotes meta characters
rtrim()	Strips whitespace from the right side of a string

Continued	
Function	**Description**
setlocale()	Sets locale information
sha1()	Calculates the SHA-1 hash of a string
sha1_file()	Calculates the SHA-1 hash of a file
similar_text()	Calculates the similarity between two strings
soundex()	Calculates the soundex key of a string
sprintf()	Writes a formatted string to a variable
sscanf()	Parses input from a string according to a format
str_ireplace()	Replaces some characters in a string (case-insensitive)
str_pad()	Pads a string to a new length
str_repeat()	Repeats a string a specified number of times
str_replace()	Replaces some characters in a string (case-sensitive)
str_rot13()	Performs the ROT13 encoding on a string
str_shuffle()	Randomly shuffles all characters in a string
str_split()	Splits a string into an array
str_word_count()	Counts the number of words in a string
strcasecmp()	Compares two strings (case-insensitive)
strchr()	Finds the first occurrence of a string inside another string; alias of strstr()
strcmp()	Compares two strings (case-sensitive)
strcoll()	Locale-based string comparison
strcspn()	Returns the number of characters found in a string before any part of some specified characters are found
strip_tags()	Strips HTML and PHP tags from a string
stripcslashes()	Unquotes a string quoted with addcslashes()
stripslashes()	Unquotes a string quoted with addslashes()
stripos()	Returns the position of the first occurrence of a string inside another string (case-insensitive)
stristr()	Finds the first occurrence of a string inside another string (case-insensitive)
strlen()	Returns the length of a string
strnatcasecmp()	Compares two strings using a "natural order" algorithm (case-insensitive)
strnatcmp()	Compares two strings using a "natural order" algorithm (case-sensitive)
strncasecmp()	String comparison of the first n characters (case-insensitive)

Continued	
Function	**Description**
strncmp()	String comparison of the first n characters (case-sensitive)
strpbrk()	Searches a string for any of a set of characters
strpos()	Returns the position of the first occurrence of a string inside another string (case-sensitive)
strrchr()	Finds the last occurrence of a string inside another string
strrev()	Reverses a string
strripos()	Finds the position of the last occurrence of a string inside another string (case-insensitive)
strrpos()	Finds the position of the last occurrence of a string inside another string (case-sensitive)
strspn()	Returns the number of characters found in a string that contains only characters from a specified charlist
strstr()	Finds the first occurrence of a string inside another string (case-sensitive)
strtok()	Splits a string into smaller strings
strtolower()	Converts a string to lowercase letters
strtoupper()	Converts a string to uppercase letters
strtr()	Translates certain characters in a string
substr()	Returns part of a string
substr_compare()	Compares two strings from a specified start position (binary-safe, and optionally case-sensitive)
substr_count()	Counts the number of times a substring occurs in a string
substr_replace()	Replaces part of a string with another string
trim()	Strips whitespace from both sides of a string
ucfirst()	Converts the first character of a string to uppercase
ucwords()	Converts the first character of each word in a string to uppercase
vfprintf()	Writes a formatted string to a specified output stream
vprintf()	Outputs a formatted string
vsprintf()	Writes a formatted string to a variable
wordwrap()	Wraps a string to a given number of characters

String Constants

Constant	Description
CRYPT_SALT_LENGTH	Contains the length of the default encryption method for the system; for standard DES encryption, the length is two
CRYPT_STD_DES	Set to one if the standard DES-based encryption with a two-character salt is supported; zero otherwise
CRYPT_EXT_DES	Set to one if the extended DES-based encryption with a nine-character salt is supported; zero otherwise
CRYPT_MD5	Set to one if the MD5 encryption with a 12-character salt starting with 1 is supported; zero otherwise
CRYPT_BLOWFISH	Set to one if the Blowfish encryption with a 16-character salt starting with 2 or $2a$ is supported; zero otherwise

XML Parser Functions

Function	Description
utf8_decode()	Decodes a UTF-8 string to ISO-8859-1
utf8_encode()	Encodes an ISO-8859-1 string to UTF-8
xml_error_string()	Gets an error string from the XML parser
xml_get_current_byte_index()	Gets the current byte index from the XML parser
xml_get_current_column_number()	Gets the current column number from the XML parser
xml_get_current_line_number()	Gets the current line number from the XML parser
xml_get_error_code()	Gets an error code from the XML parser
xml_parse()	Parses an XML document
xml_parse_into_struct()	Parses XML data into an array
xml_parser_create_ns()	Creates an XML parser with namespace support
xml_parser_create()	Creates an XML parser
xml_parser_free()	Frees an XML parser
xml_parser_get_option()	Gets options from an XML parser
xml_parser_set_option()	Sets options in an XML parser
xml_set_character_data_handler()	Sets handler function for character data
xml_set_default_handler()	Sets default handler function

Continued

Function	Description
xml_set_end_namespace_decl_handler()	Sets handler function for the end-of-namespace declarations
xml_set_external_entity_ref_handler()	Sets handler function for external entities
xml_set_notation_decl_handler()	Sets handler function for notation declarations
xml_set_object()	Uses the XML parser within an object
xml_set_processing_instruction_handler()	Sets the handler function for processing instructions
xml_set_start_namespace_decl_handler()	Sets the handler function for the start-of-namespace declarations
xml_set_unparsed_entity_decl_handler()	Sets the handler function for unparsed entity declarations

JDBC Data Types

Type	Recommended Method	Allowed Methods
BIGINT	getLong	getByte, getShort, getInt, getFloat, getDouble, getBigDecimal, getBoolean, getString, getObject
BINARY	getBytes	getString, getAsciiStream, getUnicodeStream, getBinaryStream, getObject
BIT	getBoolean	getByte, getShort, getInt, getLong, getFloat, getDouble, getBigDecimal, getString, getObject
CHAR	getStgring	getByte, getShort, getInt, getLong, getFloat, getDouble, getBigDecimal, getBoolean, getDate, getTime, getTimestamp, getAsciiStream, getUnicodeStream, getObject
DATE	getDate	getString, getTimestamp, getObject
DECIMAL	getBigDecimal	getByte, getShort, getInt, getLong, getFloat, getDouble, getBoolean, getString, getObject
DOUBLE	getDouble	getByte, getShort, getInt, getLong, getFloat, getBigDecimal, getBoolean, getString, getObject
FLOAT	getDouble	getByte, getShort, getInt, getLong, getFloat, getBigDecimal, getBoolean, getString, getObject
INTEGER	getInt	getByte, getShort, getLong, getFloat, getDouble, getBigDecimal, getBoolean, getString, getObject
LONGVARBINARY	getBinaryStream	getString, getBytes, getAsciiStream, getUnicodeStream, getObject
LONGVARCHAR	getAsciiStream	getByte, getShort, getInt, getLong, getFloat, getDouble, getBigDecimal, getBoolean, getString, getDate, getTime, getTimestamp, getObject

Continued		
Type	**Recommended Method**	**Allowed Methods**
NUMERIC	getBigDecimal	getByte, getShort, getInt, getLong, getFloat, getDouble, getBoolean, getString, getObject
REAL	getFloat	getByte, getShort, getInt, getLong, getDouble, getBigDecimal, getBoolean, getString, getObject
SMALLINT	getShort	getByte, getInt, getLong, getFloat, getDouble, getBigDecimal, getBoolean, getString, getObject
TIME	getTime	getString, getTimestamp, getObject
TIMESTAMP	getTimestamp	getString, getDate, getTime, getObject
TINYINT	getByte	getShort, getInt, getLong, getFloat, getDouble, getBigDecimal, getBoolean, getString, getObject
VARCHAR	getString	getByte, getShort, getInt, getLong, getFloat, getDouble, getBigDecimal, getBoolean, getDate, getTime, getTimestamp, getAsciiStream, getUnicodeStream, getObject
VARBINARY	getBytes	getString, getAsciiStream, getUnicodeStream, getBinaryStream, getObject

HTML Colors

In the following table of HTML colors, an asterisk (*) after a color name indicates a standard Windows color. A name in bold indicates an HTML 4.0 named color. Browser-safe colors are those with each pair of hex codes in the RGB value selected from the following: 00, 33, 66, 99, CC, or FF.

Named Color	Hexadecimal Code
Antiquewhite	#FAEBD7
Aqua*	00FFFF
Aquamarine	#7FFFD4
Azure	#F0FFFF
Beige	#F5F5DC
Bisque	#FFE4C4
Black*	#000000
Blanchedalmond	#FFEBCD
Blue*	#0000FF
Blueviolet	#8A2BE2
Brown	#A52A2A
Burlywood	#DEB887
Cadetblue	#5F9EA0
Chartruse	#7FFF00
Chocolate	#D2691E
Coral	#FF7F50
cornflowerblue	#6495ED
Cornsilk	#FFF8DC
Crimson	#DC143C

Continued	
Named Color	**Hexadecimal Code**
Cyan (same as aqua)	#00FFFF
Darkblue	#00008B
Darkcyan	#008B8B
Darkgoldenrod	#B8860B
Darkgray	#A9A9A9
Darkgreen	#006400
Darkkhaki	#BDB76B
Darkmagenta	#BD008B
Darkolivegreen	#556B2F
Darkorange	#FF8C00
Darkorchid	#9932CC
Darkred	#8B0000
Darksalmon	#E9967A
Darkseagreen	#8FBC8F
Darkslateblue	#483D8B
Darkslategray	#2F4F4F
Darkturquoise	#00CED1
Darkviolet	#9400D3
Deeppink	#FF1493
Deepskyblue	#00BFFF
Dimgray	#696969
Dogerblue	#1E90FF
Firebrick	#B22222
Floralwhite	#FFFAF0
Forestgreen	#228B22
Fuchsia*	#FF00FF
Gainsboro	#DCDCDC
Ghostwhite	#F8F8FF
Gold	#FFD700
Goldenrod	#DAA520
Gray*	#808080
Green*	#008000
Greenyellow	#ADFF2F
honeydew	#F0FFF0
Hotpink	#FF69B4

Continued	
Named Color	Hexadecimal Code
Indianred	#CD5C5C
Indigo	#480082
Ivory	#FFFFF0
Khaki	#F0E68C
Lavender	#E6E6FA
Lavenderblush	#FFF0F5
Lawngreen	#7CFC00
Lemonchiffon	#FFFACD
Lightblue	#ADD8E6
Lightcoral	#F08080
Lightcyan	#E0FFFF
Lightgoldenrodyellow	#FAFAD2
Lightgreen	#90EE90
Lightgray	#D3D3D3
Lightpink	#FFB6C1
lightsalmon	#FFA07A
Lightseagreen	#20B2AA
Lightskyblue	#87CEFA
Lightslategray	#778899
Lightsteelblue	#B0C4DE
Lightyellow	#FFFFE0
Lime*	#00FF00
Limegreen	#32CD32
Linen	#FAF0E6
Magenta (same as fuchsia)	#FF00FF
Maroon*	#800000
Mediumaquamarine	#66CDAA
Mediumblue	#0000CD
Mediumorchid	#BA55D3
Mediumpurple	#9370DB
Mediumseagreen	#3CB371
Mediumslateblue	#7B68EE
Mediumspringgreen	#00FA9A
Mediumturquoise	#48D1CC
Mediumvioletred	#C71585

Continued	
Named Color	**Hexadecimal Code**
Midnightblue	#191970
Mintcream	#F5FFFA
Mistyrose	#FFE4E1
Moccasin	#FFE4B5
Navajowhite	#FFDEAD
Navy*	#000080
Oldlace	#FDF5E6
Olive*	#808000
Olivedrab	#6B8E23
Orange	#FFA500
Orangered	#FF4500
Orchid	#DA70D6
Palegoldenrod	#EEE8AA
Palegreen	#98FB98
Paleturquoise	#AFEEEE
palevioletred	#DB87093
Papayawhip	#FFEFD5
Peachpuff	#FFDAB9
Peru	#CD853F
Pink	#FFC0CB
Plum	#DDA0DD
Powderblue	#B0E0E6
Purple*	#800080
Red*	#FF0000
Rosybrown	#BC8F8F
Royalblue	#4169E1
Saddlebrown	#8B4513
Salmon	#FA8072
Seagreen	#2E8B57
Seashell	#FFF5EE
Sienna	#A0522D
Silver*	#C0C0C0
Skyblue	#87CEEB
Slateblue	#6A5ACD
Slategray	#708090

Continued	
Named Color	**Hexadecimal Code**
Snow	#FFFAFA
Springgreen	#00FF7F
Steelblue	#4682B4
Tan	#D2B486
Teal*	#008080

Index

$ indicator for PHP variables, 311

<%> tag in, 447–448, **448**
<%@> tag, 450

/ continuation character in JavaScript, 211

& special character/escape code, 52–53, **52**, **53**, **54**

A

A language, 19
<a> anchor tag, 81–82, **82**, 85–88, **85**, **86**, **87**, **88**. *See also* links, 81
<abbreviation> tag, 545*t*
absolute property, 109
Access, 11, 175
AccessDataSource, 432, **432**
<acronym> tag, 545*t*
actions, JSP, 435, 452–464, 453*t*. *See also* individual jsp:*xxx* listings
ActionScript, 19
Active Server Pages. *See* ASP/ASP.NET and VB Script
Ada95, 19
<address element> tag, 545*t*
adware, 189*t*
Ajax, 16–17, 23, 170
    asynchronous interactions in, 17
    DOM, 17

JavaScript and, 17
XML and, 17
alert boxes, 238, **238**, **239**
alert function, 238, **238**, **239**
align attribute, 31, 41
alink attribute, 30
alt/alternate font, 31–32, 58, 71–72
ampersand (&, special character/escape code)
    characters, 52–53, **52**, **53**, **54**
<anchor> tag, 545*t*
anchors. *See* links, anchors for, 81
and/or conditions, in ASP/ASP.NET/VB Script,
    403–404, **404**
ANSI standards, 175
Apache, 288, 335
APIs, 172, 184
    CGI and vs., 281, 283
apostrophes, 5
appearance controls, 116–120
AppleScript, 19
<applet> tag, 545*t*
application methods, JSP and, 467*t*
Application Program Interface. *See* APIs
application scope, 466–468, **467**
application servers, 168–169, 169*t*. *See also* servers
applications for HTML, 1, 3–4
<area inside image map> tag, 545*t*
<area> tag, 71
arguments, in PHP, in brackets, 337

Note: Boldface numbers indicate illustrations and code; *t* indicates a table.

Note: Boldface numbers indicate illustrations and code; *t* indicates a table.

Note: Boldface numbers indicate illustrations and code; *t* indicates a table.

Note: Boldface numbers indicate illustrations and code; *t* indicates a table.

Note: Boldface numbers indicate illustrations and code; *t* indicates a table.

Note: Boldface numbers indicate illustrations and code; *t* indicates a table.

Note: Boldface numbers indicate illustrations and code; *t* indicates a table.

Note: Boldface numbers indicate illustrations and code; *t* indicates a table.

Note: Boldface numbers indicate illustrations and code; *t* indicates a table.

Note: Boldface numbers indicate illustrations and code; *t* indicates a table.

Note: Boldface numbers indicate illustrations and code; *t* indicates a table.